COMMUNICATION
SCIENCES AND
DISORDERS

COMMUNICATION SCIENCES AND DISORDERS

An Introduction to the Professions

DALE F. WILLIAMS

Psychology Press
Taylor & Francis Group

New York   London

Psychology Press
Taylor & Francis Group
711 Third Avenue
New York, NY 10017

Psychology Press
Taylor & Francis Group
27 Church Road
Hove, East Sussex BN3 2FA

© 2012 by Taylor & Francis Group, LLC
Psychology Press is an imprint of Taylor & Francis Group, an Informa business

Printed in the United States of America on acid-free paper
Version Date: 20110817

International Standard Book Number: 978-0-8058-6181-5 (Hardback)

Library of Congress Cataloging-in-Publication Data

Williams, Dale F.
    Communication sciences and disorders : an introduction to the professions / Dale F. Williams.
        p. ; cm.
    Includes bibliographical references and index.
    ISBN 978-0-8058-6181-5 (hardback : alk. paper)
    1. Speech therapists--Practice. 2. Communication disorders. I. Title.
    [DNLM: 1. Speech-Language Pathology. 2. Communication Disorders. 3. Communication. 4. Hearing Disorders. 5. Voice Disorders. WL 340.2]

RC428.5.W55 2012
616.85'5--dc23   2011014074

Visit the Taylor & Francis Web site at
http://www.taylorandfrancis.com

and the Psychology Press Web site at
http://www.psypress.com

*To anyone studying communication sciences and disorders,
regardless of whether you make it your career.*

CONTENTS

ACKNOWLEDGMENTS

There are aspects of communication sciences and disorders about which I know far less than others. Because of my deficiencies, I must first thank the people (aside from my coauthors) who either filled in the blanks or helped me find the information I needed. These individuals include James L. Coyle, Peter Dugan, Floyd Emanuel, Jamie Heidenreich, Suzanne Hungerford, Peggy Larson, Jerilyn A. Logemann, Jose Lozano, Jennifer Peragine, Cathleen Petree, Nancy Ribbler, Bob Quesal, Peter Ramig, Aimee Schulz, Kay-Frances Slattery, and Misty Williams. There are others, too, but confidentiality restrictions keep me from listing them. I hope you know who you are and how appreciative I am.

At Taylor and Francis, I would like to thank Paul Dukes, for his efforts at pulling it all together, Lee Transue, who managed the review process, and Judith Simon, for all her editing help.

Finally, I also thank my family, which includes both the current one and the one in which I grew up. You had more to do with this project than you might think.

ABOUT THE AUTHOR

Dale F. Williams, PhD, CCC-SLP, BRS-FD, is professor of communication sciences and disorders at Florida Atlantic University, where he also serves as Director of the Fluency Clinic. In addition, he is a consultant for Language Learning Intervention and Professional Speech Services. Dr. Williams has worked as a speech-language pathologist in a variety of settings and has presented clinical and research seminars to clinicians in schools, hospitals, university clinics, and private practices. A board-recognized fluency specialist of the American Speech-Language-Hearing Association since 1999, he served as Chair of the Specialty Board on Fluency Disorders from 2008 to 2010. Dr. Williams has been an editorial consultant and reviewer for numerous professional journals. His publications address a wide range of communication disorders and include the book *Stuttering Recovery: Personal and Empirical Perspectives* (published by Psychology Press [www.psypress.com]). Dr. Williams lives in Boynton Beach, Florida with his wife Misty, sons Brennan and Blaine, daughters Cayley and Caysey, and an ever-changing array of pets.

An Introduction to Communication Sciences and Disorders

So you want to be a speech-language pathologist.

That is impressive, particularly when one considers that most people do not even know what a speech-language pathologist is. But your wanting to be one raises an obvious question.

Why?

But maybe I am reading you wrong. Perhaps you instead long to become an audiologist, to offer your talents to those whose hearing difficulties interfere with their desires for satisfying and meaningful communication.

Okay. But again, why?

To be fair, many people reading this likely have no desire to enter either profession. Some simply wish to learn about communication sciences and disorders (which, for reasons of efficiency and laziness, I abbreviate as CSD). Whatever the case is for you, I suspect the answer to the question of *why* lies someplace within the following statements:

- You want to help people.
- You want to teach one on one.
- You are fascinated by velopharyngeal physiology as it relates to the myoelastic-aerodynamic theory of phonation (admittedly, this one is less likely than the first two).
- You have a friend or relative who is having difficulty communicating.
- You have a friend or relative who was aided greatly by a communication disorders specialist.

- *You* were aided greatly by a communication disorders specialist.
- You *were not* aided all that much by a communication disorders specialist and now wish to change the field for the better.
- You have read or heard about seemingly miraculous devices that allow people who could not communicate an opportunity to do so.
- You know a speech-language pathologist (SLP) or an audiologist, and you have heard him or her talk about the job.
- You have observed an SLP or audiologist at work and were interested in what you saw.
- You heard there are lots of jobs available.
- You are taking an introductory course to fulfill a requirement.

All of these are good reasons for learning about the field. CSD specialists do help some folks, often (although not exclusively) in individualized sessions. They learn about science, which, for some, does lead to working with special devices that can aid people's communication. They do find jobs in their field—more are available than people to fill them (Bureau of Labor Statistics, 2011)—and have interesting on-the-job experiences.

Finally, CSD professionals appreciate it when others learn about their professions, even if it is only to complete a requisite elective course. At least in part, this appreciation stems from the fact that so many people have the wrong idea about the professions. For example:

- We do not teach basic vocabulary to clients who do not need it (as in the movie *Regarding Henry*).
- Nor do we give every stuttering client an electronic device and send them on their way, as seems to be occurring on a lot of television shows lately.
- CSD specialists diagnose and treat according to their own plans, not what teachers or doctors tell them to do.
- The field of speech-language pathology is not limited to correcting how people talk. As the name suggests, SLPs deal with speech *and language*.
- We do not all work in schools.
- Audiologists do not simply assess, and SLPs do not just administer drill work; both counsel their clients as well.
- In everyday conversation, we do not sit in judgment of people's communication skills (well, not always anyway).
- We actually do make more money than guys who search for unclaimed quarters in vending machine change slots.
- Speech-language pathology is very different from forensic pathology, and as such, SLPs do not have the opportunity to perform autopsies.

To be fair, that last one is not that commonly held of a misconception. Most people know that our preference is to treat the living. Those outside the field do, however, hold other false beliefs about the disorders we work with. I am guessing you have heard at least one of the following at some point in your lives:

- Bad parenting can cause communication disorders.
- Childhood communication problems will go away on their own if you just wait them out.
- Any communication disorder, no matter how severe, can be over-come if you are willing to work at it hard enough.
- Hearing aids can amplify the sounds you want to hear and filter out the ones you do not.

OK, so I have spent a lot of space telling you what *is not* true about communication sciences and disorders. Let us discuss what is. It is a relatively new field encompassing speech-language pathology, audiology, and communication sciences[1] (Powers, 2000). It requires education in anatomy, physiology, neurology, and psychoacoustics, among other hard sciences. Along with this, there is course work in human behavior, counseling, and teaching. Add all that to the linguistics, phonetics, research design, statistics, multiculturalism, ethics, professional issues, and whatever else your chosen school requires, and it becomes clear that CSD specialists have to keep a lot of stuff in their heads (Figure 1.1).

As you will see in this book, while a solid knowledge base is important (critical, actually) to being a CSD professional, other features are needed as well. In fact, various texts (e.g., Guilford, Graham, & Scheuerle, 2007; Leith, 1993) include lengthy lists of what talents, skills, or attributes make up a successful SLP or audiologist. Entries include such features as sensitivity,

FIGURE 1.1   The CSD professional's expanding head (a dramatization). Note: There are two pictures because when one has twins, one cannot ask one to do something and not ask the other. (Artwork by Cayley Williams and Caysey Williams.)

FIGURE 1.2   Melody and Bill. (Artwork by Blaine Williams.)

compassion, patience, enthusiasm, insight, and common sense. Of course, exhibiting all of these simultaneously is a tall order, particularly for those of us who tend toward insensitivity, moodiness, impatience, apathy, ignorance, and irrationality. But, rather than viewing such lists as a reminder of where you fall short, read them (and the ones in this book) as goals to strive for. For one thing, there is nothing wrong with trying to be more sensitive, compassionate, patient, enthusiastic, insightful, and sensible. Second, if you are anything like me, one or all of these features might be missing at times when they really should be there. Therefore, some reminders do not hurt. As a final note on professional attributes, understand that there is no clinical "personality" that one achieves once these traits are evident. I say this because I have seen effective practitioners from all over the personality map. The key is to take your strengths and make them work for you. Figure 1.2 shows us that Melody is loud, personable, and a strict taskmaster. Children do what she says, and parents follow through on all she asks them to do. Bill is soft spoken and laid back. His geriatric clients appreciate the time he allows them to answer questions, as well as the quiet encouragement he offers when the task is not going well. Who is the better therapist of the two? I have no idea. Both are better than me, the only standard I use.

Along with being sensitive, compassionate and all, CSD professionals need to understand the job itself, one that differs somewhat from setting to setting but will surely include varying amounts of paperwork, meetings,

What Makes a Good SLP? One Professional's Take

Deena Wener

Let us assume that there is no speech-language pathology sprite to confer competence on you. What, then, is involved in gaining access to this unbelievably varied and challenging career? First, you must be realistic about whether you have "the right stuff" to be a speech-language pathologist (SLP). Although there is no one type of personality that was born to be an SLP, there are a number of characteristics that appear to predominate in students who navigate their academic and clinical programs capably. Successful students have a genuine interest in working with individuals with communication disorders and come equipped with interpersonal abilities that include sensitivity, sincerity, friendliness, tolerance, the ability to listen, flexibility, and patience. In addition, the majority of SLPs are not only effective but also strong communicators both orally and in writing. Generally, individuals selecting this field have an above-average intellectual aptitude. In addition, well-suited students display persistence, independence, scientific aptitude, emotional steadiness, creativity, and imagination as well as the ability to work well with others.

family and professional conferences, advocacy, and continuing education seminars, in addition to—oh yeah—treating clients. As a young field, CSD is ever changing, with myths being countered and new controversies arising almost daily. And, as with most professions, some days are considerably rewarding, others mundane.

The last point—monotony—brings me something else this chapter should cover: basic vocabulary. It is not only important for you, the reader, to understand common terms in CSD, but I figured that since I have been using many of them for a couple of thousand words now, maybe it is time I let you know what I am trying to say.

I begin with the most general and work my way deductively to more specific terms.

communication—the processes by which information is exchanged (speaking, writing, semaphore, etc.).
disorder—a disturbance of structure, function, or both (Dirckx, 1997) (or, to state it differently: *something is wrong*).
communication disorder—impairment in the ability to receive, process, represent, or transmit information (Nicolosi, Harryman, & Kresheck,

1989) (*something is wrong with communication*). (More specifically, *something is wrong with speech, language,* or *hearing*.) By the way, the term *communication disorders* often applies to the field of study that encompasses speech-language pathology and audiology. I have been using communication *sciences and* disorders because (1) I strongly believe that the element of science is crucial to our understanding of communication, and (2) that is the name of the department in which I am employed.

language disorders—disorders affecting (1) the way you say (or write) your message or (2) your ability to understand the messages of others.

speech disorders—disorders affecting how one verbally produces language. These include impairments of articulation (sound pronunciation), fluency (most often stuttering), resonance (such as nasality—think Fran Drescher), or voice (e.g., hoarseness such as that of Rod Stewart; or breathiness, like that of Marilyn Monroe [sorry youngsters; I could not think of a more recent example]).

hearing disorders—impairment of the sense through which sound is received (I believe that, by this definition, the tree that fell in the forest did not make a sound.)

CSD professional—speech-language pathologist, audiologist, or communication scientist.

speech-language pathologist—someone who practices speech-language pathology.

speech-language pathology—study of diagnosis, treatment, and prevention of communication and swallowing disorders.

audiology—the science of hearing, balance, and related disorders (practiced by *audiologists*).

communication scientist—investigators of the anatomical, physiological, and perceptual factors of speech, language, and hearing (Powers, 2000).

And these are just the basics. Each chapter has additional vocabulary words specific to whatever topic is covered. For your convenience—and mine—these words will be both in **bold** type and separately defined.

As you read the definitions, some questions may pop into your brain. With the terms given in this chapter, for example, you might wonder whether there is overlap across them. Doesn't language expression include speech? Wouldn't a disorder of one necessarily result in a disorder of the other? What about understanding versus hearing?

These are all good questions, if I do say so myself. Yes, there is overlap. I hope, as you read the book, that you will begin to understand why the field is categorized according to the terms given. And with any luck, these chapters examine some of the overlaps and attempt to bring the material together.

PERSONAL ESSAY

As chair of the admissions committee for a communication sciences and disorders graduate program, I have read (well, skimmed) my share of essays by prospective students wishing to enter the field. Many of these essays point to applicants' people skills or desire to help others. Experiences in CSD or related fields are also noted with great frequency, as is volunteer work. Those with lawyers or senators in the family often mention this in passing, an implied warning, I suppose, that there might be depositions or tax audits involved should a particular applicant suffer rejection. And while desires and experiences are appropriate to include (family members' occupations, not so much), I am nevertheless awaiting the day when the following essay crosses my desk.

Dear Admissions Committee:
I believe that those who work with communication disordered individuals should be required to answer the following questions:

- How do you spell the word representing the letter h? Achsh? Achhe?
- Who wrote the book of love?
- Who invented the spork?

Okay, I don't really think that. Nor do I care what the answers to these questions are. I just wanted to see whether anyone actually reads these things and figured that, if so, I'll get a response to this introduction. I mean, come on: I sent you transcripts, recommendation letters, and an application listing my name, everywhere I've ever lived, everything I've ever done, and even a list of my favorite 1980s haircuts (the list is the one that begins with 1. *The mullet*). You truly do know all there is to know about me. It seems just a bit unlikely at this point that a one-page essay is going to make or break the deal. Besides, can you really rank these things? Do people actually write to you and say, "As a candidate, I'd rate myself about a 6 out of 10. So if you get through the sevens, I'm your guy!"?

(And while I'm at it: What's the deal with making us get all those letters of recommendation? How do they help you decide who's good and who isn't? It's not like people are going to ask their enemies to write one.)

Anyway, to the matter at hand: why I want to enter the field.

continued

I'd like to tell you I'm a good person, but quite often I'm not. I don't always clean up after my dog if nobody is looking, and I squeeze the toothpaste tube in the middle.

I'd like to say that I care about others, but just this morning I was in a hurry, saw someone with her hands full, and only pretended to try to hold the elevator door for her (by pressing the wall next to the *Open* button, then shrugging my shoulders as if to say "Hey, I tried. The stupid thing has a mind of its own.").

I could tell you that a lifetime of relevant experiences has prepared me for this type of work, but it's a stretch to claim that sleeping late and watching *Saved by the Bell* reruns is sufficient preparation for any profession other than felon or blogger.

I could try false candor and say that, hey, I'm doing this for the money, but I know those of you in university positions would laugh me right out of committee.

So, I'll just tell you that I think your field is cool. Why? Well, lots of reasons:

- I'll get to work in a variety of settings. The field is so short-handed that I don't even have to feign loyalty to any one employer. I can leave, and a new job will always be waiting.
- When I talk to people at parties, I'll for once be an expert in something they might actually care about.
- I'll be able to take my master's degree and scream "Loser!" in the face of all my bachelor's-level friends who razzed me about going back to school.
- I'll finally solve the mystery of velopharyngeal physiology as it relates to the myoelastic-aerodynamic theory of phonation.

Just joking about that last one.

At this point—oh, who am I kidding? Nobody reads this far into application essays. You people have stuff to do. But if you had, you'd surely be asking yourself, "How can we get this guy into our program?" Well, you're in luck. Based on the nonresponses from the other 58 programs I applied to, I'm not in as much demand as you might think. Give me a spot, and we'll see each other in the fall.

On the topic of the rest of the book, here is a partial list of what else the chapters include. Each provides an overview of a topic, including some of the pervasive myths and current controversies. Additional material, such as firsthand accounts of CSD professionals and those they treat, is used to amplify central themes. Finally, helpful visuals such as

WHY I ENTERED THE FIELD

I was working in marketing for a company that did a lot of phone sales. I didn't like it, but that alone was not enough to spur a career change. That process began with a head cold.

Yes, a head cold.

What happened was I missed a few days of work, and, when I came back, I realized something. Just as much got done when I wasn't there as when I was.

My contribution to society didn't even register.

It was time to look for a new job.

I called a headhunting agency and told them my qualifications (leaving out the part about not contributing to the good of anything). They set up an interview for me—another marketing position—in Tampa.

As Tampa was approximately 2,000 miles away, I thought it prudent to arrange an airline flight. The best (that is, the cheapest) one I could find had a 4-hour layover in St. Louis. I knew exactly one person in St. Louis, sort of. He was a friend of a friend (FOAF), and I hadn't spoken to him more than a half dozen times in my life.

I called him anyway, to see if he lived close to the airport and wanted to waste 4 hours in the middle of a weekday. He liked the idea and asked me why I was flying cross-country. This led to a conversation about career paths, during which FOAF told me he was going back to school to earn a graduate degree. He was quite excited about it and made the idea sound so appealing that the following afternoon I went to the local university library and began researching graduate programs. That was the day I discovered that there was such a thing as a master's in communication sciences and disorders. I wrote some letters and filled out some applications.

In the meantime, the Tampa interview fell through, so my flight to St. Louis never materialized. And FOAF decided against getting a master's. But less than 4 months after our telephone conversation, I was sitting in my first graduate course, learning what communication sciences and disorders professionals do.

Figure 1.3 are utilized to illustrate important concepts. It is hoped that by presenting the basic, important, and remarkable aspects of CSD, this book will provide a balanced picture of the profession.

That is it in a nutshell, although the firsthand accounts require some explanation. These are personal stories collected from others. I wrote them of course, but the stories nevertheless belong to the tellers. For purposes of confidentiality, however (and to appease the institutional review

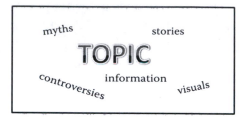

FIGURE 1.3 Organization of chapters in this book. (Artwork by Brennan Williams.)

board of my university), it was necessary to rid them of identifying information. Obviously, this sort of purging would leave the stories with gaps large enough to drive an SUV through. The solution I came up with is the same as that used in my first book:

> "I chose to fill these voids with new details (read: stuff I made up) to keep the flow of the story going. In all cases, however, the final draft was approved by the individual who related the account, on the bases that 1) the spirit of the story was not violated and 2) I agreed to stop calling at 3 a.m. to request this approval." (Williams, 2006, page xvii)

☐ Discussion Questions

1. What do you hope to gain by learning about CSD?
2. Write down something you believe to be particularly interesting about a specific communication disorder. Do a little research. How accurate was your statement?
3. Write down something you believe to be true about a CSD professional. Then determine the accuracy of this statement.
4. Describe the perfect job in CSD.
5. Compose a list of 10 or more traits or features that together would make up the perfect CSD professional.
6. Write two practice essays about why you want to enter the field—one that people will read and one they will not. What is the difference between them? What, if anything, does this tell you about yourself?

☐ Note

1. Prior to the development of speech pathology and audiology (in the 1920s and 1940s, respectively), knowledge of how humans communicated was

housed in a variety of disciplines, including psychology, medicine, linguistics, and education (Powers, 2000). The influences of these areas of study are very much present today, given how CSD requires education in a variety of disciplines.

☐ Recommended Reading

American Speech-Language-Hearing Association (2008). About the professions. Retrieved from http://www.asha.org/students/professions/.
    Good for anyone very interested, somewhat interested, or even potentially interested in a CSD career, this site lists resources, describes market trends, and illustrates employment settings for budding SLPs and audiologists.
Anderson, N. B., Shames, G. H., & Chabon, S. (2006). Introduction: Human communication disorders: A philosophy and practice of service. In N. B. Anderson & G. H. Shames (Eds.), *Human communication disorders: An introduction.* Needham Heights, MA: Allyn & Bacon, 1–21.
    A valuable overview of the field.
Bowen, C. (2007). The SLP "start page." Retrieved from http://members.tripod.com/Caroline_Bowen/slp-eureka.htm.
    This site is particularly valuable for its FAQs (frequently asked questions) and resource lists.
Duchan, J. F. (2006). Getting here: A short history of speech pathology in America. Retrieved from http://www.acsu.buffalo.edu/~duchan/new_history/overview.html.
    Beginning in the 19th century and going to the 21st, Duchan provides an outline for how theory and practice have evolved in the field of speech-language pathology.
National Dissemination Center for Children With Disabilities (2007). Speech and language impairments. Retrieved from http://www.nichcy.org/pubs/factshe/fs11txt.htm.
    An overview of communication disorders, with particular attention paid to their educational implications.
TeensHealth (2007). Speech problems. Retrieved from http://www.kidshealth.org/teen/diseases_conditions/sight/speech_disorders.html.
    Common speech production problems are viewed from the perspective of a teenager. Included are tips for dealing with the problems.

Normal Communication

We humans are interesting machines when you think about it. During the time it takes to reach adulthood, we turn the goo's and gaa's of infancy into a complex process by which thoughts are formed into language, which in turn is related to others through a synchronous process involving the ears, brain, lungs, vocal cords, and tongue, among other parts.

As the auditory system is explained in great detail in Chapter 11, let us take ears out of the equation for the time being and look at the part of the communication process that involves thought, language, and speech. We all know the basics: People think of things to say, transfer those thoughts into language, and say them. And, even though a good deal of what we say is not all that useful, it is nonetheless mysterious how it all works.

☐ How It Works

How it all works is a good place to start. The problem, however, is that I do not really know how it all works. Despite the apparent ease with which we say all of our questionable stuff, human communication is a complicated and often-puzzling process that people have been researching for hundreds of years. Even with centuries of examination, however, there is plenty we still do not understand. And this knowledge—that is, knowing that we are lacking knowledge—is true with respect to all the parts of the system previously noted—thought, language, and speech. Assuming that we think before we speak (a large assumption, I will grant you, for anyone who has ever listened to talk radio), I provide a one-paragraph overview of thought before discussing language and speech.

Thought

Think of the term *thought* as the conceptualization of ideas. It requires **cognition**, in large part because we have no choice but to base our thoughts on what we know. It is probably not news to you that thought takes place in the brain, but you might be surprised to learn that numerous cortical areas are involved, primarily because conceptualization involves so many subfunctions, such as attention, data gathering, and motor processing, among others.

Language

Because thoughts occur in the cortex, it is rather efficient that there is additional brain space devoted to **language**. That way, thoughts can become meaningful symbols, useful for expression, without ever having to leave the neighborhood.

The language center of the brain is usually referred to as **Wernicke's area**. It is here that the aforementioned symbols are attached to our thoughts, essentially turning them into language. Still, it is important to note that language is more than just symbols. After all, without some rules governing the use of these symbols, we would all be using them differently, and no one would know what anyone else was talking about. Therefore, it is both shared symbols and rules that make up a language.

Learning a language, then, requires the ability to detect recognizable symbols (formed into words) in a stream of spoken sounds, attach meaning to those words, and then create your own meaningful symbols in response (Alvares & Williams, 1995). The enormity of this challenge would be overwhelming without brains that are preprogrammed to learn language. Language acquisition is thus a nature-nurture process, involving a biological capacity to acquire language and an environment that is brimming with it.

Symbols and the rules that govern language allow for the creation of a boatload of ways to express ideas. For example, we use colloquialisms, common expressions, and figurative language (clichés, hyperbole, idioms, metaphors, similes, and the like) so much that people just learning the language are sometimes unable even to determine the context of the conversation.

"Sounds like it's really peppering down out there!"
"Oh man, it's cats and dogs."

Notice that nowhere in that exchange can you find the actual topic—rain—mentioned. Imagine hearing it from the perspective of someone who learned numerous English words, but little about their everyday usage.

In addition to the creative ways language is employed across a culture, there are interesting variations from place to place and time to time. You rarely hear, for example, a Bostonian say, "I reckon it's fixin' to rain," or anyone under 40 describe an object or idea as "groovy." Language is clearly not a static entity, but a varied and ever-changing system of communication.

Given that language is complex, symbolic, dynamic, rule bound, and often abstract, it follows that it can also, at various times, be difficult to grasp. For this reason, it is perhaps instructive to break language down into its components. Most simply, one can think of **receptive language** as understanding and **expressive language** as production. Logically, expressive language will be at the same level or less advanced than receptive language skills (we do not produce more than we can understand). Similarly, receptive skills do not exceed cognitive level (meaning we cannot understand more than we know).

Language—both receptive and expressive—has been traditionally separated into five domains: phonology, semantics, morphology, syntax, and pragmatics. Although each of these domains is addressed separately here, in reality they interact (see Chapter 17). As perhaps the most straightforward example of such interaction, we all know how meaning can be completely altered by very slight differences in pronunciation (e.g., *pickle* vs. *pimple*), which brings us to **phonology**, the language domain concerned with speech sounds, or phonemes. While there are over 100 (really) speech sounds that humans are capable of making, only around 43 are used in general American English (see Table 2.1). And, English speakers are further restricted by the rules regarding their use. For example, the sound at the start of the second syllable of "leisure" is never used to begin a word (unless, I suppose, you count *Zsa-Zsa*). When developing language, children learn both individual speech sounds and the rules that govern their use, also known as **phonological processes**.

Of course, making sound combinations is a waste of time if we do not attach meaning to them. This is where **semantics** comes into play. Early on, for example, toddlers learn that saying "no" has definite consequences on their environment. Later, they begin to associate nouns to sound combinations, often using overextension (e.g., calling every round object a ball). Getting from this rather simple beginning to an adult language model is in many ways an exercise in expanding classification schemes. With little effort, adults can point out the similarities and differences of *ball, baseball, basketball, circle, wheel*, the number *zero*, and the letter *o*.

Morphology, another language domain, is the study of **morphemes**, the smallest units of meaning in language. A morpheme may be a free morpheme, which is a word that can stand alone, such as *fish*. A

TABLE 2.1 The International Phonetic Alphabet for American English Phonemes

	Symbol	Key Word
Vowels	/i/	b<u>e</u>
	/ɪ/	p<u>i</u>n
	/e/	<u>a</u>te
	/ɛ/	r<u>e</u>nt
	/æ/	h<u>a</u>t
	/u/	sp<u>oo</u>n
	/ʊ/	b<u>oo</u>k
	/o/	b<u>oa</u>t
	/ɔ/	<u>jaw</u>
	/a/	f<u>a</u>ther
	/ə/	<u>a</u>sleep
	/ʌ/	<u>o</u>ven
	/ɚ/	fing<u>er</u>
	/ɝ/	b<u>ir</u>d
Diphthongs	/aʊ/	c<u>ow</u>
	/aɪ/	fl<u>y</u>
	/ɔɪ/	t<u>oy</u>
	/eɪ/	tr<u>ay</u>
	/oʊ/	g<u>o</u>
Consonants	/p/	<u>p</u>ig
	/b/	<u>b</u>oy
	/t/	<u>t</u>ea
	/d/	<u>d</u>oll
	/k/	<u>k</u>ey
	/g/	<u>g</u>irl
	/f/	<u>f</u>all
	/v/	<u>v</u>an
	/ɵ/	<u>th</u>erapy
	/ð/	<u>th</u>is
	/s/	<u>s</u>oup
	/z/	<u>z</u>ipper
	/ʃ/	<u>sh</u>oe
	/ʒ/	trea<u>s</u>ure
	/h/	<u>h</u>ouse
	/tʃ/	<u>ch</u>in
	/dʒ/	<u>j</u>udge
	/m/	<u>m</u>ap
	/n/	<u>n</u>ose
	/ŋ/	thi<u>ng</u>
	/w/	<u>w</u>in
	/j/	<u>y</u>ellow
	/l/	<u>l</u>ift
	/r/	<u>r</u>amp

TABLE 2.2 Words with 1–7 Morphemes

Word	Number of Morphemes
Establish	1
Establishment	2
Disestablishment	3
Antidisestablishment	4
Antidisestablishmentarian	5
Antidisestablishmentarianism	6
Antidisestablishmentarianismist	7

morpheme may also be a bound morpheme, such as the plural marker *-es* (see Table 2.2). When added to the first example, the new word (*fishes*) has two units of meaning: fish + plural.

Syntax refers to the rules that dictate the order in which words may be combined into sentences. We all remember from those middle school diagramming exercises that sentences must have a subject (a noun) and a verb. If articles appear, they go before the noun, while adverbs modify the verb. Even simple English sentences rely heavily on word order for their meaning.

Married people can't be flirty.
Can't married people be flirty?
Flirty people can't be married.

Each of these sentences express very different thoughts from the others, even though the variations in word order are slight.

Pragmatics refers to the rules governing the use of language. Language is a social tool used to communicate information to others. For a child to be an effective communicator, he or she must learn to use language to express a wide variety of communicative intents. For example, people use language to request objects, request actions, comment, acknowledge, and engage in social amenities. They learn to take turns in conversation, to use the vocabulary appropriate to the situation, and to start, maintain, and change topics, among other pragmatic skills. Language users also need to understand the social appropriateness of different language forms and content. "Hold your horses" is fine among a group of friends but less so when your professor is waiting for you to answer a question.

Speech

Speech is one of two ways in which language is expressed (the other being writing). It is a complex process that begins after the language symbols

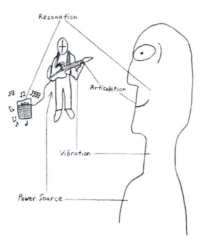

FIGURE 2.1 The sound systems of a bass guitar and human speech. (Artwork by Blaine Williams.)

travel from Wernicke's to **Broca's area**. The latter brain structure then activates the muscles of respiration, voicing, and articulation, which coordinate their movements to make recognizable speech.

If you stood in your favorite public setting and started asking people how speech works, I would be willing to guess that most would describe it this way: We have these vocal cords in our necks, and we pluck them in various ways, sort of like a bass guitarist plucks the strings of his or her instrument to make different notes. The result is the sounds we use to speak.

This is not correct, but it is not totally off base either. The human speech mechanism does have a lot in common with a bass guitar (Figure 2.1).

Instruments utilize a power source, vibrator, and the processes of resonance and articulation. A power source supplies energy to a vibrator to put it into motion. The bass guitarist (i.e., the one member of every band whose name you cannot remember) is the source of the instrument's notes. A vibrator sends periodic energy particles traveling through space. The strings of the guitar serve this purpose. Resonance is the process by which portions of the sound are amplified. Most bass guitars have an electronic amplifier that serves this purpose (if this seems too far from the image of the speaking mechanism, think about an acoustic guitar, which has a hollow body to act as a resonator). Articulation occurs by changing the vibration rate of the vibrator. The guitarist's fingers do that.

The power source for human speech has two parts. Air from the lungs is utilized for all sounds. In addition, the **vocal folds** (commonly called the *vocal cords*), located in the larynx (what we sometimes call the *voice box*), are used in the production of 34 of the 43 speech sounds in the English language. Using the air from the lungs, the vocal folds release air pulses by rapidly moving together and apart (by "rapidly," I mean over 100 times a second for men and twice that for women). These pulses vibrate a column of air (i.e., the vibrator) located above the folds, resulting in a tone that is the voice, the primary sound used in speech. It is not all that different from how fingers vibrate guitar strings. Before being heard by a listener, the tone produced by the vocal folds is modified by the resonating characteristics of the vocal tract—the pharynx and the oral and nasal cavities. In addition to the resonation it receives in the vocal tract, the voice is modified by the process of articulation. The articulators—the tongue, lips, jaw, palate, teeth, and pharynx—move to change the shape and size of the resonator. The positions of the different articulators, and thus the specific resonating features of the resulting tone, depend on the sound being produced (e.g., the positions of the tongue and teeth are very different when saying "ah" than they are for a /v/ sound). The speaker determines the sound he or she wishes to say and, without conscious effort, adjusts the articulators accordingly. This, in turn, changes the characteristics of the vocal fold tone. Because of the large number of sounds required for speech, it is fortunate that the articulators can shape the vocal tract in numerous ways.

Structurally, then, speech can be viewed as consisting of four systems: respiration, the breathing that supports speech; voicing, the sound powered by the vocal folds; resonance, the means by which sound is changed as it travels through the cavities of the neck and head; and articulation, the formulation of speech sounds by the lips, tongue, and other structures. More specifically, it is the integration of these four systems that is needed for the production of normal speech. One interesting (to me, anyway) side note of this arrangement is that because all voiced sounds begin as the same tone, which is then changed as it makes its way up and out of the mouth, what you think of as your voice is really the end product of voicing, respiration, resonance, and articulation.

This four-prong description omits certain elements important to everyday speaking. One such element is *fluency*, the forward flow of speech. Fluent speech is rhythmic and smooth, lacking pauses, repetitions of speech units, or any other interruptions of speech flow. Another aspect of conversational speech, *prosody*, is the ability to utilize elements such as stress, pitch, timing, and loudness to impart meaning. One common example of prosody is the rise in pitch used at the end of a question. Then, there is speech rate, which is exactly what it sounds like—how fast we talk. Obviously, if the rate is too fast, speech can be hard to understand. And if it is too slow, it also calls attention to itself simply because it sounds so unnatural. In conversation, the normal range (i.e., what we hear as natural-sounding speech) is 4.4–5.9 syllables per second (Goldman-Eisler, 1961).

What follows are some other interesting notes about the process:

- Speech is essentially a series of overlaid functions. The main purpose of the lungs, larynx, and resonating tubes is not phonation, but breathing. The articulators are really there so we can eat. Yet, even though all of the structures exist to help keep us alive, humans have made efficient use of these structures, allowing us to communicate in almost unlimited ways.
- **Loudness** refers to the amount of sound the listener perceives. With speech, its value depends on the amount of lung air behind the sound and the tightness of the vocal folds (greater tension there can make the resulting tone louder). As would be expected, sounds of greater **intensity** are perceived to be louder.
- **Pitch** is the subjective quality that listeners use to order tones from low to high. It is a perception based on **frequency,** or vocal fold vibration rate. Because the vocal folds typically vibrate 100–125 times per second for adult males and about twice that for adult females and children, we perceive men as having lower pitches than women and kids.
- The third voice parameter, **quality,** is, like loudness and pitch, a subjective judgment on the part of the listener. Quality is best understood as the perception of how the patterns of loudness and pitch combine to make a person's voice recognizable. Two individuals, talking with the same average pitch and loudness, can sound very different. One may sound hoarse or breathy in comparison to the other. These are differences of quality.
- An individual speech sound is not always made the same way. Research has shown us, for example, that articulator movements vary with repeated productions of the same words (Gracco & Abbs, 1986). Maybe the tongue does not move as far or as fast for a sound as it did the last time it made the exact same sound. So, why do listeners still perceive it as the same sound? Simple: The other articulators compensate for the difference (maybe the lips moved a little further or faster for the second production).
- You could individually record the sounds /f/, /ɪ/, and /ʃ/ and then combine them into one recording. It might resemble the word *fish*, but it would not sound like speech. That is because speech involves not just sounds, but all that goes on in the transitions between sounds.
- Related to the previous two items is **coarticulation.** If we look at sound features such as length of time and intensity, we will see that, for example, the /s/ at the beginning of "sausage" is not the same as the one at the end of "mongoose." This is due to the process of **assimilation**—the first /s/ is more "aw-like" than the second, which more resembles the phoneme /u/.

DOUBLE TROUBLE! (OR BETTER YOU THAN ME)

For those of you who did not have the opportunity to experience an ultrasound, circa 2001, the procedure went something like this: The ultrasound tech picked up a tube and squeezed what looked to be liquid nails onto my pregnant wife's stomach. Why her belly required translucent goo at that point in time I wasn't sure. Maybe it *was* liquid nails, and they were making certain that the contents didn't leave the container.

In any case, what I remember next is the tech taking one of those paddles from an air hockey game and squishing it around within the liquid, creating both a mess and some indiscernible images on a nearby television.

"How are you doing?" she asked.

"*I'm* fine," I answered, not wanting to speak for my wife. After all, I wasn't the one with liquid nails and an air hockey paddle on my abdomen.

The tech continued making conversation. "Is there a history of twins in your family?"

"No." I looked at my wife. She shook her head.

"Well," said the tech, "*there is now!*"

That moment will stay with me forever. It could not have been any more memorable had the tech taken her little TV and smashed it over my head.

Twins?! How was I going to handle twins? I didn't even remember to feed the dog every day. And babies can't put their bowls in their mouths and bring them to you as a reminder.

I also began to recall stories I'd heard about twins and how creepy they can be, communicating through telepathy, marrying people with the same names, those sorts of things. I know of twins who were each traveling—on two different continents—who sent their mother the exact same birthday card.

I was clearly entering a new world.

I stayed in shock for a number of days, during which I found it difficult to even tell people the news. When I did, their reactions pretty much fell into three categories—joy, laughter (mostly my family), and the line, "Hey, better you than me!" I heard that one so often that I decided that the next person to say it would receive a double load of dirty diapers in the mail (I was convinced it was the most unoriginal joke ever until the twins were born and I had to listen to passersby shout "Double trouble!" a few quadrillion times).

continued

There were a couple of folks who opined that watching twins develop would be interesting. After all, they noted, not many people get to experience two children of the exact same age influence each others' maturity.

Thinking that these folks were trying to put a happy face on a disaster, I responded with grunts to let them know that I had better things to do than listen to uninformed theories.

Once my daughters were born, however, I have to say that the experience was different from living with single babies (which I had done twice before). Of course, I didn't realize this, or much of anything else, for several months, as the girls rarely let me sleep more than 15 consecutive minutes. Then, I began to notice some things. Most strikingly, one daughter was a snuggler, the other a wiggler. Maybe, I surmised, they aren't so much parts of a set as they are two separate individuals.

The one who crawled first was the last to walk, but the first to run. She's the one who liked to sit and read, while her sister roughhoused with their brothers. One twin was more selfish, yet had a greater dislike of being alone. The other was quite content to play by herself.

Their communication developments took diverse tracks as well. The snuggler's first word was *cat*, and the wiggler's was *dog*. One used a lot of function words, we think—she spoke in almost constant and unintelligible jargon. The other produced only whole words— nouns and verbs mostly—that she could say correctly. Interestingly, the latter twin was not as easy to understand by the age of 2. She also spoke with comparatively increased nasality, presented a greater variety of language forms, and produced far more breaks of fluency even though she talked less.

One proved to be more of a risk taker with language, willing to guess when she didn't know and to try complex words that she really didn't have the capacity to produce. Her sister simply told us "I can't say that." Oddly, the one who gave up on words was the more daring when it came to swimming, trying new foods, and riding roller coasters.

One always talked to people in stores, work, and so on. When preschool began, she separated easily and joined the other children, assuming that they were awaiting her participation. Her sister held Dad's hand until she *had* to separate and, teary-eyed, walk away with the teacher. The good news was that after a few weeks, the teacher reported that she was coming out of her shell.

"Great," I said. "What about her sister?"

"Her sister doesn't *have* a shell."

Oh, right.

The girls mastered their sounds at different times, but eventually got them all. Neither could produce a decent /s/ for the longest time, but they distorted the sound in such different ways that we could tell them apart a room away (provided they were talking, of course). In addition to these differences, there were articulation patterns that were strikingly similar. Both put "lickstip" on their mouths. They used "napkumes" to wipe their faces after eating "skapetti" or "yogret." Being Florida girls, they knew that "topical storms" can form into "hurkacanes."

Both girls learned early how to use language to manipulate. Statements that resulted in little but disinterest from my sons could elicit great emotion from their sisters.

"Don't put the glass on the edge of the table. It'll spill."
"Mommy! Daddy's being mean to me!"

Their manipulation skills evolved in different ways. One was sneaky, preferring to mislead her parents away from any wrongdoing she may have performed. Often, in fact, she misled through her teeth. The other manipulated from the comfort of a unique logic scheme.

"Sissy took my dolly away from me."
"Why?"
"She wanted it back."
"Did you take it from her first?"
"Uh-huh."
"Well, then she gets to play with it now."
"But I wanted it!"

I never came up with anything that convinced her that my reasoning was any better than hers.

Learning to read and write illuminated their differences as much as speech and language had. One had no worries that she'd eventually catch on; the other found these tasks quite stressing. There were good and bad points to each approach. Being laid back gave one daughter the confidence to learn. Unfortunately, it also made her lazy.

"What comes after c?"
"I don't know. Seven? Can I go out and play now?"

continued

The other twin's perfectionism held back learning, in that it made her reticent to guess or to ask for help. Once she got it, however, she continued to work hard. Maybe she didn't learn to write as quickly as her sister did, but 2 months later she was filling up pages with a wide variety of information.

> Misty costume is a Ladbug.
> Misty costume is red.
> Misty costume is pitty.
> I love Misty costume.
> And so on.

Sis, on the other hand, wrote stories consisting of variations of the same few sentences, as this completed the assignment faster (which, in turn, got her out to play faster).

> Costume is Mistys I like the antlears.
> I like the red shrt.
> I like the antlears so much.
> I like the red shrt so so so so much.
> (You get the idea.)

Can these sorts of things be challenging? Well, yeah, at times. But now that I see how it works, I have little doubt that they will both eventually get to where they need to be.

☐ How It Develops

Although *thought* is the foundation of our model of communication, this has more to do with how I sequenced the process of expression (thought to language to speech) than it does with development. In truth, the skills of cognition, language, and speech develop simultaneously, starting at birth and proceeding gradually toward an adult model. Not only do they develop concurrently, but also they all influence one another (Wener, 1998). Highlights of this development include the following:

- At birth, infants have little control over starting and stopping their voices. The upside to this is that they do not really need it, given that they are completely dependent on a caretaker who jumps at every sound they make. The most well known of these sounds is, of course, crying. It is reflexive and used to express pain, displeasure, and hunger. Later, parents often report that their babies have different cries to express different desires. In other words, the infant learns how to use sound (the crying one, anyway) to manipulate the environment.

- Six to 8 weeks after birth, and continuing to about 3–4 months of age, babies engage in **cooing**—small, miscellaneous throaty sounds, made in response to some physical state such as hunger. Typically, cooing sounds are vowels, with limited variability. Still, they are more speech-like than crying and thus pave the way to eventual word production.

- Infants respond to some sounds, most notably mom's voice. They also recognize commonalities in the language around them, such as patterns of stress and intonation. This recognition eventually helps them determine word boundaries (Anderson & Shames, 2006).

- At 3 months of age, infants can visually track objects.

- Children begin to laugh around 16 weeks of age.

- Between 3 and 6 months, babies start putting everything they get a hold of in their mouth. By doing so, they both explore and learn shapes, textures, and other characteristics (e.g., that thing the dog left behind tastes yucky).

- Between 4 and 6 months is a period of vocal play (Stark, 1986), when children sound pretty much like frat boys, producing raspberries, squeals, growls, and laughter. They also begin to use longer strings of sound combinations.

- By 5 months, infants recognize their own language, responding to it differently than to other languages (Nazzi, Jusczyk, & Johnson, 2000).

- At 5–6 months, infants begin to realize that not just crying, but also other behaviors (vocalizations, smiles) can be used to manipulate others.

- **Babbling** occurs by month 6 and continues to about 10–12 months of age. At this point, a noticeably greater variety of sounds is being produced. Often, sound combinations are reduplicated (e.g., sa-sa or the one that gets Mom excited: ma-ma). Babbling sounds more like language than does cooing. Although controversial, some researchers (e.g., Boysson-Bardies, de Sagart, & Durand, 1984) have concluded that listeners can often tell if a baby's babbling comes from their language.

- Around 8 to 11 months, vocalizations are different enough that parents can easily distinguish the infant's intentions (Smiley & Goldstein, 1998).

- **Echolalia**—the exact repetition of what someone else says—starts around 9 to 12 months and continues to about 18 months of age. Essentially, the infant is trying to imitate an adult speech model. Although this is considered a normal part of language development, it can also represent a problem if it persists too long.

- From 9 to 18 months of age, children use a lot of **jargon**. This sounds very much like running speech, as it contains syllables strung together with inflection, but the kid is not saying anything meaningful. As with echolalia, should jargon persist (i.e., if the child does not move past it by a year and a half or so), it can signal a delay in language development.
- A child's first real word usually occurs around 10–14 months of age. When I ask parents about this, I specify that I am inquiring about the first word other than "mama" or "dada," given that these may occur randomly during the aforementioned syllable reduplication phase.
- Many early words refer to classifications (e.g., "cat" means all animals) or have multiple meanings ("Mommy" as a name and a way of getting Mom's attention).
- From 12 to 18 months, children will request objects, actions, and sometimes even information. They begin to acknowledge, answer, greet, and even show off (Smiley & Goldstein, 1998). On average, a child will produce about 75 words during this time.
- Around 18 months, children start putting two words together.
- In the second year of life, the toddler learns to associate phonological patterns with actions and objects, such as saying "uh-oh" when something falls or saying "baba" for bottle (Alvares & Williams, 1995).
- While many early words are nouns, the toddler also learns some verbs and adjectives, particularly between 18 months and 2 years of age, as this is a period of rapid vocabulary growth. Different types of words can be combined into short phrases (e.g., "Go bye-bye"). During this time, speech is about 25% intelligible (Bowen, 1998), and voice is used in increasingly sophisticated ways to convey meaning (such as using rising pitch at the end of questions), express moods (louder means angry or excited), and recognize situations (e.g., indoor vs. outdoor voice).
- At 24 months, toddlers can (although they often do not) follow simple verbal commands. They develop **object permanence**, an understanding that when items disappear from sight they still exist. Although this understanding makes it harder for Dad to do magic tricks, it also signifies a higher level of awareness. In addition, 2-year-olds engage in active and independent problem solving, often expressing their intention to do so in less-than-charming ways ("You go 'way—I do it!"). Speech is now about 50–75% intelligible. Disfluency can occur in as many as 25% of words spoken.
- By the time they are 27 months old, most children can point to and name familiar objects in pictures.
- Between 27 and 30 months, they begin to present the following: regular plurals, past tense (regular and irregular), possessive /s/, regular past tense, negation, and questions. My kids were best at the last two—they

responded "no" to most everything I said and asked endless streams of *why* questions ("Why going?" So we can get home. "Why?" It's time to go home. "Why time go home?" It's late. "Why?" It's past your bedtime. "Why?" Shut up. And so on.).

- At 31 to 34 months of age, articles and adjectives emerge.
- At 33 months, toddlers can often identify simple action pictures.
- Prepositional phrases normally come in between 35 and 40 months. Intelligibility at this age is about 75–100%.
- By 39 months, many kids can identify the primary colors. By the way, I stopped here with the color learning, which now makes it tough when furniture salespeople use descriptions like "taupe with melon highlights" ("with" is the only part of that I understand).
- At 42 months, children can give their full name on request.
- At 45 months, many children enjoy pretending, which they incorporate into much of their play.
- By the age of 5 years, children have acquired 90% of adult brain weight and most rules of language. This includes **metalinguistic skills**, which begin to develop late in the preschool years.
- By age 9, all English sounds have generally been acquired.
- During the school years, children learn to use and understand words that are used metaphorically, such as using personification to express an idea (e.g. "March comes in like a lion") (Alvares & Williams, 1995).
- The school environment places different academic and social language demands on the child than does the home. Haynes, Moran, and Pindzola (1999) described a number of skills the child needs to learn, including rules of behavior, how to ask and answer questions, turn taking, and maintaining a topic of conversation. The language used is different as well, often focusing on ideas such as letters, colors, and numbers.
- With age comes an increasing sense of personal identity, as children become concerned about how they present themselves—what sort of an impression they make on others and what they should and should not say about themselves.
- New communicative demands continue to crop up during later school years. These demands include impressing members of the opposite sex and changing one's language depending on the situation or listener (we do not say the same things—or at least not the same way—when talking to friends and family as opposed to being at school or work).
- After the school years are over, additional demands—getting a job, changing jobs, moving to new locations, and the like—force language to keep growing in terms of vocabulary and uses.
- Vocal pitch at about age 18 is what it will be through middle age and beyond. Fluency will not change a lot either; adults are about 95%

fluent, but with much variability—your favorite TV anchor is higher, and that guy you know who drops an "um" or "y'know" after every third word of conversation is lower.

- Communicative improvements do not go on forever, of course. As adults age, they gradually lose **inhibition**, information-processing speed, and memory. Shortly after age 60, the voice may decline as well, evidenced by a decreased ability to control both pitch and loudness.

The following are some interesting notes about the development process:

- Communication functions—**instrumental, regulatory, interactional,** and **personal**—begin early and continue throughout life.
- One of the more amazing aspects of development for parents is hearing infants start to shape random sounds into words. They can hear articulation getting more precise and purposeful while witnessing the onset of semantic skills.
- Speaking of parents, what they do (for instance, simplifying their own language or expanding on the child's utterances) can benefit the child's language development. This is not to say that language-disordered children are the product of bad parenting or that obsessive parents produce the most linguistically gifted children. Rather, it simply points out that environmental influences can be positive ones.
- During initial word acquisition, children use overextension. To use the previous example, a child may call all animals "cat." In this way, the word *cat* refers to a classification (all animals). As classification schemes expand, more words are needed. For example, my son called all land animals *cat* and all water creatures *duck* (except for the black bear at the zoo, which for some reason was a duck). In time, of course, he developed a more sophisticated classification scheme where *cat* included everything from a Bengal tiger to our useless tabby.
- Children can also do the opposite and undergeneralize. That is, if a toddler knows that Asti (the aforementioned tabby) is a cat, he or she might argue that *only* Asti is a cat. Show the kid another cat, say "cat," and you will get a firm "No!" because only one entity is associated with the word *cat*.

☐ Synopsis

Communication is a complex process. The components of thought, language, and speech develop concurrently and influence one another in terms of both development and implementation.

☐ Vocabulary

assimilation—effect of one phoneme on another when uttered in close sequence, such that they become more like each other (Nicolosi et al., 1989)

babbling—prelinguistic vocalizations typically occurring during the second 6 months of life characterized by repetition of syllables and intonational patterns

Broca's area—brain structure responsible for programming the motor events required to carry out the production of language units

coarticulation—influence of phonetic environments on articulatory sequences (Minifie, Hixon, & Williams, 1973)

cognition—the act or process of knowing

cooing—production of vowel-like sounds, often in isolation

echolalia—repetition of sounds without modification

expressive language—the communication an individual produces, expresses, or encodes as output, that is, the *language performance* (Alvares & Williams, 1995)

frequency—the number of repetitions of compressions and rarefactions of a sound wave that occur at the same rate over a period of time, expressed in hertz

inhibition—loss of ability to filter out that which is irrelevant or should not be said

instrumental communication—language functioning to satisfy wants and needs

intensity—magnitude of force, energy, power, or pressure acting to produce a sound (Nicolosi et al., 1989)

interactional communication—language utilized to establish or maintain interpersonal contact

jargon—verbal behavior that contains a variety of syllables that are inflected in a manner approximating meaningful connected speech (Nicolosi et al., 1989)

language—the symbolic formulation of thought, encompassing understanding, integration, and expression of information in either a verbal or graphic form (Alvares & Williams, 1995)

loudness—the psychological parameter (i.e., perception) of intensity

metalinguistic skills—ability to reflect language and to comment on it, as well as to produce and comprehend it (i.e., language about language) (Nicolosi et al., 1989)

morpheme—unit of meaning (Brown, 1973)

morphology—study of the structure or forms of words, primarily through the use of the morpheme construct (Brown, 1973)

object permanence—awareness that an object is relatively permanent and is not destroyed if removed from the visual field (Nicolosi et al., 1989)

personal communication—language employed to express attitudes, emotions, or interest

phonological processes—rules kids use to make productions fit into their understandings and abilities

phonology—the study of the rules governing speech sounds/phonemes

pitch—the psychological parameter of frequency

pragmatics—the rules governing the use of language in context; how language is used

quality—subjective impression of the patterns of frequencies and relative intensities of the voice (Nicolosi et al., 1989)

receptive language—the language that the individual understands, comprehends, processes, or decodes as input (Alvares & Williams, 1995).

regulatory communication—language used to control others' behavior

semantics—the study of the meaning in language

speech rate—medium of verbal communication (as opposed to *writing*, the graphic production of language)

syntax—study of the rules governing the combination of words to form sentences (Brown, 1973)

vocal folds—twin pliable tissue structures involved in breathing, protection of the airway, and producing voice

Wernicke's area—posterior portion of superior temporal gyrus; responsible for forming, understanding, and storing language

☐ Discussion Questions

1. How much of your day-to-day language is figurative? List some examples.
2. Infant-directed speech (also known as *motherese*) is characterized by simplified speech, lots of inflection, and accompanying facial expressions and gestures. How (if at all) might this help the infant understand what is being said?
3. Give an example of something you commonly say to friends that you would not say to a professor? How about the other way around?
4. The vocal folds vibrate over 100 times a second for men and twice that for women. Why do females' folds vibrate faster?
5. See if you can determine which of the items listed in the "How It Develops" section are cognitive milestones, which are language, and which ones refer to speech.

☐ Recommended Reading

Alvares, R. L., & Williams, D. F. (1995). Students with speech and/or language impairments. In R. L. Taylor, L. Sternberg, & S. B. Richards (Eds.), *Exceptional children: Integrating research and teaching* (pp. 191–216). San Diego, CA: Singular.

OK, maybe it is tacky to cite one's own material, but we did spend a lot of time putting together the "how it all works" stuff.

American Speech-Language-Hearing Association (ASHA) (2007). Your child's communication development: Kindergarten through fifth grade. Retrieved from http://www.asha.org/public/speech/development/communicationdevelopment.htm. One of many good sources of development on the ASHA Web site, this link provides a quick and accurate checklist for developmental milestones.

Bowen, C. (1998). Brown's stages: The development of morphology and syntax. Retrieved from http://www.speech-language-therapy.com/BrownsStages.htm.

The author clearly presents Roger Brown's stages of expressive language development.

Smiley, L. R., & Goldstein, P. A. (1998). *Language delays and disorders from research to practice*. San Diego. CA: Singular.

This text bridges the research–practice gap in readable fashion.

CHAPTER

Research

Note: This chapter is based in large part on *How to Read Research (and Non-Research),* a chapter in my 2006 book *Stuttering Recovery: Personal and Empirical Perspectives.* It is not exactly the same chapter, but portions are close enough that I figured I had better get permission from the publisher (Lawrence Erlbaum Associates, Inc., Mahwah, NJ) before this one came out. Rest assured this has been done.

Anyone who wants to keep up on advances in communication sciences and disorders (CSD) needs to read the research. This is true whether your interest is theory (such as looking for causes of disorders) or practice. In fact, research is more relevant to the latter than you might think, given the moves of the professions toward **evidence-based practice.** That is, it is not enough for treatments to show face validity (i.e., to seem logical). Increasingly, they will be required to substantiate their claims of effectiveness (Feeney, 2006).

Some view the importance of research (theoretical or practical) as bad news. The reason is that they find published studies about as easy to understand as those light-speed disclaimers at the end of drug commercials. Although we do not get every word of these stipulations (something about side effects, vomiting, or death), we do get the general idea: This medication is not for everyone. Similarly, the aim of most research is relatively easy to comprehend, even if we do not decipher each and every term. One thing that helps us with this understanding is that all studies use the same format. That is, every one begins with a literature review followed by sections on methods, results, and discussion. This chapter follows the same order, beginning with the literature review.

☐ Literature Review

As Robey and Schultz (1993) explained it, research is driven by theory building. In essence, this means that it is based on the scientific method: develop, test, and if necessary, modify a hypothesis. Thus, the basis for research should not be "let's see what happens to x when we do y." Sure, doing so might result in some interesting findings:

- What would happen to a kid's language development if we made him talk like a pirate?
- How would shock treatments affect someone who talks out of turn?
- Would people swallow less in the presence of a smelly wet dog?

Nevertheless, random questions are not the basis for proposed research. Rather, it is what we know up to now, the current state of theory, that determines what comes next. Ideally, then, the authors of a research study can make a case that their experiment is the foremost investigation to advance our understanding of communication (or at least some aspect of it) at this point in time. In other words, everything that has happened in the past has led us to their experiment. They convince us of this important point via a review of the literature on which the theory is based.

Because the literature review is meant to support the study in which it resides; it progresses deductively toward a purpose statement (explaining why this particular experiment is being done; see Figure 3.1). One result of this general-to-specific succession is that just about anything might appear at the beginning. Adding to the confusion is that this section necessarily includes numerous citations, which can make it difficult to read. Note the following (fictitious) example.

For years, researchers have been investigating the Freudian slips of midshipmen (Jones, 2004; Jones & Jones, 2001; Jones & Smith, 1983; Jones, Smith, Smith, & Jones, 2002; Jones, Smith, Smith II, Jones, & Jones, 1993; Smith, 2002; Smith & Jones, 2003; Smith, Jones, & Jones, 1977; Smith, Jones, Smith, & Jones, 2002; Smith, Smith, & Jones, 1987; Smith, Smith, Jones, Jones, & Jones, 2002; Smith, Smith, Smith, Smith, Smith, Jones, Smith, Smith II, and Duffy, 2004; Williams, 2003). While much of this literature is written to advance theoretical notions about this phenomenon (Duffy, 1995; Duffy & Jones, 1991; Duffy, Jones, & Smith, 2002; Duffy & Smith, 1999; Duffy, Smith, & Jones, 1993; Smith, Jones, & Duffy, 1944; Smith, Jones, Duffy, & Herbert, 2003; Williams, 2003), other researchers have focused on limiting their occurrences (Herbert, 2002; Jones, 2004; Smith, 2000; Smith &

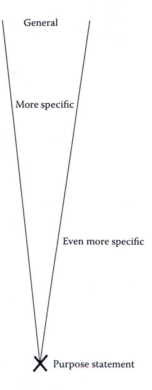

General

More specific

Even more specific

Purpose statement

FIGURE 3.1   Progression of the literature review.

Duffy, 2001; Smith & Herbert, 1987; Smith & Jones, 2000, Smith & Smith, 2002; Smith, Smith, Jones, & Herbert, 1999).

The numerous articles cited may have little in common, other than they are all somehow related to the sentences that they follow. It is even possible, in fact, that some have only slight relevance to the study they are introducing. So, why are they there?

If questioned, the author would likely put forth variations of the following claims:

- A broad overview provides a historical foundation for the theory under test.
- Classic studies form a basis for present research.
- After the introduction is balanced with a discussion of the relevance of the study, the reader will understand how it adds to the overall knowledge base.

Cynical observers might point out additional benefits of this format. For one, it gives the appearance that the authors have read a ton of research, even if in reality they only skimmed a few abstracts. Second, they had ample opportunity to cite their friends, which one day could lead to reciprocation. Third, the accepted format for introducing a research study allows the authors to reference their own research. In many cases, it can even be cited alongside the most seminal works in the field, suggesting that it belongs there.

> Much has been written on the topic of communication sciences and disorders (Bloom & Lahey, 1978; Van Riper, 1973; Williams, 1993).

Note that nothing about this citation format gives away that I am grouping a major contribution to the understanding of language development, a landmark treatment text, and a 2-page article I wrote for an in-house newsletter.

Finally, the introductory paragraphs provide a place for the authors to mention articles with which they are unfamiliar or even dislike. This is an unfortunate, albeit sometimes necessary, evil of the publication process. Once a manuscript is submitted for publication, it is sent to experts in the field for review; often, these reviewers suggest that the author cite specific articles.

> The topic is worthwhile, but needs to be couched in a historical context, that is, how does it further the landmark work of Moe (1944, 1946), Larry (1945), and Moe, Larry, and Curly (1947)?

Rather than risk annoying a reviewer by asking who Moe, Larry, or Curly are, or waste time wondering which one the reviewer is, the authors might decide to include these works in a nebulous manner that appears respectful without actually allowing the studies in question to interfere with the present one.

> Research in this area has been going on for decades (Moe, 1944, 1946; Larry, 1945; Moe, Larry, & Curly, 1947).

It is worth noting that extraneous information added to placate reviewers is not limited to citations. Nonsequiturs appear throughout research articles. For example, when reading a study, you might come across a paragraph similar to the following:

> Fletcher (1914) noted differences in speech-related breathing when comparing samples of stuttered and nonstuttered speech. It should be noted, however, that there were people treated by Moe, Larry, and Curly (1947) who did not fit this pattern.

Actually, it should not have been noted, but now you know why it was.

Despite the potential for self-aggrandizement, the review process is a necessary element of the scientific method. Some (Bartley, 1984; Herbert et al., 2000) even view it as the most important feature of science. How better to advance a hypothesis than to feed it to ravenous critics who will tear it apart and leave the remains for theorists to reconstruct into a (it is hoped) superior form?

Does that mean the reader can trust the infallibility of published research? Read on.

☐ Purpose

The whole point of the introduction/literature review is to lead to the purpose of the study, a statement of how the outlined theory will be put to test. Figure 3.1 shows how the introduction progresses from the general to the specific. Think of the purpose statement as the point at the bottom (the one handily labeled "Purpose statement"), the final level of specificity. For example, an introductory sentence referencing communication disorders sets up mention of research on misarticulated sounds, which leads to articulation disorders, which falls nicely into testing for articulation disorders, which brings the reader to research utilizing articulation tests that the author knows how to use, which, finally, results in the purpose statement for this particular study.

The following are examples of purpose statements similar to what you are likely to find in CSD research journals:

1. *The purpose of the present study is to determine whether sample groups of adults who do and do not stutter differ with respect to alpha-wave suppression under visualized speech conditions.* The purpose here is to advance our understanding of a particular phenomenon.
2. *The purpose of the present study is to determine whether focused practice results in improved performance on objectives related to established outcomes.* This time, the purpose is more practical—examining the application of therapy.
3. *We decided to address the lack of clarity observed in past research by stopping the first five people we saw and asking, "So what's the deal with communication?"* Here, the author really needed a publication to keep his or her job.

☐ Methods

The purpose statement generally concludes the introduction and paves the way for the next section, the one that describes the methods used to test the theory. These are necessarily presented in great detail so that other researchers can, if they so desire, replicate the study themselves. Unfortunately, this specificity may turn readers glassy eyed as they plow through procedural descriptions, trying to absorb a general idea of how the experiment was set up without spending excessive time and energy concentrating on sentences such as "Respiratory, electroglottographic, and air flow signals were digitized at 1000 samples per second by a 12-bit analog-to-digital conversion board" (Williams, 1992) (yes, this is an actual sentence that appears in my doctoral dissertation, originally titled "A Series of Convoluted Sentences").

Despite its propensity for detail, however, this section should not serve as a cue to stop paying attention, given the importance of the methods used to achieve the stated purpose of the study. Readers of research often pontificate on the topic of validity,[1] wondering aloud whether the researchers really accomplished what they set out to accomplish. The "Methods" section is the focus of such pontification, the place where validity can be established. For example, determining genetic influences on deafness by tracking gene markers would be far different from doing so by asking people, "Anyone else in your family have problems hearing?" Moreover, it does not require excessive concentration to figure out research methods. For most, the trick is to lose the wall of resistance to anything technical. Ask your professor—he or she is accustomed to feeling this wall go up whenever something scientific is mentioned.

"I can't do that," students explain. "I'm not a science person."

Yes, you can. Sure, methods can be complex, but so can a lot of things. Many will say they cannot keep scientific complexities straight, yet these same people can describe in great detail how an eight-cylinder engine works, or why Misty was crying when Bud responded to the statement, "I love you," with, "Back at ya."

☐ Results

The "Methods" section is followed by the presentation and analysis of the raw data of the study. This section, headed "Results," is where the researcher reports numbers, statistical analyses, and concrete observations of what happened when the authors' hypothesis was put to test. Sounds good, right? I mean, nothing could be more objective than that, right?

Again, read on.

Think of "Results" as the foundation on which the conclusions of the study will be based. While there is nothing inherently wrong with this sequence, there is, unfortunately, room for creative foundation building.

See, there are many ways to present results. The means by which it is done in a given study might depend on whether the authors have a theory they are just dying to tell you about (see discussion in Park, 2000). And, believe me, many do. In fact, it is often possible to accurately predict the conclusions of the study knowing only the title and author's name.

It should be noted here that results (and the conclusions drawn from them) are usually based on **statistical significance**. That is, before running any statistical analysis, an author will set a significance level, indicating the acceptable probability that any differences found could have occurred by chance alone (Schiavetti & Metz, 2006). Common criterion levels are .05 (a 5% probability, which equates to a 95% likelihood that the differences were real and not random) and the more stringent .01.

Even using such objective criteria, however, the same results can be reported differently, as the next examples illustrate:

- The descriptive data indicate that the sample consisting of people with language deficits scored lower on all tests than did the subjects with no disorders. However, when t tests were applied to the sample means, it was found that none of the differences was statistically significant.
- One obvious trend from the data is that the subjects with language deficits scored consistently lower on all tests than did the no disorder group. In fact, in all cases, these differences approached statistical significance.

The first example informed the reader what happened. When the data were eyeballed, there appeared to be a trend. But, when it was analyzed, the trend was not a meaningful one.

In the second example, the writer is also reporting what happened, but in this instance, the trend is made to appear consequential. The problem with this example is that, by the author's own criterion, the differences between the groups are not meaningful. That is, the author defined a difference as group means that vary to a statistically significant degree. That did not happen. Now, the reader is told that any difference is suitable. In other words, the author decided to change the rules. Mind you, there are times I would like to do things in reverse order myself. I would be rich if, for instance, I could place a parlay on the Kentucky Derby after it has been run. Unfortunately, that is considered bad form. So is setting the criterion level after you have tried to meet it.

Notice also that if the author leaves out the second sentence, the motive is even less apparent.

- One obvious trend from the data is that the subjects with language deficits scored consistently lower on all tests than did the no disorder group.

Now, the reader is being told that statistical analyses need not be applied (or at least not reported). Just take the author's word that the difference is really a difference.

This same strategy can be manifested in other forms. The following examples show the same results reported three ways:

- Significant results were found for variables A, B, and C ($p < .05$). Analysis of variable D did not indicate a significant difference ($p > .05$).
- Significant results were found for variables A, B, C ($p < .05$) and D ($p < .10$).
- Significant results were found for variables A, B, C ($p < .05$). In addition, significance was approached for D ($p = .09$).

Remember that before running any statistical analysis, an author will set a significance level. In these instances, the level was set at .05. Using this very standard criterion, significant differences were found for three variables. End of story. In the first example, the author says so. In the second, the significance level is changed to get a fourth difference. The third example is a little better than the second in that the author does not overtly fudge the significance level. It is likely, however, that the results are reported as such because, in the "Discussion" section, the author intends to sell the reader on four differences, not three.

☐ Discussion

The "Discussion" section exists for exploration of the import of the study. Prior to this section, the authors have given the reader an overview of current theory and research (literature review), the means by which they attempted to add to this body of research (methods), and what happened during this attempt (results). What is left is to tie it all together, to explain how the current results complement present theory. In other words, what do the results mean?

The interpretation of data can be a tricky business. For example, there is the problem of directionality (Neale & Liebert, 1986). Does A cause B, or does B cause A? Does team camaraderie lead to winning, or do teams that win tend to get along? Do differences in brain function cause stuttering, or does a lifetime of stuttering influence how the brain functions?

The answer might be none of the above. Sometimes, there is a third variable influencing both A and B (Neale & Liebert, 1986). Does the presence of mittens cause an increase in car accidents, or does a larger number of wrecks cause people to wear mittens? Probably neither, at least in any universe that includes an as-yet-unmentioned factor—snow—that could be responsible for both. Similarly, correlations between different communication disorders might not reflect one causing the other, but rather some underlying difference in the overall system that influences both.

To be fair, directionality and third-variable issues are difficult to assess. The same cannot be said for other forms of misinterpretation, however. We have all heard that, with statistics, anyone can say anything. Actually, inventive conclusions do not even require any statistics, as the following old joke illustrates. (Note: This particular joke has been retold in many forms. In honor of my brother and dad's affiliation with the University of Michigan, I tell it this time as a Wolverine joke.)

Two boys are playing football in Ann Arbor. Suddenly, one is attacked by a rabid rottweiler. Thinking quickly, the other boy rips a big board off a nearby fence, wedges it down the dog's collar and twists it, breaking the dog's neck.

A reporter happens to be strolling by. He sees the incident and rushes over to interview the boy.

"Young Michigan Wolverine Fan Rescues Friend From Vicious Animal," he starts writing in his notebook.

"But I'm not a Michigan Wolverine fan," the little hero replies.

"Sorry. Since we're in Ann Arbor, I just assumed you were," says the reporter. Crossing out his notes, he starts again: "Little Michigan State Spartan Fan Rescues Friend From Deathly Attack."

"I'm not a Michigan State fan either," says the boy.

Puzzled, the reporter looks at the boy. "I assumed everyone who lives in Michigan was either for the Wolverines or Spartans," he explains. "What team do you root for?"

"I'm an Ohio State fan," the boy replies.

The reporter starts a new sheet in his notebook and writes, "Little Redneck Buckeye Kills Beloved Family Pet!"

Of course, it is not just football rivalries that are subject to skewing. In a similar fashion, research findings can be viewed in a variety of ways. Take, for instance, a previous example of reported results:

The descriptive data indicate that the sample consisting of people with language deficits scored lower on all tests than did the subjects with no disorders. However, when t tests were applied to the sample means, it was found that none of the differences was statistically significant.

The "Discussion" section would, ideally, include a statement that no evidence was found of differences between groups and an examination of how this progresses or detracts from current theory. In this way, the results of the investigation have provided a legitimate foundation for the authors' conclusions.

Unfortunately, the ideal is not always the reality. If it were, I would have a mansion on Palm Beach Island, and you would be rolling your eyes at someone else's book. The reality here is that a shaky foundation is sometimes used to support a straw house. If the results are reported in a deceiving manner, expect the discussion to follow in kind, likely spelling out the authors' pet beliefs and favorite theories.

The following are two additional examples from the previous discussion of results:

- One obvious trend from the data is that the subjects with language deficits scored consistently lower on all tests than did the no disorder group. In fact, in all cases, these differences approached statistical significance.
- Significant results were found for variables A, B, C ($p < .05$). In addition, significance was approached for D ($p = .09$).

What these examples have in common, as noted, is that nonsignificant results are reported as meaningful. In fact, it is quite possible that the author will treat them exactly as he or she would have had they been significant, particularly in a "Discussion" section where numbers need not be listed. For example:

One obvious trend from the data is that the subjects with language deficits scored consistently lower on all tests than did the no disorder group. In fact, in all cases, these differences approached statistical significance. The obvious question raised by these data is why the disordered subjects were inferior with respect to every measure taken in this experiment.

Actually, the more obvious question is this: Given that the authors did not find any differences, using their own ground rules for what constitutes a difference, why are they acting as if they did? The answer is that the authors simply *know* a difference exists and want to tell us about it.

The problem is that they did not provide evidence for its existence.

Believe it or not, fitting the results to the discussion (rather than vice versa) is even done when no differences are found whatsoever. In this instance, the reader may come across a sentence such as

Descriptive data indicate that the groups are roughly equivalent in their scores, a result unsupported by previous research. This raises the question of how this experiment differed from earlier ones. Perhaps it was the ages of the subjects under test. Indeed, when the four oldest subjects are compared to matched control group subjects, distinct differences emerge.

Nice try—but again a researcher is not allowed to create one set of rules and then play by another. Stated differently, one cannot set out to compare adults who are and are not disordered, then throw out the subjects who do not fit the predetermined conclusions the author wished to discuss.

Can a real difference exist even if statistical significance is not reached? Sure. Just like significance can occur when there actually is no real difference (see "My Greatest Research Fear" below). Any system based on probability is subject to some flaw. In fact, when authors report "mixed results," they are often referring to differences that sometimes reach significance and sometimes fall short. For example, studies comparing how adults who do and do not stutter visually process language are mixed with respect to group differences (Hand & Haynes, 1983; Hardin et al. 1992; Moore, 1976). So, is processing somehow related to stuttering? Quite possibly, it is. At the very least, it is a relationship worthy of additional exploration. More to the point of this chapter, it is perfectly legitimate to view mixed results from a body of literature in this manner. But, that is far different from failing to find a difference in a single study and claiming that one exists nonetheless.

Whether it is done fairly or unfairly, the discussion includes what the author feels the results mean and whether they support the current state of theory, add to it, or force reanalysis of it. This leads to a concluding sentence, which, more often than not, is a call for further research. For example:

In attempting to determine the efficacy of the treatment program I named after myself, it appears that more questions were raised than answered. Thus, future research should focus on the types of clients best served by this treatment as well as its long-range efficacy.

As far as I am concerned, the inventor of the call for future research deserves a bust in the Researchers Hall of Fame. This helpful device can be utilized whenever the discussion gets so thick with theory that the author cannot find his or her way out. In addition to that, it can be dropped in if the author simply gets tired. In fact, it works best when both conditions are present. Even better, it does not have to make sense.

This raises the obvious question of why the present study found A when each and every other study ever completed on this topic found B. Of course, the answer is impossible to determine at this time. Perhaps future research can examine issues of methodology and data collection procedures as they relate to sample variance.

MY GREATEST RESEARCH FEAR

Suppose, just suppose, that a speech-language pathologist (SLP) made the discovery that all of her articulation-disordered kids ate cream-filled doughnuts for breakfast. Now suppose further that she mentioned this discovery while giving a presentation to an audience that included exactly 20 researchers.

"Aha," think all of the researchers simultaneously. "I'm going to study this phenomenon."

Thus, 20 studies are undertaken to examine the possible relationship between cream-filled doughnuts and articulation disorders. All use a .05 level of significance, meaning that there is only a 1-in-20 chance that a relationship could be found where none actually exists.

Remember that 20 studies are being run.

Now, let us say that the 1-in-20 chance becomes a 1-in-20 actuality. That is, one of the researchers actually finds a statistically significant correlation between doughnuts and speech. Nineteen do not.

Which study is most likely to be published?

Let us fast forward a few months to the inclusion in a scientific journal of an article purporting the aforementioned relationship. It is now part of the knowledge base of the field that a fattening breakfast food is related to mispronounced sounds.

But, you ask, with replication (i.e., other people doing the same study), before long we would realize that this study is in error, right?

Not so fast.

A lot of research is carried out by doctoral students. Because they are students, they have to get their designs approved by a committee of professors. These professors are not looking for replication but, rather, original research ideas. Thus, a doctoral student is less likely to investigate cream-filled doughnuts versus articulation as he or she is to examine (to name just a few possibilities)

- The relationship between doughnuts and other speech production deficits.
- The relationship between other breakfast foods and articulation disorders.
- Elements of the cream-filled doughnut (i.e., isolating its components). Does the doughy, deep-fried shell by itself lead to speech breakdowns? What about the sugar on top? Or, how about that indistinguishable cream-like substance they somehow jam into the middle?

Now, we have an entire line of scholarship devoted to clarifying an inaccurate relationship. Yes, given the scientific methods, the relationship will, over time, be discredited. I just wonder how much time and energy will be wasted chasing the imaginary doughnut-articulation association.

Or

This concludes the section on how to read research. Future investigation may one day add to our understanding of this important topic, as well as provide a suitable conclusion.

☐ How to Read Nonresearch

Obviously, there is much written about communication disorders aside from that in research journals. Given that much of this material is not peer reviewed or even much concerned with the scientific method, it should be divorced from the problems outlined, right?

No, this is not right—not even close.

Actually, much of the nonresearch purported to solve communication disorders presents the same problems and more. By "more" I mean additional themes that are cause not only for concern but also terror and dread.

One of the most disconcerting of these themes is anti-intellectualism, a disregard for those who pursued the education and professional training necessary to research and treat communication disorders. Disdain for those with conventional training takes many forms, from contempt for recognized experts in the field to a reliance on undefined "common sense." Teach yourself to be careful when you come on variations of the following phrases.

- Like Galileo, my ideas challenge the establishment.
- So-called experts might not like me but remember that they have a vested interest in maintaining the status quo.
- It is likely that my idea is so good *because* I didn't study in the field.
- I don't need to run studies. I have a disorder. That makes me a walking laboratory.
- What I do works. The happy faces of my clients tell me all I need to know.

- I don't have trouble speaking when I'm alone or talking to my dog. So, common sense tells me it's not a physical problem or I'd be doing it all the time. That's how I know it's mental.

Let us start with Galileo. Questioning stodgy and stale ideas can lead to positive outcomes, particularly when those holding the ideas have not experienced an original thought since their last show-and-tell session. Challenging such individuals can be so worthwhile, in fact, that it might one day result in innovations that could greatly benefit humankind, such as new modes of transportation or elevator "Open" and "Close" buttons that are actually hooked up to something. The problem, of course, is that simply defying old theory is insufficient evidence of the viability of a new theory. Remember that for every Galileo, there have been thousands of bad ideas, many of which were explained solely to padded walls.

It is interesting, not to mention ironic, when ideas that do not advance theory are nevertheless proclaimed as progressive (Herbert et al. 2000; Scott, Clark, & Brady, 2000). In such instances, the proponents of the ideas often fall victim to one of the benchmarks of anti-intellectualism, the *maverick syndrome* (Saul, 1989). Numerous individuals who have been reprimanded, left unhired, criticized, or had their views rejected claim that their troubles are due to their insurgency. In all fields of study, countless bad ideas have been defended on the grounds that the originator is a rebel and, as such, subjected to unfair criticism from envious or repressive authoritarians. When someone suggests that there are flaws in the person's thinking, he or she simply claims to be an iconoclast and, as such, unpopular because of a propensity to challenge authority (Quesal, 1999). This ignores an alternative explanation, namely, that there are flaws in the person's thinking.

There are probably countless reasons why unpopular ideas are defended as unfairly outcast. One is simple defensiveness. When a person takes ownership of an idea, he or she tends to protect it like mother to a child or a face painter to his school's athletic teams. Thus, when rejected, it is preferable to look for an alternative explanation than it is to admit that the idea is flawed. Attributing the rejection to an admired personality trait is perfect in that the originators of the idea can feel good about both the idea and themselves. This brings me to the second reason for the popularity of the maverick syndrome: Many cultures value boldness and confidence, the hallmarks of rebellion. Thus, people like to think of themselves as rebels. Think about it—when is the last time you heard someone say any of the following?

- I always did what I was told.
- When someone gets in my face, I turn the other cheek.
- I like to think of myself as a yes-man.

It's likely that you never did. We tend to boast more about our independence and brazenness. Apparently, nonresearchers are no different.

In addition to its use as ego feed, whining can provide a substantial smoke screen. When the debate can be shifted away from ideas, it is always good for the more ambiguous ones (Green, 1996; Herbert et al. 2000). Even better for the self-proclaimed mavericks of the world, such manipulation is not particularly difficult to do.

A: Your ideas are garbage, B.
B: You don't like me.
A: This isn't about you ... B? Where'd you go?

B is gone, telling the world what a nonconformist genius he is, based on the dislike he engenders in the A's of the world.

Of course, it is possible that a valid concept *was* unfairly rejected. After all, Galileos do come along. And, while there is no comparable story in CSD, it is true that good ideas have come from those with unconventional backgrounds and varied knowledge bases who looked at matters in new ways. The main point of all this is not that all outside suggestions need be accepted or discarded, but rather, they should be approached carefully. Being an outsider should render someone neither instant scorn nor instant credibility. There is nothing wrong with raising questions from a fresh perspective. There is in declaring answers from a questionable knowledge base.

This raises a question: When current research and theory are ignored, on what basis are the resulting ideas supported? The answers are testimonials and the accounts of the originators (Quesal, 1999), whether it is the proponents' own experiences as walking laboratories or something they see in their clients' faces. Such "evidence" is more emotional and, as such, may well be more convincing than data and statistical analysis (Herbert et al. 2000). Even better, the use of personal accounts allows one to present the good and withhold the bad (Popper, 1965).

To be fair, experiences and observations are important (Green, 1996), just not as a cover for poor substance. Often, such reports are not only missing objective support, but also displaying a disheartening lack of knowledge. The example statement implying that research studies need not be done when personal experience is readily available shows an ignorance of one of the primary characteristics associated with human communicative disorders: their individuality.

While, generally speaking, some knowledge is better than none, incomplete knowledge leads to trouble when solutions are based on it (Quesal, 1999). We all know that in life, the people furthest removed from a problem have the easiest solutions. When a nonparent says, "Just tell your kid to stop or else," you know this is easy for the person to say, a person who knows neither the child in question nor anything whatsoever about parenting. Similarly, limited knowledge of communication allows for definitive statements. The problem, of course, is that communication is filled with intricacies and gray areas. Myths, controversies, and mixed results abound. But if you ignore all that, solutions become rather easy.

Unfortunately, simple and direct hypotheses are sometimes worn as badges of honor. This has been going on for centuries, dating at least to the time of Occam's razor, a philosophy frequently translated from its Latin origins as "The simplest explanation is probably the right explanation" (Occam's razor, 2004). Oddly, simplicity has been used as evidence of a theory's validity (i.e., my theory has to be the correct one because it is the simplest).

While Occam's razor has merit, there are at least three problems with its general use. Most obviously, it is not always true. A theory that teaches that articulation disorders are caused by bad breakfast foods is quite simple, yet is not in the same area code as the truth. Second, theories appear comparatively simpler depending on the reader's knowledge base. Stated differently, simple is in the eye of the beholder. In the aforementioned attempt to explain variability (the guy who talks to his dog), the speaker knows something about environmental influences (or at least that they exist) and nothing about the neurology of speech. From his perspective, then, the former is a far simpler explanation for the variability he experiences. Obviously, one's unique perspective is a shaky scaffold on which to rest a theory. Finally, Occam's razor, directly interpreted as "Entities should not be multiplied more than necessary," may well be intended to instruct theorists to offer explanations that are as simple and direct as possible (Occam's razor, 2004). That is, give us the easy version, not the more complicated one. This is not only good advice, but also a far different recommendation from choosing the simpler sounding of two competing theories.

In addition to Occam, another frequent defense of simple theories is common sense. Although there is certainly nothing wrong with common sense, it is insufficient evidence for theory. For one thing, it has more interpretations than Occam's razor. The theorist who converses with his dog is, after all, offering a common sense argument based on his knowledge of the subject. To others, his argument may be common, but far from sensible.

Finally, nonresearch is likely to make massive leaps from present theory (Bunge, 1967; Herbert et al. 2000). As a function of the scientific method, research is a step-by-step process designed to improve understanding gradually (Sagan, 1995). When the restrictions of the scientific method are not present, an author can make giant bounds beyond what is commonly accepted. Yes, research often points out the obvious, but that alone should not allow nonresearchers to make uninformed rushes to judgment. Good researchers know they do not have all the answers. What are the odds that nonresearchers do?

A COMPARATIVE INVESTIGATION OF
TWO ATHLETIC TEAMS

Throughout the years, humans have engaged in sporting events of various types (Doubleday, 1869; ESPN, 2006; Olympic Program, 776 B.C.). One way in which winners of such events have been decided is by determining which participant or team of participants first reached a predetermined location, such as a "finish line." That is, sports such as skiing, track, and swimming are based on how fast competitors arrive at a point in space, sometimes moving at the same time (Andretti, 1969) and other times across the same course at different times (Heiden, 1980).

In addition to being fastest to a given spot, athletic activities have declared as their victors those individuals or teams who earn a comparatively favorable number of "points" (Riley, 2006; Stengel, 1962; Stoops, 2000). These points have been awarded in two separate ways: Participants perform an objectively established task, such as scoring a goal, or they are judged subjectively by those determined to possess expertise in their particular sport. Examples of the latter scoring system include boxing, figure skating, and of course, synchronized swimming. Although such sports are popular, objectively measured games such as football, baseball, hockey, basketball, golf, tennis, and poker have been observed more readily by American researchers (e.g., ESPN, 2004–2008).

In recent years, however, the notion that the superior participant is the one who achieves a greater point total has been challenged (Cuban, 2006; Leinart, 2006; Every junior tennis player in the state of Florida, 2002–2010). In essence, the research question being asked is this: "Is total number of points an accurate indicator of an athlete's or a team's comparative skill level?" This is an important question to answer, given the rewards associated with being a publicly declared winner. Such rewards can be monetary (Jordan, 1998) or personal. For example, winning teams have been assumed to have "character" (Rudy, 1993) and possess "what it takes" (Every sports talk radio host, beginning of time–2008). Losers, on the other hand, are widely viewed as not having had "the horses" (Guys in sports bars, personal correspondence, 1994–1999) or enough "heart" (The loudmouth who sits behind me at every sporting event, 1968–2010), among other body parts apparently necessary for victory.

Given that those who consistently score more points than their opposition may become wealthy and will almost certainly be viewed

continued

as also possessing comparatively exceptional personality traits, it is worth investigating whether a higher score is really indicative of a superior team. The purpose of the following study was to determine whether the point totals scored by two basketball teams in a regulation game established which team was better.

METHODS

Subjects

The subjects for this study were two basketball teams, heretofore referred to as Team A and Team B. Both teams consisted of 12 male players between the ages of 22 and 34. The mean age of Team A was 26.7, with a standard deviation of 6.1. For Team B, the mean and standard deviation were 25.5 and 7.4, respectively. All players were trained by their team's coaching staffs so they would completely understand the rules of the game.

Procedure

Teams A and B were instructed to engage in a basketball game using standard rules of international competition (source unknown). That is, both teams attempted, over the course of 40 minutes of playing time, to outscore the other. The dependent variables collected by the researchers were number of points scored per team. Points were awarded as follows: 2 points per basket, operationally defined as putting the ball through a metal hoop; 3 points for each basket made from a distance greater than 6.25 meters; and 1 point for each "free throw" (a basket made from 4.6 meters in which the player is unguarded). Thus, if Team A were, for example, to score a free throw, 1 point would be added to their total, but no points would be added to the point total for Team B.

Following this task, a chi square statistic was utilized to analyze and compare the two point totals. A standard probability level of .05 was used to determine significance.

RESULTS

At the conclusion of the game under test (and as can be seen in Table 3.1), Team A had accumulated 64 points (seven 3-point baskets, fifteen 2-point baskets, and 13 free throws). Team B was awarded 59 points (five 3-point baskets, fifteen 2-point baskets, and 14 free throws). As

TABLE 3.1 Team Designation Versus Total Points	
Team	**Total Points**
A	64
B	59

per the aforementioned game rules, the fact that the accumulated totals were not equivalent limited the game time to 40 minutes. That is, no overtime periods were added due to the 5-point discrepancy (i.e., 59 subtracted from 64) observed in the descriptive data.

When the chi square analysis was applied to these data, no significant difference emerged ($\chi^2 = 1.24$, $p > .05$). Thus, no evidence was found that the variation in the teams' point totals was due to any factor other than chance occurrence.

DISCUSSION

The results of this study challenge the notion that the team that scores the most points is necessarily superior and even calls into question whether they should be declared the winner. Of course, had one team scored, say, 5,000 points and the other none, the point total difference may well have been statistically significant and the resulting conclusions straightforward. Nevertheless, this study clearly demonstrates that a greater descriptive point total alone is not necessarily indicative of supremacy.

Also called into question is basketball's, and arguably all sports decided by points, standard of using overtime only when two teams' points are equal. After all, if the purpose of overtime is to continue play because a better team has not yet been determined, it must also be employed when nonsignificant differences are present at end of regulation time. Perhaps such analyses should be run at the conclusion of all sporting events and continue until such time as significance is reached. After all, if the superior team is to be rewarded financially and assumed to possess high-quality personality traits, it is important to determine unequivocally which team this is.

Finally, it should be noted that the conclusions drawn from this research can only be applied to games based on point totals. More research is needed to determine the viability of subjectively judged sports and those in which participants race to a finish line.

☐ Synopsis

Research follows (to varying degrees) the scientific method to advance theory. While imperfect, this research presents far fewer problems than nonresearch writings, with their questionable bases and lack of rigorous evaluation. Those who wish to read about CSD should know the difference between research and nonresearch, as well as the idiosyncrasies inherent in both, to make informed decisions about what to accept and reject. Those who wish to follow developments in the field from afar require simpler advice: Don't believe everything you hear.

☐ Vocabulary

evidence-based practice—the conscious and clear use of the current best evidence, practitioner experience and patient concerns and expectation in making decisions toward individualized patient care (Martin & Clark, 2006)

statistical significance—in statistics, a property of the results of an empirical investigation suggesting that they are not due to chance alone (Colman, 2001)

☐ Discussion Questions

1. As noted in Chapter 1, many myths surround communication disorders. From a research perspective, why might misleading statements get passed along as if they were true?
2. The point of evidence-based practice is that evidence is needed to show the effectiveness of a treatment. How would you gather convincing evidence? Would, say, surveys be convincing, or would you insist on empirical data from a controlled experiment?
3. Is it possible that simple solutions to human communication disorders exist? Explain your answer.
4. Where do *you* typically get information on communication (language development, speech disorders, etc.)? What are the strengths and weaknesses of your sources?

☐ Note

1. *Validity* refers to the accuracy of the measurement instrument. This differentiates it from *reliability*, which is the consistency of a result. An example offered by Emanuel (1985) is useful for illustrating the difference. Suppose you find a ruler, measure a tabletop, and find it to be exactly 4 feet long. You measure again and get the same result. You measure it 10 more times and keep getting exactly 4 feet. You have a very reliable measure. Now suppose someone points out to you that your ruler is only 11 inches long. This, of course, means that your measure is inaccurate (i.e., the table is not exactly 4 feet long, but rather 44 inches). That is, as a result of a faulty instrument, you did not determine the table length correctly. Your experience resulted in a measure that was reliable but not valid.

☐ **Recommended Readings**

Justice, L. M., & Fey, M. E. (2004). Evidence-based practice in schools: Integrating craft and theory with science and data. *The ASHA Leader, 9*(17), 4–5, 30–31.
This short article provides an easy-to-read explanation of evidence-based practice plus an interesting account of how it is applied to school-based therapy.

Quesal, B. (2005). "Empathy based practice" in stuttering. Paper presented at the International Stuttering Awareness Day Conference. Retrieved from http://www.mnsu.edu/comdis/isad8/papers/quesal8.html.
Although this paper is specific to stuttering, it raises many general questions about evidence-based practice.

Schiavetti, N., & Metz, D. E. (2002). *Evaluating research in communicative disorders.* Boston: Allyn & Bacon.
This text offers detailed descriptions of research practices common to CSD. Excerpts from research studies are effectively utilized to illustrate points.

CHAPTER 4

Diagnosing Communication Disorders

Note: Although there are similarities in the diagnoses of speech-language and hearing problems, issues related to the latter are addressed in Chapter 11. Thus, this chapter deals primarily (albeit not exclusively) with speech-language evaluations.

Diagnosis is like creating a sculpture from a cloud.

At least that is the mental image I always get. Information is floating about in a seemingly random and unpredictable manner. My job is to gather it, condense it, and turn it into something concrete and useful.

But that is just me.

Other communication sciences and disorders (CSD) professionals will tell you that diagnosis is a three-step process:

1. Find out if there is a problem.
2. If so, find out about the problem.
3. Make recommendations.

This sounds easier than sculpting a cloud (Figure 4.1) until you begin to look at what is really involved. To begin, you have to get the terms straight. **Diagnosis, evaluation, assessment**, and **differential diagnosis** are all commonly used words in the field of communication disorders. Knowing what they mean and which are (mistakenly or not) used inter-changeably can help make sense of the cloud—a little, anyway.

Forgetting about clouds and sculptures for the moment, diagnosis could also be seen as akin to cleaning up a messy desk. It involves organizing and classifying bits of information, some of which are necessary, others of which are clearly not, and still more that initially seem important, but in reality are not so (like the memo I recently found on my desktop that began, "IMPORTANT! Please respond before April 15, 1999").

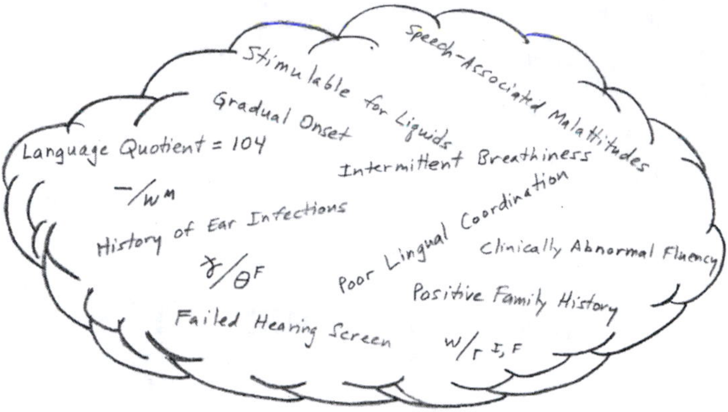

FIGURE 4.1   A cloud of information following a diagnostic evaluation.

Among CSD folks, a more common analogy for diagnosis is solving a puzzle, and there is certainly merit in this comparison. Diagnosis is a process that involves drawing conclusions based on the weight of the evidence. I state it that way because no client ever fits any one diagnostic profile perfectly. Instead, some expected symptoms will be present, others not, and the rest will appear ambiguous.

A big reason for the inherent imprecision of the process is that we do not diagnose communication as much as we diagnose communicators (Haynes & Pindzola, 2004). That is, we deal with people, not just problems. And with people, 1 plus 1 does not always equal 2. Moreover, even if someone were the exact sum of his or her parts, that is no guarantee that this will be the case tomorrow.

On the subject of people, it is worth pointing out that, while an evaluator might view the assessment in terms of information and symptoms, the disordered individual is more likely to see it as the first sign of hope that the problem can be helped. He or she may well be looking for complete recovery, and even if this is not the case, the client is surely expecting help in some form. Disappointment may well set in if the kind of help that the client is hoping for is not realistic (Haynes & Pindzola, 2004). The professional must be sensitive to these emotions.

One way of gaining such empathy is to learn as much as possible about the client, present and past. The person is not a language, speech, or hearing disorder, but an ex-accountant who is frustrated at her loss of function that is now compounded by people treating her like a child. On one level, the evaluation may seem like just another diagnostic session to the speech-language pathologist (SLP) or audiologist, but to the client and family, it is a new and important experience that will yield answers about the future.

Relating to clients is not just a form of courtesy, but a crucial part of the clinical progression. In fact, the interpersonal relationship between client and professional can be viewed as the catalyst of the diagnostic process (Haynes & Pindzola, 2004). Put simply, the more comfortable the client is, the more he or she communicates, and the more data the clinician can gather. This level of comfort, however, does not always come easily. Young children, for example, may be scared and react by being wild or going to the other extreme and clamming up completely. Adolescents might retreat to a shell of false bravado, saying little other than that their communication problems are no big deal. Older adults may be experiencing diminished hearing or memory, making it difficult to get information from them. In these and all other instances, the professional must determine the best strategies for communication.

Because people are not static entities, it is important to remember that the conclusions drawn from the evaluation session (e.g., the diagnostic classification, recommended goals for therapy, etc.) are not cast in stone. Often, they must be adjusted over time, as new observations are made and additional information related. Thus, it is best to think of diagnosis as an ongoing, open-ended venture. Yes, an evaluation session is done for the purpose of diagnosing the client's problem, but later testing may also be needed to revise therapy or to monitor progress.

☐ The Role of the Clinician

Because the diagnostic process is comprehensive and somewhat indefinite in nature, clinicians must employ numerous skills and knowledge from their training. The following list includes just a few areas of proficiency that the professional must synthesize when evaluating a client.

- Testing techniques
- Observational skills
- **Counseling**
- Creative intuition
- Problem-solving abilities
- Data collection
- The ability to scrutinize all aspects of behavior

Because so much is expected of them, diagnosticians rely on left brain and right, science and art, objective analysis and hunches. As noted, diagnosing humans is a complex and comprehensive process that may seem difficult to understand, but the same holds true for a lot of other things. Consider that a batter is out after three strikes unless the third one is a type of strike called a foul (except when this foul is caught by the team on defense) or unless the catcher drops the third strike, provided it is not a foul, and the batter runs to first base before the ball gets there (a rule not in place for strikes 1 and 2). No, I am not comparing the complexity of evaluating a human being to striking out. I have done both and can assure you they are not the same. Rather, I am merely pointing out that, although the complex might always remain complex, it can still be understood.

☐ Gathering Information

To help with the understanding of the diagnostic process, let us think of it as an information-gathering procedure. This is how we determine whether a problem exists, and if so, what it is and what we can do about it.

The gathering of information often begins with the client's first contact. The initial phone call or e-mail provides the clinician with a statement of the problem and likely of additional concerns. It is also the first chance to establish **rapport** with the client. When the clinician and client are face-to-face, far more information can be obtained with case history forms (Figure 4.2). Whether they are general (that is, paperwork that is sent to all clients, regardless of presenting complaint) or specific to a particular disorder, these forms are a means of collecting basic data such as the client's description of the problem, medical history, social history, and education. These documents might be mailed out and returned prior to the face-to-face evaluation, or they can be filled out just before the client meets the clinician. Either way, information obtained is not only important but also, unfortunately, incomplete. For this reason, the CSD professional will also do a **history interview** with either the client or, in the case of children, the client's parent(s).

The history interview covers much of the same ground as the case history form but allows the clinician to unearth specifics. If a mother says that her child's first word was "mama," uttered at 6 months of age, the SLP (thinking that Mom was observing the syllable reduplication phase noted in Chapter 2, while at the same time engaging in wishful thinking) can follow up by asking "What was the first word besides 'mama' or 'dada'?" Also, information that is incomplete (say the client reported that he eats a lot of sweets) can be filled in with follow-up questions such as "Does this particular diet have any effect on your speech?"

By the time the history gathering is complete, the CSD professional should have information about the onset, development, and variability of the communication problem as well as any factors that might have caused it (structural or genetic) or contribute to it (such as work demands, habits,

LANGUAGE LEARNING INTERVENTION
&
PROFESSIONAL SPEECH SERVICES

Speech and Language Case History Form – Child Form

Child's Name: _____   Date of Birth: _____

Address: _____   Sex: Male _____ Female _____

_____   Phone: _____

Mother's Name: _____ Age: _____   Last Grade Completed: _____

Mother's Occupation: _____   Work Phone: _____

Father's Name: _____ Age: _____   Last Grade Completed: _____

Father's Occupation: _____   Work Phone: _____

Legal Guardian: _____

Guardian's Address: _____   Home Phone: _____

_____   Work Phone: _____

Email: _____

Statement of problem: _____

When was problem first noticed? _____

Brothers & Sisters:

Name	Age	Grade	Speech/Hearing/Medical Problems
_____	_____	_____	_____
_____	_____	_____	_____
_____	_____	_____	_____
_____	_____	_____	_____
_____	_____	_____	_____
_____	_____	_____	_____

What languages does the child speak? _____

What is child's primary language? _____

Emergency Contact: _____   Relationship to Child: _____

Home Phone: _____   Work Phone: _____

FIGURE 4.2   Example of a case history form.

or learning limitations). As a bonus, the client's motivation for therapy
will also begin to become apparent as the interview progresses.

More often than not, the history interview is done at the beginning
of the evaluation. This is because the clinician wants to know as much
as possible about the client before he or she begins the testing. However,
there are professionals who prefer to wait until later to gather this information, particularly with children. The reasons for the latter sequence are
that the tester is uncomfortable talking to the parents about a child he or

MEDICAL HISTORY:

Provide the approximate ages at which the child has had the following illnesses/conditions:

Allergies_____ Asthma_____ Chicken Pox _____

Colds _____ Convulsions _____ Croup_____

Dental Problems _____ Dizziness _____ Draining ear _____

Ear aches _____ Ear infections _____ Encephalitis_____

German measles _____ Headaches_____ High fever _____

Influenza _____ Mastoiditis_____ Measles _____

Meningitis_____ Mumps_____ Rheumatic fever_____

Scarlet fever _____ Tinnitus _____ Tonsilitis _____

Describe any surgeries your child has had _____

_____

Describe any major injuries your child has suffered _____

_____

Describe any major illnesses or physical problems not mentioned above_____

_____

_____

List any medications your child is currently prescribed _____

_____

Child's Doctor _____ Phone Number _____

Address _____

DEVELOPMENTAL HISTORY:

1. Pregnancy and Birth History

   Illnesses/accidents during pregnancy_____

   _____

   Medications during pregnancy _____

   Smoking/alcohol/drug use during pregnancy_____

   _____

   Length of pregnancy_____ Length of Labor _____

   Type of delivery: head first_____ feet first_____ breech_____ Cesarean _____

   Unusual problems during delivery _____

   _____

   Were drugs used?   Yes _____ No _____

   Were instruments used?   Yes _____ No _____

   Was infant blue?   Yes _____ No _____

   Did infant require oxygen?   Yes _____ No _____

FIGURE 4.2 (continued)

Was infant jaundiced?   Yes _____   No _____
Were there bruises/abnormalities?   Yes _____   No _____

Infant's weight at birth _____
Describe health problems during first weeks/months of infant's life _____
_____

2. Developmental Milestones
MOTOR

At approximately what age did the following occur?

Holds head erect while lying on stomach   _____
Sits without support   _____
Stands without support   _____
Creeps or crawls without assistance   _____
Walks without support   _____
Uses toilet   _____

Does child do the following?

Drinks from a cup/glass without assistance   Yes _____   No _____
Feeds self with spoon/fork without assistance   Yes _____   No _____
Dresses/undresses without assistance   Yes _____   No _____
Colors or draws independently   Yes _____   No _____
Uses scissors to cut paper   Yes _____   No _____
Generally uses _____ right/ _____ left hand

SPEECH AND LANGUAGE

At approximately what age did the following occur?

Babbling and cooing   _____
First word ("mama", "dada" not included)   _____
Uses 2 word sentences   _____
Uses 3 word sentences   _____

INFANTS (answer only if your child is birth to 18 months of age)

Smiles and vocalizes in response to an adult   Yes _____   No _____
Turns head toward source of sound   Yes _____   No _____
Plays peek-a-boo/pat-a-cake/so big, etc.   Yes _____   No _____

FIGURE 4.2 (continued)

Associates spoken words with objects/actions	Yes _____	No _____
Greets familiar adult spontaneously	Yes _____	No _____
Approximately how many different words does child say	_____	
(attach list if under 25 words)		

TODDLERS (answer only if your child is 18–36 months of age)

Separates easily from parent	Yes _____	No _____
Expresses emotion	Yes _____	No _____
Shows affection toward people/pets/possessions	Yes _____	No _____
Enjoys having stories read	Yes _____	No _____
Knows his/her name	Yes _____	No _____
Knows his/her age	Yes _____	No _____
Plays alongside another child	Yes _____	No _____
Plays independently	Yes _____	No _____
Generally understands what is said	Yes _____	No _____
Responds "yes" or "no" appropriately	Yes _____	No _____
Pays attention to activity for at least 5 minutes	Yes _____	No _____
Approximately how many different words does child say	_____	
(attach list if under 50 words)		

PRESCHOOL (answer only if your child is 3–5 years of age)

Cooperates in group activities	Yes _____	No _____
Takes turns and shares	Yes _____	No _____
Has special friend(s)	Yes _____	No _____
Generally follows directions	Yes _____	No _____
Follows 3 or more verbal commands	Yes _____	No _____
Uses imagination in play	Yes _____	No _____
Knows whether he/she is boy/girl	Yes _____	No _____
Knows the difference between right and wrong	Yes _____	No _____
Occupies self for 10 or more minutes	Yes _____	No _____
Looks at/points to/touches pictures in a book	Yes _____	No _____
Pays attention for at least 10 minutes?	Yes _____	No _____
Understands in, on, out, under, in front of, behind	Yes _____	No _____
Understands mine, yours, his, hers, theirs	Yes _____	No _____
Understands how and why questions	Yes _____	No _____
Points to pictures when named	Yes _____	No _____

FIGURE 4.2 (continued)

Recalls events from stories read aloud   Yes _____   No _____
Uses sentences of 5 or more words   Yes _____   No _____
Identifies circle, square, and triangle   Yes _____   No _____
Identifies red, blue, yellow, and green   Yes _____   No _____
Identifies big and small shapes   Yes _____   No _____

SCHOOL AGE (answer only if your child is over 5 years of age)

Knows address and phone number   Yes _____   No _____
Participates in meaningful conversation   Yes _____   No _____
Identifies right and left   Yes _____   No _____
Speech is clear and easily understood   Yes _____   No _____

_____

Does your child make any sounds incorrectly?   Yes _____   No _____
   If yes, which ones? _____
Do you think your child stutters?   Yes _____   No _____
   If yes, please describe _____
_____
_____

Do you think your child has a voice problem?   Yes _____   No _____
   (e.g. hoarseness, high/low pitch, loudness)   If yes, please describe_____
_____
_____

Do you think your child has a hearing problem?   Yes _____   No _____
   If yes, please describe _____
_____
_____

What are your child's favorite toys/activities? _____
_____

Is there anything else you would like us to know about your child (special skills,
exceptional fears, problems, etc.)? _____
_____
_____
_____
_____

FIGURE 4.2 (continued)

EDUCATIONAL HISTORY:

Child's school _____

Address _____ Phone _____

Grade _____ Teacher _____

How does your child seem to feel about school? _____
_____
_____

How is your child is doing academically? _____
_____

Any specific problems in school? _____
_____
_____

Is your child currently receiving any special services at school?

Yes _____ No _____

   If yes, please describe _____
_____

Has your child received any previous speech-language-hearing therapy?

Yes _____ No _____

   If yes, where and by whom? _____

If therapy is required, I give my consent for LLIPSS to provide speech/language/hearing services for my child.

Person completing form _____

Relationship to child _____

Signature _____ Date _____

FIGURE 4.2 (continued)

she does not know or the clinician does not want the child to have to wait (possibly increasing the anxiety and decreasing the amount of attention for later testing).

When the client—child or adult—is finally face to face with the clinician, whether it is for the history interview or another task, first impressions are critical in a number of ways. Although largely unstructured, the initial portion of the evaluation is a time for the CSD professional to meet several responsibilities. One is establishing rapport with the client (for a full discussion of rapport, see Chapter 5). This helps the clients to develop trust in the clinician and reassures them that they have nothing to fear (this is especially important with children). In addition, this is the time when the clinician can make initial observations of not only the client's communication, but also of mood and motivation. If, for example, it appears that an antsy child will not sit still for long, the professional can prioritize the scheduled tests to get as much information as possible in the potentially limited time available.

☐ Testing

At some point during the evaluation, the client will be asked to engage in tasks designed to assess communication. Such tasks are often in the forms of formal, commercially produced tests and screens, although additional tasks may be done so that the clinician can make less-formalized observations.

Formal testing materials are either **criterion referenced** or **norm referenced**. Criterion-referenced assessment tells us how well clients are performing on specific tasks. A "cutoff" score is used to determine who is performing adequately and who is not. The examinations in the class for which you are reading this book are undoubtedly criterion referenced. In communication sciences and disorders, this type of assessment can be useful in helping diagnosticians plan later therapy (Wildemuth, 1984).

Norm-referenced tests, on the other hand, compare their takers to one another. They are derived from testing samples of individuals similar to the client being evaluated. That is, they make use of a **norming sample**, hopefully one that is representative of the client's age and other variables, such as socioeconomic status, gender, and geographic area. By using such samples, the tests provide a range of values against which the client can be compared. Thus, the tester can determine the individual's **percentile score**, **age equivalency**, or other values that help us determine whether the skills are within or outside normal limits.

Regardless of the type of test selected, it is important to remember that these are tools and not definitive measures. That is, they result in data that can be added to other information (history records, clinician's observations, and the like) to arrive at a differential diagnosis and plan of treatment.

Fortunately, there are many testing materials available (for all ages and areas of communication) that can help us in this endeavor. Professionals determine which ones to use partly on the basis of what is known about the client (e.g., age, cognitive level, etc.). They also select the tests they are most comfortable using, although caution is urged here. Clinicians must be careful not to use their pet tests as a drunk uses a street lamp—for support rather than illumination. The job is, after all, to diagnose a communication problem, not to stay within one's comfort zone.

Less comprehensive than formal tests are **speech and language screens**. Screening tasks are designed to identify whether a client needs further testing. While there are formal screens available for all areas of communication, often screens are done informally.

One common screening done during speech-language evaluations is the **hearing screen**. This involves the presentation of tones at the outer edge (i.e., loudest level) of normal limits. In this way, the tester can observe

TEACUP AND PIE PAN

I experienced my first speech evaluation when I was in the sixth grade. It was an encounter that took all of 20 minutes.

I was called to the elementary school library, a grimy, one-room storage space for outdated hardbacks. The therapist sat opposite a cold gray table that was only slightly smaller than a regulation soccer field. There were rows of rectangular windows behind her chair, allowing in unimpeded sunlight. Because of this, a dusty glare obstructed my view of this new authority figure.

I remember her as a kindly old woman with a pleasant, competent manner. Unfortunately, her knowledge of my particular disorder could have fit in a teacup.

"Are you getting along with the other children?" she asked me.

I told her I had friends.

"What kinds of things do you like to do?"

"Sports."

"Are you good in sports?"

I excitedly told her about winning the 50-yard dash during the previous spring's "Field Day," a track meet for fifth and sixth graders.

"What about your other classes?"

"Four A's and a B."

She asked me about my home life. Mom, Dad, brother. A dog named Bill. A cat named Cat. Three goldfish (unnamed). Could not have been more normal.

"Well, I'm stumped," she admitted. "You seem to be popular, good in sports, good in school, and there are no problems at home. I can't see any reason why you should have any trouble talking."

After writing something on a form, she concluded matters by saying, "If you ever feel like you're going to mess up a word, just replace it with one you can say. Lord knows there are plenty of those."

No therapy was recommended as a result of this evaluation.

A year later, I was assessed again, by a different therapist. This one was younger, more energetic, and might have been attractive were she not sporting one of those ridiculous shag haircuts so popular at the time. It gave her chin and cheeks the appearance of three balloons stuck to a pie pan. In any case, she asked me if I needed anything before we started. I said no. Actually, I had to go to the bathroom but figured I could wait 20 minutes.

Like the teacup lady, Pie Pan began with numerous questions about my life, although she did not seem anywhere near as interested in my popularity or athletic prowess. At one point, she asked what I do when I cannot say a word.

"I change it to one I can say."

I thought I saw her visibly shudder at that answer.

After the questioning, she had me read several passages aloud. She tested my ears and looked in my mouth. Then, I named pictured objects, repeated sentences, followed commands, and a bunch of other stuff, all of which took a good hour and a half. I really wished I had gone to the bathroom when I'd had the chance.

Finally, she gave me her conclusions. I had a speech disorder (I already knew that). I needed therapy (not a total surprise, despite Tea Cup's proclamations about my normalcy). And, finally, I wasn't going to get any better by avoiding all the tough words (it took me a while to see the value of this one).

I was seen for therapy twice a week for the next 6 years.

whether a tone that probably should be heard actually is heard. As with all screens, no conclusions can be drawn if the client fails (yes, it could be poor hearing, but it could also be lack of attention to the task). It is simply a way of determining whether to refer a client to an audiologist for further testing.

While administering tests, the clinician continues to make observations of the client, trying to gain as much insight as possible about communication, mood, motivation, and other factors that could affect either the diagnosis made or the treatment recommended. It is not all that infrequent for additional (i.e., unplanned) testing to be done on the basis of observations. In one instance, an adult client with above-average cognition and language (and a PhD in physics) was observed performing basic language tasks correctly, but with numerous delays. When the clinician added some extra tests to determine how well he processed spoken material, it was found that he exhibited numerous deficiencies in this area, deficiencies for which we were able to make subsequent recommendations.

☐ The Evaluation Session

To this point, there has been much discussion on what an evaluation is, but little about what is being tested, screened, or observed or how. In an audiological evaluation, the **auditory system** is clearly the focus (see Chapter 11). Similarly, in a full speech and language evaluation, all aspects of the speech-language system (articulation/phonology, fluency, hearing, language, and voice) are under test. How is this done? A common sequence is as follows:

- Hearing screen
- History interview
- Speech/language sample
- Testing of speech and language
- Oral-motor assessment
- Recommendations

To this point, three of these items have not been discussed. The sample of spoken language gives the tester an opportunity to observe communication in a regular conversation. The length of the sample needed depends in large part on what the SLP is looking for. With a child who mispronounces /s/, one would like to hear the sound in all word positions in a variety of phonetic contexts. The disfluent classmate, on the other hand, might be led toward producing speech at various levels of complexity, from single words to conversation, to see where speech begins to break down.

The **oral-motor assessment** is usually performed in conjunction with an **oral-peripheral assessment**. These examinations are done to ensure that both the configuration and movement of the speech structures are adequate for the production of spoken language. These assessments vary in length and complexity but will likely involve lingual structure and function (looking at the tongue and testing whether it can do maneuvers necessary for speech), labial structure and function (same deal for the lips), observation of the **hard palate** (is it high enough not to interfere with lingual movement without being too high for the tongue to reach?), and movement of the **velum** ("Open your mouth and say 'ah.'"). In addition, the SLP will look for differences such as missing teeth, enlarged **tonsils**, or **adenoids**. Often, no abnormalities are found, but that is also helpful in that the SLP can rule out structural deficits and consider other **etiological factors**, such as learning limitations, environment, or hearing loss.

The final segment of the evaluation (the recommendations of the SLP or audiologist) is, from the client's point of view, the most important part. This is, after all, why he or she showed up in the first place: to learn what is wrong and what can be done about it. Of course, before answering that, the clinician has to determine *if* something is wrong. A client's (or his or her caregiver's) perceived difference in his or her own speech might not be a difference at all. And even if it is, it may not be a difference that makes a difference. For example, a 3-year-old who misarticulates /s/ is exhibiting speech that is dissimilar to what we generally hear. Yet, preschoolers are not necessarily expected to produce all sounds, and it is not certain that any child will produce a perfect /s/ at such a young age. In this instance, there is a "difference" that does not warrant intervention.

Then, there are the people with perfectly normal speech and language who nevertheless sound different. A guy from Georgia who speaks with a southern dialect could move to New York and sound quite unlike any of his listeners. But in this case, the difference reflects no deficiency whatsoever. After all, the southerner did what all language learners do: picked up the speech and language in his environment. His language learning system performed exactly what it was designed to do.

In determining whether a difference makes a difference, it is important to realize that surface features may not reflect the entirety of a communication disorder. The three-part classification scheme of the World Health Organization (WHO), the International Classification of Impairments, Disabilities, and Handicaps, defines disorders in terms of **impairment** (for our purposes, the communication disruptions), **disability** (inability to perform specific communicative tasks), and **handicap** (failure to fulfill everyday needs, be they occupational, economic, or social) (Yaruss, 1998). This design indicates how speech and language disorders can extend far beyond surface features. In fact, one could argue that an impairment concerns an individual only because of the resulting disability and handicap. For example, the repetitions associated with stuttering might be less troublesome to a client than the resulting fear of talking to people.

☐ Recommendations

Of course, recommendations following a diagnostic evaluation often involve therapy. This is not always the case, however. It is difficult, for example, to recommend treatment in the following instances:

- The client's speech, language, or hearing are within normal limits.
- A client does not view his or her communication as disabling or handicapping.
- The **prognosis** for improvement is poor.
- Altering the client's environment might allow for the necessary communication changes to be made.
- A referral to another professional is a more reasonable first step than is formal therapy.

Of course, speech or language therapy often *is* recommended. In these instances, the clinician will be specific about the nature of said therapy. "Treatment for communication" is essentially meaningless to the client. "Treatment three times per week for 60-minute sessions to focus on production of /s/ and /z/" gives the client the information he or she has been waiting for. No guarantees are made with respect to the outcome of this treatment (remember again, we are dealing with people and all their variability), but the clinician is clear that this is his or her professional opinion about what is best.

In formulating recommendations, the professional has to draw on his or her knowledge base about the condition observed (e.g., what causes it, available treatments and track records with it, etc.) and what is known about the client (such as strengths, weaknesses, and the impact of the disorder). Other professionals and what they can do (referrals or consultations) will also be considered. Parents of disordered children might need to be counseled. For example, the mother who feels responsible for her child's condition may need reassurance that she did nothing wrong and a direction of focus for the future.

At this point, the clinician has turned a substantial amount of data and observations into concrete recommendations. To my way of thinking, he or she has sculpted a statue from a cloud.

☐ Synopsis

Diagnosing communication disorders involves taking copious bits of information (the client's relevant history, test results, and observations, among others) and determining whether a client has a problem and, if so, what to do about it. It is a complex process that requires the professional to administer various tasks and employ numerous skills. Diagnosis is also ongoing, a continuous exercise in refining and learning about the client and his or her communication.

☐ Vocabulary

> **adenoids**—lymphoid tissue within the nasopharynx (Seikel, King, & Drumright, 2005)
>
> **age equivalency**—age reflective of achieved score
>
> **assessment**—evaluation
>
> **auditory system**—neurological system responsible for hearing and balance
>
> **counseling**—process by which a professional guides an individual toward understanding and resolving personal matters
>
> **criterion referenced**—an assessment in which performance is compared to an objective or standard and not to the performance of others
>
> **diagnosis**—identification of a disorder by analysis of the symptoms presented (Nicolosi et al., 1989)

differential diagnosis—distinguishing between similar looking conditions

disability—inability to perform specific communicative tasks

etiological factors—the causes of, or factors related to, the development of a disorder (Gerrig & Zimbardo, 2002)

evaluation—process of determining a diagnosis as well as of monitoring progress

handicap—the social consequence of impairment (WHO, 1980)

hard palate—the roof of the mouth

hearing screen—testing administered to determine the necessity of a complete audiological evaluation

history interview—process by which a clinician obtains information from the client in person

impairment—an abnormality of a structure or function (WHO, 1980)

norming sample—a sample used to standardize a test (Schuler, 1998)

norm referenced—an assessment in which performance is compared to that of other people in a specified group

oral-motor assessment—evaluation of the movement of the speech structures

oral-peripheral assessment—evaluation of the speech structures void of movement

percentile—any of 100 points measured within the range of a plotted variable, each of which denotes that percentage of the total cases lying below it in value (Nicolosi et al., 1989)

prognosis—prediction of judgment concerning the course, duration, termination, and recovery from a disease or disorder (Nicolosi et al., 1989)

rapport—a feeling of mutual trust, understanding, and confidence

speech and language screens—evaluative items utilized to determine if further testing is warranted

tonsils—prominent masses of lymphoid tissue that lie one on each side of the throat (Stedman, 2006)

velum—soft palate, located behind hard palate

☐ Discussion Questions

1. What would you consider to be essential characteristics for a diagnostician? Why?
2. What are the advantages and disadvantages of both criterion-referenced and norm-referenced tests?
3. In Chapter 7, it is noted that oral motor therapy is a source of controversy in the field of CSD because little evidence exists that practicing

general oral movements leads to improved speech movements. Why would oral-motor assessments be any less controversial?

4. Would you recommend therapy for an individual presenting a communication impairment without a resulting disability or handicap?

☐ **Recommended Reading**

Haynes, W. O., & Pindzola, R. H. (2004). *Diagnosis and evaluation in speech pathology*. Boston: Allyn & Bacon.

Haynes and Pindzola's work serves as an effective source of information and offers insights into the clinical process.

Shipley, K. G., & McAfee, J. G. (2004). *Assessment in speech-language pathology: A resource manual* (3rd ed.). Clifton Park, NY: Delmar Learning.

Although primarily used as a graduate text, this source is clear and understandable for all readers. Included are descriptions of diagnostic procedures, as well as sample forms, reading samples, and more.

5
CHAPTER

Treatment

Note: As with the chapter on diagnosis, this one primarily (but not exclusively) addresses the world of speech-language pathologists (SLPs). Audiology is not mentioned as often, as hearing treatments are covered in Chapter 11.

Sculptures can be refined, even those that began as clouds.

With this proclamation comes the topic of **treatment** (also known as **therapy** or **management**). Although treatment begins with a concrete plan, where it goes from there can involve enough turns, stops, detours, and roadblocks to confuse a Formula 1 race car driver.

Despite its complexity, treatment can be whittled down to two essential processes: the teaching of the clinician and the learning of the client. Among other things, these basics mean that communication sciences and disorders (CSD) professionals must learn how to teach. Fortunately, there are many ways to go about gaining this skill:

- Course work in teaching helps us to understand what works in general, if not necessarily for the next client we treat.
- Discussions with peers allow us to hear new insights and ideas about improving the clinical interaction.
- Observation of others' teaching can show us what some basic teaching methods look like from the outside.

Then, there is actually doing it. As a classroom teacher once told me, you learn the most by teaching. Actually, what she said was, "The *only* way you learn to teach is by teaching," but that position negates the value of one of the classes I teach (not to mention this chapter). The point, as I see it anyway, is that nothing really makes as much of an impact as being across the table from a client and trying out your skills. That is where you learn what works and, just as important, what does not. It is where making mistakes has the proper impact ("I'll always remember how dumb I feel right now"), and you learn to make adjustments ("I'll always remember to pay attention when the client is talking").

The other part of the equation—the client's learning—is really the whole point of the clinical interaction. CSD professionals need to have a basic knowledge of how people learn, understanding that individual variations require different teaching. Such knowledge begins with general learning theories.

☐ General Learning Theories

Behavior can be changed via both **classical conditioning** and **operant conditioning**. We begin with classical.

The best-known, and quite possibly only, example ever used for classical conditioning is Pavlov's dogs. For the handful of your classmates who do not know the story, Pavlov understood that the presence of meat powder essentially turned the saliva glands of dogs into Niagara Falls. His discovery was that if he rang a bell just before presenting the animals with the meat powder, they eventually learned to open the saliva floodgates as soon as they heard the ring. In other words, something as neutral as a bell can evoke a strong response, provided it is paired with a stimulus that someone (in this case, one dog) will respond to automatically.

Because our clients are not dogs, there are two additional points to consider here:

1. Classical conditioning also works with people (think doorbell and pizza rather than bell and meat powder).
2. Individuals (people and dogs) can just as easily learn to *fear* a neutral signal if it is paired with something negative. Say the bell was rung just before an MMA fighter stomped on your foot. Unless you are pretty slow, you would learn to dislike that bell.

What does any of this have to do with CSD? A lot. For one, some behaviors we treat are learned via classical conditioning (e.g., the telephone comes to represent a feared situation to the person who stutters; talking in groups is equated with embarrassment for the guy with a language disorder). For another, because of how these associations are learned, it takes classical conditioning therapies to unlearn them. Strategies such as **systematic desensitization** and **counterconditioning** are applicable to these instances.

Whereas in classical conditioning, a response is elicited (i.e., drawn out), in operant conditioning it is emitted, then strengthened or weakened via **reinforcement** or **punishment**. Thus, it is the recipient controlling the environment, not vice versa.

In therapy, it works like this. The clinician presents a stimulus, and the client responds. If the response is the behavior the clinician was hoping for, it is reinforced (the clinician says "Good job!" or stuffs a piece of candy in the kid's mouth, or does whatever else the client views as a reward). Assuming the client likes the reinforcement (i.e., if it is actually reinforcing), the behavior will recur. Thus, a client can learn a new skill through a system of rewards.

One important point in all of this is that the reinforcement has to be rewarding to the client. Van Riper (1957) writes of an SLP using kissing as a reinforcer. That is, on instances of a desired behavior, the clinician kissed the client (I am not really sure who came up with this idea—or why—but that is what was written). As expected, the frequency of the behavior changed. *Unexpectedly*, however, it decreased. For some undetermined reason—the clinician was not the client's type, she was a lousy kisser, or whatever—the client viewed this "reinforcement" as an aversive stimulus.

The flip side of reinforcement, punishment, is also presented after a response, and if it is really punishing, the response it follows should decrease. If, for example, I insulted my clients after each misarticulation, the overt instances of these errors would likely diminish.

Punishment is rarely used by CSD professionals. For one thing, it is not particularly helpful toward building and maintaining rapport. Moreover, it is not always easy to determine what is punishing for a given individual (consider the lonely client who might have liked being kissed by Van Riper's clinician) or to know what behavior is being extinguished. On the last point, I once had a dog who was punished every time she got up on the good sofa (back before kids, when I actually *had* a good sofa and cared about stuff like that). No big deal—the dog just found someplace else to fulfill her apparent 20-hour daily requirement of sleeping. Or, so we thought. The problem was that when my wife and I were gone for the day, upon our return we found ample evidence that the dog had been on the good sofa. What had she learned through our punishment efforts? She would avoid that one sofa when people are around.

Another reason we generally steer clear of punishment is that we may have to keep increasing it to keep it effective. Using a previous example, this could result in either insulting the misarticulating client too much or, worse, getting a return insult. Also, punishment may only inhibit, rather than extinguish, behaviors. That is, the insults may reduce misarticulations, but only because the client stops talking.

All of this is not to say we never use punishment. Occasional **time-out** or **response cost** methods can help get kids in line. It is also important to note that we cannot avoid negative responses. Part of teaching, after all, is pointing out mistakes. It is just that the clinical model is more about the positive—having a good rapport, being enthusiastic, and, yes, reinforcing success—than the negative.

☐ Organization

The ability to elicit and reinforce (and occasionally punish) responses is but one technical skill needed to be an effective CSD professional. Another is the ability to organize information. I mention this here because organization is a skill employed before word one of any teaching begins (and thus before the client learns anything). Evaluation recommendations need to be turned into goals, and goals need to be prioritized and converted to tasks. Ideas must cease being ideas and instead become concrete materials, activities, and instructions.

☐ Goals

The task most associated with organizing data is the setting of both **short-term goals** and **long-term goals**. That is, professionals need to determine goals for where the client will eventually be as well as for the next scheduled session. Often, these are straightforward (i.e., if a little boy cannot pronounce /s/, the goal is that he learn how to say /s/). Other times, however, deficiencies cannot realistically be alleviated. Instead, the client must learn to compensate for them. For example, a client whose speech mechanism is wholly or partially paralyzed must learn alternative forms of communication. In this case, the goal might be to transmit ideas via alternative methods (such as gestures, writing, or pointing to words and pictures).

Goals consist of, at bare minimum, the skill to be learned:

Client will improve word-finding ability.

In most settings, however, you won't get away with that. You will need more, namely, a **criterion level** and specific information about what the client's objective is.

Client will name functional objects in her environment with an 80% level of accuracy.

The long- and short-term goals make up the **treatment plan**, which is a list of desired outcomes along with the steps needed to reach them. Will therapy unfold exactly according to this plan? No, it will not; the treatment plan is no more exact than any other type of plan (business, school, career, etc.). In fact, one could think of it as a statement of what probably *is not* going to happen. Even so, the plan offers some structure to therapy, a place to start.

With speech production issues, short-term goals often move through **operational levels of therapy**. How this works is that the SLP will teach the target behavior first in, say, words (or, in some cases, syllables or individual sounds) and progress to language levels that are increasingly longer and more complex and spontaneous. For example, once words are mastered, the client may get bumped up to phrases, then sentences, and so on until the target is produced in conversation in all settings. From the client's point of view, then, each time a task is completed, the "reward" is a new, more difficult, task.

As the treatment plan is unlikely to come off exactly as created, it is important to remember that, once goals (short or long term) are created, they are not cast in platinum. What I mean is that, with proper justification—new observations, change in client status—goals can be altered. With short-term goals, such change might occur on the fly. That is, sometimes the client just is not experiencing success, and the clinician has to come up with an **intermediate goal**—something tougher than the goal already mastered but easier than the one the client is struggling with. Perhaps a client can use newly learned speech techniques in sentences but not conversation. Possible intermediate goals are production of two sentences ("Tell me two things you like about baseball") or describing pictures. In either case, the language expected is longer and more complex than single sentences but less so than conversational speech.

☐ Tasks

To make goals useful, the clinician must, of course, create learning activities designed to achieve them. This means selecting materials and tasks appropriate for the particular client and whatever it is that he or she needs to learn. Factors that might impact these selections include the obvious one, client age (we do not use toy trains with adults, after all), and the cognitive level, gender, experiences, and likes/dislikes. The clinician should also consider whether the tasks help or hinder **response level**. A kid might really love blocks, but if he or she plays with them at the expense of learning new skills, they are not really effective therapy materials.

☐ Rapport

Once in the room with the client, the CSD professional will often begin by establishing rapport (or, if this has already been accomplished in earlier sessions, *maintaining* rapport). As a clinical concept, rapport can be difficult to grasp. For one thing, it is not measurable (i.e., you cannot add 10 units of rapport when a session needs a boost). Furthermore, there is no universal way to set or continue it. Still, it is clearly essential to the clinical interaction. After all, treatment tasks administered on your enemies are unlikely to be effective.

Some things that help rapport include being enthusiastic about therapy (not necessarily doing the wave after each correct response; just projecting an interest in the client and his or her progress) and clinical competence (clients are nicer if they think you know what you are doing). Basic courtesy does not hurt either.

Rapport is the reason why sessions often begin with chitchat: "How are things going?" "Did you buy that hybrid you were talking about last session?" "And how about that weather we're having lately, huh?" The purpose of this banter is not necessarily to hear the client's opinions on the mundane, but more so to make him or her comfortable and allow the clinician to observe communication in everyday conversation.

☐ Attention

As noted, rapport must be both established and maintained. The same can be said for the client's attention to the therapy objectives. This requires clearly presenting goals and tasks and preventing interferences and redirecting the client to the task when necessary. Depending on the client, interferences can mean anything from too many toys on the table to flashy clothing. CSD professionals learn early on to keep the therapy space clear and the distractions to a minimum.

Adult clients may well be motivated to learn new skills, and as a result, attention to task might not be a pressing issue. With children, however, the clinician may have to work harder to keep the therapy activities interesting. For instance, an SLP might incorporate the targets into games. The problem here is when the game, and not the target, becomes the objective ("Yeah, sure—remember to slow my rate. Whatever you say. It's your turn. Go!"). If this happens, it does not mean one should abandon the idea of making treatment fun. It just means that the clinician must find a new means of holding the client's attention while teaching a skill. Perhaps a small adjustment such as awarding extra turns for using the targeted skill can refocus the client to what he or she is supposed to be doing. The inattentive client, after all, is not learning anything.

Unfortunately for CSD professionals, inattentiveness is an easy state to achieve. Attention for most of us is limited; we literally have only so much. Worse yet, most of what we do have is utilized in **gross attending behaviors**, a relatively *inattentive* state of attentiveness. To understand gross attending behaviors, think about students in a college class. They are hearing the lecture, nodding, taking notes, and could tell you the general topic and maybe even the subtopic under discussion. For the most part, however, details are being written down without actually being absorbed.

Imagine that, in the same classroom, the professor announces that new material is about to be presented, after which there will be an exam. Now, the students turn on their **fine attending behaviors**. This increased state of focus is when real learning takes place. Thus, the more often a student (or a client) can find it, the better. For this reason, clinicians strive to keep the client concentrating as much as possible on the skill being taught.

☐ Behavior Modification

Of course, sometimes attention can wander. Other times, it refuses to show up at all. It is on these occasions that clinicians are forced to utilize their **behavior modification** skills. Such skills are different for CSD practitioners than they are for many other professions in that we cannot start off with a power play. "Don't smile until Thanksgiving" is not an option for us. Because rapport is so crucial to what we do, it is actually quite important that we do not come across as Attila the Hun, even temporarily. Rather, we strive to create an environment that is warm, nonthreatening, and often informal. We approach the clinical interaction not expecting behavior problems. Still, if we are not prepared to deal with them, we end up with kids and materials flying about the room while we sit in one place pulling our hair out.

Given our approach, it really helps to avoid behavior problems before they start. Some things that can help with this have already been mentioned:

- Keep the environment clear of objects that are easy to toss.
- Keep the task at a level so that the client can experience at least some success.
- Utilize materials that are interesting.
- Keep the clients busy.

Many clinicians also aim for what I would term a democratic relationship—sort of. Yes, both parties are involved in decision making, but the clinician is ultimately in charge. For example, the SLP can offer choices, but limited ones. Asking a client, "What do you want to do now?" gives the impression that the client actually gets to choose. In other words, it grants the client control of the session. Asking the client instead: "Do you want to do another word list or your swallowing exercises?" allows the client some input but keeps the session within the limits of the treatment plan. Furthermore, allowing clients to choose makes them accountable for their behaviors. Kids are less likely to misbehave during tasks they selected.

Sometimes, of course, we make all the right preventive moves and behavior problems still occur. As any clinical professional will tell you, sometimes good clients have bad days. And bad clients always do. Whatever the case, there are times we have to enforce our rules for appropriate behavior. With kids, such enforcement is accomplished more with action than words. Arguments and sermons take time, after all, and we prefer to spend our time teaching. Threats are often made in haste and with great emotion, which almost always results in them being empty (you have all seen the kid acting up in the grocery store, to which Mom says something like, "One more word and you're grounded for a year!"). Rather than saying something I cannot back up, or deliver a speech that will not be heard, I try to quickly administer a time-out or remove the problem stimulus (e.g., the block that just glanced off my head) or some other solution that allows me to get back to teaching.

☐ Teaching

Just as with behavior modification, the teaching of new communicative skills involves giving the client the appropriate information (here is what you did right; here is what you need to change). In addition, we teach by other means, such as **modeling** the behavior ourselves and **shaping** the new skill from one the client already has. An example of the latter method is a client who cannot say /k/ but can say similar sounds, such as /g/; in such a case, the client can be instructed to make a /g/ with an adjustment (i.e., remove the voicing) to get the /k/.

When the client does not exhibit the desired behavior, the clinician often provides **cues**. Although there are many different ways to cue a client—additional information, gestures, and leading questions, to name a few—the goal of cueing is always the same: to teach the client to one day cue him- or herself. Thus, clinicians may discard very effective cues because the client cannot use them. For example, a client who has difficulty finding the word he or she wants to say might be greatly aided by having the clinician provide the first sound of the answer. But, if the client cannot learn to produce the first sound on his or her own (i.e., self-cue), this method of cueing cannot be considered effective.

☐ Counseling

The most recent clinical examples given (i.e., shaping a /k/, using cues to help a client find a word) refer to managing **overt behaviors**. It is worth mentioning that clinicians also address what is beneath the surface. Examples of **covert behaviors** presented by clients include anxiety about speaking, embarrassment over listener reactions, and fear of difficult words, demanding people, or situations that might result in teasing. SLPs may administer counseling designed to bring these thoughts and emotions to the surface so the client can deal with them. After all, one cannot confront a disorder as long as part of it remains hidden.

Unfortunately, most CSD programs do not require counseling training. Thus, professionals often have to gain these skills via continuing education and other resources.

☐ Making Adjustments

A skill that crosses counseling, teaching, behavior modification, and other clinical competency areas is the ability to adjust to unexpected occurrences. In therapy, change can happen quickly. A client finds a previously difficult task to be suddenly easy (or vice versa). Or, perhaps the client's behavior takes a quick turn for the worse. In these instances, it is important for CSD professionals to think on their feet. In the view of many supervisors, in fact, the ability to make immediate and appropriate adjustments is what separates the good from the great clinician. Although this is debatable, it is certainly true that making the right modifications results in more efficient sessions. Doing so requires a thorough understanding of both clinical methods and the specific treatment plan.

☐ Response Recording

At this point in the chapter, we have a clinician who is maintaining rapport and holding the client's attention while teaching and obtaining targeted behaviors. Now, add to this that the clinician has to keep track of how well the client is doing. This aspect of therapy is known as **response**

recording, and like pretty much everything else discussed in this chapter, it can take various forms. At the least (i.e., to chart basic progress), it will involve keeping track of correct and incorrect answers.

$$+ - + + + - + + + +$$

These scores are not bad—80% right. That is some important information right there. It is hoped, though, that most clinicians keep track of more than just right versus wrong. Knowing which items were cued, for example, and how effective the cues were, would certainly help with later teaching. Keeping track of which strategies or activities did and did not work can also help to make adjustments for the next session. The following are marks taken from an actual response recording form.

$$N N - G N + G D N (C) - D N$$

What happened? Well, the client was asked to communicate pictured ideas, and this was accomplished with 80% accuracy. A cue (noted with the C) was used to elicit one answer. Of the eight correct communications, four were named (N) (one of these with the help of the aforementioned cue), one was communicated with a gesture (G), another with a combination of naming and gesture (N + G), and two were described (D). The point here is not that this client likes to talk more than gesture, but rather, that response recording can be efficient while still yielding a lot of information.

☐ Transfer of Skills

From response recording come new goals and adjustments to the therapy plan, as the client continues the trek toward the long-term goals. It is hoped that this trip will lead not only to improved skills but also habituated ones. That is, the client will develop skills not reliant on the clinician's reinforcement and those that can be used anywhere, anytime.

This brings us to the trickiest aspects of treatment, **transfer** and **generalization**. Clients can do wonderful things inside therapy rooms. However, many of these same skills run and hide the moment the client steps out the door. Unfazed by this disappearance, we try different things to expand their presence.

A home program is one means of extending therapeutic goals to different settings. Such programs range from simple word lists (for practicing speech tasks) to informal activities, such as reading essays, watching videos, or searching for information on the Internet.

JOCK TRANSFER

I worked with surly people. Lots of them.

The offices surrounding the private practice were seemingly packed with young drones dressed in their Saturday worst doing jobs that apparently required a lot of sneering and grunting, not to mention endless smoke breaks. Most of the time, this did not matter much to me, as I was secluded within a treatment setting. The problem was that sometimes therapy takes one out of the clinic and, in this case, among the noncommunicative.

Let me point out a couple of things here. One is that what I'm referring to—transfer activities (i.e., tasks designed to take skills into new locations and listeners)—can get dull in any private practice setting. Because people in office complexes are busy and only see each other infrequently, forced conversations tend to be short, repetitive, and quite often, uninteresting. How many times can your clients ask for directions or the correct time? Still, this setting was worse. Not only, as I mentioned, were people not particularly friendly, but many of their conversations featured vocabulary that was not all that appropriate for the kids I was seeing, for example:

Person 1: "Hey [expletive as noun], what the [same expletive as adverb] [new expletive as noun] is that [original expletive as adjective] [other expletive as noun]?"
Person 2 (laughing): "[All-purpose expletive]!"

And the men were even worse.

Adding to all that, the clients were mostly middle school males who would not have been at all intrigued by the topics of these conversations. Mind you, I was never really able to discern what these topics actually *were*; I just knew they were not sports. And sports were what these kids were interested in, almost to the exclusion of everything else. In fact, their speech was quite controlled when talking about school, family, and pretty much anything else. Sports presented bigger challenges, however, because they were *important* and thus involved streams of thoughts that must be expressed rapidly.

It occurred to me that what I needed were not grunting strangers, but rather, people who could talk about sports and get my clients talking as well. That was when I came up with the idea of calling athletes.

It seemed like a good idea the moment it hit me.

continued

All I needed were some athletes.

I started asking around and was surprised by what I found. A friend played college baseball. A friend of a friend played professionally. A colleague directed me to a football coach. Tennis pros said they would lend a hand (they never turned me into much of a player, so I guess they felt like they owed me this) (just kidding; they and everyone else I contacted were willing to help with no reservations whatsoever).

It worked like this. I called the jock and explained what I wanted to do. When the session began, I told the client that we were calling a baseball, tennis, whatever player and to write down some questions or topics to discuss with him or her. Then, I labeled the questions/topics according to what techniques I wanted the client to use. I dialed the number and asked for Joe (or Jo) Jock. This afforded me an opportunity to model the targets, usually in an exaggerated fashion (e.g., if I asked for Dwyane Wade, I could use, for example, voluntary stuttering and say, "Mmmmy name is D-D-D-Dale Williams, and I'm ssssitting here with K-K-Kyle who has ssssssome questions. Do you have a few moments?"). (No, he was not one of the ones we called, but I figured some students just skim these sidebar essays, and one of them might come away thinking that I know Dwyane Wade.) Anyway, it was at that point that I passed the phone to my client.

I have to tell you that the kids were impressive. Employing their techniques, they asked their questions and made their comments without intimidation or avoidance. Furthermore, they loved the activity, even asking to make more calls. So, we expanded the list to include sportswriters, peers, and support group members, among others.

During one session, the client got off the phone with a baseball player and said, "That was the coolest thing! Can we stop now so I can tell my mom what I did?"

"We'll be done soon."

"Can I have his [the player's] number?"

"Uh, no," I answered. "Why would you even ask me that?"

"I know my brother won't believe me, so I want to be able to call and verify."

Another time a client called a favorite author, and I couldn't get him off the phone. They discussed my client's school, career aspirations, vacation plans, and I think they were getting into favorite snack foods ("Pretzels? No way!") when I finally told him it was time to go.

As with all transfer activities, this task was a step toward the finish line but was not the line itself. For one thing, I was there listening, which by itself affected the clients' speech. Still, the fact that they were able to handle this situation said volumes about their progress. It also visibly improved their confidence.

Looking back, I am now thankful for those surly people.

Transfer of skills can also be aided simply by leaving the treatment room now and then. In doing so, clients can employ new skills with a variety of listeners. Although some of these listeners might turn out to be jerks, clients learn that most are not, and that the ones who are can be dealt with.

There are also transfer activities that are possible to do in the regular therapy setting. Bringing in new listeners is one way to change the communication environment. Another is role play (Susca, 1997), during which the therapist can take the role of the boss, peer, parent, massage therapist, or whoever else is involved in difficult speaking situations for a particular client. This can help with the development of strategies for addressing such situations.

☐ Group Therapy

The sequence outlined in this chapter—from initial therapy planning to generalization of learned skills—is relevant whether treatment is individualized or administered in groups. Although individual therapy is often better for learning new skills, there are some advantages to seeing clients en masse. These advantages include the following:

- If the caseload is heavy, group therapy is more efficient than individualized treatment for the obvious reason that the SLP sees a comparatively greater number of clients in the course of a workday.
- Group therapy allows clients to observe (and it is hoped learn from) feedback given to others.
- With children, there may be less stigma associated with being in a group, as they discover that some of their peers also have communication problems.
- For clients in need of mutual aid and emotional support, therapy groups can offer both.
- Groups also provide a built-in set of listeners on which to try new skills (Williams & Dugan, 2002), making group therapy conducive to skill transfer.

It is important that any sort of collective treatment follow a **shaping group** format (Leith, 1993) in which participants are encouraged to offer feedback to one another. In this way, each client stays involved throughout the entire session. This format assumes both open and equal participation. All group members should feel free to contribute, but no one should be allowed to dominate the session (Ramig, 2003).

Possible disadvantages of group therapy include

- High caseloads can result in large groups, which can be difficult to manage (Leith, 1993). The clinician's job feels more like crowd control than helping people communicate.
- If a shaping format is not utilized, groups can also lead to less treatment time per client. That is, if every client is not engaged throughout the session, group therapy can become individual therapy done in a crowd. By way of example, if a group of four is seen for 1 hour and each member takes part in therapy tasks only when it is his or her turn, it can be argued that each client received 15 minutes of therapy, not 60.
- Finally, because of scheduling concerns, children are sometimes grouped by classroom/grade and not by disorders. This can result in multiple disorders being treated at the same time.

☐ Interpersonal Skills

In addition to the technical skills needed to teach, there are other areas of aptitude that help make a good clinician. Probably the most obvious of these are interpersonal skills. We are, after all, dealing with real people. How one presents oneself makes a difference. Ideally, CSD professionals will appear motivated, poised, and knowledgeable without coming across as condescending (i.e., using words like *oneself*). They are good communication models who do not give long and technical (that is, rambling and boring) answers to their clients' questions. They use their overinflected Steve-from-Blue's-Clues voices only when addressing children and not adults. They do not roll their eyes at heartfelt statements uttered by teen clients.

You think I am just pointing out the obvious, but I have witnessed all of these examples firsthand. I have also heard each of the following statements, all made by clinicians to clients:

- "How was it growing up in the South? I heard all the schools are really bad down there!"
- "So, you're from India. How exciting! I don't know anything about India. Do they, like, have electricity there?"

- "Me and my friends was going to go to the football game this weekend."

Then, there was this gem of an exchange:

Clinician: You grew up in Cleveland? You poor thing.
Client: I'm curious. What was it about Cleveland that you didn't like?
Clinician: Oh, I've never been there.

Let us call this Rule 1: Avoid saying stupid things. It is a rule that can serve clinicians well not only with clients but also with others. After all, CSD personnel take part in regular conferences with families and with other professionals, either of which can test their interpersonal skills. Let us examine these separately.

Family conferences are a place to obtain information about the client's everyday life, as well as give loved ones a chance to ask questions and discuss referrals. Interpersonal skills are crucial in such a setting, especially when one considers that family members may not always hear things exactly as the professional means them:

The clinician says: I made a referral to a psychologist as I feel your husband's anxiety may be more than just speech-related.
The client's spouse hears: You think my husband is crazy.

The clinician says: I've observed some instances where your son had difficulty coordinating his movements. I'm going to consult with a neurologist since they really know the brain. Now is the time to rule out any bigger problem.
The client's mom hears: You think my kid is stupid.

Staffings allow the SLP or audiologist to meet with professionals from other disciplines. These meetings range from small, informal groups to large, pressurized question-and-answer sessions. However it is done, the idea is to have everyone come together and get a complete picture of the client. In this way, the various specialists can help each other. For example, the SLP can tell the physical therapist to use short utterances and repeat instructions because the client has trouble processing information. The physician can report changes of medication that might have an impact on therapy.

Problems that can arise in staffings include:

- Know-it-alls who show up less for the good of the clients than to display their knowledge of, well, everything. Generally speaking, they are both annoying and ignored. If time constraints are tight, someone may tell them to shut up. Make sure it is not you, as we like people to associate our profession with some measure of dignity.

- Arguments about what is best for the client. Disagreements expressed in a civilized manner can be resolved and may even be beneficial if people learn new information that can help a client. Arguments consisting of one rude comment after another benefit no one. You might want to ask the know-it-all doctor, "Where did you get your degree in audiology?" But, it is unlikely to get the client's hearing needs met.

If Rule 1 is to avoid saying stupid things, Rule 2 is: Be yourself. Unless, of course, you are prone to saying stupid things. If that is the case, be a better version of yourself.

Part of being the best you that you can be is utilizing whatever listening skills you possess. Give the client your fine—actually, your *finest*—attention. And, leave your personal problems outside therapy. If you woke up late, missed breakfast, had a flat tire, and your cat threw up all over your shoes—all in one morning—you still do not have a right to take out your aggressions on the client. None of these occurrences were the client's fault, after all. And even if they were, the clinician still has an obligation to remain professional.

☐ Self-Evaluation Skills

A final set of competencies that a good clinician must develop are **self-evaluation skills**. As a young field, theories and techniques in it change regularly. We need to keep up and sharpen our skills. This involves not only making use of our strengths but also addressing our weaker areas (and we all have some).

It is worth noting that self-evaluation is an active process, requiring a degree of effort on the part of the professional. We do not just work and mysteriously absorb knowledge. Those who claim that "experience is the best teacher" are just kidding themselves. Yes, experience offers insights into our teaching skills—what works and what does not. But passive existence does not build the knowledge base so crucial to professionals in a young and dynamic field. A clinician with 40 years experience estimated that 75% of what he learned in graduate school is now considered wrong. "Not a different perspective or new attitudes that changed with the times. I mean it was flat wrong."

Thus, CSD professionals need to make an effort to improve. They could, for example, ask colleagues to observe their sessions. After all, those with similar knowledge bases and experiences can provide feedback to improve technical, interpersonal, and any other sets of skills.

In many settings, however, there is exactly one SLP or one audiologist. If it is you, it follows that you are the only one monitoring you. In these instances, meaningful self-evaluation becomes trickier, but there are some undertakings that can help. One is simple introspection. Reviewing goals and progress and thinking about (and researching) new approaches can offer novel insights into treatment.

Obviously, effective self-evaluation will also involve stepping outside one's own thoughts. Feedback from clients is one means of obtaining a different perspective of one's skills. This can be done via confidential satisfaction survey questions (e.g., "How well does the clinician explain tasks?") or through less-formal discussions. Either way, the clinician is likely to learn something; in my experience, clients are not shy about expressing their feelings about the treatment they are receiving.

Audiotaping and videotaping sessions can also be learning experiences. They provide the clinician with an opportunity to view the session as an outsider would. Items that go unnoticed when providing therapy—the client's posture, the clinician's tone of voice, and how often the interjections "um" and "y'know" are used, among others—are out in the open for the viewer to observe and ponder.

To increase their knowledge foundations, CSD professionals need continuing education. This involves a variety of learning experiences—reading professional journals, attending workshops, listening to teleseminars, attending online conferences, and just about anything else that utilizes a known means of delivering information. In these ways, those in the field can continue to update their educations and, in doing so, provide the most up-to-date services for their clients.

Because of the complexity of the therapeutic process, when one self-evaluates, there are a number of issues that must be addressed. The following is a list of questions a clinician can ask him- or herself. It is hoped that the answers help with the self-improvement process.

- Am I planning the sessions appropriately?
- Are my goals appropriate? How about my tasks, materials, and feedback?
- How well do the clients understand my instructions?
- Am I getting enough responses from the client?
- Is my client getting frustrated? Why?
- Did I remember to wear deodorant?
- What else can I do to improve my performance as a clinician?

☐ Synopsis

Treatment is a process of teaching and learning. Clinicians develop sets of skills—technical, interpersonal, self-evaluation, and others—that help them become effective teachers. The hope is that they can use these skills to help clients learn and habituate necessary communication skills.

☐ Vocabulary

behavior modification—the systematic use of principles of learning to increase the frequency of desired behaviors or decrease the frequency of problem behaviors (Gerrig & Zimbardo, 2002)

classical conditioning—type of learning in which an initially neutral stimulus becomes a conditioned stimulus (positive or negative) when presented together with an unconditioned stimulus (i.e., something you do not have to learn to love or hate)

counterconditioning—technique used to replace a negative response with a positive one by repeated association of a stimulus that has evoked the negative response with a positive experience

covert behaviors—thoughts or feelings that cannot be observed (Leith, 1993)

criterion level—minimal level of performance that meets a goal

cues—an aid that promotes a correct response (Nicolosi et al., 1989)

family conferences—meetings involving the clinician, members of the client's family, and when appropriate, the client; the purpose is to discuss the client's treatment

fine attending behaviors—analytical focus to task

generalization—transferring and maintaining behaviors in new environments

gross attending behaviors—general awareness

intermediate goal—something tougher than the goal already mastered but easier than the one the client is struggling with

long-term goals—terminal behaviors, that is, those expected when the client is dismissed from therapy or after a given period of time

management—therapy; also treatment

modeling—emulation or following the example of another (Nicolosi et al., 1989)

operant conditioning—method of changing behavior in which the client or learner is rewarded or punished after the response (to be conditioned) occurs

operational levels of therapy—stages of language progressing from simple and structured (e.g., word lists) to complex and spontaneous (such as conversation)

overt behaviors—actions or movements that can be observed (Leith, 1993)

punishment—aversive stimulus following an unwanted behavior

reinforcement—positive event occurring after a behavior is performed (Leith, 1993)

response cost—reward is given for certain behaviors, but also taken away for others

response level—frequency of responses during an activity or session

response recording—written documentation of individual responses

self-evaluation skills—the ability to assess one's own performance

shaping—creating a behavior the client cannot do from one he or she can

shaping group—group therapy in which members are directly involved in the therapeutic process, in terms of both receiving therapy and providing therapy (Leith, 1993)

short-term goals—steps leading to long-term goals

staffings—an exchange of information with other professionals

systematic desensitization—learning of alternative responses through graduated steps

therapy—treatment of any significant condition to prevent, alleviate, or cure it; Nicolosi et al., 1989)

time-out—period during which client does not respond to stimuli, usually because the task has stopped

transfer—extending target behaviors to new environments

treatment—therapy

treatment plan—specific plan of care that includes all long-term goals to be attempted with a particular client

☐ Discussion Questions

1. When I first moved into my new house, every time the phone rang, I groaned because I knew it was somebody wanting money (electric company, telephone company, mortgage company, etc.). Shortly thereafter, salespeople started calling, and I learned to say no firmly because only that ended the conversations. Now you relate lessons you've learned through both classical and operant conditioning.
2. Give an example from your own life when you were punished. Did the punishment work? Why or why not?
3. The following are two short-term goals. Create appropriate tasks for each.

   - Client will produce /s/ in the initial position of words with 90% accuracy.
   - Client will correctly use irregular plurals in sentences with 80% accuracy.

4. When do you exhibit gross attention skills? How about fine attention skills?

5. People learn in many different ways. Describe the teaching style of someone from whom you learned a lot.

6. You need to refer a client to a psychologist. How can you do this in a way that is professional, compassionate, and clear?

7. You are an SLP who is seeing a client with severely limited speech but given a good prognosis to one day carry on normal conversations. During the staffing, a psychiatrist says, "I asked the client how he was, and he said fine. Then I asked him if he was sure, and he said yes. Since all his answers were appropriate, I don't see why this guy is wasting his time in speech therapy." How do you respond?

8. Aside from the skills listed in this chapter (organization, ability to set goals, etc.), what talents do you feel make a good therapist?

9. At the end of the chapter, there is a list of questions that a clinician could use for self-evaluation. Can you think of any others?

☐ Recommended Reading

Leith, W. R. (1993). *Clinical methods in communication disorders*. Austin, TX: Pro-Ed.
I have used this text in my own courses for a number of years, and students never fail to remark about its clarity and fine use of examples.

Roth, F. R., & Worthington, C. K. (2001). *Treatment resource manual for speech-language pathology*. Albany, NY: Singular.
A comprehensive work, this text includes client profiles, sample activities, and helpful hints, as well the basics of treatment (teaching, data collection, generalization, etc.).

6 CHAPTER

Language Disorders

Although I had no diagnosed language disorder, as a child or teen, I made all of the following statements.

- "It bugs me when he just stands there and be's annoying!"
- "That put a monkey in the wrench!"
- "She has a bad altitude"
- "There are numerous, uh, well, contradictory I should say, for they are not just numerous in the context in which I'm about to extrapolate on their, uh, essence I guess you could say. In other words ... " (actually, I still say a lot of stuff like this; ask my students).
- "Look what my mom bought us for dessert. What is this—cherry slop over cow chips?" (Not that bad a sentence, until you realize that the listener was a dinner guest who, unbeknownst to me, had been nice enough to bring us a cherry-chocolate pastry for dessert.)

Yes, my own language skills are not always perfect. In fact, I have made mistakes within and across all five language domains noted in Chapter 2, and so have you. This is not particularly surprising, when you consider that not only is language complicated, but also the machine producing it (humans) is quite multifaceted. Because of all this complexity, a wide variety of things can go wrong—in one domain or in an almost endless set of domain combinations.

☐ Language Delay

For a variety of reasons, sometimes language development is hindered. The child with a *language delay* follows a somewhat orderly sequence of development (see Chapter 2), but not at a normal pace. The result is that language skills are consistently below what is expected for his or her age. A 5-year-old boy with a delay could say, for example, "I wear shoes on my foots." The missing form (the irregular plural) is one he should have at his age. By not using it, his statement sounds more like something a 3-year-old might say. It is likely that the rest of his language does as well, given that this sort of immature language can affect any domain.

There are a variety of potential causes for language delays. These may be prenatal (for example, they may be tied to a positive family history of developmental delays), perinatal (delays occur often with premature births), or postnatal (e.g., chronic ear infections). Whatever the cause or causes, the essential jobs of the speech-language pathologist (SLP) are to get the delayed child caught up to his or her age level and to determine whether further evaluation (for more serious disorders) is warranted.

☐ Characteristics of Language Disorders

In contrast to language delays, individuals with language disorders do not follow an orderly pattern in developing a language code. The disordered child is more likely to use grammar and forms outside normal development, that is, ones that kids do not typically say at any age (e.g., "Foot shoe in").

As with delays, disorders can affect expression, reception, or be mixed (i.e., involve both). They can be deficits of writing (*dysgraphia*), reading (e.g., *dyslexia*), speaking, or understanding speech. In fact, there is growing speculation that disorders of **literacy** are closely associated with spoken language disorders, perhaps even deriving from the same sources of memory deficits or deficiencies in the ability to process linguistic information (Baddeley, 2003; Gillam, Cowan, & Day, 1995).

Many language diagnostic classifications (e.g., phonological disorders, central auditory processing disorders) are handled in depth in other chapters. There are other diagnoses, however, that can affect the language system. These are described in the following pages.

Specific Language Impairment

Specific language impairment (SLI), also known as developmental language disorder, is impaired language in the absence of other learning difficulties (Alvares & Williams, 1995). SLI clients comprise the greatest number of children receiving language intervention services. It is diagnosed in 7% of 5-year-olds (most of them males) and affects more than a million kids in public schools alone (Flax et al. 2003; Merril Advanced Studies Center, 2004).

As with a lot of communication disorders, the cause of SLI is **idiopathic**, which means, essentially, that we do not know what it is. In defense of communication sciences and disorders (CSD) professionals, however, let me point out that the reason we do not know is not ignorance, but because the cause is likely complex, with many factors contributing to the condition. Such factors can be genetic (Crago & Gopnik, 1994; Tomblin & Buckwalter, 1994) and environmental (Hammer, Tomblin, Zhang, & Weiss, 2001). That is, children can be born with differences that restrict their ability to learn language; indeed, with SLI, there is usually a positive family history of language or learning problems; on the other hand, children may suffer from a lack of exposure to language, which gets them in a vicious circle of less language, leading to fewer language experiences, resulting in less language, and so on.

SLI may also be tied to medical/physical aspects, such as chronic middle ear infections during infancy and toddlerhood. Such a factor could delay early and speech sound development (Menyuk, 1992) and make it difficult to acquire the underlying grammatical rules necessary for language.

Memory deficits and SLI is an active area of study. Researchers have found that these children present diminished *phonological working memory* (Montgomery, 1995) and *verbal working memory* (Evans & Mainela-Arnold, 2005; Marton & Schwartz, 2003; Montgomery, 2002; Ellis Weismer, Evans, & Hesketh, 1999). It may be that poor **working memory** skills serve as a barrier to the acquisition of language. That is, an inability to temporarily store verbal, especially phonological, input may prevent the child from processing its meaning (Archibald & Gathercole, 2006; Baddeley, 1986; Gathercole, Alloway, Willis, & Adams, 2006; Leonard et al., 2007; Montgomery, 2002; Westby & Watson, 2004). This processing difficulty would, in turn, impair the development of language.

Children with SLI commonly experience difficulties with all areas of language. In the domain of semantics, they may show problems with word retrieval and vocabulary. Their expressive speech and writing may include **circumlocution** or reliance on nonspecific words (e.g., overusing the word *thing*). They may have trouble understanding words with multiple meanings, such as *spring* or *saw*. Also, the child who has SLI may have difficulty identifying central concepts, using metaphoric language, and reading complex material that requires the ability to understand the perspective of the writer. Syntax errors may include incorrect use of **morphologic markers**, frequent use of starters such as "ah" or "you know," and problems with subject-verb agreement (Alvares & Williams, 1995).

In the area of pragmatics, a child with SLI may show difficulties understanding listener perspective, maintaining a topic, identifying themes or concepts, and using humor. Such pragmatic difficulties can result in poor social skills (Conti-Ramsden & Botting, 2004; Fujiki & Brinton, 1996; Fujiki, Brinton, & Isaacson, 2001), including difficulty understanding situational demands in the classroom (Haynes et al., 1990). Further, children with SLI may have difficulty using language to interact socially, which may result in exclusion or rejection by peers (Rice, 1993).

As all domains of language can be affected, SLI has educational implications beyond socialization. Associated learning and reading problems may be present in school. Difficulty with spoken and written language will impact numerous, if not all, areas of academic performance. Interestingly, SLI could be tied to math problems as well, as memory for complex tasks may well have an impact on the ability to carry out calculations (Gathercole et al., 2004).

Language Disorders in Special Populations

SLPs and audiologists provide services to populations with cognitive, motor, or sensory limitations that can result in unique language profiles. In general, clients with special needs require collaborative intervention involving family members and professionals.

Intellectual Disability

As intellectual disability is manifested in different types and severity levels, the effects on language can be varied (McCauley, 2001). For example, Down syndrome can affect morphology and syntax while preserving semantics and pragmatics (McCauley, 2000). Still, there are some general statements that can be made. Individuals with intellectual disabilities tend to develop language skills in the same sequence as other children, but progress at a slower rate and, because of cognitive limitations, do not attain the same level of proficiency. Moreover, in addition to their belated language abilities, these clients may exhibit weaknesses in auditory processing and pragmatic skills (Taylor, Smiley, & Richards, 2009), limiting their opportunities for exposure to language. Thus, an already-deficient system may not be allowed to develop to capacity.

Pervasive Developmental Disorder/Autism

The spectrum of **pervasive developmental disorders** (**PDDs**) goes from barely perceptible all the way to severe and includes a wide variety of conditions marked by difficulties communicating, playing, or relating to others. **Autism** is the best known of these disorders, in large part because of the movie *Rain Man*. In reality, however, few individuals with autism have brains that work like high-speed calculators. In fact, about 80% present IQ scores in the deficient range (below 70), although it is important to note that (1) intelligence testing requires communication on the part of the person being tested, and (2) autism is not defined by intelligence, as these individuals can fall anywhere from impaired to genius (Alvares & Williams, 1995). More typically, the characteristics include less Hollywood-friendly symptoms, such as deficits in using communication for social interaction and stereotypical and repetitive behaviors (Anderson & Shames, 2006; Mundy & Stella, 2000). Social communication deficits include difficulty sharing experiences, poor eye contact, and infrequent use of greetings, all of which negatively affect the client's ability to establish meaningful relationships with other people.

Autism is considered to be a neurological condition, although the exact type of brain dysfunction is unknown (Akshoomoff, 2000). The **incidence** is anywhere from 2 to 21 cases per 10,000 live births, with about 80% of those affected being males (Scott et al., 2000). It is usually diagnosed between the ages of 18 and 36 months in babies who lack babbling or meaningful gestures, do not respond to their names, maintain poor eye contact, and exhibit repetitive movements (hand flapping, rocking), among other unusual behaviors.

Children with autism use communication to request objects or actions but rarely to comment. Some do not speak at all. Others may exhibit any or all of the following: **echolalia**, a tendency to comment off topic, avoidance of social interactions, and abnormalities of pitch, stress, rate, rhythm, and intonation (Alvares & Williams, 1995). Because they engage in relatively few social interactions, children with autism have fewer opportunities to acquire language. Therefore, the SLP and other education professionals often attempt to increase the child's awareness of others in an effort to keep the child from falling even further behind his or her peers.

Hearing Impairment

Individuals with hearing impairments have a wide range of speech, language, and communication abilities. As noted in Chapter 11, some communicate primarily through verbal expression, relying on amplification and speech reading for receptive language. Others depend in part or completely on manual communication.

It is not unusual for children with impaired hearing to present language deficits. Simply stated, if a child cannot hear the language in the environment, he or she cannot learn it. As might be expected, the resulting deficits have an impact on all domains of language. In such cases, audiologists and SLPs often work together to help the child catch up to peers.

THE DIAGNOSIS AND TREATMENT OF BILLY

To his father, Billy seemed different right from the start. The trouble was, Dad could not put his finger on exactly what was unusual. Billy smiled at his parents like any good toddler should. Eye contact was fine, and he played with the toys his family bought for him.

Played with the toys. Looking back, that was a key. Not that Billy played with toys, of course; all toddlers do that. It was more the *way* he played. To Dad, Billy seemed overly cautious, at times even fearful. The only example Dad could point to, however, was that Billy let other kids take his toys away without protest. The responses to that concern were predictable: "So what? He's shy." "He'll learn. Nothing to worry about."

As Billy progressed through toddlerhood, the shyness began to look more like social anxiety. He made noticeably little eye contact with anyone and became quite upset any time his mother left the house. By the time he was 2 and a half, he was spending most of his time with adults and seemed to be retreating into a tiny comfort zone. Speech, which had consisted of one-word utterances, stopped completely. When he was around other children, Billy showed little interest in what they were doing.

His parents tried preschool to see if that would get Billy out of his shell. When they visited the classroom and observed other 3-year-olds, it hit them how different Billy was from his peers. The boys in the classroom related to each other via laughter, shouting, and periodic aggression. Billy, on the other hand, barely interacted at all, preferring to engage in activities such as throwing leaves up in the air and spinning around or rolling plastic cars back and forth along the same path. He used only a few of the toys available and always played by himself.

His play at home was also becoming more unusual. When manipulating toy animals, for example, he did not pretend they were galloping or making noises; he just set them down and stared at them. Sometimes, he would follow the staring with a physical activity, such as flapping his arms or running around the house. His parents referred to these as self-stimulating behaviors because it seemed like Billy needed to do them to satisfy whatever was going on inside his brain. Looking back, they realized these behaviors started a few months before enrollment in preschool but were relatively infrequent at that time.

As the self-stimulation became more pronounced, his parents brought Billy to a psychologist for testing. Unfortunately, the tester had no idea what, if anything, was going on. They ended up getting him tested twice more, which resulted in two separate diagnoses: autism (moderate in severity) and pervasive developmental disorder/not otherwise specified. The latter diagnosis is somewhat ill defined, meaning, in essence, that some but not all features of autism or another developmental disorder are present. Even so, this is the one they went with, primarily because they had the most confidence in the tester.

The decision was made to pull Billy out of school and have Dad, who had some experience with developmental differences, work with Billy at home. At first, this plan involved a part-time job for Dad, with afternoons at home being Billy's teacher. Unfortunately, this arrangement did not work as well as both parents had hoped (Billy's early progress was minimal), and Dad eventually stayed home full time.

Billy's father described the teaching he did as "walking a fine line between pushing the language system and keeping things fun." One behavior addressed early on was the inappropriate play. To begin with, Dad and Mom (when she was home) self-stimulated with their son. Billy flapped his arms, the parents flapped their arms. He ran in circles, they followed. Although they were mimicking Billy's behavior, both parents were careful not to come across as mocking it. Their goals were to (1) get into his world and (2) let him know that his behaviors were okay with them. As they had previously been punishing inappropriate play, this new tack was a pleasant surprise for Billy. He often laughed at his parents' antics, an early sign of interaction.

When the three of them were all performing an activity together, the parents engaged in more appropriate play. Billy did likewise. In time, he learned that the typical play was more fun, which reinforced its occurrence. The appropriate participation also allowed the parents to stimulate language development.

The same basic approach was used to teach Billy functions beyond just play. Other missing behaviors—using a fork to eat, making eye contact with people, and others—were also taught via shaping existing actions. Each one took time, but the parents' hard work eventually paid off.

Almost 3 years after the initial diagnoses, Billy is back in preschool and, interestingly, in a school where children are tested to ensure that they are within normal limits in terms of cognition, language, and other measures of school readiness. He is reading at a

continued

fourth-grade level and is demonstrating a talent for drawing. Is he recovered? Dad says no, but noted that, if you saw him, at first glance he would look like just another kid in the classroom, adding, "If you didn't know, you wouldn't know, you know?" Yet, there are clear differences:

- Billy's language system still shuts down on occasion. For reasons not entirely clear, aspects of language (often sentence structure) will decline for a time, then return to age-appropriate level.
- Although Billy is old enough to engage in team sports, his parents believe that he is not yet ready for the level of social interaction required.
- The parents specifically chose a school with small class sizes because they worried that a large number of classmates would be overstimulating—more distractions, more conflict, and more instances of other kids being loud, all of which make Billy withdraw.
- The fact that there are still situations that overwhelm him, along with a newly developed ability to recognize them, results in Billy passing up some events (e.g., birthday parties) that other children look forward to attending.
- Mom and Dad still work with him regularly, in the form of therapeutic play designed to further stimulate language development. Sessions are now less structured and, on the surface, not that different from what other parents do with their children (play with blocks, draw pictures, color, etc.). But, Billy's parents ask a lot of questions and make a lot of comments about whatever the activity is to make certain that he is hearing and using language as much as possible.

As would be expected, Billy's parents have surfed some emotional tidal swells. At first, there was surprise at the unusual behaviors. As their son's differences became more prominent, there was anger directed at Billy (e.g., "Why can't you do this?") and at others, such as family members who appeared doubtful about their plan of treatment and other parents who boasted about the wonderful accomplishments of their children.

The anger gave way, but lingering depression and feelings of inadequacy remained. At times, it felt as though everything they did centered on Billy, yet results were gradual and not always apparent. They looked for sources to blame. Was there something in the environment? What about medicines or vaccinations? What about us—is this our fault?

On top of all that was confusion about what to do. A lot of information exists on PDD, much of it conflicting and even inaccurate. Until they figured out how to read the research critically, it often served to increase their frustration.

Billy's father says it took about 2 years to gain acceptance of the situation, to conclude that Billy is not like the other children, but is who he is, which on balance is pretty positive. Maybe, when all is said and done, this acceptance will emerge as the most important outcome of all.

☐ Diagnosing Language Deficits

As with all communication disorders, language deficits are identified through diagnostic evaluations. As noted in Chapter 4, this is an information-gathering process that includes standardized, norm-referenced tests; informal observation; and reports from those who are significant in the client's life. The clinician's job is to assess which domains are affected, determine what particular skills, if any, are in need of remediation, and make the necessary recommendations.

Both SLPs and audiologists may work with other professionals as part of a multidisciplinary language assessment team. The choice of assessment procedures depends on the

- preferences of the professional doing the testing,
- client's age,
- aspect of language being assessed,
- materials that are available, and
- requirements of specific agencies, such as a school district or insurance company (Alvares & Williams, 1995).

Some language-testing materials are comprehensive in that they can be used to assess receptive and expressive language in several language domains. Other tests are domain specific (e.g., phonology tests). For the domain of pragmatics, there are no widely used standardized measures; thus, the SLP may rely on informal measures, such as observational checklists and teacher reports.

In addition to test results and reports, SLPs also frequently obtain a language sample, which is an analysis made of elicited conversational speech. The language sample allows the SLPs to observe how the child uses all domains of expressive language and conversational abilities in spontaneous utterances.

Language Delay

As you might expect, diagnosing language delay can be tricky, given the variability in language acquisition across children. Compounding this are the findings that delays in language development can be an early sign of disorders such as SLI, autism, or PDD. Still, testing all domains can help determine whether a child's language is following an orderly but slowed sequence in the absence of additional PDD characteristics (e.g., repetitive behaviors, difficulties with socialization).

Specific Language Impairment

Specific language impairment can have a significant academic impact on a child's life if it is not addressed early (i.e., during the preschool years). Thus, early identification is critical.

Thorough testing is also necessary to diagnose SLI, given the variety of skills and domains that can be affected. The apparent connection between SLI and working memory has given rise to an interest in **processing-dependent measures** (e.g., phonological working memory tasks) (Campbell, Dollaghan, Needleman, & Janosky, 1997; Dollaghan & Campbell, 1998; Weismer et al., 1999), which have an added benefit of not being culturally biased. For example, short-term memory tasks (e.g., repeating letter or word sequences) can provide an index of phonological working memory (Montgomery, 2002).

Similarly, the language and literacy connection has led to the suggestion that SLPs assess reading and writing skills in addition to speech and oral language (Apel & Masterson, 2001). Skills ranging from spelling to reading comprehension have been suggested as areas of potential (and future) difficulty (Apel & Swank, 1999; Masterson & Crede, 1999).

Finally, it has been suggested (e.g., Kaderavek & Sulzby, 2000) that **emergent literacy** could help with the diagnosis of SLI. That is, children with SLI were found to be less able than their normally developing peers to produce language features associated with written language (e.g., past tense verbs, personal pronouns).

Individuals With Intellectual Disability

Any time there are cognitive limitations, language testing will be challenging to some degree simply because such limitations may interfere with standardized instructions. McCauley (2001) noted the importance of accommodating the client to get a complete picture of language. That is, standardized testing may give way to informal measures and test adaptations, such as repeated and uncomplicated instruction, allowing reinforcement, and using large visual stimuli. In some cases, these accommodations are more likely to reveal the client's overall language.

Because language and cognition are strongly linked, the speech and language skills of an individual with intellectual disabilities will generally be commensurate with (and no higher than) the cognitive abilities. Within one's language, expression is unlikely to exceed understanding but should be close to it. Thus, intervention is recommended when language skills are significantly below cognition or expressive language is well under receptive. Children with Down syndrome, for example, often exhibit an expressive language delay that is greater than would be expected for their level of cognitive and receptive language performance (Greenwald & Leonard, 1979; Mundy, Sigman, Kasari, & Yirmiya, 1988). In such cases, treatment would be initiated based on the client's language potential.

Pervasive Developmental Disorders

As with intellectual disability, the variability associated with PDD results in different types and levels of language impairment, from no or almost no deficiency (Asperger's) to limited or no language skills (Rett's). This heterogeneity, combined with possible intellectual disability and difficult social interaction on the part of children with PDD, can make the use of standardized tasks both difficult and invalid (McCauley, 2001). Formal language instruments are based on reciprocal communication, a skill often missing for individuals on the PDD spectrum. As a result, history questionnaires, parent history interviews, and communication checklists often play a major role in assessment.

Because of the complex nature of some PDDs, language assessment is often part of a global evaluation involving medical, educational, and other pertinent professionals. In this way, people with different areas of expertise can witness other assessments and judge the implications against their own areas (Scott et al., 2000). For example, an occupational therapist can discover how communicative limitations might keep a client from efficiently learning needed exercises.

Hearing Impairment

With hearing-impaired individuals, there are a number of diagnostic factors to consider when planning a valid evaluation. As the primary modality for receiving instructions is not the usual one (hearing), the evaluator must determine how the client communicates. After doing so, the examiner must be extra certain that instructions are understood. Modifications such as eliminating as many possible distractions as possible may also be called for. In addition to these rather straightforward concerns, McCauley (2001) noted that American Sign Language may be needed for some profoundly impaired clients, and that, partly because of this, there may not be valid norms available with which to compare these clients' scores.

☐ Treatment

As with assessment, there is no shortage of materials available for language intervention. The CSD professional often works with clients on individual skills, such as phonology or syntax, generally using activities that the client finds enjoyable and that provide focused practice. Ideally then, the manner in which services are provided depends on the needs of the individual client.

In addition to work with the SLP or audiologist, language treatment often involves the participation of others, such as peers, family members, and with child clients, their teachers. These individuals can serve as important agents for language intervention. Given that any communicative act can potentially enhance communication skills, it follows that the more one interacts with others, the more opportunities one has to practice language skills. Peers and family members can serve as models of appropriate speech, language, and social skills. In addition, they can provide positive communicative experiences. Some will even take a more direct role in the intervention process by helping the client complete home program assignments. Similarly, teachers can aid in the generalization of newly learned skills by becoming involved in specific assignments or by simply monitoring language performance in the classroom.

Language treatment routinely employs techniques outlined in Chapter 5, such as modeling, shaping, and cueing. Although there are commercially produced programs (e.g., Dunn et al., 1981), much language-based therapy is developed by the CSD professional so it can be specific to the individual client and his or her language profile. Even when formal, specific curricula are utilized, in fact, it is usually more as a guide than a script. That is, those items deemed appropriate are used, while others are changed to better suit the client or not utilized at all.

In addition to printed materials, there are computer intervention programs designed for language-impaired children. Two well-known and widely used examples are *Fast ForWord* and *Earobics*. Computerized language instructions allow for individualized practice and, with some programs, online collection of data that permits the clinician to document progress automatically. In addition to these benefits, computer programs can be motivating for clients simply because they find using a computer to be fun.

Despite these advantages, computer language programs are not advocated by all CSD professionals. For one thing, many of them are expensive.

Moreover, critics point to studies in which effectiveness is not necessarily supported (e.g., Rouse & Krueger, 2004), raising the question of whether there is an advantage to their use in comparison to traditional intervention.

Language therapy is most often administered in the operant conditioning format of stimulus, response, and reinforcement. As language skills need to be internalized (as opposed to simply learned), home programs are essential to further reinforce them. Partly because of their importance, conferences with parents or spouses will be frequent.

For children experiencing delayed language development, therapy may consist of **language stimulation**. This approach utilizes language-enrichment techniques such as **expansion, child-centered language, open-ended questions**, and description to help expand the child's language. That is, by using such techniques with everyday materials, the clinician exposes the child to new vocabulary and language forms, which the child, over time, internalizes.

For SLIs, Montgomery (2002) advocated incorporating working memory activities into therapy with children. For example, naming tasks focus the child's attention on the structure of language, as does using children's stories. Even with older children and adults, activities featuring nonsense or rhyming words afford practice of the working memory system.

Individuals with mild intellectual disability may have communication differences similar to those with SLI, in which case the CSD professional would focus intervention on areas of need. In addition, the treatment plan might include social communication goals, particularly with clients who qualify for vocational training. For those more severely impaired, therapy is likely to concentrate on enhancing communication skills rather than the development of speech and language. That is, the focus of intervention will be functional: teaching the skills necessary to communicate in the client's everyday environments.

While clients with autism/PDD also represent a wide range of language and cognitive abilities, they share a common problem with those suffering from intellectual disability: They present difficulty in the use of speech and language for social interaction. Their highly specialized needs require comprehensive programming that will include social communication skills. Intervention efforts should focus on teaching how language is used to interact with others.

☐ Synopsis

Language deficits can occur in any, or across many, domains. An individual's language can be delayed or disordered. Problem areas can be isolated to specific language skills, or they can occur alongside conditions such as intellectual disability, autism, or hearing impairment. Whichever the case, standard diagnostic procedures should result in a valid language profile, provided adjustments are made for special populations. Treating language deficits involves challenges as well, as CSD professionals must decide which materials—commercially produced, computer based, or informal—best serve their clients.

☐ Vocabulary

autism—severe developmental disability with symptoms that are present before a child's third birthday. The three hallmark characteristics of autism are difficulties with social interactions with others, severe impairment of communication skill, and restricted and stereotypical behaviors and interests (Justice, 2006)

child-centered language—describes what the child is doing, seeing, hearing, as he does it (Wachter, 2007)

circumlocution—talking around a topic

echolalia—repeating words, sounds, or sound patterns with no communicative intent, meaning or understanding; this repetition may occur immediately or even days later. (Smith, 2006)

emergent literacy—moving from picture-governed attempts at reading to print-governed attempts (McKenna & Stahl, 2003)

expansion—repeat the child's "baby sentences" the way an adult would have said them, thus providing a good model for the child by revising and completing his or her speech (Wachter, 2007)

idiopathic—of no truly identifiable origin (Martin & Clark, 2003)

incidence—the frequency with which a condition appears in a particular population

language stimulation—language enrichment techniques that can be incorporated into everyday activities to facilitate language development. Examples include describing objects, expanding the child's utterance, and use of open-ended questions

literacy—use of visual modes of communication, specifically reading and writing (Owens et al., 2007)

morphologic markers—inflectional or derivational morphemes. Inflectional morphemes are the grammatical endings that mark verb tense and person (like third-person singular and past tense) and also plurals and possessives. Derivational morphemes nearly always change the part of speech, for example, -ly, -ment, un-, re-

open-ended questions—questions that are broad in their context; that allow for multiple responses and that do not limit the child to single word responses

pervasive developmental disorder—one of the autism spectrum disorders (ASDs); either not all three ASD characteristics (problems in communication, social interaction, and repetitive or manneristic behaviors) are present or they are mild (Smith, 2006)

processing-dependent measures—language measures designed to minimize the contributions of prior knowledge on performance (Campbell et al., 1997)

specific language impairment—significant limitations in language functioning that cannot be attributed to deficits in hearing, oral structure and function, general intelligence, or perception. No obvious anatomical, physical, intellectual, or perceptual cause seems to exist (Owens et al., 2007)

working memory—temporary storage of information during information processing. This can be visuospatial (nonverbal) information or linguistic information (Hungerford & Gonyo, 2007)

☐ Recommended Reading

American Speech-Language and Hearing Association. (2007). Language-based learning disabilities. Retrieved from http://www.asha.org/public/speech/disorders/LBLD.htm.
>   This short summary defines learning disabilities due to language deficits and takes the reader from early warning signs to options for treatment.

McCabe, P. C. (2005). Social and behavioral correlates of preschoolers with specific language impairment. *Psychology in the Schools, 42*, 373–387.
>   In this research study, the author explores the relationship among language, social skills, and behavior problems.

Mosheim, J. (2006). Figurative language: A different model of comprehension. *Advance for Speech-Language Pathologists & Audiologists, 16*(46), 6–8, 18.
>   The large amount of idioms, similes, irony, and other forms of figurative language used in everyday conversation can be difficult for those with impaired language. How this idea applies to CSD professionals is outlined in clear fashion.

Ramirez, J., & Bain, M. (2006). Unlocking the secrets of autism. *Newsweek*, November 27, 50–51.
>   A short primer on the neurology of autism, this two-page outline is one of three features on autism within this issue of the news magazine.

Scott, J., Clark, C., & Brady, M. (2000). *Students with autism: Characteristics and instructional programming*. San Diego, CA: Singular.
>   This text on autism is clear and innovative and includes entries on numerous related topics, written by guest experts.

Neurogenic Disorders

Deena Louise Wener and Dale F. Williams

Deena Louise Wener, PhD, CCC-SLP, is an associate professor in the Department of Communication Sciences and Disorders at Florida Atlantic University. Dr. Wener has served as chair of the Department of Communication Sciences and Disorders for 16 years. She teaches in the area of adult communication disorders. In her personal life, Dr. Wener is involved in advocacy efforts to increase public awareness of the prevention and treatment of colorectal cancer.

Many students are confounded by communication disorders that have neurological etiologies. One reason for this may be that, in the authors' experience, students prefer "absolutes." Unfortunately, however, there are few unconditional conclusions when it comes to the brain. There are instead abundant individual differences resulting from diverse experiences, development, nutrition, general health, education, culture, and a host of other factors too numerous to mention. These individual differences account for a wide variability of characteristics when areas of the brain suffer neurological damage. In fact, two people suffering the same brain injury can present very different symptoms. So, before embarking on the study of the speech and language disorders associated with neurological injury, let us provide the following absolute: There are absolutely no absolutes in the study of speech and language disorders associated with neuropathologies.

Now you may proceed.

This chapter discusses the speech and language disorders that result from neurological damage. These are not **developmental disorders** or **functional disorders**, but rather **acquired disorders**. This is an important distinction. With an acquired disorder, the individual loses speech and language skills

TABLE 7.1 Neurological vs. Nonneurological Speech and Language Problems

Neurological Disorders With Associated Speech and Language Problems (Acquired)	Nonneurological Disorders With Associated Speech and Language Problems (Developmental/Functional)
Aphasia	Developmental language delays
Dementia	Development delays in speech sound production
Traumatic brain injury	Laryngectomy
Right hemisphere brain damage	Cleft lip and palate
Sensory deficits (e.g., tactile, kinesthetic, proprioceptive disorders)	Psychogenic disorders (e.g., depression, schizophrenia)
Parkinson's disease	Vocal abuse
Huntington's chorea	Head and neck tumors (excluding brain tumors)
Amoyotrophic lateral sclerosis (ALS)	Age-related speech & language changes

that existed prior to neurological damage. That is, the skills developed normally and fully but are no longer available to the individual. Table 7.1 provides some examples of what are, and are not, neurological disorders that are commonly associated with acquired communication disorders.

The next section of the chapter addresses disorders of language due to neurological damage. Then, the chapter addresses speech disorders due to neurological damage. It should be noted that while these disorders are divided into and discussed in two separate sections, neurologically based speech and language disorders often co-occur.

☐ Adult Language Disorders

Language disorders in adults are generally associated with aphasia, right hemisphere brain damage, traumatic brain injury (TBI), or dementia. Each of these disorders affects speech and language function in varying ways. Symptoms for each disorder are not discrete, necessarily, and may be found to exist in any of the other disorders. However, there are features that distinguish language disorders caused by each condition. It is these distinguishing features that aid in the differential diagnosis of the disorders.

☐ Aphasia

There are numerous definitions of **aphasia**. These definitions are based on the theorist's concept of what aphasia is. For example, the *localization theory of aphasia* holds that the speech and language difficulties exhibited with aphasia are dependent on the site of lesion in the brain (Shuster, 2005). On the other hand, the *social perspective of aphasia* views the disability from a social rather than a medical viewpoint. The degree to which a person is disabled by physical, mental, or emotional differences from the norm depends on the interaction between the individual and the environment in which he or she lives. For this reason, the disabling nature of aphasia is likely to be different among individuals even if their symptoms are similar in type and severity. In addition, a person with aphasia will experience different disabilities in different aspects or interactions of life (Goodwin, 2003).

Simply stated, an individual with aphasia is without utterance (*phasia*) or, more directly, unable to produce language as a result of neurological damage to the brain. It is probably most helpful to consider *aphasia* as a general term that describes a number of different syndromes, each syndrome having a variety of symptoms.

Aphasia results from damage to specific areas of the brain. The most frequent cause of aphasia is a *cerebrovascular accident*, or CVA. A CVA is commonly referred to as a *stroke* (Table 7.2). Although there is a correlation between the location of the brain damage and the symptoms exhibited, this correlation is by no means 100%. In essence, two individuals who have suffered damage to the same areas of the brain may nevertheless exhibit different symptoms. This is one place where the aforementioned lack of absolutes reveals itself. Further, not every individual who has a stroke will have aphasia. Students of neurogenic communication disorders must accept the fact that, despite identification of the localization of brain damage, it is not always possible to identify precisely the type (or severity) of aphasia that will occur.

The onset of aphasia may be *insidious* (developing gradually over time) or *acute* (sudden onset). Insidious pathologies include brain tumors, hydrocephalus, infections, progressive diseases, toxicities, nutritional disorders, and metabolic disorders. A CVA is an acute event. It occurs when there is an interruption of the blood supply to the brain. This can happen different ways. An *ischemic stroke* is caused by a complete or partial blockage of blood in the arteries, resulting in the blood not making it to the brain. The blockage is often caused by a condition known as *arteriosclerosis* (or *atherosclerosis*). There is a thickening of the walls of the arteries in an individual with arteriosclerosis. This thickening is caused by the accumulation of *plaques*, or fatty particles, along the arterial walls. When these plaques adhere to and build up on the walls of the arteries, elasticity is lost or reduced, blood flow is restricted, and the walls may be weakened. If the blockage is temporary or partial, a **transient ischemic attack (TIA)** may occur and cause short-lived or mild symptoms. However, if the blockage is complete, lasting permanent damage and destruction of brain tissue occurs.

Another cause of an ischemic stroke is an *embolism*. An embolism is a traveling blood clot that has broken off a larger clot and is composed of

---

TABLE 7.2 Statistics Related to Strokes in the United States

Prevalence

- Among adults age 20 and older, the estimated prevalence of stroke in 2005 was 5.8 million (about 2.3 million males and 3.4 million females).

Incidence

- Each year, about 780,000 people experience a new or recurrent stroke. About 600,000 of these are first attacks, and 180,000 are recurrent attacks.
- On average, every 40 seconds someone in the United States has a stroke.
- Each year, about 60,000 more women than men have a stroke. However, men's incidence rates are greater than women's at younger ages but not at older ages.
- Blacks have almost twice the risk of first-ever stroke compared with whites.
- The Brain Attack Surveillance in Corpus Christi (BASIC) project clearly demonstrated an increased incidence of stroke among Mexican Americans compared with non-Hispanic whites. The crude cumulative incidence was 168/10,000 in Mexican Americans and 136/10,000 in non-Hispanic whites.

Mortality

- Stroke accounted for about 1 of every 16 deaths in the United States in 2004.
- Stroke ranks number 3 among all causes of death, behind diseases of the heart and cancer.
- On average, every 3 to 4 minutes someone dies of a stroke.
- The 2004 final overall death rate for stroke was 50.0. Death rates were 48.1 for white males and 74.9 for black males; 47.2 for white females and 65.5 for black females; 41.5 for Hispanic or Latino males and 35.4 for females; 44.2 for Asian or Pacific Islander males and 38.9 for females; and 35.0 for American Indian/Alaska Native males and 35.1 for females.
- Because women live longer than men, more women than men die of stroke each year. Women accounted for 61.0% of U.S. stroke deaths in 2004.

Stroke Risk Factors

- The risk of ischemic stroke in smokers is about double that of nonsmokers.
- High blood pressure is the most important risk factor for stroke. Individuals with blood pressure lower than 120/80 mm Hg have about half the lifetime risk of stroke compared to subjects with high blood pressure.

Source: This information was compiled and excerpted from American Heart Association. Heart Disease and Stroke Statistics—2008 Update. Dallas, Texas: American Heart Association, 2008. ©2008, American Heart Association. http://www.americanheart. org/downloadable/heart/1200078608862HS_Stats%202008.final.pdf

---

arterial waste. When that traveling clot becomes stuck in an artery that has been narrowed by arteriosclerotic plaques, a blockage results, and the brain is deprived of oxygen.

A *thrombus* is another type of clot that blocks blood supply to the brain. A thrombus does not travel. Rather, it develops at the site of arteriosclerotic plaque buildup, becomes trapped in that plaque, and continues to grow until the artery is occluded.

A *hemorrhagic stroke* is so called because it is caused by a hemorrhage. A *hemorrhage* is when the wall of an artery bursts, usually because of increasing pressure, and blood flows out of the artery, flooding the brain tissue. The direct bleeding into brain tissue is what causes the stroke.

Some of you may have personal experience with aphasia because you have a relative or friend who has the disorder. More of you will gain experience as your grandparents, parents, friends, and neighbors age. One of the authors of this chapter has had a profoundly personal experience with aphasia, as her mother suffered a massive stroke at 59 years of age and was rendered bed bound, with very limited capability for speech.

The current convention is to classify aphasias as either fluent or nonfluent. Fluent and nonfluent designations are, most often, based on the localization of brain damage. **Fluent aphasias** are associated with the more posterior regions of the brain (temporal or parietal lobes). **Nonfluent aphasias** are associated with damage to the frontal lobe. Clearly, then, fluency is important to the categorization of aphasia. More specifically, factors tied to fluency, such as phrase length, effort, rate, pauses, articulation, and prosody, are used help assess the type and severity of aphasia an individual may be exhibiting. In terms of aphasia, fluency is considered normal if rate, prosody (melodic line), lexicon (vocabulary), and sentence length are all within normal limits. An individual with aphasia who struggles to initiate speech, has abnormal pauses and hesitations, and speaks in a sort of shorthand (nouns and verbs only) is considered nonfluent.

The severity of an individual's aphasia is related to a number of variables. These variables include the etiology, the location and extent of the brain damage, the type of aphasia, whether there is a single injury or multiple injuries due to recurrent strokes, and patient variables such as age and overall health status. Aphasia may affect all language modalities (listening, speaking, reading, and writing), one modality, or any combination. It is important to remember that aphasia is not reflective of motor speech disorders (MSDs), dementia, or loss of intelligence.

Despite the variability of aphasia, there are some general symptoms of the disorder. Some of these symptoms are defined and discussed next.

Paraphasias are word errors. An individual with aphasia may have difficulty retrieving the words that he or she wants to say. Sometimes, no words can be produced. At other times, and depending on the type of aphasia, the individual may produce a word or word-like utterance in place of the intended word. A paraphasia sounds like the intended word, a word related in meaning to the intended word, or a nonsense word.

The term *anomia*, while used to identify a symptom of aphasia, also specifies a type of fluent aphasia characterized by the inability to retrieve words when speaking. Naming problems are particularly apparent during activities that involve **confrontation naming** and **word fluency tasks**. Individuals exhibiting anomia may have less difficulty with words that have a higher frequency of occurrence in our daily language usage (e.g., house, dog) than those that have a low frequency of occurrence (e.g., plethora, giraffe).

The ability to repeat language is also variously impaired in aphasia. Some individuals retain a good ability to repeat words, phrases, and even sentences. Others are unable to repeat or, conversely, exhibit a disorder of repetition called *perseveration*. With perseveration, the individual fixates on and produces the same utterance repeatedly even after the original stimulus (i.e., whatever initially prompted the response) is no longer present.

Clients with aphasia have difficulties not only producing language, but also understanding it. Depending on which definition or theory of aphasia one subscribes to, either all individuals with aphasia have some level of **auditory comprehension** deficit or only those with specific aphasia syndromes do. Regardless of which opinion one holds, all speech-language pathologists (SLPs) can agree that deficits in auditory comprehension are common to individuals with aphasia. These deficits may range from very mild to profound. They appear to be more pronounced in the fluent aphasias, although an individual with a global aphasia (a nonfluent aphasia) generally will have severe deficits in auditory comprehension.

Because aphasia may cross all language modalities, language functions related to reading, writing, gesturing, mathematical problems, recognizing sounds in the environment (e.g., doorbell, ringing telephone), or telling time may be affected. Deficits in reading and writing most often mirror in severity the deficits that occur in speaking and understanding. Although individuals with aphasia may exhibit sensory disorders such as hearing loss, deficient visual acuity, or failed tactile sensation, aphasia is not a sensory disorder. Even though aphasia is generally associated with older adults, and declines in hearing and vision are often age related, it is possible that an individual with aphasia will have normal hearing or vision. It is common for someone with aphasia to suffer from depression and experience seizure activity following a stroke.

In addition to their language issues, individuals with aphasia may have concomitant physical or sensory impairments. For example, both **hemiparesis** and **hemiplegia** frequently accompany the other symptoms that occur in the nonfluent aphasias. This co-occurrence is attributed to the proximity of the motor cortex (motor strip) to the language areas in the frontal lobe of the left hemisphere of the brain. Individuals with nonfluent aphasias rarely exhibit hemiparesis or hemiplegia but may experience a *hemisensory impairment* whereby they cannot sense pain or temperature. The loss of the ability to sense temperature becomes problematic for many individuals with aphasia because they are not able to detect extremes in the temperature of bathwater. Those individuals living in areas of the country with extreme winter climates may not recognize that they are becoming too cold and could risk frostbite.

FIGURE 7.1   Hemianopsia: right visual field impairment.

Another sensory impairment that accompanies aphasia is the visual impairment **hemianopsia**. Hemianopsia is the impairment of the same half of the visual field in each eye (see Figure 7.1).

As noted in Chapter 13, **dysphagia** is another impairment that may result from a stroke. When paresis or paralysis is present, nerves that supply the head, face, oral, and neck structures may be impaired. A possible result of this impairment is the client being unable to handle swallowing food without drooling and gagging. Of particular concern for individuals with dysphagia is the **aspiration** of liquids and food into the lungs. Aspirated substances cannot be expelled and can eventually result in the development of bacteria and infection, leading to **aspiration pneumonia**.

An individual with *agnosia* has lost the ability to recognize people, body parts, and other items and to understand input related to recognition. The deficit is not due to sensory impairment. The individual is able to see, hear, and feel but unable to make connections between the incoming sensory information and the identification of what they are hearing, seeing, or touching. For example, with *auditory agnosia*, one will hear the sounds but be unable to identify them as coming from dog barking or a ringing phone. An individual with *tactile agnosia* cannot identify an object by touch. Female readers will relate to the importance of recognizing things by touch every time they delve into a handbag or tote to locate their keys, cell phone, or a package of tissues. *Prosopagnosia* is a deficit that impairs facial recognition, leaving the individual unable to recognize faces—from family members to celebrities.

Agrammatism is a hallmark of nonfluent aphasias. The individual with agrammatism omits grammatical elements when speaking. He or she may use only nouns and verbs, omitting articles and prepositions. Because of the clipped and abbreviated style of this type of speech it is frequently referred to as *telegramese*. Morphological endings, such as the plural -*s*, may also be absent.

Agraphia can be defined as a difficulty with writing due to neurological injury. Clients may be unable to form letters, write to dictation, or compose what they are able to say easily. As noted previously, writing problems usually mirror language and speech deficits, resulting in written products that contain neologisms, jargon, and agrammatism.

Alexia occurs when neurological injury results in impairment in the ability to read. Alexia is an acquired disorder; a loss of a previously learned skill. This differentiates it from *dyslexia,* which is a developmental disorder characterized by a child's inability to acquire the skills needed to read.

Jargon is described as meaningless speech that is produced with normal prosodic patterns. Young children often engage in babbling, or jargon, when they are developing speech and language. In the adult with aphasia, jargon appears as long strings of sounds, words, or neologisms strung together using correct syntax. It sounds as though the individual is actually communicating thoughts and ideas when, in fact, all that is being produced are nonsensical utterances.

The most severe and limited form of verbal expression, with the exception of not being able to speak at all, is the use of *verbal stereotypes.* A verbal stereotype is an utterance—it could be a neologism or a recognizable word or phrase—that becomes the speaker's sole means of expression. The first author has worked with several clients who exhibited this profound impairment. One client was a young woman in her early 30s. During an angiogram performed to locate the possible source of unremitting neck pain, the catheter used to deliver the dye developed a kink and subsequently blocked an artery. This caused a cessation of blood flow to the brain that resulted in a stroke. When the individual woke from her coma, she repeated the syllable "lud" in rapid succession (lud-lud-lud-lud) in response to any question or when attempting to communicate.

Recovery from stroke and the damage and deficits that result vary from patient to patient and differ depending on the type and severity of the stroke. Individuals who have suffered ischemic strokes appear to have greater and more rapid recoveries than individuals who have had hemorrhagic strokes. After an ischemic stroke, there is noticeable recovery within the first few weeks. Maximum recovery (at whatever level that may be for the individual) is realized from 3 to 6 months poststroke. In contrast, recovery from a hemorrhagic stroke is slower. When the individual's progress plateaus (reaches a stable, consistent level with little or no improvement), there are still remaining deficits of a significant magnitude. Following a hemorrhagic stroke, little recovery is seen in the first 3 to 6 months. More significant recovery is recorded after the initial 3 to 6 months poststroke.

Syndromes of Aphasia

Fluent Aphasias

The fluent aphasias are characterized by multiple paraphasias (mostly semantic and neologistic), excessive verbal output, comprehension deficits ranging from mild to profound, and articulation and prosodic elements that are within normal limits. Individuals with fluent aphasia produce abundant quantities of speech. A common symptom seen in these individuals is *press for speech*. Press for speech, also referred to as *logorrhea*, describes a mode of speech in which the individual appears driven to speak rapidly (almost compulsively) and excessively, often without conveying any specific meaning or intent. The individual rambles on without regard to turn taking, maintaining the topic, and other conventions of conversation. The speaker is, literally, unable to control his or her speech.

The four types of fluent aphasias are Wernicke's, anomic, conduction, and transcortical sensory. Each of these types is discussed.

Wernicke's Aphasia

Wernicke's aphasia was first described in 1874 by a German neuropsychiatrist named, coincidentally, Wernicke. Carl Wernicke called it *sensory aphasia*, and it was (and is) characterized by speech that is fluent, often rapid, and excessive. With this condition, speech is grammatical but replete with paraphasias and neologisms. Auditory comprehension deficits are in the moderate-to-severe range. Articulation and prosody are within normal limits. Individuals with Wernicke's aphasia often employ **circumlocution** to compensate for word retrieval problems.

Location of Neurological Damage
Primary
- lesions in the left hemisphere, specifically in *Wernicke's area* (see Figure 7.2)
Secondary
- damage may be subcortical or in parietal regions, among other sites

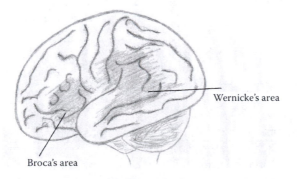

FIGURE 7.2 The locations of the major language (Wernicke's) and speech (Broca's) areas of the brain. (Artist: Barbara Fries, EdD.)

General Characteristics
- no paresis or paralysis
- **anosognosia**
- psychiatric disorders: paranoia, depression, suicidal tendencies
- exhibit little frustration (most likely associated with lack of awareness)

Prominent Speech and Language Characteristics
- rapid rate of speech
- **prosodic features**, phrase length, and articulation within normal limits
- severe word-finding/word retrieval deficits
- "empty speech" because of numerous neologisms and paraphasias
- poor auditory comprehension
- impaired conversational skills, such as the inability to take turns or maintain a topic
- poor repetition ability
- impaired reading and writing
- speech fluency ranging from normal to abnormal (press for speech or logorrhea)

Anomic Aphasia

As discussed, *anomia* is a symptom of most aphasias and describes a difficulty in naming. Anomic aphasia is an aphasic syndrome that has anomia as its most dominant symptom. That is, although most language skills are within normal limits, severe naming problems will be present.

Location of Neurological Damage   Lesions resulting in anomic aphasia are not identified with a high degree of certainty. Multiple lesion sites may be involved. One of those sites most commonly associated with the occurrence of anomic aphasia is the juncture of the temporal and parietal lobes.

General Characteristics   There are no general neurological features or characteristics associated with anomic aphasia.

Prominent Speech and Language Characteristics
- severe, and often debilitating, word-finding problems
- semantic (or verbal) paraphasias
- good articulation and auditory comprehension
- normal or near-normal syntax, repetition ability, reading and writing skills

Conduction Aphasia

Conduction aphasia is considered one of the more controversial aphasia syndromes with regard to its neuroanatomical bases. This controversy stems from the rather wide range of symptoms that are associated with it. The range of symptoms stems primarily from the sites of damage. The more anterior lesions produce a less-fluent aphasia with better auditory comprehension, and the more posterior lesions result in a more fluent aphasia and poor auditory comprehension. Conduction aphasia is relatively rare and is characterized, generally, by fluent speech with abundant paraphasias and poor repetition ability. Unlike the other fluent aphasias, individuals with conduction aphasia exhibit good-to-normal auditory comprehension. One of the authors' mother had conduction aphasia. Her severely impaired repetition skills made it challenging to find treatment approaches that could be effective. Her ability to comprehend was excellent, with problems only at the most complex levels of syntax or language processing. She also had a right-sided hemiplegia and mild-to-moderate oral and verbal apraxias.

Location of Neurological Damage   As mentioned, there is still a great deal of controversy and disagreement about the lesion sites associated with conduction aphasia. The most commonly suspected sites of lesion are as follows:

- damage to the *arcuate fasciculus*; considered the most important association fiber tract for speech and language connecting Broca's area (motor speech area) to Wernicke's area (sensory speech area)
- one or multiple lesions anywhere between Broca's and Wernicke's areas
- also mentioned are lesions to the left parietal lobe, supramarginal gyrus, inferior parietal gyrus, and the lower, postcentral sulcus area

General Characteristics
- varied neurological symptoms most likely attributable to variable sites of lesions
- physical neurological symptoms ranging from no impairment to right-sided paresis in the mild to severe range
- oral and limb apraxias possible

Prominent Speech and Language Characteristics
- markedly impaired repetition abilities
- phonemic paraphasias and, less frequently, semantic and neologistic paraphasias
- significant word-finding deficits
- possible speech fluency problems

- good-to-normal syntax, prosody, and articulation
- near-normal auditory comprehension
- variable reading and writing problems

Transcortical Sensory Aphasia

Transcortical sensory aphasia (TSA) is also known as *posterior isolation syndrome*. Individuals with TSA have mostly intact repetition ability, which distinguishes it from Wernicke's aphasia. However, this repetition ability is most often characterized by **echolalia**. The individual with TSA is able to parrot what he or she hears but usually has a severe comprehension deficit for spoken language. Commonly, symptoms appearing in the initial stages of TSA may not be apparent in later stages of recovery.

Location of Neurological Damage:
>   Primary
>   - lesions to the temperoparietal region, which isolates Wernicke's area from the rest of the cortex but spares the arcuate fasciculus connecting it to Broca's area
>   Secondary
>   - lesions in the occipital or temporal lobes

General Characteristics
- onset associated with hemiparesis, which resolves, leaving no significant physical impairment
- may initially resemble a patient with *dementia* (to be covered in this chapter)
- possibility of *Gertsmann syndrome,* which is characterized by **finger agnosia**, **agraphia** (inability to write), **acalculia** (inability to do math), and left-right confusion
- neglect of one side of the body

Prominent Speech and Language Characteristics
- fluent, well-articulated speech
- copious semantic and neologistic paraphasias resulting in empty speech
- good repetition skills with little comprehension of what is repeated
- echolalia
- automatic speech (e.g., counting, reciting rhymes, days of the week) often within normal limits if assisted in starting the recitation
- impaired auditory and reading comprehension but mostly preserved oral reading skills

Nonfluent Aphasias

Individuals with nonfluent aphasia exhibit speech that is slow and labored. They struggle to retrieve words and form sentences. They exhibit a reduced speech rate (less than 50 words per minute), limited phrase length, difficulty initiating speech, and impaired prosody. Speech is primarily composed of content words (nouns, verbs), while function words (articles, prepositions) are omitted. The three nonfluent aphasias—Broca's, global (or mixed), and transcortical motor—are described next.

Broca's Aphasia

In 1861, Paul Broca, a French neurosurgeon and physical anthropologist, described a nonfluent aphasia associated with damage to the lower portion of the frontal lobe in the left hemisphere of the brain.

This area is known as *Broca's area* (the third frontal convolution/gyrus in the left hemisphere) and is associated with motor speech function. Broca used the term *aphemia* to describe the language disorders he associated with damage to the lower portion of the left frontal lobe. A number of other terms have been used to describe the syndrome of Broca's aphasia: **expressive aphasia**, motor aphasia, agrammatic aphasia, and anterior aphasia. Damage solely to Broca's area is most likely to produce temporary mutism and mild apraxia.

Location of Neurological Damage   The site of the lesion responsible for causing Broca's aphasia is still being debated. The advent of neuroimaging (computed tomographic [CT] scans, positron emission tomographic [PET] scans) has revealed that damage to Broca's area alone would not be sufficient to explain the symptoms associated with the syndrome. In addition, these same symptoms can be caused by lesions to areas other than Broca's. In other words, an individual may have Broca's aphasia without having any damage to Broca's area, and damage limited to Broca's area is not enough to account for the symptoms associated with the syndrome. Some of the areas that, when damaged, are associated with Broca's aphasia are

- the lower portion of the motor strip
- areas anterior to and inferior to Broca's area
- deep cortical damage in addition to damage to Broca's area

General Characteristics
- right-sided hemiparesis or hemiplegia of upper and lower limbs as well as facial muscles

- **emotional lability** (vast emotional swings), also referred to as *catastrophic reactions*

Prominent Speech and Language Characteristics
- effortful, labored speech filled with pauses, revisions, and sound and syllable repetitions
- agrammatism
- slow rate, limited output, reduced length of utterances
- impaired skills with regard to repetition, naming, oral reading, and writing
- mild auditory comprehension deficits
- prosodic deficits
- associated speech problems of apraxia and dysarthria

Global or Mixed Aphasia

Global aphasia is considered to be the most severe form of aphasia and affects all modalities of communication. The overall effect on communication is devastating in that no skill is spared impairment, not even nonverbal communication. Damage occurs to all the speech and language centers in the left hemisphere.

Location of Neurological Damage   Lesions resulting in global aphasia are widespread and may well involve both Broca's and Wernicke's areas.

General Characteristics
- right-sided hemiparesis or hemiplegia
- apraxia
- neglect of one-half of the body

Prominent Speech and Language Characteristics
- profoundly impaired verbal and nonverbal communication skills
- language limited to very few utterances that may or may not be recognizable (e.g., verbal stereotypes)
- impaired repetition, naming, reading, writing

Transcortical Motor Aphasia

Transcortical motor aphasia (TMA) may be referred to as *isolation syndrome*. It is a type of aphasia characterized by repetition skills that are startling in contrast to the degree of impairment of other skills. Individuals with TMA are extremely nonfluent, and spontaneous speech is very limited. There is a notable discrepancy between the individual's spared ability to repeat and overall language output.

Location of Neurological Damage
  Primary
  • frontal lobe with deep lesions below or above Broca's area
  Secondary
  • lesions to association pathways that connect Broca's area to other areas of the brain

General Characteristics
  • motor disorders, including rigidity of the upper extremities, loss of movement (*akinesia*), slowness of movement (*bradykinesia*)
  • behavioral symptoms (e.g., apathy, withdrawal)

Prominent Speech and Language Characteristics
  • mutism that slowly resolves to echolalia and perseverative speech
  • paucity of spontaneous speech
  • intact repetition skills
  • comprehension is better than production; good for simple conversation
  • agrammatism
  • telegramese

Atypical Syndromes of Aphasia

As research into and knowledge about adult language disorders has increased, it has become obvious that not all patients with aphasia will fit into the fluent/nonfluent paradigm. In fact, Hegde (2006, p. 180) stated that "up to 50% or more patients with aphasia do not fit the description of standard syndromes."

Examples of atypical syndromes may be those that occur rarely or aphasias in which reading (alexia) and writing (agraphia) problems are greater than the language and cognitive deficits. Also categorized as atypical are aphasias that occur in specific populations, such as individuals who are bilingual, left handed, or deaf.

Subcortical Aphasias

Aphasic disorders have long been associated with cortical damage and pathology. Current research has reported a number of speech and language disorders that are related to subcortical damage. Damage to the basal ganglia or the thalamus produces the speech and language deficits that have come to be associated with the subcortical aphasias. The role of subcortical structures in language is not well defined. Therefore, there are still questions regarding where, how extensive, and if lesions to subcortical areas are responsible for some of the language deficits attributed to them. Most investigators believe that damage to the subcortical structures alone is not sufficient to produce aphasia. Lesions to cortical areas must exist as well.

Prominent Speech and Language Characteristics   Depending on the site of lesions, characteristics might include

- severe dysarthria
- mild deficits in the ability to repeat
- moderate deficits in word finding
- deficits in auditory comprehension
- moderate reading and writing deficiencies
- global aphasia
- one-word productions and monosyllabic stereotypy
- mutism during initial recovery

Aphasia in Special Populations

As mentioned, the term *atypical aphasia* encompasses aphasia that occurs in different "special" populations. This section discusses the unique concerns, issues, and characteristics of aphasia in individuals who are bilingual and left handed. Also discussed is a rare form of aphasia called *crossed aphasia*.

The Bilingual Individual and Aphasia   Individuals who are bilingual and acquire aphasia may experience deficits in both languages. It is interesting to note that the deficits in one language may not be identical to the deficits in the other. Unfortunately, there is very little research reported in this area despite the fact that "in the United States, it is estimated that more than 150,000 patients are bilingual and 45,000 new bilingual cases may be reported each year" (Hegde, 2006, p. 195).

In most bilingual individuals, one language is considered the dominant or primary language. This is generally the first language an individual learns and speaks. A bilingual individual may not have complete knowledge of both languages but still be equally proficient in speaking them. Conversely, that individual may have speech and language deficits in both languages or be more proficient in one language over the other.

Left hemisphere damage (LHD) is responsible for aphasia in individuals who are bilingual just as it is in individuals who are not. Moreover, the types of aphasia and their progression appear the same whether an individual is a speaker of one language or many. In general, SLPs assess and treat the bilingual individual in what is considered to be the dominant language.

As mentioned, there is limited research on individuals who have aphasia and are bilingual. While the knowledge base is constantly changing, it is presently based in large part on clinical reports. Consequently, information on recovery in these individuals is still considered speculative and not fully substantiated. With that stipulation in mind, one may make the following observations:

- The severity of the aphasia does not predict whether the individual will recover one or both languages.
- There is no current evidence to confirm that the language recovered will be the dominant or first language.
- Some individuals may recover both languages, some only one language, and with others, one may be recovered more completely than the other.
- Some bilingual individuals with aphasia may mix words, phrases, or idioms from both languages in their recovered speech.

It is important that the clinician gather a detailed case and language history to be better able to assess and treat the bilingual individual with aphasia. The clinician must monitor which language(s) emerge during recovery and adjust treatment goals to accommodate any changes. SLPs who are not bilingual or proficient in a second language will need to employ the services of a translator to assist them in planning and monitoring treatment. Although family members may be useful in this capacity, the clinician must make sure to train the family member in what is required of a translator. Often, in an effort to be helpful, a relative will interpret, rather than translate literally, what their loved one is saying or trying to say. For obvious reasons, this can complicate assessment or therapy.

The Left-Handed Individual and Aphasia   Approximately 10% of the population is either left handed or ambidextrous (Tanner, 2007). There is a higher incidence of left-handedness in men (Raymond, Pontier, Dufour, & Moller, 1996) and in certain neurological disorders (e.g., Down syndrome, autism, and dyslexia) (Lewin, Kohen, & Mathew, 1993). McManus (2004) argued that the proportion of left-handed people is rising most likely due to the fact that schools are no longer forcing children to switch to their right hands for writing. He further stated that, historically, left-handed people have produced an above-average quota of high achievers, and that the brains of left-handed people are structured to widen their range of abilities, and that the genes that determine left-handedness also govern neurological language development.

Most left-handed people are left brain dominant for language, and some exhibit mixed dominance. Only a very small percentage of left-handed individuals—somewhere around 19%, as opposed to about 3% of righties—appear to use their right brain for language (Coon & Mitterer, 2008). According to Hegde (2006, p. 198), there is no solid research indicating that there are significant differences between right- and left-handed clients or that these differences would affect diagnosis or treatment.

Crossed Aphasia   A right-handed individual with clearly established left hemisphere dominance for language can acquire aphasia following a lesion to the right hemisphere. This is an example of crossed aphasia, and there is no single theory supported for why it occurs. The fact that it is rare makes it difficult to acquire a body of knowledge about the disorder. The only consensus about its cause is that it is probably attributable to a number of different etiologies. Some of the ideas proposed for *crossed aphasia* are

- Crossed aphasia may occur when there is right hemisphere, bilateral, or diffuse representation of language in the brain.
- There may be an undiscovered lesion in the left hemisphere of individuals exhibiting crossed aphasia.
- Right-sided subcortical lesions may account for crossed aphasia.
- Crossed aphasia results because a right hemisphere lesion has spread to the left hemisphere.

However, none of these ideas has gained acceptance as a viable explanation for the occurrence of crossed aphasia.

The Evaluation and Treatment of Aphasia

Considerations

Given the current costs of health care and the shift to evidence-based practice to validate procedures used in the field of speech-language pathology (see Chapter 3), SLPs must carefully plan the diagnostic and intervention approaches used with these clients. Comprehensive diagnostic tests for aphasia often take 2–4 hours to administer. This is problematic, given that insurances and other third-party payers are unlikely to reimburse for that much time and because practicing clinicians are generally expected to evaluate an individual in under an hour, often bedside. This is a far cry from the training students receive in graduate programs, where diagnostic evaluations are scheduled for 2 hours, and an additional diagnostic session might be scheduled if needed. Despite the time constraints, however, the SLP must accumulate the information needed to make a correct diagnosis, determine prognosis, and if warranted, recommend treatment directions. The primary purposes of assessment and diagnosis are to

1. establish the individual's current level of functioning,
2. determine strengths and weaknesses, and

3. ascertain the probable degree of success (i.e., the prognosis) should intervention be recommended and undertaken.

The purpose of treatment is to aid the individual in acquiring the functional communication abilities needed for his or her environment. Before the skyrocketing costs of rehabilitation, the goal of treatment was to return the individual to functioning that was as close as possible to the **premorbid state**. That goal is no longer feasible within the time constraints of insurance reimbursement. The goal of necessity has become rehabilitation that allows the person to function well enough to leave the hospital or rehabilitation unit and return to the home, assisted living facility, or nursing home in which the individual lives.

Other factors that must be considered when deciding if an individual is an appropriate candidate for treatment include age, medical condition, spontaneous recovery (discussion to follow), type of aphasia, cause of the aphasia, severity, family/living situation, communication needs, concomitant disorders (e.g., dementia, apraxia, etc.), vision, hearing, and psychological status. In addition, it is important that the SLP make recommendations about the time, intensity, and outcomes of treatment.

Medical Considerations

Individuals who have a history of smoking, alcohol use, poor diet, lack of exercise, high blood pressure, elevated cholesterol, diabetes, obesity, and previous strokes are at a greater risk for a CVA, and thus for aphasia, than the general population. Generally, aphasia is considered to be a disorder occurring in adulthood. However, children and young adults may become aphasic following a head injury or due to a brain tumor. As noted, the onset may be sudden or insidious. Regardless of the etiology, an individual who develops aphasia does so because the brain is deprived of the blood and oxygen it needs.

During the onset or first few minutes of a stroke, the individual may experience dizziness, **diplopia**, weakness in the limbs, headaches, or slurred speech. Some individuals may lose consciousness completely.

Transient ischemic attacks (TIAs) are often referred to as "ministrokes." The effects of a TIA are temporary, lasting from a half-hour to several hours, after which function returns. Often, TIAs go unnoticed by the individual because the symptoms are shrugged off as from another cause (e.g., spoiled food, too much alcohol, fatigue). However, TIAs are considered to be a precursor of a more serious cerebrovascular event.

About 2 of 10 people who have a stroke die within the first month, 3 of 10 in the first year, and 5 of 10 die within the first 5 years (Stroke Education Ltd., 2006). Thus, it can be said that the majority of individuals who suffer a stroke will survive for a reasonable period of time. Even so, however, they are likely to present some residual impairment of one or more functions.

Following a stroke, the individual may be comatose. The duration of the coma varies depending on the seriousness of the stroke and the amount of damage suffered by the brain. It is generally believed that recovery is poorest for those who have deeper and long-lasting comas and periods of unconsciousness. The *Glasgow Coma Scale* (Teasdale & Jennett, 1974) is commonly used to measure levels of consciousness. Following a stroke, the individual will most likely require acute care in the hospital until his or her medical condition is assessed as stable. Depending on assessments by doctors, nurses, physical and occupational therapists, SLPs, social workers, and other allied health professionals deemed relevant, the individual may be transferred to a rehabilitation unit within the hospital or to an outside rehabilitation facility. Those who are well enough to go home can be treated with follow-up visits by in-home or outpatient rehabilitation services. Others may be transferred to a nursing home for long-term care.

The neurological effects of a stroke are most severe immediately following the event. Recovery is a gradual process and occurs over many months and sometimes years. *Spontaneous recovery* is a period of healing lasting anywhere from 3 to 6 months after onset of the stroke. This spontaneous recovery occurs naturally as swelling (or *edema*) in the brain is reduced and the individual's medical condition is stabilized. As this recovery occurs, the client and his or her significant others may notice a gradual return of some functions that were absent or impaired following the stroke.

For all of the reasons mentioned, it is important to realize that an individual's status immediately poststroke will not provide an accurate picture of his or her impairment and intact functions. Recovery tends to be most rapid during the first 6 months after the onset of the neurological injury and slows, to varying degrees, after that point. Factors such as age, medical status, and overall severity of the injury will affect both the extent and rate of recovery. Some individuals may reach a plateau of functioning after 6 months, while others may continue to show improvement well after that time. It is not possible to predict how quickly or how well any individual will recover because each stroke patient has his or her own pattern of symptoms and recovery. It is this unpredictability, mentioned at the very start of this chapter, that families, significant others, therapists, and the patient find so very frustrating.

It is generally accepted that both assessment and intervention should begin as soon as possible following a stroke. The SLP must be aware that the individual being assessed, and potentially recommended for intervention services, will be going through the process of spontaneous recovery and will be changing in function as time from onset expands. The SLP must be flexible enough to modify goals and prognosis on a regular basis.

A PERSONAL ENCOUNTER WITH A STROKE

The mother of one of the authors of this chapter suffered a massive stroke at 59 years of age and was rendered bed bound, with limited capability for speech. This was a harsh wake-up call for this author. Considering herself an "expert" in the assessment and treatment of aphasia, the author assumed that she would be able to provide her mother with the intervention needed to return her to the maximum functioning she could achieve. The reality was very different and emotionally shattering. It gave this author a much greater appreciation for what the family and friends of a stroke patient go through when a loved one suffers a neurological injury.

The author and her father decided to care for her mother in their home. Once her mother had stabilized, the author gathered her clinical bag of tricks and went to her mother's bedside to begin what she believed would be a magical recovery of speech and language skills based on her unique interventional talents. Having spread some stimulus items on her mother's bed table, the author began to explain to her mother what they were going to do. Or perhaps, a more accurate description would be what the author expected she and her mother would do. But, Mom had other plans. She gave the author a rather withering look and then proceeded to sweep the stimuli from the bed table to the floor with her unaffected left arm. When the author recovered from her shock and tried again, her mother once again swept the items from the table, and this time, for good measure, stuck out her tongue. It was clear that Mom had no intention of working with her daughter as a therapist. Unable to express her wishes in words, Mom nonetheless clearly made her point. The author conceded to her mother's wishes and asked a colleague to provide therapy. The author's mother had been a vibrant, funny, intelligent, and caring individual who worked full time alongside her husband. What remained of that individual following her stroke was mostly trapped inside, although glimpses of her personality came through during a number of instances. The impact on the author's father was overwhelming. His independent, take-charge, strong spouse was now completely dependent on him for all of her physical, medical, and emotional needs. The partnership that had existed was now a patient/caregiver relationship. Friends, who were initially attentive and visited, became uncomfortable with the chronic nature of their friend's condition and the changes that resulted because of her lack of speech (her comprehension remained mostly intact) and, as the years went on, disappeared. She was no longer the mother, wife, and friend of memory. It is not possible to adequately describe, in a limited context, the tremendous impact this stroke had on everyone involved.

It is likely that some individuals will not be good candidates for intervention following a stroke. Most commonly, these are the ones with coexisting conditions, a history of multiple strokes, degenerative conditions, or individuals who are unresponsive to testing. However, the SLP must be tuned-in to the possibility that an individual initially felt to be a poor candidate for intervention may become a better one as the process of spontaneous recovery occurs and progresses. It is not uncommon to reevaluate a potential client several months after onset to determine if the original assessment is still valid.

Assessment

Assessment of the individual who has survived a stroke usually begins once he or she has stabilized and been moved out of the intensive care unit. The SLP is one component of a multidisciplinary team. This team will be comprised of the medical and allied health professionals involved in the patient's care.

The composition of this team will depend on the specific patient's needs but generally includes (in addition to an SLP and audiologist)

- a neurologist,
- the patient's primary care physician,
- nursing staff,
- physical and occupational therapists,
- a social worker, and, often,
- a family member or significant other.

If indicated, the team may also include a psychiatrist, registered dietician, respiratory therapist, recreation therapist, neuropsychologist, and pharmacist.

The critical first element of any assessment is a careful and detailed case history. Understanding that the patient may be unable to provide the information needed, the SLP reviews the patient's medical record and fills in the gaps by speaking with family members and significant others. It is important to obtain as clear a picture as possible of the client as he or she was before the stroke to identify any changes that have occurred. During one spouse interview, a woman complained bitterly that her husband was cranky and irritable all the time. When asked if this represented a change in status, the wife replied, "Oh, he's always been a cranky and irritable son-of-a-gun! I just thought maybe this stroke would improve his mood." Humorous as that may be, it is important to note that neurological injury can indeed change an individual's behavior, but rarely does it improve it. This helps to emphasize another important element of the assessment process—communicating about the patient's conditions with loved ones. There is no "cure" for aphasia, and the ethical clinician will never promise one. It is important to communicate to family and significant others in an honest and compassionate fashion the level at which their loved one is functioning and provide a best estimate of prognosis and projected outcomes. There is a fine line between honesty and brutal, harsh reality. The clinician must always be honest, but must do so with an understanding of how very emotionally fragile, frightened, and confused the significant others may be.

The assessment of function is achieved through both formal and informal measures of the patient's abilities and skills. Patients are assessed across all modalities: oral communication, auditory comprehension, reading, writing, and even gestural. Assessment measures may include informal or structured observations, screening measures, or comprehensive test batteries. The most important element of the assessment is to determine whether the patient has aphasia. Once that determination is made, the severity and type of aphasia are identified, and prognosis and intervention plans, if indicated, are developed. Although not etched in stone, while in the hospital, the SLP will use an aphasia screening tool, often administered at the patient's bedside, leaving more comprehensive assessments to rehabilitation units or outpatient rehabilitation programs. Because screening tests require shorter administration times and scoring procedures, they are most often used for the initial determination of aphasia.

Both screening and comprehensive aphasia tests focus on the assessment of the patient's skills. There is a long list of skills that can be assessed and evaluated. The most common ones are conversational speech skills, speech fluency, auditory comprehension, repetition of language units, naming abilities, grammatical structure, automatic speech (e.g., counting), reading aloud, reading comprehension, writing, and nonverbal communication (such as use of gestures). The extent to which each of these skills is assessed will be dependent on the degree of impairment the individual exhibits. It must be stressed that assessment is not a one-shot activity. Because of the frequently changing nature of recovery from neurological injury, assessment must be ongoing throughout the patient's recovery.

Some of the more commonly used bedside or screening tools and comprehensive diagnostic tools are provided in Table 7.3.

There are also a number of aphasia assessment tools that focus on specific modalities or areas of deficit. The more commonly used and their purposes are provided in Table 7.4.

Intervention

General Observations

Following assessment, the next job of the SLP is to plan and execute intervention. The primary goals of intervention with adults who have aphasia are to

1. aid the client in recovering lost speech and language skills,

TABLE 7.3 Screening and Comprehensive Diagnostic Tests for Aphasia

Name of Assessment Measure	Reference	Screening Test	Comprehensive Test Battery
Acute Aphasia Screening Protocol (AASP)	Crary, Haak, & Malinsky (1989)	X	
Aphasia Diagnostic Profiles (ADP)	Helm-Estabrooks (1992)		X
Aphasia Language Performance Scales (ALPS)	Keenan & Brassell (1975)	X	
Aphasia Screening Test (AST), 2nd ed.	Whurr (1997)	X	
Bedside Evaluation Screening Test, 2nd ed. (BEST-2)	West, Sands, & Swain (1998)	X	
Boston Diagnostic Aphasia Examination, 3rd ed. (BDAE-3), long and short forms	Goodglass, Kaplan, & Barresi (2001)		X
Communicative Abilities of Daily Living, 2nd ed. (CADL-2)	Holland, Frattali, & Fromm (1998)		X
Communicative Effectiveness Index (CETI)	Lomas, Pickard, Bester, Elbard, Finlayson, & Zoghaib (1989)		X
Frenchay Aphasia Screening Test, 2nd ed.	Enderby, Wood, & Wade (2006)	X	
Functional Communication Profile-Revised	Kleiman (2003)		X
Minnesota Test for the Differential Diagnosis of Aphasia (MTDDA)	Schuell (1973)		X
Porch Index of Communicative Ability-Revised (PICA-R)	Porch (2001)		X
Quick Assessment for Aphasia	Tanner & Culbertson (1999)	X	
Reitan-Indiana Aphasia Screening Test	Reitan (1991)	X	
Sklar Aphasia Scale (SAS)-Revised	Sklar (1983)	X	
Western Aphasia Battery-Revised (WAB-R), includes bedside	Kertesz (2006)	X	X

2. provide compensatory strategies (or alternative modes of expression) to make up for those abilities that are not responsive to remediation, and
3. enable the individual to communicate sufficiently well to make needs, wants, and desires understood.

Unfortunately, these goals are not always attainable for all clients. Further, as mentioned, individuals with aphasia are not a homogeneous group. Therefore, each one will require intervention goals that are tailored to the severity of the disorder and his or her communication needs. It is important also to consider whether there are any medical or other

TABLE 7.4 Specialized Aphasia Assessment Tools

Name of Assessment Measure	Reference	Purpose
Revised Token Test	McNeil & Prescott (1978)	Auditory comprehension
Psycholinguistic Assessments of Language Processing in Aphasia	Kay, Lesser, & Coltheart (1992)	Auditory comprehension, naming, reading, writing
Boston Naming Test, 2nd ed.	Goodglass & Kaplan (2001)	Naming/word finding
The Reporter's Test	DeRenzi & Ferrari (1978)	Syntax
Reading Comprehension Battery for Aphasia, 2nd ed.	LaPointe & Horner (1998)	Reading

coexisting deficits or disorders that will affect the ability of the client to respond to treatment.

To ensure participation of the client and his or her significant others, it is critical that they be involved with the SLP in goal setting and the relevancy of activities. No treatment program exists in a vacuum. Likewise, no SLP waves a magic wand and makes disorders disappear. The involvement of the family and significant others in identifying goals of treatment will assist the SLP with home programs and carryover into activities of daily living. Just as it is important to include those close to the clients in planning and assisting treatment, it is equally important that the SLP inform and interact with all members of an individual's treatment team regarding his or her progress and prognosis.

For many individuals with aphasia and their significant others, the only goal that is acceptable and desired is the return of prestroke speech and language skills. Given the neurological damage associated with this condition, however, full recovery may well not happen. It is very important to be clear in communicating a realistic prognosis to family and significant others and for the disclosure to be tempered by compassion and understanding. As noted in Chapter 5, the SLP who says only what the clients want to hear will soon lose credibility.

Even when the prognosis for improvement is favorable, no promises can or should be made about the outcomes of treatment or the amount of progress an individual will make. Prestroke functioning is still unlikely, a concept that is difficult for both the individual with aphasia and the significant others to grasp. An analogy that can soften the message that a loved one will most likely not be restored to prestroke functioning is to liken the individual with aphasia to a pie, stating that a terrific pie is still terrific even with a piece missing. The intent is to help significant others see that their loved ones are still there and should not be discounted, ignored, or worse, treated as babies. Many individuals with aphasia have complained about being treated like children by their spouses or significant others. People rush to fill in their sentences or assume their intent.

Their children no longer confide or discuss things with them. Friends do not come by just to chat and visit. It is bad enough that the individual is isolated by the loss of communicative abilities; it is worse to be isolated by family and friends who are themselves uncomfortable with the individual post-CVA.

What Intervention Is Right for Whom

In selecting intervention techniques or programs, most SLPs will decide on those approaches that best align with their beliefs about the nature of aphasia. Following an assessment that is as detailed and extensive as necessary, the SLP is faced with identifying the skills that will be most responsive to remediation and provide the individual with the best outcome for communication. The SLP might select specific areas of deficit for remediation, such as naming or reading, or select skills that underlie communication, such as auditory comprehension and memory. The SLP must evaluate whether the individual would be best served by an alternative or augmentative system of communication (see Chapter 12) or if communication skills will be best achieved through speech or writing. In selecting the modalities to teach, as well as those through which treatment will be delivered, the SLP must be cognizant of coexisting conditions affecting treatment. Examples include hemiparesis or paralysis of the dominant hand, visual deficits, and hearing impairment.

☐ Right Hemisphere Injury

Deficits that result from damage to the right hemisphere (RHD) of the brain are referred to as *right hemisphere injury* (RHI) or *right hemisphere syndrome*. Although the right hemisphere is not the dominant hemisphere for most language functions, damage to it may result in both linguistic and perceptual disorders.

Split-brain studies, investigations of the independent functions of the right and left hemisphere following surgery, were instrumental in identifying the particular skills of each hemisphere. These studies enabled investigators to determine that the left hemisphere was primarily responsible for analytical and verbal tasks, while the right hemisphere was specialized for orientation and attention, visual perception, and emotional expression and experience. In addition, the right hemisphere controls the perception of time and the sequence of events, as well as musical harmony and language functions affecting an individual's pragmatic ability (i.e., how language is used). Patients with RHD can experience personality and mood changes and exhibit indifference to events and once-enjoyed activities. Damage in the right hemisphere can also result in right-sided hemisensory impairment, hemiparesis, or hemiplegia.

The same neurological injuries responsible for LHD are responsible for the loss of abilities in the right hemisphere. Assuming you have not memorized what those injuries are, they include CVAs (strokes), tumors, head injury, and neurological disease. The degree and nature of the impairment are dependent on the location, type, and severity of the neurological injury (Table 7.5).

General Characteristics

Individuals with RHD exhibit a variety of deficits that are grouped, generally, into three categories: perceptual/attentional, affective, and communication.

Perceptual and Attentional Deficits

- *Left neglect.* This refers to a decreased or complete lack of awareness of stimuli on the left side of the body. It also affects the individual's awareness of "space" on the left side of the body and awareness of the left visual fields. Damage to the posterior parietal cortex in the right hemisphere results, most often, in left neglect. However, damage to the prefrontal cortex in the right hemisphere may also result in left neglect. Individuals exhibiting left neglect may exhibit the following deficits:
  - difficulty in shifting attention from the right to the left
  - seeing only the right side of a picture or object (apparent when the individual draws only the right half of the object) (see Figure 7.3)
  - lack of awareness or no awareness of stimuli on the left side
  - attention to items, text, or facial features on the right side only
  - denial of the existence of the left side of the body and failure to recognize objects worn on that side of the body
  - lack of awareness of left spatial relations, causing the individual to bump into people on the left side
  - failure to cross midline (not crossing to the left side of the page) when reading and writing
  - failure to respond to sounds from the left side
  - failure to move the left side, resulting in problems with balance or injury to a limb because of failure to move it away from a damaging or painful stimulus
- *Facial recognition deficits (prosopagnosia)*
  - difficulty in or failure to recognize familiar faces in photographs
  - failure to recognize the face of a known individual or family pet
  - problems in naming famous individuals from pictures of their faces

TABLE 7.5 Aphasia: Differential Diagnosis

Aphasia	Dementia	Traumatic Brain Injury	Right Hemisphere Damage
Sudden onset (most common)	Slow onset	Sudden onset	Sudden onset (most common)
Left hemisphere damage; focal lesions	Bilateral/diffuse brain damage	Bilateral damage, diffuse	Right hemisphere damage, usually diffuse lesions
Neurologically based language disorder	N/A	Language of confusion	Neurologically based; perceptual disorders predominate
CVA (usual etiology); tumors; head trauma; neurologic disease	Variable etiology	Head trauma	CVA; tumors; head trauma; neurologic disease
Fluent or nonfluent speech	Fluent until dementia worsens	Variable speech	Mild speech problems
Typically late onset (adult or old age)	Typically late onset; progressive (adult or old age)	Onset variable (most common: males 15–24 years old)	Onset variable
Mood usually appropriate (occasionally depressed)	May be moody, withdrawn, agitated	Mood often inappropriate	Mood variable, sometimes inappropriate
Cognitive deficits not typical	Mild to severely cognitively impaired	Severe cognitive deficits	Cognitive deficits not typical
Most memory functions typically intact	Memory impaired to varying degrees; often severely	Loss of memory for events before/after trauma; associated with reduced consciousness or excessive arousal	Variable degrees of memory loss
Generally relevant speech, socially appropriate, organized	Often irrelevant, socially inappropriate, disorganized	Speech typically irrelevant	Speech often irrelevant, excessive, rambling; inappropriate humor
Semantic, syntactic, phonologic performance simultaneously impaired	Progression of deterioration from semantic to syntactic to phonologic performance	Little or no syntactic difficulties	Mild problems with syntax
Deficits in auditory comprehension	Progressive deterioration	Mild to severe	Mild comprehension problems; understands only literal meanings; left neglect of auditory stimuli

TABLE 7.5 (continued) Aphasia: Differential Diagnosis

Aphasia	Dementia	Traumatic Brain Injury	Right Hemisphere Damage
Reading, writing affected	Progressive deterioration	Mild to severe reading problems	Mild problems, usually due to left neglect
Communication better than demonstrated language skills	Communication may be good initially but deteriorates significantly with progression; individual may be withdrawn and uncommunicative	Communication worse than demonstrated language skills	Possesses good language skills, but communication may be very poor; no integration (may retell only nonessential, isolated details)
Pragmatic impairment: mild	Progressive deterioration of pragmatic ability	Pragmatic impairment moderate to severe	Striking pragmatic impairments
Anosognosia (denial of illness) seen occasionally in fluent aphasias	May be unaware, rather than denying	May not be aware	Denial of illness; lack of insight into problems; indifference
Some prosodic defects	Not generally a problem	Not generally a problem	Pronounced prosodic defects
Generally stable, unless multiple strokes occurring	Generally progressive (unless reversible dementia)	Generally stable unless secondary conditions cause problems	Generally stable, unless multiple strokes occurring
No disorders of perception	Progressive deterioration	Mild to severe disorders of perception	Left-sided neglect; may not recognize familiar faces (prosopagnosia); perceptual deficits more dominant
Possible attentional deficits	Progressive deterioration of attention	Attentional deficits possible	Pronounced attentional deficits and distractibility
No confabulation	Confabulation	Confabulation	Confabulation
No disorientation (may occur for short period after stroke)	Progressive disorientation to time, place, people	Disoriented to time, place, people	Disorientation to space and surroundings
No significant behavioral (personality) change	Progressive behavioral (personality) change	Significant behavioral (personality) change	Impulsive behavior
Normal emotional responses, interpersonal relations	Emotional responses and interactions deteriorate over time	Often inappropriate	Difficulty expressing own emotions; lack of appreciation of others' emotions

FIGURE 7.3 Left-side neglect. The client was asked to reproduce the drawing and the sentence on the right. The client's reproductions are on the left.

- *Constructional deficits*
  - difficulty in constructing block designs
  - difficulty with stick figures and two-dimensional drawings
  - difficulty with drawing and copying
- *Attentional deficits*
  - difficulty in being attentive, maintaining attention, and attending selectively
- *Disorientation*
  - difficulty in finding one's way around one's house, room, or neighborhood
  - confusion regarding directions and physical locations (street, city, or state)
- *Visuoperceptual deficits*
  - difficulty recognizing line drawing but not actual objects
  - production of distorted drawings with regard to size or shape

Affective Deficits

Deficits in **affect** are reflected by the individual's inability to express or understand normal states of emotion or experiences. Our actual experiencing of emotions is governed by the limbic system. However, it is the right hemisphere that controls our expression of emotions and our ability to recognize the emotions being expressed by others. An individual with RHD may exhibit the following affective deficits:

- difficulty in understanding emotions that are verbalized or expressed by facial expression
- difficulty describing emotions in pictures or videos
- difficulty understanding emotions expressed through the pitch, loudness, or stress of speech

Prominent Communication Characteristics

The speech and language deficits following damage to the right hemisphere are not similar to those due to left hemisphere lesions. It is important to remember that in the majority of people, it is the left hemisphere that is dominant for language (this is true for most left-handed individuals, as well). Therefore, the incidence of word-finding problems, paraphasias, sound production errors, and agrammatism is not significant with right-sided damage. While an individual with RHD might exhibit **circumlocution**, it is not because of a difficulty finding the word or initiating sound production. Rather, the cause of circumlocution is the cognitive, attentional, and perceptual deficits associated with the damage. The speech and language deficits occurring most prominently in an individual with RHD are

- prosodic deficits
  - monotonous speech or impaired variability of pitch
  - abnormalities in stress patterns
  - slow rate
  - failure to convey emotion in speech, as well as failure to understand the emotional content of speech
- impaired narration, description, and conversational abilities
  - inability to distinguish relevant from irrelevant information
  - difficulty using sarcasm, humor, and abstractions
  - excessive, rambling, production of speech
- semantic deficits
  - literal interpretation of implied and abstract information, proverbs, idioms, and metaphors
  - lack of understanding of a situation, event, or story
  - difficulty understanding sarcasm, humor, and subtlety of expression
- pragmatic deficits
  - difficulties in conversation with turn taking, topic maintenance, eye contact, and sensitivity to the communication environment

TABLE 7.6 Speech and Language Deficits Associated with LHD and RHD

Speech and Language Deficits Associated With Left Hemisphere Neurological Damage	Speech and Language Deficits Associated With Right Hemisphere Neurological Damage
Focal or localized pattern of deficits	Diffuse deficits
Concrete deficits (e.g., naming problems, agrammatism)	Abstract deficits (e.g., difficulty expressing/understanding emotion)
Direct result of brain injury and specific lesions	Result of deficits in attention, perception, and affect
Fewer behavioral deficits	Complications associated with denial of symptoms, indifference, left neglect, impulsivity, attentiveness, and poor reasoning abilities

Table 7.6 provides a quick comparison of the differences and similarities in the speech and language deficits associated with RHD and LHD.

☐ Traumatic Brain Injury

Hegde (2006), in the third edition of *A Coursebook on Aphasia and Other Neurogenic Language Disorders*, defines traumatic brain injury (TBI) as follows:

The term traumatic brain injury excludes cerebral damage from strokes, tumors, infection, progressive neurological diseases, metabolic disturbances, toxic agents and inherited or congenital conditions. Traumatic brain injury is injury to the brain sustained by physical trauma or external force. It is brain injury that impairs various skills and general behavior, requiring extensive and often prolonged rehabilitation services.

According to the National Center for Injury and Prevention Control (NCIPC) (2009), 1.4 million individuals sustain a TBI each year in the United States. These injuries are the cause of a substantial number of deaths (around 50,000) and permanent disability annually. Close to a quarter million are hospitalized long term, and over a million are treated and released from emergency rooms.

It is not known how many people with TBI go untreated. We do know that males are twice as likely as females to sustain a TBI, and that the two age groups at highest risk are children from 0 to 4 years of age and adolescents aged 15 to 19. Other groups at risk, according to the NCIPC (2009) are as follows:

- Adults age 75 years or older have the highest rates of TBI-related hospitalization and death.
- Certain military duties (e.g., paratrooper) increase the risk of sustaining a TBI.
- African Americans have the highest death rate from TBI of any race or ethnic group.
- TBI hospitalization rates are highest among African Americans and American Indians/Alaska Natives.

The leading causes of TBI are falls (28%); motor vehicle-traffic crashes (20%); struck by/against events (19%); and assaults (11%) (NCIPC, 2009).

Falls leading to TBI have the highest rates for children ages 0 to 4 years of age and adults ages 75 years of age and older. Motor vehicle and traffic crashes account for the greatest number of TBI-related hospitalizations. Adolescents between the ages of 15 and 19 years have the highest rate of motor vehicle-related TBIs. Another susceptible population is motorcycle riders who do not wear helmets (National Highway Safety Administration, 2008). Many elderly individuals suffer such injuries in the bathroom when they fall and hit their heads on the sink, tub, or floor.

Sports and recreation accidents are responsible for approximately 1.6–3.8 million of the TBIs that occur in the United States each year. Fortunately, most of these injuries are mild, and a number do not require treatment in a hospital or emergency department. One of the authors clearly remembers when she received a call from her brother, telling her that her nephew had sustained a moderate head injury during his karate class. Her brother was extremely concerned and wanted assurances from the author that his son's disorientation, grogginess, and **amnesia** about the event would be temporary. Of course, no such assurances can be given, but most of the information on TBI bears out the temporary nature of these types of injuries. Fortunately, the effects of her nephew's TBI resolved within a week, and the author is proud to report that her nephew is currently in college, majoring in aeronautical engineering. The obvious conclusion might be that a TBI leads one to become a rocket scientist, but the sounder conclusion is that the effects of the TBI were transitory and caused no permanent impairment.

Regardless of the causative factor, a significant number of individuals who sustain a TBI require care, often long term, and intensive rehabilitation services. For many of them, the TBI will cause damage that is permanent and forever alters their lives.

Types of Brain Injuries

Traumatic brain injuries are broadly classified as either *penetrating injuries/open-head injuries* or *nonpenetrating injuries/closed-head injuries*.

Surprisingly, it is the nonpenetrating brain injuries that have the most debilitating and long-lasting effects, requiring substantial and costly rehabilitation treatment.

Penetrating/Open-Head Injuries

Penetrating or open-head injuries involve an injury to the head wherein the skull is opened, and a foreign object penetrates the brain tissue. As would be expected, the degree of penetration correlates with the severity of the injury. Bullets, knives, arrows, and nail guns are some examples of items that cause penetrating head injuries. Such injuries are termed *high-velocity injuries* when caused by an automatic weapon, rifle, or bomb debris. *Low-velocity injuries* occur when the projectile travels at a slower speed (such as an arrow, knife, or nail gun). When the foreign object crashes through the skull and enters the brain tissue, it carries with it skin, hair, dirt, and other debris, such as material from a hat or scarf, leading to a high possibility of infection in addition to the damage to the brain tissue. Without doubt, the higher the speed of the object entering the brain, the more severe will be the damage and injury to the brain. The size of the invading object and the path the object takes within the brain also affect the degree of injury. Objects traveling in a straight line produce less severe injuries than objects that "yaw" or zigzag through the brain. Although it appears obvious, it should be stated that multiple injuries will increase the amount of damage sustained by the brain.

Although it is possible to survive a penetrating TBI, the overall death rate from them is high. For one thing, there is an increase in pressure in the brain caused by the force of the object that has entered it. In addition to this increase in intracranial pressure, a penetrating head injury may cause fluctuations in blood pressure, a reduction or interruption of the normal blood flow throughout the brain, and edema (swelling) of the brain tissue, sometimes leading to hydrocephalus, infection, and bleeding (i.e., a hemorrhage) within the brain. For those who survive, brain tissue may be permanently destroyed, leading to long-term deficits in movement, cognitive function, behavior, and communication.

Nonpenetrating/Closed-Head Injuries

Although the skull may be fractured in a nonpenetrating or closed-head injury, there is no opening from the skull into the brain. That is, the brain tissues are not invaded by any foreign object or substance. However, the aftermath of a closed-head injury produces symptoms and deficits that are lifelong and more complex than those observed following a penetrating head injury.

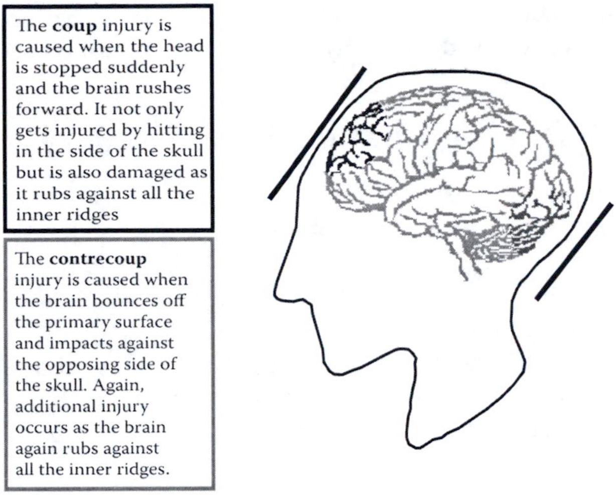

The **coup** injury is caused when the head is stopped suddenly and the brain rushes forward. It not only gets injured by hitting in the side of the skull but is also damaged as it rubs against all the inner ridges

The **contrecoup** injury is caused when the brain bounces off the primary surface and impacts against the opposing side of the skull. Again, additional injury occurs as the brain again rubs against all the inner ridges.

FIGURE 7.4 Coup and contrecoup brain injuries.

The brain is not firmly fixed within the skull. It is perched atop the brainstem, a rather slender structure relative to the size and weight of the brain. Think of a cantaloupe balanced on an upside-down celery stalk.

While the brain does not roll around in the skull, it is able to "wobble" on the brain stem when an individual receives a blow to the head. Consequently, a strong blow to the head may cause the brain to twist and wobble so much that brain tissue can tear.

There are two types of nonpenetrating head injuries. A *coup* injury occurs at the site of impact. In a coup injury, the brain is pushed in the direction of the impact or blow and smashes into the inside of the skull.

Because the inside surface of the skull is not smooth, the brain is injured not only by its compression against the skull but also by the jagged and sharp projections on the inner surface of the skull. A *contrecoup* injury is caused when a blow to the head causes the brain to strike the skull opposite from the site of impact. In a contrecoup injury, damage occurs to the brain at the original site and at a site opposite the original site. A *coup-contrecoup injury* "describes contusions that are both at the site of the impact and on the complete opposite side of the brain. This occurs when the force impacting the head is not only great enough to cause a contusion at the site of impact, but also is able to move the brain and cause it to slam into the opposite side of the skull, which causes the additional contusion" (Brain Injury Association of America, 2009) (see Figure 7.4).

Some of the causes of nonpenetrating head injuries are work-related and sports-related accidents; banging the head against an object or the ground when falling, for example, off a ladder or chair; a blow to the head with a blunt object such as a two-by-four or a shovel; car accidents; and injuries that may occur during physical abuse or fighting.

Primary Effects of a Traumatic Brain Injury

- injuries and fractures to the skull
- widespread damage to nerve fibers in the white matter of the brain
- injury to the brain stem
- injury to the vascular (blood flow) system
- damage to cranial nerves
- bruising or abrasions to the brain caused by its rubbing against or hitting the uneven surface on the inside of the skull
- injuries to specific sites (focal injury) within the brain

Secondary Effects of a Traumatic Brain Injury

- intracranial hematoma
- increased pressure within the brain
- hypoxia
- difficulties caused by damage to the brain or brain stem such as breathing, seizures, reduced blood pressure, and inflammation or infection of the linings of the brain

General and Behavioral Characteristics Following TBI

- ranges in consciousness from coma to grogginess or slight disorientation
- persistent vegetative state resulting from severe and widespread brain damage
- amnesia
- problems with memory
- general confusion or bewilderment
- swallowing disorders (dysphagia)
- changes in mood, behavior, and mental state

Prominent Speech and Language Characteristics

The degree and complexity of the communication disorders associated with TBI will vary depending on the extent of damage, the sites of damage, and the type of head injury sustained. The speech and language characteristics will therefore occur in a range from mild to extremely severe and debilitating. These characteristics include

- dysarthria, which may cause problems with phonation, stress, pitch, accuracy of articulation, rate, and breath support for speech
- varying degrees of confused language, anomia, and perseveration
- semantic and pragmatic deficits in turn taking, initiation of conversation, topic maintenance, narrative sequencing, use of vague terms, and circumlocution
- difficulties in comprehension
- reading and writing problems

Some individuals who have sustained a TBI may recover most of their lost skills over time, while others will have ongoing, chronic deficits that do not resolve. Coexisting medical problems and injuries will also affect recovery.

☐ Dementia

Kinsella and Wan (2009) provide 20 questions and answers about global aging in the 21st century. The answers to some of the questions may surprise you:

Question: The world's older population (65 and over) was increasing by approximately how many people each month in 2008?
a. 75,000
b. 350,000
c. 600,000
d. 870,000
Answer: d. The estimated change in the total size of the world's older population between July 2007 and July 2008 was more than 10.4 million people, an average of 870,000 each month.

Question: True or false? Current demographic projections suggest that 35% of all people in the United States will be at least 65 years of age by the year 2050.
Answer: False. Although the United States will age rapidly when the baby boomers (people born between 1946 and 1964) begin to reach age 65 after the year 2010, the percentage of the population aged 65 and over in the year 2050 is projected to be 20% (compared with 12% today).

TABLE 7.7 Commonly Held Myths About Older Adults

Myth	Fact
Most older people are pretty much alike.	They are a very diverse age group.
They are generally alone and lonely.	Most older adults maintain close contact with family.
They are sick, frail, and dependent on others.	Most older people live independently.
They are often cognitively impaired.	For most older adults, if there is decline in some intellectual abilities, it is not severe enough to cause problems in daily living.
They are depressed.	Community-dwelling older adults have lower rates of diagnosable depression than younger adults.
They become more difficult and rigid with advancing years.	Personality remains relatively consistent throughout the life span.
They barely cope with the inevitable declines associated with aging.	Most older people successfully adjust to the challenges of aging.

Source: APA (2011). Reprinted with permission from the American Psychological Association APA (2011).

Question: True or false? The number of the world's "oldest old" (people 80 and over) is growing more rapidly than the older (65 and over) population as a whole.

Answer: True. The oldest old are the fastest-growing component of many national populations. The world's growth rate for the 80-and-over population from 2007 to 2008 was 4.3%, while that of the world's older (65 and over) population as a whole was 2.1% (compared with 1.2% for the total [all ages] population).

Any way you slice it, the number of elderly adults is growing. As more and more baby boomers reach 65, the United States will realize an 8% growth in older adults by 2050.

A certain amount of memory loss is considered normal as one ages (Table 7.7). We have all had the experience of walking into a room and forgetting why we went there in the first place, losing our train of thought, or not being able to retrieve the name of a movie or actor. Brain cells decrease as we age, so a certain degree of cognitive decline is to be expected. But, how does one determine when forgetfulness has progressed to something that is beyond normal? What is the cutoff between mild cognitive decline and dementia?

The National Institute of Neurological Disorders and Stroke (NINDS; 2009a) describes **dementia** as follows:

Dementia is not a specific disease. It is a descriptive term for a collection of symptoms that can be caused by a number of disorders that affect the brain. People with dementia have significantly impaired intellectual functioning that interferes with normal activities and relationships. They also lose their ability to solve problems and maintain emotional control, and they may experience personality changes and behavioral problems such as agitation, delusions, and hallucinations. While memory loss is a common symptom of dementia, memory loss by itself does not mean that a person has dementia. Doctors diagnose dementia only if two or more brain functions—such as memory, language skills, perception, or cognitive skills including reasoning and judgment—are significantly impaired without loss of consciousness.

One important feature of this definition is that it shows dementia is not a part of the normal aging process. Many adults live into their 80s and 90s without developing it. Still, the difference between normal age-related memory loss and dementia is not always easy to discern. The general guideline used in making this distinction is whether the loss is interfering with everyday functioning and life. In general, age-related cognitive and memory declines are considered normal if the oldster can still handle activities of daily living and remains active and engages with his or her environment. Memory problems that are not part of the normal aging process are

- forgetting things more often than you are used to,
- forgetting how to do things you have done many times before,
- trouble learning new things,
- repeating phrases or stories in the same conversation,
- trouble making choices or handling money, and
- not being able to keep track of what happens each day (Psychiatry24x7. com, 2009).

The NINDS (2009a) stated that, "All forms of dementia result from the death of nerve cells and/or the loss of communication among these cells." These conditions can result from a number of factors:

- reactions to medications
- metabolic problems and endocrine abnormalities
- nutritional deficiencies
- infections
- subdural hematomas
- poisoning
- brain tumors
- anoxia
- heart and lung problems

Alzheimer's disease (AD) is named for Alois Alzheimer, a German doctor who first described the disease in the early 1900s. AD is the most common form of dementia but is not the only type. Research over the past 30 or so years has identified a number of different types and causes of dementia. The sections that follow provide a survey of the different dementia types that have been identified, as well as conditions that may cause dementia.

How Are Dementias Classified?

Dementias or dementing disorders are classified into groups by the features they have in common or by the parts of the brain that are affected. The most commonly used classifications are primary and secondary.

- Primary dementia. A primary dementia is not caused by any mitigating disease or factor such as medication or physical injury.
- Secondary dementia. A secondary dementia is caused by a disease or injury.

Other types include the following:

- Cortical dementia. In a cortical dementia, it is the cortex of the brain that is damaged or affected. Individuals with cortical dementia may exhibit problems with memory, language, thinking, and social behavior.
- Subcortical dementia. Subcortical dementias are caused by damage to areas of the brain that are below the cortex and may cause problems with emotions, movement, and memory.
- Progressive dementia. A progressive dementia is one that increases in severity as the individual ages. An individual with a progressive dementia may begin at a very mild stage that then develops into a severe or profound dementia.

Not all dementias fit precisely into one category; in fact, a number of dementia types will fit into several categories. AD, for example, is a primary, progressive, cortical dementia.

Dementia Types: Primary Dementias

Alzheimer's Disease

The most common cause of dementia in people over 65 is Alzheimer's dementia. According to the NINDS (2009a):

Experts believe that up to 4 million people in the United States are currently living with the disease: one in ten people over the age of 65 and nearly half of those over 85 have AD. At least 360,000 Americans are diagnosed with AD each year and about 50,000 are reported to die from it.

Individuals with AD and their families notice a gradual decline in the individual's cognitive abilities. This decline occurs over a period of 7 to 10 years and affects memory, movement, language, judgment, behavior, and abstract thinking.

Patients in the early stages of AD may exhibit memory impairment, lapses of judgment, and changes in personality. As time passes, the memory and language problems become more severe, and the individual is unable to handle daily living. Simple functions such as bathing, dressing, meal preparation, and taking daily medications become difficult to perform or are forgotten. As the disease progresses, individuals with AD become disoriented and do not recognize places or the passage of time. Some report hallucinations and events that have not occurred. Unfortunately, in a number of instances the individual with AD will be easily angered and physically aggressive and violent. In the final stages of the disease, individuals are incontinent and may exhibit poor motor control and difficulty chewing and swallowing. The individual with AD does not recognize significant others, although there may be one family member or friend of whom the individual retains memories. However, these memories may be vague. The first author's grandmother, who had dementia, would often say, "I know I love you, but I don't know who you are." It was both heartbreaking and heartwarming. This same grandparent would show the author pictures of her father as a young man and ask her if she wanted to meet her son. When told that her son was the author's father, Nana would look at the author totally confused and ask, "He got married?" On a number of occasions, the author would come into her Nana's room to find her hiding in her closet because she did not recognize the old man sitting in her room. When told it was her husband, she would appear stunned and say, "That's Ell? He's old. What happened to him?" While perhaps amusing, these scenes were replayed almost daily as if they had not occurred before.

Individuals with AD may also develop depression and exhibit agitation or anxiety and have difficulty sleeping. They may wander aimlessly, and if not kept within familiar surroundings will wander off with no knowledge of where they are going or how to return. According to the NINDS (2009a), "Patients with AD live for 8 to 10 years after they are diagnosed. However, some people live as long as 20 years. Patients with AD often die of aspiration pneumonia because they lose the ability to swallow late in the course of the disease."

Vascular Dementia

The second most common type of dementia is vascular dementia, and it makes up approximately 20% of all dementias. Vascular dementias are caused by brain damage following a stroke, heart disease, and genetic diseases. The incidence of vascular dementias increases with age. Because of its etiologies, vascular dementias often begin suddenly. Unlike AD, a vascular dementia may not be progressive but, rather, remains stable over time. As with recovery from the disabilities that result from stroke, a vascular dementia may decrease over time. A primary difference between individuals with AD and vascular dementias is that individuals with vascular dementia seem to retain their personalities and normal emotional responses.

If there are changes in personality and emotional responsiveness, those changes occur in the later stages of the dementia.

Lewy Body Dementia

Lewy body dementia (LBD) is a progressive dementia named after masses that disrupt the normal functioning of neurons. Individuals with LBD exhibit many of the same symptoms as individuals with AD. Because it often co-occurs with Parkinson's disease, symptoms characteristic of this condition may be present as well.

Frontotemporal Dementia

Frontotemporal dementia (FTD) is also referred to as *frontal lobe dementia*. It results from diseases that cause nerve cells in the frontal and temporal lobes to degenerate. These lobes control judgment and social behavior. Therefore, individuals with FTD will exhibit problems maintaining appropriate social behavior. They may present compulsive behaviors, neglect responsibilities, or be excessively rude or crude.

A type of FTD that may manifest in individuals as young as in their early 40s is *primary progressive aphasia* (PPA). As indicated by its name, PPA is a progressive disorder that affects language functions. The symptoms of PPA begin gradually and progress slowly over time. In addition to difficulties with communication as the PPA progresses, the individual may exhibit problems with memory and personality changes.

Dementia Pugilistica

Those with dementia pugilistica are sometimes referred to as "punch drunk." This condition results from the chronic swelling of the brain that occurs when someone has been punched in the head repeatedly.

Symptoms of Parkinson's disease commonly occur with the dementia. Boxers, wrestlers, football players, and martial arts fighters may also sustain the type of head trauma that leads to dementia pugilistica. Well-known fighters who have been identified as having the disease include Jack Dempsey, Joe Louis, Floyd Patterson, Jerry Quarry, Sugar Ray Robinson, and Muhammad Ali (Kindred, 2006; Minigh, 2007; Sabbagh, 2008).

Other Types of Primary Dementias

- **HIV-associated dementia:** occurs when the HIV virus causes the destruction of the white matter of the brain.
- **Huntington's disease:** is a hereditary disorder that causes the degeneration of cells in many areas of the brain and spinal cord. Individuals with Huntington's disease have a life expectancy, after diagnosis, of approximately 15 years. Onset of the disease generally occurs between 30 and 50 years of age.
- **Corticobasal degeneration (CBD):** is progressive and is characterized by both nerve cell loss and the atrophy of multiple areas of the brain. There are no specific treatments available for CBD. The symptoms often do not respond to medications. Occupational, physical, and speech therapy can help in managing the disabilities associated with this disease.
- **Binswanger's disease:** is a rare form of vascular dementia. In Binswanger's disease, the blood vessels in the white matter of the brain are damaged, leading to memory loss, disordered cognition, and mood changes.
- **Pick's disease:** is a form of FTD in which nerve cells become balloon-like and eventually die. Pick's disease tends to run in families and results in changes to the individual's personality and behavior. These changes become worse as the disease progresses.
- **Creutzfeldt-Jakob disease:** is a progressive, degenerative disease. It is rare, affecting approximately 1 in every 1 million people per year, and it is fatal. An individual with Creutzfeldt-Jakob disease may experience the following symptoms: muscular incoordination, personality changes, impaired memory and judgment, impaired vision, insomnia, and depression. As the disease progresses, individuals lose all ability to move and go blind before slipping into a coma and eventually dying.

Dementia Types: Secondary Dementias

Dementias that co-occur with disorders affecting movement or other functions are referred to as *secondary dementias*. A good example of this is the dementia associated with Parkinson's disease. One of the authors' father had a mild Parkinson's-related dementia. He was able to recognize family members, assist with self-care, and converse socially. However, his short-term memory was poor. A typical evening went as follows:

> After dinner, Dad was settled in front of the TV to watch say, *Law & Order*. The author would go to her computer to do some work or answer e-mail. Having been left alone for all of 10 or 15 minutes, her father would call, and they would engage in an exchange that was replayed on a daily basis.

Dad: Uh ... Deena? What am I going to watch when this is over?
Deena: I'll put something on for you when the program you're watching ends.
Dad: Okay, that's good.

Five minutes pass.

Dad: Honey? What am I going to watch when this is over?
Deena: I'll put on channel 10 for you.
Dad: Oh, I can do that. Okay, channel 10.

Five minutes pass.

Dad: Deena? What station am I switching to when this is over?
Deena: Dad, put on channel 10 at 10:00. Got it? 10 at 10:00.
Dad: Okay, that's fine. You don't have to get up.

Five minutes pass.

Dad: I think this show is going to end soon. What am I going to watch when it's over?
Deena: Would you like to watch *Law & Order* at 10:00?
Dad: Yeah, I like that one. What station is it on?
Deena (at this point with a slight edge to her voice): Channel 10 at 10:00. Don't try to remember; I'll come in and change the channel for you. Just watch your show, and I'll change the channel when it ends. Just watch the show.
Dad: What are you getting so irritable about? I just asked what I should watch when my show is over. Forget it.

Five minutes later:

Dad: Deena, I don't know what to watch when this program ends.
Deena (finally acknowledging defeat and feeling guilty for getting cranky): Okay, Dad. I'm on my way. I'll watch TV with you and change the stations.
Dad: Oh, that would be nice. I don't like watching alone.

It is no surprise that caregivers burn out and lose patience. They feel that they are living out the movie, *Groundhog Day*. Every day, the same conversations are repeated, the same topics are discussed, and the same events transpire. The next day begins the cycle anew.

☐ Motor Speech Disorders

Duffy (2005) defined motor speech disorders (MSDs) as "speech disorders resulting from neurologic impairment affecting the motor planning, programming, neuromuscular control, or execution of speech. They include the dysarthrias and apraxia." By this definition, speech disorders caused by sensory deficits, psychogenic disturbances, and cognitive and linguistic disorders are not motor speech disorders.

Apraxia of Speech

Individuals with apraxia of speech (AOS) have lost the ability to exercise volitional control over the positioning of speech (Figure 7.5). The sequences of movements for speech are also often affected, as are the sequence of phonemes in words.

Unlike the dysarthrias (discussed further in this section), individuals with AOS do not have significant problems with muscle weakness, slowness, or coordination when producing automatic and reflexive movements. This is an important distinction to understand. An individual who has an AOS may not be able to protrude the tongue on command. The individual will struggle to produce the movement, start and stop and restart the movement, and may or may not achieve the target behavior. However, that same individual, when given an ice cream cone or a lollipop, will extend the tongue to lick the ice cream or lollipop. This clearly illustrates that the

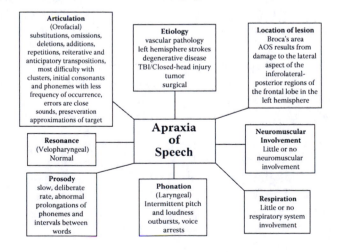

FIGURE 7.5 Etiology, neurology, and motor speech aspects of apraxia of speech (AOS).

problem is not due to an impairment in the muscle, but rather in the ability to program the commands sent to that muscle. Because of the location of the lesion resulting in AOS, individuals may have a coexisting Broca's aphasia. In addition, AOS is often accompanied by *limb apraxia* (usually the upper limbs) and *buccofacial apraxia* (apraxia involving the oral musculature).

Individuals with AOS exhibit the following speech characteristics:

- Slow, effortful speech. The individual exhibits a slow rate and appears to be groping for sounds and struggling to produce those sounds as indicated by false starts and difficulty initiating phonation.
- Distorted, inconsistent, and imprecise articulation of sounds. The individual with AOS may not produce the same sound substitution each time a word is said. For example, when shown a picture of a "coat," the individual may variably produce "poat," "doat," or "soat" or may perseverate on the incorrect production, saying it over and over, for example, "poat-poat-poat."
- Distortion of sounds due to poor differentiation in the production of voiced-voiceless sounds, slurring, sound prolongations, and trial-and-error attempts at correct articulatory placement.

Flaccid Dysarthria

Flaccid dysarthria is associated with damage to the brain stem, motor neurons, or motor cranial nerves. Individuals with flaccid dysarthria may have problems in the areas of respiration, phonation, resonance, and articulation. Because of these problem areas, this condition is characterized by hypernasal speech, poor articulation, and a breathy voice. Deficits may occur in any one speech production area or any combination of areas. The primary deviant speech characteristics are attributable to muscular weakness and reduced muscle tone, which affect the speed, range, and accuracy of speech movements (Figure 7.6).

Specifically, individuals with a flaccid dysarthria will exhibit

- reduced vital capacity of the lungs and increased breaths per minute
- sluggishness of the vocal folds bilaterally or unilaterally
- incomplete glottal closure, unilaterally or bilaterally, causing breathiness of vocal quality
- reduction in syllables or words produced per breath for speech
- reduced loudness, pitch range, and stress patterns
- nasal emission and hypernasal voice quality
- weakened or no movement of the tongue, palate, and pharyngeal walls, leading to imprecise articulation

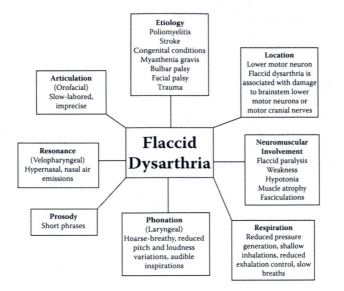

FIGURE 7.6   Characteristics of flaccid dysarthria.

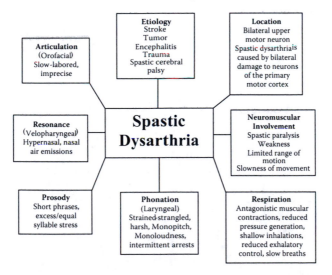

FIGURE 7.7   Areas of speech production affect by spastic dysarthria.

Spastic Dysarthria

Spastic dysarthria is caused by damage to the primary motor cortex of the brain. Its hallmarks are extremely poor articulation, a strained-strangled voice quality, and vocal low pitch. As seen in Figure 7.7, any or all areas of speech production may be impaired (and usually more than one is).

Individuals with spastic dysarthria exhibit the following speech and speech-related characteristics:

- reduced volume of inhalations and exhalations, resulting in short phrases with monotony of pitch, loudness, and stress
- a harsh, strained-strangled voice quality
- a slow rate of speech and imprecise vowel and consonant articulation attributable to the reduced speed and range of the tongue, jaw, and palate musculature
- increased pauses between syllables and words

Ataxic Dysarthria

Ataxic dysarthria is associated with damage to the cerebellum, a structure responsible for the modulation and coordination of movement when performing skilled motor behaviors (such as speech). The effects of the damage are most pronounced in the individual's articulation and prosodic patterns (see Figure 7.8), specifically:

- bursts of loudness due to poor coordination of respiration;
- imprecise and irregular breakdowns of articulation attributable to decreased speech muscle coordination;

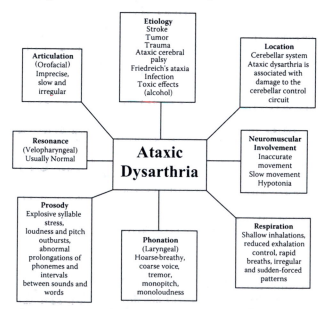

FIGURE 7.8　Characteristics of ataxic dysarthria.

- speech with a "drunken" quality that includes frequent stumbling over words, slurring, and slowed rate; and
- monotony of pitch, loudness, and stress.

Hyperkinetic Dysarthria

Hyperkinetic dysarthria is associated with diseases that affect the basal ganglia, a structure strongly involved with motor control. This condition is characterized by involuntary muscle movements that affect speech (Duffy, 2005). Such movements include lip smacking; sticking the tongue out and then back in; opening and closing the jaw; quick, jerky motions; and rhythmic, repetitive movements. Although the effects of hyperkinetic dysarthria may be seen throughout the process of speech production (see Figure 7.9), the most prominent effect is on prosody. Specific deficits may include

- imprecise articulation,
- abnormal vocal quality,
- sudden stops in voicing,
- variations in rate within an utterance,
- monoloudness and monopitch,
- alternating loudness,

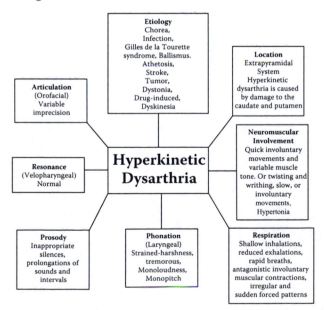

FIGURE 7.9   Characteristics of hyperkinetic dysarthria.

- abnormal pausing,
- reduced, equal, or excess stress, and
- hypernasality.

Hypokinetic Dysarthria

Hypokinetic dysarthria, like the hyperkinetic variety, is caused by damage to the basal ganglia. Parkinson's is the disease most closely associated with hypokinetic dysarthria (but not the only one). The most prominent effects of this dysarthria are heard in the client's voice, articulation, and prosody (see Figure 7.10). The deviant speech characteristics are attributable to the effects of **rigidity** and to the inconsistent (sometimes slow, sometimes quick) repetitive movements. Individuals with hypokinetic dysarthria produce speech characterized by weak vocal quality, frequent hesitations, and brief, rapid bursts of speech.

Mixed Dysarthrias

Mixed dysarthrias occur when there are compounded neurological events (e.g., multiple strokes or the co-occurrence of two neurological diseases). Amyotrophic lateral sclerosis (ALS or Lou Gehrig's disease) is often associated with mixed forms of dysarthria (see Figure 7.11).

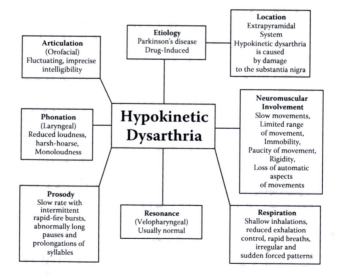

FIGURE 7.10   Characteristics of hypokinetic dysarthria.

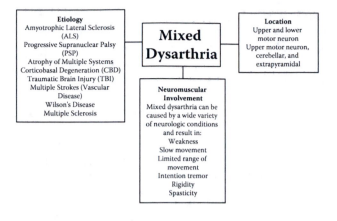

FIGURE 7.11   Characteristics of mixed dysarthria.

☐ Vocabulary

acalculia—inability to do math

acquired disorder—disorder that occurs, most often, after normal speech and language skills have been developed fully

affect—a set of observable manifestations of a subjectively experienced emotion (*Merriam-Webster*, 2009)

agraphia—inability to write

amnesia—loss of memory

anosognosia—ignorance of the presence of disease

aphasia—partial or total loss of language due to brain injury

aspiration pneumonia—pneumonia infection that develops as a result of foreign material entering the airway

aspiration—the inhalation of food or fluid into the lungs

auditory comprehension—the ability to decode and understand stimuli that one hears

circumlocution—talking around the subject

confrontation naming—providing the name of an item in response to a question, such as "What is this?"

dementia—significant loss of intellectual abilities, such as memory capacity, severe enough to interfere with social or occupational functioning (MedicineNet.com, 2009)

developmental disorder—disorder in which the individual has not developed, during normal acquisition periods, the speech and language skills expected

diplopia—double vision

dysphagia—disorder of swallowing

echolalia—the parroting of words or phrases

emotional lability—a neurologic disorder that causes sudden and unpredictable episodes of high emotion (e.g., crying or laughing)

expressive aphasia—difficulty in conveying thoughts through speech or writing (as opposed to *receptive aphasia*, a difficulty understanding spoken or written language). The patient knows what he or she wants to say but cannot find the words needed (NINDS, 2009b).

finger agnosia—inability to recognize fingers

fluent aphasia—aphasias characterized by word substitutions, neologisms, and often verbose verbal output (Owens, Metz, & Haas, 2007)

functional disorder—disorder in which the structure, and therefore function, of the oral mechanism is impaired

hemianopsia—impairment of the same half of the visual field in each eye

hemiparesis—weakness on one-half of the body

hemiplegia—paralysis of one-half of the body

hypoxia—loss of oxygen to the brain tissue that can lead to brain damage

intracranial hematoma—a collection or pool of blood within the brain resulting from a hemorrhage

nonfluent aphasia—aphasia characterized by slow, labored speech and struggle to retrieve words and form sentences (Owens et al., 2007)

premorbid—occurring or existing before the occurrence of the condition

prosodic features—intonation, stress, and rhythm in speech

receptive aphasia—difficulty understanding spoken or written language. The patient hears the voice or sees the print but cannot make sense of the words (NINDS, 2009b)

rigidity—condition in which both the active and passive movements of a joint are restricted because of the abnormal, involuntary contraction of one or more muscles (About.com:Stroke, 2009)

transient ischemic attack—a neurological event caused by a temporary lack of adequate blood and oxygen (ischemia) to the brain and in which stroke-like symptoms regress within a short period of time

word fluency tasks—naming as many items as possible in a category or providing as many words as possible beginning with a specific letter

☐ Recommended Reading

In 2002, the National Council on Aging (NCOA) provided an update to its continuing study, American Perceptions of Aging in the 21st Century: The NCOA's Continuing Study of the Myths and Realities of Aging™. In that update, the NCOA provided information on the myths and realities of aging. You may think you know what *old* means, but wait until you reach the age that you thought was old. Suddenly, it does not seem as old anymore.

CHAPTER

Speech Sound Disorders

Cynthia Core and Dale F. Williams

Cynthia Core, PhD, is an assistant professor in the Department of Speech and Hearing Science at The George Washington University. Dr. Core's research focuses on the development of speech and language skills in young bilingual children and young children with cochlear implants. Dr. Core is a licensed SLP and a member of the American Speech-Language Hearing Association and the International Association for the Study of Child Language.

Read this story carefully. When the second author's son was learning to talk, he pointed to each and every round object and said, "Baw" (meaning ball). On one occasion, Dad answered, "Is that a baw?" (yes, he said—and meant—*baw*). Son excitedly replied, "No, baw. *Baw*!"

So, what was that all about? Several things actually:

1. Despite not being able to produce it, he knew the correct pronunciation of the word.
2. He could not hear his own mispronunciation.
3. He thought Dad was a dope (or at least someone unable to correctly say the word *ball*).

In defense of Dad, some kids with sound production errors do not know how the sound should be said. Others do hear their errors but are unable to correct them. And, more to the point of this chapter, there are those for whom such errors persist beyond the early stages of speech.

Speech sound disorders (SSDs) include both articulation and phonological disorders and are characterized by errors in sound production. A disorder exists when a child's sound productions differ from other children of the same age and negatively affect the child's ability to communicate. A SSD may be severe enough to greatly reduce a child's **intelligibility**, or it may only affect a few sounds and not be all that noticeable. Although SSDs are most often associated with children, they can also occur in adults.

SSDs have traditionally been categorized as **disorders of articulation** or **disorders of phonology**, although the distinction between the two is not easily made. When the disorder is characterized by the way a sound is produced, it is categorized as an articulation disorder. When the disorder affects the production *and* an individual's ability to store or represent speech sounds in the mental lexicon, the disorder is categorized as a phonological disorder. That is, phonological disorders are believed to be more linguistic in nature, whereas articulation disorders are viewed as motoric. However, the two types are not mutually exclusive, and these disorders can coexist in a child. For example, a child with cleft lip or palate may have articulation difficulties due to the structural changes of his or her oral mechanism. The same child may also use **phonological processes** (e.g., deleting all final consonants), indicative of a phonological disorder. Since articulation and phonological disorders are not always distinguishable, and since they can both affect an individual child, the current preferred term for disorders of speech production is *speech sound disorders*.

Previous terms for speech disorders with unknown origin (that is, no identified physiological or neurological basis) have included *articulation delay, articulation disorder, phonological delay, phonological disorder, phonological impairment, functional phonological disorder, speech disorder, speech impairment,* and *speech delay*. The term *speech sound disorders* (SSDs) encompasses articulation disorders, phonological disorders, and mixed articulation and phonological disorders, regardless of etiology. It also includes **childhood apraxia of speech (CAS)**, a child motor speech disorder. This chapter addresses mainly child speech disorders of unknown origin.

SSDs are not sound errors due to dialect differences (e.g., think /r/ in New England accents), foreign accent (e.g., pronunciation of English "thing" as "sing" by native speakers of French), or common errors of speech development produced by young children. There is no clinical marker for SSDs; they must be described and diagnosed with respect to a child's age and developmental level (see Table 8.1). For example, my infant son substituting "baw" for "ball" does not constitute a disorder. If he is still doing it when he is 16, that is a different story.

☐ Etiology

SSDs can result from a variety of known origins, such as Down syndrome, autism, craniofacial dysmorphologies, and fragile X syndrome. SSDs can

TABLE 8.1 Ages of Sound Acquisition

Early-Developing Sounds[a]

Phoneme	Age of Acquisition (years:months)[b]	GFTA-2 Standardized Sample Ages[d]
/p/	3:0	2:0 to 3:0
/b/	3:0	2:0 to 3:0
/d/	3:0 to 3:6	2:0 to 3:0
/m/	3:0	2:0
/n/	3:0 to 3:6	2:0 to 3:0
/j/	4:0 to 5:0	5:0
/w/	3:0	3:0
/h/	3:0	2:0

Middle-Developing Sounds[a]

Phoneme	Age of Acquisition (years:months)[b]	GFTA-2 Standardized Sample Ages[c]
/t/	3:6 to 4:0	3:0
/k/	3:6	3:0
/g/	3:6 to 4:0	3:0
/f/	3:6 to 5:6	3:0 to 4:0
/v/	5:6	5:0 to 6:0
/tʃ/	6:0 to 7:0	5:0
/dʒ/	6:0 to 7:0	5:0
/ŋ/	2:0 to 6:03	3:0 to 5:0

Late-Developing Sounds[a]

Phoneme	Age of Acquisition (years:months)[b]	GFTA-2 Standardized Sample Ages[c]
/θ/	6:0 to 8:0	7:0 to 8:0
/ð/	4:6 to 7:0	7:0
/s/	7:0 to 9:0	5:0
/z/	7:0 to 9:0	5:0 to 7:0
/ʃ/	6:0 to 7:0	5:0
/ʒ/	6:0 to 8:0[d]	N/A
/l/	5:0 to 7:0	5:0
/r/	8:0	5:0 to 6:0

[a] Order of acquisition (Shriberg, 1993).
[b] Age of acquisition (Smit, Hand, Freilinger, Bernthal, & Bird, 1990).
[c] Age at which 85% of Goldman-Fristoe Test of Articulation-2 (GFTA-2) standardization sample correctly produced the consonant and consonant cluster sounds,.
[d] Age of acquisition (Sander, 1972).

be associated with a general developmental delay or with specific physiological, cognitive, and neurological deficits. More commonly, however, SSDs have no known origins. These SSDs of unknown origin have also been called *functional disorders of speech*.

Recent studies suggested that genes may be responsible for SSDs, SSDs with accompanying language impairment, and SSDs and literacy difficulties such as dyslexia. Lewis et al. (2007) identified familial aggregation as a cause for SSDs and reported that there is likely more than one gene responsible for these disorders. Some genes may be responsible only for SSDs, and others may affect written and spoken language disorders (e.g., dyslexia). Smith, Pennington, Boada, and Shriberg (2005) found that SSD and reading disability are linked in at least three chromosomal regions, suggesting that one subset of genes influences both disorders.

Several researchers have suggested that SSDs have complex multifactorial etiologies involving both genetic and environmental factors (Campbell et al., 2003; Lewis et al., 2007; Shriberg et al., 2000). According to Shriberg and colleagues (2006), genetic risk factors (risk or susceptibility genes, such as *FoxP2*, for those who know their genes) can interact with environmental factors to affect overall risk for SSDs. Some risk factors for speech delay that have been studied include low maternal education, low socioeconomic status, and prolonged **otitis media with effusion (OME)** (Campbell et al., 2003; Shriberg et al., 2000). Gender would also have to be considered a risk factor, given that boys are about 1.5 times more likely than girls to present SSDs (Lewis et al., 2007).

Intermittent hearing loss as a result of otitis media is often named by speech-language pathologists (SLPs) and pediatricians as a cause for speech and language delays and disorders. However, several recent studies have shown that, although there is the aforementioned correlation for OME and SSD, there is no statistically significant causal relationship between duration of otitis media resulting in fluctuating hearing loss and speech sound production skills (Campbell et al., 2003; Paradise et al., 2000, 2001; Shriberg et al., 2000). In other words, just because they occur together, there is insufficient evidence to say one causes the other. However, such a conclusion is not convincing to everyone, given other reports of differences in **babbling** and early word forms in infants and very young children during and following episodes of fluctuating hearing loss due to OME (e.g., Mody & Schwartz, 1999; Miccio, Gallagher, Grossman, Yont, & Vernon-Feagans, 2001; Miccio, Yont, Davie, & Vernon-Feagans, 1999; Petinou, Schwartz, Gravel, & Raphael, 2001).

Childhood Apraxia of Speech (CAS) is a type of speech disorder that affects some children with SSDs. Researchers estimate that 3–5% of preschool children diagnosed with SSDs have CAS. CAS differs from other SSDs in that it is primarily a deficit of speech motor control rather than a deficit in linguistic knowledge. Children with CAS have difficulty producing sound sequences accurately and transitioning their articulators between sounds rapidly. The etiology of CAS is unknown; however, it differs from adult apraxia of speech in that it is not the result of an acquired injury or brain lesion in the motor cortex. CAS is also not caused by weakness or paralysis of the articulators. It is often accompanied by deficits in receptive and expressive language, which slows progress in intervention.

☐ Prevalence

Children with SSDs are common enough to be found on the caseloads of most school SLPs. In fact, a recent American Speech-Language-Hearing Association (ASHA) survey found that 91% of SLPs employed by schools reported treating children with phonological impairment (ASHA, 2006).

So just how common are these disorders? That is difficult to pinpoint. Estimates of SSD prevalence in children range from 3% (Winitz & Darley, 1980) to 13% (Peckham, 1973). More recently, Shriberg and colleagues (1999) used data from a large epidemiological study of specific language impairment (SLI) in kindergarteners (Tomblin et al., 1997) and also collected speech samples from some of the children. According to their estimates, the prevalence of SSDs in 6-year-old children is about 4% (3.1% for girls and 4.5% for boys).

One reason that prevalence of SSDs in children is difficult to estimate is that young children present a lot of variability in their productions of speech sounds (as well as in just about everything else). As children approach school age, their sound systems mature, and there is more consistency of sound production and in the way the sounds are organized. Children who had multiple error patterns and severe SSDs in early childhood may have only one or two residual errors by the time they are 8 or 9 years old, even without intervention. For other children with severe SSDs in early childhood, speech patterns may match their peers by 5 or 6 years of age and be considered normal for the child's age. Which children have errors that resolve with time and intervention is not yet clear.

Several conditions are **comorbid** with SSDs. Of particular interest, given the implications for academic ability, is the relationship between SSDs and language impairment. As with SSDs in general, the exact prevalence for this comorbidity has been difficult to establish, but it is clearly not uncommon. Estimates for accompanying expressive language impairment range from 32% to 62% (Lewis et al., 2006). Regarding SLI, Shriberg, Tomblin, and McSweeney (1999) reported that approximately 11–15% of 6-year-old children with persisting speech delay had SLI, and approximately 5–8% of children with persisting SLI had speech delay.

Comorbidity rates for SSDs among children who stutter are high. Blood, Ridenour, Qualls, and Hammer (2003) reported that 33.5% of 2,628 children with stuttering also had articulation disorders, and 12.7% of the children were reported to have phonological disorders.

Several studies have reported that more than half of children with SSDs also experience later academic difficulties in language, reading, and spelling (Aram & Hall, 1990; Bishop & Adams, 1990; Menyuk et al., 1991; Nathan, Stackhouse, Goulandris, & Snowling, 2004). Approximately 18% of children with isolated SSD (and no known language impairment) had reading problems in elementary school (Lewis, Freebairn, & Taylor, 2000). Reading problems affect about 75% of children with concomitant speech and language impairment (Lewis et al., 2000). SSDs can continue to affect people into adulthood, even after overt signs of the impairment have resolved, particularly if the SSD was accompanied by language impairment in childhood. Adults who received treatment for SSDs as children had poorer receptive language, reading, and spelling skills than adults who did not have a history of speech disorders (Lewis et al., 2007), and adults who had a childhood history of speech and language disorders performed more poorly than those with a history of only SSD.

☐ Phonology and Phonetics

To assess and treat SSDs effectively, an understanding of phonology and phonetics is imperative. *Phonology* is the branch of linguistic study that deals with the organization of speech sounds in a language. *Phonetics* is the study of the production of speech sounds.

Speech sounds are called *phones,* and representations of sounds that can change the meaning of a word are called *phonemes.* Phonemes are not individual sounds. Rather, they represent a larger category of sounds. Sounds are influenced by neighboring sounds and stress patterns in words, so the /t/ sounds in "top" and "kitten" are quite different. The /t/ in "top" is *aspirated,* produced with a slight puff of air (aspiration) as the sound is released. The /t/ sound most commonly used by North Americans in the word "kitten" is actually a brief pause during which vocal fold vibration stops completely. The pause in vocal fold vibration is called a *glottal stop,* and it is a common variant of /t/ in North American varieties of English. Although aspirated /t/ and the glottal stop are produced in very different ways, they both represent the sound /t/, and their occurrence is predictable by their position within a word. Most native speakers of English are not even aware that they are producing words like *kitten, curtain,* and *Martin* with a glottal stop, and many students of phonetics are quite surprised by this information.

In addition to individual speech sounds, it is important to understand the smaller components of sounds called **distinctive features**, which represent acoustic and articulatory properties of sounds. The distinctive feature paradigm allows for a unique description of each sound based on these properties. These features have been used clinically to describe patterns of sound errors and to help select treatment goals for intervention.

Understanding the phonotactic properties of a language is also part of the basic knowledge required to conduct speech assessment and to plan intervention. *Phonotactics* refers to the possible word shapes of a language, the possible sequences of sounds within a syllable or word, and the stress patterns that are possible for multisyllabic words in a given language. Word shape is the frame of consonants (C) and vowels (V) that make up a word form in a language. For example, English has complex syllable and word shapes, such as CCCVCCC in the word *sprints*, that are not found in most languages of the world.

Phonotactic knowledge allows speakers to know which sequences are possible in words of their language. In every language, there are restrictions on the environments in which sounds can occur and which sounds form possible sequences. For example, most speakers of English agree that a word beginning with /kn/ would be unusual, but that sequence is possible in Hebrew. Similarly, English words cannot start with /ng/, but Vietnamese words can.

Many sound error patterns affect syllable structure. A syllable is composed of a *nucleus*, which is a vowel or vowel-like sound; an *onset*, which is the consonant or consonants preceding the vowel; and the *coda*, consonants following the vowel in the same syllable (vowel-initial syllables have no onset as defined here). The nucleus and coda together are called the *rhyme*. In the word *sprints*, the onset is /spr/, the nucleus is the vowel /ɪ/, and the coda is /nts/. The rhyme of the word is /ɪnts/.

A sequence of consonants, such as the ones preceding and following the vowel in the word *sprints*, is called a consonant cluster. English permits two- and three-member consonant clusters in both initial and final position. English is relatively rare among languages in its variety of onset clusters beginning with /s/, such as *spot, skate, stop, smell, snake, slide, swing, string, spring, split,* and *scrape*.

The **International Phonetic Alphabet** allows for a universal system of one-to-one correspondence of symbols to speech sounds used for most of the world's languages. SLPs use phonetic transcription to transcribe what a client's speech sounds like. Using this systematic framework, information about speech sounds can easily be shared among SLPs for any language. Along with phonetic symbols, additional markers called **diacritics** are used to indicate variations of production of a sound, such as whether a sound is **dentalized**.

Speech sounds cannot be transcribed using the standard writing system (or *orthography*) of a language because there are not consistent one-to-one correspondences between sounds and symbols. For example, although English has two distinct "th" sounds (in *thing* and *that*), both sounds are represented by "th." Thus, using "th" to transcribe sound production would not allow for distinction between the two phonemes /θ/ (theta, as in "thing") and /ð/ (eth, seen in "that"). Chapter 2 includes a list of English consonant phonemes and key words for each phoneme.

Consonant sounds are organized by three primary descriptive parameters: *place* of production, *manner* of production, and *voicing*. *Place* refers to the specific articulators employed in the production of a particular phoneme or the location of the constriction in the vocal tract in production of a consonant (Small, 2005). English consonants can be produced using the lips (/p/, /b/, /m/); the lower lip and upper teeth (/f/, /v/); the tongue tip and teeth (/θ/, /ð/); and the tongue tip and the alveolar ridge (/t/, /d/, /s/, /z/, /n/, /l/). They can also be produced with the tongue and the hard palate: /ʃ/ (the first sound in "shoot"); /ʒ/ (the third in "measure"); /tʃ/ (the initial phoneme in "chop"); /dʒ/ (which begins "juice"); and /r/. Finally, some sounds utilize the back of the tongue and the soft palate: /k/, /g/, and /ŋ/ (the "ng" sound, i.e., the last sound in the word "weeping").

Manner of production refers to the way the airflow is modified in the oral/nasal cavity during speech production. English consonants can be produced as stops, fricatives, affricates, nasals, liquids, and glides. *Obstruent sounds* involve stricture in the oral cavity, and *sonorant sounds* involve a more open vocal tract with voicing. Obstruents include stops, fricatives, and affricates. Sonorants include liquids, glides, and nasals.

Stops (or *plosives*) involve a complete stricture of the oral cavity (e.g., /p/, /b/, /t/, /d/, /k/, /g/). *Fricatives* require a narrow stricture through which air flows, producing turbulent aperiodic sound waves (/f/, /v/, (/θ/, /ð/, /s/, /z/, /ʃ/, /ʒ/). *Affricates* are also known as complex segments, and they are composed of elements of stop and fricative production. The sound begins as a stop, but terminates as a fricative (/tʃ/; /dʒ/). *Nasal sounds* involve airflow through the nasal cavity (in lieu of or in addition to airflow through the oral cavity), and these sounds include /m/, /n/ and /ŋ/. *Liquid sounds* include both *lateral sounds*, such as /l/, in which air flows over one or both sides of the tongue, and **rhotic** sounds, such as /r/, which have a unique acoustic quality. *Glides* are produced with very little stricture in the oral cavity and are always voiced, such as /w/ and /j/ (the first sound in "you").

Simply describing English consonant production does not provide enough information for SLPs. Other languages use production places and manners that ours does not. For example, Bantu languages in southern Africa use clicks as speech sounds, and some speakers of French and German use a **uvular fricative** to make an /r/ sound. Typically developing

Phonology Joke

/wʌt du ju kɔl ðə stʌdi əv fʌn/ /fən ɔlədʒi/ (What do you call
the study of fun? Phon-ology.)

English-speaking children and adults with speech impairments also use
sounds that are not English phonemes. Some phonologically impaired
children, for instance, have produced consonant clusters as **bilabial trills**.

☐ Speech Development

Speech development is a process that begins before birth and culminates
with acquisition of all of the sounds of the language in question, sometime between the ages of 7 and 9. Although all of the sounds of English are
acquired by age 9, some more complex phonological rules that are related
to morphology (called *morphophonemic variations*) are realized later. For
example, stress rules for multisyllabic words are often related to prefixes
and suffixes, and these rules are learned in adolescence.

Speech development is usually divided into three main stages: prelinguistic, first words, and systematic development. Clear evidence shows that
infant speech perception and learning the sounds of their language begins
in utero (DeCasper & Spence, 1986). Prenatal maternal speech influences
newborns' perception of speech sounds. As noted in Chapter 2, infants
tend to make reflexive sounds, such as crying, hiccupping, burping, and
vocalizing on exhalation during the first several weeks of life. Although
these are not speech, the sounds are produced by the speaking mechanism, and at times, parents even respond to them as if the child were
taking a conversational turn. Around 6 to 8 weeks, children begin to make
cooing sounds when they are happy. During this stage, children begin to
laugh (around 16 weeks), and they start to string cooing sounds together
separated by a breath. The speech development between 4 and 6 months
can be described as a period of vocal play (Stark, 1986), during which children begin to experiment with their articulators, producing raspberry
sounds, squealing, growling, and laughing. Babies develop a repertoire of
consonant-like and vowel-like sounds during this period, and they begin
to use longer strings of sound combinations. After 6 months, babbling
starts to emerge, with the production of true syllables. Babies begin with
canonical or *reduplicated babbling*, producing a series of identical syllables,
such as /mama/ or /baba/. Around 8 to 10 months, babies begin using
different syllables in their babbling strings. Use of two distinct consonants

in babbling is called *variegated* or *nonreduplicated* babbling. Children begin to use more combinations of consonants and vowels during this time. They also develop the intonation, or **prosody**, of their native language. When children produce long strings of babble with prosody, they sound as though they are producing sentences of their language. These long strings are referred to as **jargon**.

At about 1 year of age, children begin to use **protowords**, or phonetically consistent forms that serve as early words. For example, a child may consistently use the syllable /ba/ to mean "bottle" or "blanket." When the child uses a form consistently to refer to an object in his or her environment, it is considered a word in the child's **lexicon**, even though it does not match the adult production of the word and may not be recognizable as the target word to most adults. Between 12 and 18 months, children produce on average about 75 different early words. These early words are usually single syllables (/ba/, /di/) or strings of reduplicated syllables /baba/. In this period of early word learning, children use a limited set of vowels and consonants (Ingram, 1989). The early sounds used by children are often the same sounds that occur in the late stages of babbling. There is some evidence that children in this single-word stage of speech and language development focus more on word learning than on individual sounds. *Phonological idioms* illustrate this hypothesis. Children may produce a word in a way that approximates the adult form early in development, then as their sound system expands, they may produce the form in a way that conforms more to their developing system and less to the adult form. The early accurate productions are called *phonological idioms*.

Around 18 months, which is about the time children start putting two words together, their need for more consistency in their sound system increases dramatically. As children's vocabularies expand rapidly, they

PHONOLOGICAL AWARENESS

Phonological awareness refers to a set of prereading skills, including rhyming, identifying, segmenting, and manipulating sounds and parts of words. It is well established that phonemic awareness skills (segmentation and manipulation of individual sounds) are necessary for learning to read and spell. Although these skills are not directly related to speech production abilities, children with SSDs often have poorer phonological awareness skills than their peers with typical speech and language and are at risk for difficulty in learning to read and spell. Gillon (2005) has established that training phonological awareness skills in young children (as young as 3 years old) can have positive and lasting effects on reading and spelling skills in children with SSDs.

need to differentiate between lexical items in their speech. The limited consonant and vowel repertoire and restricted word and syllable shapes are no longer sufficient to accommodate the demands of producing the larger vocabularies. During this period, children's productions rarely match the adult forms because all children systematically alter them. These modifications of the adult form are called **phonological processes**, and they are common to all children acquiring the same language. Many, in fact, are common across all languages. As children mature, they tend to use the processes less frequently, until eventually they no longer use them (that is, they suppress the process use). In fact, by age 3, many of the common phonological processes are no longer heard.

The following are some examples of common phonological processes.

Weak syllable deletion	banana → nana
Final consonant deletion	moon → moo
Cluster reduction	play → pay
Reduplication	water → wawa
Stopping	foot → put (i.e., the /f/ was changed to a stop sound)
Fronting	key → tee (here the first sound was made in front of where it should have been)

Some phonological processes are considered unusual or idiosyncratic, and they occur less commonly in children with typically developing speech and more frequently in children diagnosed with SSDs. However, phonological process use is not a form of speech disorder. Employment of phonological processes in early speech development is universal to all children of all languages. However, those who demonstrate persistent use (past the age at which such processes usually disappear) may have a speech impairment. Still, there is not an SSD that is characterized solely or primarily by process use.

Following the early developmental period, from about 3 to 5 years, children continue to systematically develop their phonological systems. They acquire more complex syllable and word shapes, and they use more multisyllabic words. Children in this age range gradually begin to use more phonemes from the target language, and they use fewer sound substitutions.

After age 4, only a few sounds of English remain to be acquired. Some phonological contrasts are established, such as fricatives and affricates. Although 5-year-olds may not produce some sounds, such as /s/ or /l/, as accurately as adults, the sound is still identified as matching the adult target. Smit and colleagues (1990) found that cluster production was relatively inaccurate until around age 8 for many consonant clusters. Shriberg, Kwiatkowski, and Gruber (1992) identified eight fricative, affricate, and liquid sounds that they described as late acquired. By age 9, virtually all children have mastered all of the sounds of English in all word positions, including initial and final clusters in connected speech.

PHONOLOGICAL PROCESSING

Phonological processing skills are closely related to reading abilities. This term refers to phonological awareness, phonological memory, and rapid automatic naming. Phonological memory is usually measured by nonword repetition tasks. Nonsense words are presented one at a time, and the child repeats the words. Deficits in phonological memory are associated with language and reading disabilities. The term *phonological processing* can be confusing to SLPs because it is very similar to the term that refers to speech error patterns known as *phonological processes*. In fact, the two terms refer to completely different aspects of language. Unfortunately, some SLPs incorrectly refer to SSDs as "phonological processing disorders" because a child uses phonological processes that adversely affect intelligibility.

☐ Assessment

Best practices in assessment include the use of standardized testing of sound production (as it is available and appropriate to a child's age and linguistic background), analysis of spontaneous speech samples, oral peripheral/oral motor examination, and intelligibility measures. The first of these, standardized testing, generally involves using pictures to elicit single words. That is, the child names pictures with target words such as "airplane," "bath," and "blue." The clinician **transcribes** the child's utterances or simply notes on a score sheet which speech errors—**substitutions, omissions** (Figure 8.1), **distortions**, or **additions**—were made. A standardized score is obtained by comparing the number of errors produced by a child to the number of errors produced by his or her peers. Standardized tests are usually easy to administer and score. These scores are then used to determine eligibility for speech intervention in public schools.

However, standardized testing does not always accurately identify children with speech impairment. Older children (age 8 or 9) who have only one or two residual errors may score within the normal range on a standardized test even though they have speech patterns with observable errors not expected at their age, such as a lisp or distorted production of an /r/. Other shortcomings of standardized tests are that they do not identify the severity of an error or its impact on speech. For example, standardized tests rarely use multisyllabic words or connected speech to evaluate error patterns, even though children produce more errors in those contexts than in single, monosyllabic words. In addition, such testing does not reveal the **phonetic environment** in which the errors occurred. This

What do you call a fish with no eyes?

FIGURE 8.1 Phonological awareness task that involves phoneme deletion.

can be important in that many speech sound errors are inconsistent in that they occur before or after some phonemes, but not others.

Standardized tests typically have from 30 to 60 stimulus items. This limited set of items is not sufficient to conduct a comprehensive assessment of a child's phonological system.

Most standardized articulation tests are normed on children between ages 3 and 18. For younger children, standardized testing is not feasible, primarily because the children will not comply with the examiner's requests to name or repeat stimuli. For these reasons, use of a spontaneous speech sample and an assessment of intelligibility are always recommended. By collecting (via video or audio recording) and transcribing a 100- to 250-word speech sample, a clinician can conduct a thorough phonological analysis that will enable him or her to set treatment goals. Digital video technology is recommended because it is inexpensive, has good audio quality, and provides visual information (such as placement of the articulators) that a straight audio recording does not.

Speech assessment should include an analysis of all sounds in a variety of word positions, word shapes, stress patterns, and sound production in connected speech. In addition, an examination of the structure and functions of the articulators should be conducted to determine if any physical problems, such as cleft palate, submucous cleft palate, weakness, or incoordination of articulators are affecting speech production. Assessment of hearing, receptive and expressive language, and early literacy skills is also recommended as part of a speech evaluation.

☐ Treatment

Intervention is required for 80% of children diagnosed with phonological disorders (ASHA, 1993). Given the high likelihood of subsequent academic difficulties, early intervention for SSDs and SSDs that co-occur with other conditions is critical to preventing later difficulties with reading and spelling.

As noted in Chapter 3, ASHA has been pushing for evidence-based practices. In keeping with this push, several researchers in child speech disorders have investigated the effectiveness of some phonological treatment methods (Gierut, 1998). At this point in time, none of the treatment methods investigated appears to be significantly more effective than other methods when thorough analysis of sound patterns is conducted.

Until the late 1970s, speech intervention was based on phonetic training of sound production. This approach is now known as the *traditional method*. With this method, one sound is trained at a time, first in isolation until a designated level of accuracy (generally 80% or 90%) is achieved. As the sound is produced correctly at the specified accuracy level, the sound is trained in more complex environments: syllables, words, phrases, sentences, and so on up to conversation in all settings.

By the early 1980s, a field known as clinical phonology began to influence intervention techniques. Intervention programs began to include concepts of phoneme knowledge, such as distinctive feature analysis, to determine error patterns and select treatment targets. **Minimal pair contrasts** were used to teach the errors in production that caused communication breakdowns for the listener. Phonological processes (error patterns), rather than individual sounds, were targeted in intervention.

One well-known intervention program that came out of the field of clinical phonology is the *cycles approach* developed in the 1980s (Hodson & Paden, 1991). Rather than focusing on one sound at progressive levels of language, this approach is designed to target phonological processes affecting a child's intelligibility. Treatment targets change after one or two therapy sessions, with new sounds selected based on error patterns (that is, the processes being used by the child) and the client's **stimulability** for a potential sound. A treatment cycle includes sessions that target selected error patterns. For example, if the client is deleting final consonants /n/, /m/, /d/, and /t/, this can be addressed in a session utilizing words ending in /n/. The cycles method continues to be used by clinicians, although only a few studies have been conducted on its efficacy (e.g., Gierut, 1998).

ORAL MOTOR EXERCISES

Oral motor exercises are mouth exercises that are often recommended by SLPs as part of speech intervention. They can include moving the tongue from side to side, smiling, and puckering the lips. When oral motor exercises are prescribed, SLPs indicate that they are attempting to improve oral strength and coordination of the articulators and thereby improve speech production abilities. Recently, use of oral motor exercises has come under close scrutiny. Research does not support use of these exercises to improve speech production (Guisti Braislin & Cascella, 2005; Ruscello, 2008;), and some reports indicated that using therapy time to do oral motor exercises can delay improvement in speech production (e.g., Lof, 2006). Speech intervention works best when the therapist and client work on speech sounds in the therapy setting.

Treatment for children with CAS and children with cleft lip or palate differs somewhat from treatment for children with other SSDs. CAS therapy focuses on motor learning principles and dynamic properties of speech, such as transitions from consonants to vowels and vowels to consonants. One treatment approach for CAS is *integral stimulation*, which focuses on phrases rather than sounds or words. Various levels of clinician support (saying the phrase together, providing visual cues) and prompt fading encourage the client to produce functional phrases with increased accuracy. A few studies (e.g., Strand & Debertine, 2000; Strand, Stoeckel, & Baas, 2006) have shown efficacy of this method.

Treatment for cleft lip or palate should maximize a child's use of sonorant sounds (nasals, liquids, and glides) to increase intelligibility. Although audible nasal air emission may occur when oral stops and fricatives are produced (because air rushes through the cleft and out the nose), it is important to train production and accurate placement of those sounds so that diagnostic measures for repaired surgeries will be accurate and lead to the best surgical decisions. Also, if articulatory placement is taught prior to a repair surgery, a child's speech will be more accurate postsurgery.

☐ Synopsis

SSDs are errors of sound production. They include disorders of articulation (motor production) or phonology (i.e., linguistic errors). Although the cause is often unknown, these disorders affect many children and some adults. Assessment consists of testing for sounds in error or patterns of disordered sounds. Likewise, treatment may focus on individual sounds or on features common to numerous sound errors.

☐ Vocabulary

addition—the insertion of an extra phoneme in the production of a word, usually used in reference to disordered speech (Small, 2005)

babbling—prelinguistic vocalizations typically occurring during the second 6 months of life characterized by repetition of syllables and intonational patterns

bilabial trill—vibrating the closed lips by blowing out air (making the sound of a raspberry)

childhood apraxia of speech (CAS)—lack of motor control of the oral mechanism for speech production that is not attributable to other problems of muscular control (Bauman-Waengler, 2004)

comorbid—two or more conditions occurring together

cooing—production of vowel-like sounds, often in isolation

dentalization—production of an alveolar phoneme as linguadental, that is, with the tongue tip more forward than normal (Small, 2005)

diacritics (diacritical markings)—marks added to sound transcription symbols to give them a particular phonetic value (Bauman-Waengler, 2004)

disorders of articulation (or articulation disorder)—difficulties with the motor production aspects of speech

disorders of phonology (phonological disorder)—a mental operation that applies in speech to substitute for a class of sounds or sound sequences presenting a common difficulty to the speech capacity of the individual (Stampe, 1979)

distinctive features—a subphonemic property used in the classification of the sounds of the world's languages (e.g., voicing, consonantal, vocalic, etc.) (Small, 2005)

distortion—a characteristic of disordered speech involving the production of an allophone of an intended phoneme. A "lisp," or dentalized production of /s/, would be an example of a distortion error (Small, 2005)

intelligibility—the degree to which others understand one's speech

International Phonetic Alphabet (IPA)—an alphabet used to represent the sounds of the world's languages; created to promote a universal method of phonetic transcription (Small, 2005)

jargon—verbal behavior that contains a variety of syllables that are inflected in a manner approximating meaningful connected speech (Nicolosi et al., 1989)

lexicon—an individual's personal dictionary of words and meanings

minimal pairs (contrast)—two linguistic units that differ on a single distinctive feature or constituent (as voice in the initial consonants of *bat* and *pat*) (*Merriam-Webster*, 2008)

omission—the deletion of a phoneme in a word (Small, 2005)

otitis media with effusion (OME)—fluid in the middle ear in the absence of an acute ear infection

phonetic environment—the phones surrounding (i.e., preceding and following) the sound in question

phonological processes—simplifications used by children not capable of producing adult speech patterns (Small, 2005)

prosody—the ability to utilize elements such as stress, pitch, timing, and loudness to impart meaning

protowords—vocalizations used consistently by a child in particular contexts but without a recognizable adult model (Bauman-Waengler, 2004)

rhotic—/r/-like sounds, such as /r/ or the vowel in "sure"

stimulability—the ability to produce a sound when given oral and visual modeling

substitution—the replacement of one phoneme for another

transcribe—to represent speech sounds with phonetic symbols

uvular fricative—made when the back of the tongue is raised towards the uvula, or back of the soft palate, forming a narrow passage. The uvular fricative is the most common pronunciation of /r/ in German (Hall, 1993)

☐ Discussion Questions

1. SSDs often have no known cause and no universal cure and are manifested differently in different speakers. In other words, they share many of the characteristics of stuttering (noted in Chapter 9). Why do you suppose SSDs are never considered to be as mysterious as stuttering is?
2. A coworker asks you the difference between articulation and phonology. How do you answer in layperson's terms?
3. Given how surrounding sounds affect some speech sound errors, how would an SLP discover all possible SSDs in a child's speech?
4. Taking into account all of the factors involved in SSDs, is it likely that one universal treatment will ever be found? Why or why not?

☐ Recommended Reading

Bauman-Waengler, J. (2004). *Articulatory and phonological impairments: A clinical focus*. Boston: Pearson.

This text covers everything from basic concepts to theoretical perspectives. It also includes useful clinical examples.

Small, L. H. (2005). *Fundamentals of phonetics: A practical guide for students*. Boston: Pearson/Allyn & Bacon.

For those interested in learning more about phonetic transcription, this is the book for you. Transcribing details are included, as are exercises to apply them.

Williams, A. L., McLeod, S., & McCauley, R. J. (Eds). (2010). *Interventions for speech sound disorders in children*. Baltimore: Brookes.

A complete and relevant therapy guide.

Fluency Disorders

You are on campus. Someone walks up to and says, "Please t-t-t-tell me how to get to registration."

Is that person **stuttering**?

What about these people?

- "Please tell me how to get to rrrrrrregistration."
- "Please … tell … uh … tell me how to … um … get to … uh, registration."
- "Please tell me, uh, y'know, how, y'know, how to get to, um, y'know, to, uh, registration."
- "I need to get to, well, the, um, place where, well, to register, uh uh, classes, gonna go, not, uh, sure where."

Are they stuttering?

And why is registration so hard to find?

In each case, the correct answer to whether the person is stuttering is a resounding, "Who knows?" Moreover, here is why you do not know:

1. There's more to stuttering than disrupted flow of speech.
2. Not all fluency disorders are stuttering, even though many can look like it.

Let us begin with reason one. Your average guy off the street would likely define stuttering as speech with interruptions. And technically, this is not far off the mark. Stuttering is characterized by three types of interruptions, or **disfluencies**:

- **Part-word repetitions** (buh-buh-buh-ball)
- **Prolongations** (mmmmmine)
- **Hesitations** (My name is ... Billy)

Yet, stuttering is far more than simple breaks of speech fluency. For one thing, stuttering almost always (i.e., unless it started yesterday) includes **secondary characteristics** (also known as associated behaviors) as well. These are behaviors designed to quickly escape from stuttering (for example, tensing facial muscles to push a word out) or to avoid it altogether (using an easier word in place of a feared one) (Figure 9.1). Examples of secondary characteristics include eye blinks, arm movements, foot tapping, verbalizations, and every other motor or verbal behavior known to humankind. What I mean is that I am convinced that any type of movement or vocalization you can think of has been used as a secondary behavior by some stuttering individual somewhere, sometime.

Along with those characteristics that are included in most any definition of stuttering—part-word repetitions, prolongations, hesitations, and secondary behaviors—there are trends that we see with many, but not all, people who stutter. Examples include

- preschool age of onset,
- episodic development (that is, it comes and goes),
- a tendency to show **adaptation**,
- negative **speech-associated attitudes**,
- reduced stuttering under certain conditions, including whispering, singing, speaking alone, choral speech, and conversing in noisy settings.

Such characteristics and trends are important not only to the definition of stuttering but also to its diagnosis. For example, say a client presents part-word repetitions that began around the age of 4 and displays avoidance of speaking situations, speech-related fears, and total fluency when speaking

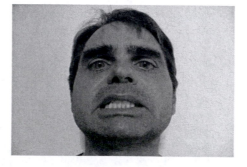

FIGURE 9.1 Escape behavior of facial tension.

in unison. In such a scenario, much evidence has been accumulated that suggests that the client fits the general profile associated with stuttering.

Evaluation tasks, then, are based on what we know about stuttering, and fortunately, we have learned much over the years. Unfortunately, despite decades of research, there remain some pieces of information that elude us—the cause, for example, and the cure.

Smaller data pieces are missing as well, as the following statements indicate:

- We do know that some kids stop stuttering, but we do not know why, we are not clear on how many and cannot predict which ones will.
- We know of treatments that are effective with small children. We just do not understand *why* they are.
- We have designed various therapies that have benefited a lot of adults, but none that helps everyone or that cures anyone. Moreover, we are not yet certain how to match client and treatment.

In a nutshell, then, other than not knowing much about the cause, development, or management, we are in good shape. For instance, we know some things that *are not* true, even though some people think they are. Read the following four statements and choose the one that has not been offered up as an actual explanation of some aspect of stuttering:

1. Stuttering is caused by tickling.
2. People who stutter are descendents of the lost continent of Atlantis.
3. Stuttering can be cured by talking with a mouth full of pebbles.
4. Exercise is the best treatment for stuttering as it relaxes the muscles of respiration and voicing.

I only made up one of these. Can you guess which? The rest, none of which are any less sensible than mine, are all beliefs people have actually held.

Really.

(I made up number 4.)

In addition to the ridiculous statements already offered, there are beliefs about stuttering that I consider equally wrong, but enough people have wondered about them over the years that they deserve some explanation.

☐ Incorrect Beliefs

Parents Cause Stuttering

Despite the well-known and influential (and now outdated) semantogenic (also known as diagnosogenic) theory that states, in effect, that "stuttering begins not in the mouth of the child, but in the ear of the parent" (Johnson, as cited in Williams, 1992), no evidence exists that parents cause stuttering. All this statement serves to do is increase parents' guilt when their children do develop the disorder.

Stuttering Is Simple

The search for a simple solution has led to other misguided theories as well. As with parental causes, there is little evidence that stuttering originates from any overt physical problem (e.g., an immobile tongue), by the mouth moving faster than the brain, or even by psychological factors (more on that in this chapter). While the exact cause is, as noted, unknown, current research indicates that stuttering results from a complex interaction of multiple factors—genetic, linguistic, neuromotor, environmental, and others. In other words, it is anything but simple.

People Who Stutter Are Jittery Wallflowers

In 1970, Yairi and Williams determined that speech-language therapists identified children who stutter as anxious, nervous, shy, quiet, and withdrawn, among other comparable traits. Subsequent studies of speech and language professionals have yielded similar results (Cooper & Cooper, 1985; Woods & Williams, 1976). Moreover, people who stutter also have been stereotyped in this manner by the general public (Craig, Tran, & Craig, 2003; Silverman & Paynter, 1990); employers (Hurst & Cooper, 1983a); vocational rehabilitation counselors (Hurst & Cooper, 1983b); teachers (Yeakle & Cooper, 1986); school administrators (Kiser et al. 1994; Lass et al. 1994); college professors (Dorsey & Guenther, 2000); nurses (Silverman & Bongey, 1997); and pediatricians (Yairi & Carrico, 1992).

Different researchers have speculated on the existence of this "stutterer stereotype" (White & Collins, 1984). Their conjecture includes the ideas that:

- listeners react to the high anxiety of the stuttering moment, then generalize that the speaker is always anxious (Woods & Williams, 1976), and
- all people experience anxiety and tend to withdraw when they are disfluent; thus, people overtly and abnormally disfluent are often seen as perpetually anxious and withdrawn (White & Collins, 1984).

Perhaps a more sensible speculation for the stutterer stereotype emerges from the research on attitudes toward speech. From an early age (somewhere around 7 years), people who stutter present increased speech-associated anxiety in comparison to nonstutterers (DeNil & Brutten, 1987). This anxiety continues to grow with age, as speech comes to increasingly represent failure.

Given their negative experience histories with speech, it makes sense that stuttering individuals are, overall, less likely to be verbally outspoken or serve as the storytellers within their peer groups. From this, it is an easy overgeneralization to assume that similar traits exist in nonspeech situations. Based on current knowledge, it is also incorrect. The lawyer who stutters will not negotiate less aggressively than fluent opposing counsel. A teacher may well be a strict disciplinarian, even if he or she stutters. Stuttering athletes are as apt to battle to the finish as their nonstuttering opponents.

Everybody Stutters Sometimes

Yes, everybody is disfluent at times, but this does not mean they stutter. Again, stuttering is defined by the part-word repetitions, prolongations, and hesitations. Everyday speech, on the other hand, is characterized by such disfluencies as interjections ("I, *um*, want to, *you know*, go along"); revisions ("I have, I want to go"); incomplete phrases ("I want—and then—"); and broken words ("I *w-[pause]-ant* to go") (Alvares & Williams, 1995). These momentary bobbles do not call attention to themselves the way that stuttering does. In fact, listeners are so accustomed to them that they rarely even notice their occurrence. Moreover, people do not attempt to hide or escape from these disfluencies, another important distinction.

Related to the belief that all speech breaks are stuttering is the claim some people make that they "used to stutter" or "stutter themselves sometimes." These folks either do not know what stuttering is or they are feeding their listeners self-serving drivel (as in "Look what I overcame"). The truth is that someone who "stutters sometimes" can no better identify with true stuttering than someone who sings in the shower can relate to being Mick Jagger.

Sometimes articles about stuttering perpetuate the idea that all children stutter while developing speech (e.g., Bender & Small, 1994). Stuttering is, by definition, a communication disorder and therefore not part of normal development (Alvares & Williams, 1995). While it is true that young children typically present numerous disfluencies, normally developing kids display part-word repetitions, prolongations, and hesitations on a comparatively infrequent basis.

All Abnormal Fluency Is Stuttering

Stuttering is a big fish in a small pond. It is the fluency disorder most frequently treated by speech-language pathologists (SLPs) (and researched by PhDs). Yet, among all communication disorders, it is takes up a relatively small percentage of cases. Among the population as a whole, it has a **prevalence** of just 1%.

Although it is the biggest fish in the fluency pond, it is not the only one. There are additional disorders of fluency, some of which can look like stuttering, but vary in terms of onset, development, and symptoms (both overt and secondary).

Neurogenic dysfluency, sometimes called *acquired stuttering*, is disordered fluency that results from strokes, head injuries, or neurological disease. Characteristics of neurogenic dysfluency vary with the extent and location of the brain damage. Clinical reports have generally noted few secondary behaviors, little concern about specific words and situations, and less improvement under conditions that enhance fluency for developmental stutters (singing, choral reading, and such) (Ringo & Dietrich, 1995). Onset of neurogenic dysfluency is typically sudden, further differentiating this condition from stuttering.

Psychogenic dysfluency can also happen overnight, but in these cases, the client does not present any neurological damage. Although few examples of this condition exist in published literature, in general it appears that psychogenic dysfluency can be quite severe and occur under all speaking conditions, even miming speech (Deal, 1980). The good news is that it tends to respond quickly to treatment.

Another recognizable fluency disorder is **cluttering**. As are many other fluency disorders, cluttering is difficult to characterize. In terms of speech production, cluttering individuals often present a rapid, dysrhythmic, and unorganized speech pattern that is not easily understood (Daly, 1993). Words may be mispronounced and entire syllables omitted or repeated. These speech characteristics are usually accompanied by an impaired ability to formulate language (Daly, 1993) and often by poor social skills, improved speech under stress, and a complete lack of awareness on the part of the client that his or her speech sounds any different (among other associated deficits).

Stuttering Is Psychological

Another common misconception about stuttering is that it is a psychological condition. This myth is partly the result of **repressed needs theories**, a collection of old suppositions suggesting that people stutter to satisfy unresolved oral-erotic needs of childhood (Coriat, 1928) or because they are fixated at the anal-sadistic level (Fenichel, 1945). Stuttering is thus viewed as a pleasing oral experience or as symbolic diarrhea and constipation, depending on which end of the digestive tract one chooses to compare to a speech production disorder. Such theories are unsupported

(Bloodstein, 1993) and no longer widely believed, clear attempts to search where the light is better.[1] Nevertheless, repressed needs hypotheses do arise from time to time (mostly in casual conversation or pop culture), indicating that some people are having trouble letting go of them. The harm is in the perception of stuttering as an emotional disorder, cured, presumably, by fulfillment of basic needs. It is worth noting that attempts to eliminate stuttering via emotional counseling have not been particularly effective (Bloodstein, 1981).

Related to repressed needs theories is the idea that stuttering results from some emotional occurrence in childhood. Incidents ranging from changing schools to childhood discipline have been offered as causes. In truth, there is little to support the notion that stuttering arises suddenly from one notable event. Again, the onset of developmental stuttering is gradual (Starkweather, 1987).

This is not to say that significant events cannot further the development of stuttering. But, that is very different from attributing one as the cause. Research (e.g., Smith & Kelly, 1997; Wall & Myers, 1995) suggests that certain children are biologically susceptible to stuttering. Such susceptibility, however, requires an environmental agent for manifestation, and these agents have not been isolated. Therefore, even if it could be determined that a child's stuttering began right after Dad yelled at him for slam dunking the basketball into the toilet, this does not place the blame squarely on the child's father. If the child was that predisposed, it is almost a certainty that if the punishment had not brought it out (if indeed it even did), something else would have.

Of course, none of the evidence against sudden onset will stop people from asking an individual what happened to trigger his or her stuttering. The answer to this question is nobody knows. The answer to what they are really asking is that the stuttering is nobody's fault.

The other side of the psychological continuum from repressed needs includes the idea that those who stutter are experiencing a sort of mental block, similar to the infielder who can no longer throw the ball to first base. In fact, many people who stutter have voiced this opinion. Usually, it is phrased something like this: "I can speak fluently when I'm alone. In other situations too. That proves that I am capable of talking without stuttering. The fact that I don't do it everywhere shows that it's all in my head."

Actually, this *proves* and *shows* nothing, other than stuttering is variable across situations. It is just as easy to attribute this phenomenon to a physical difference as to a psychological one. Within the human brain, many neural sites (hundreds actually) are involved in speech. The extent to which one site is involved in a given speech output, or whether it is at all, depends on the circumstances surrounding the speech—phrasing, emotions, body activity, and numerous others (Webster, 1999). Thus, if stuttering is the result of a small neurological deficit, one would expect it to be situational.

☐ Controversies

In addition to what we know and what we clearly do not, there are many areas of controversy. The following are two that have been kicked around in the research literature for years.

Children Who Stutter Eventually Stop

Many believe that, generally speaking, stuttering in children is nothing to worry about because it eventually goes away on its own. This idea is based on investigations of spontaneous recovery in children. However, the actual rate of spontaneous recovery is unclear (Curlee &Yairi, 1997; Ramig, 1993). Moreover, for those older than preschool age, complete cessation of stuttering is rare (Bloodstein, 1981).

There Is a Best Treatment Option

The topic of treatment includes disagreements about both preschoolers and those older. These disagreements center on, respectively, indirect versus direct therapy and fluency shaping versus stuttering modification. We begin with the former.

Indirect Therapy

While there are various forms and definitions of **indirect therapy** (e.g., Hegde & Davis, 1999; Roth & Worthington, 2001; Yaruss & Quesal, 2001), for the purposes of this discussion, I define it simply as the implementation of therapy without any feedback from the therapist. In essence, what this means is that intervention is based primarily on **modeling** and **environmental changes**. In many cases, parents are trained to (1) utilize a speech model that is fluency enhancing (in the hope that the child picks up on it and begins using it also) and (2) effect subtle changes in the child's day-to-day life that make the experience of communication easier.

The speaking model conducive to fluency involves decreasing both the loudness and the rate of speech. The latter is controlled not by slowing the movement of the articulators (and thus sounding like a robot), but by adding pauses (Guitar & Conture, 2006; Williams & Williams, 2000).

The resulting rate should still sound natural; it is just on the slower end of the normal range. Television's Mr. Rogers is often used as an example. The intent is to let the child know that speech need not be rushed but can instead be done in a relaxed and deliberate manner.

This idea of making communication comfortable is also the basis of the aforementioned environmental changes. Examples of such changes include the following:

- Allowing the child plenty of time to respond.
- Stressing turn taking in speech and other activities.
- Being a patient listener who responds in a calm, unemotional manner.
- Asking yes/no questions or at least those that can be answered with relatively few words.
- Asking only one question at a time.
- Encouraging slow and thoughtful answers.
- Paying attention to the content of the child's speech rather than to the presentation.
- Rephrasing disfluent utterances prior to responding to them as a means of showing the child that the content of the message is important and was received.
- Occasionally modeling a dysfluency to demonstrate that speech need not be perfect in its presentation.

Making communication a relaxed activity keeps the disfluent child from rushing, encouraging instead the production of speech at a manageable pace. As this is a goal of indirect therapy, there are also certain actions that parents are warned to avoid whenever possible, such as interrupting and finishing the child's sentences. Such behaviors, no matter how well intentioned, rush the child, forcing him or her to speak in a manner that is difficult for any preschooler, let alone one susceptible to stuttering.

Many SLPs like to begin stuttering therapy with this sort of an indirect approach. A justification for using it is the concern that small children often do not have the **metalinguistic skills** necessary to understand instruction related to slowing or relaxing speech (McKeehan & Child, 1990). Another is that it works. That is, based on treatment guides (e.g., McKeehan & Child, 1990) and at least one review of case reports (Williams, 1999), indirect therapy has helped many preschool children eliminate stuttering.

Direct Therapy

Direct therapy includes many of the same aspects as indirect therapy. For example, parent participation and environmental changes will almost surely be components of the treatment plan. Unlike with indirect therapy, however, parents may be able to address their child's speech in more overt ways. This can take the form of reinforcing relaxed speech (McKeehan & Child, 1990) or reinforcing fluent speech (Onslow, Packman, & Harrison, 2003).

Some clinicians use direct therapy right from the start, noting that no evidence exists that indirect therapy is any more effective. Other SLPs use both approaches, selecting the one they use at the beginning based on such factors as the following:

- Client age—The window of opportunity for eliminating stuttering does not stay open forever. If the child is an older preschooler (e.g., close to 6 years of age), this window may be a narrow opening.
- Secondary behaviors—Their presence indicates that awareness and concern about speech are high (thus nullifying the justifications for using an indirect approach).
- Previous therapy—Perhaps an indirect approach was already attempted, and the client did not respond to it.

Clearly, the reasons and rationale for using direct therapy are varied, and the same can be said for the methods used. The main goal, however, is always the same: the reduction of stuttering-like disfluencies.

Fluency Shaping Versus Stuttering Modification

For clients school age and older, stuttering involves more than the occasional breaks of speech seen with preschoolers. There are also fears, frustrations, anxieties, and all the other leeches lying in wait beneath the surface. In the face of such formidable foes, it follows that treatment must somehow address both the speech and nonspeech components of stuttering.

In general, stuttering therapies for these clients can be divided into two categories (Keys & Ruder, 1992). The first of these is **fluency shaping**. The idea behind this approach is that, using the appropriate physiological techniques (proper breathing, gentle initiation of voicing, light contact of the articulators, etc.), speech can be stutter free. In other words, if a person learns to speak in a fluency-enhancing manner, almost by definition disfluency will disappear. If this sounds familiar, it should. The aforementioned approaches for preschool children come from a fluency-shaping perspective.

The justifications for this overall goal of enhancing fluency (that is, decreasing stuttering) include the beliefs that (1) this is what most clients really want from therapy (Schwartz, 1999; Shames & Florence, 1980; Shenker, Kully, & Meltzer, 1998), and (2) stuttering involves learned behaviors that can be unlearned (Siegel & Gold, 1999) and replaced by those more conducive to fluency. Furthermore, proponents can point to published evidence of the effectiveness of such techniques, even with adults (Andrews, Guitar, & Howie, 1980; Davidow, Crowe, & Bothe, 2004). Despite these reports of success, however, there are concerns about fluency-shaping approaches. Some (e.g., Ramig & Dodge, 2005) maintain that the learned therapy targets will not hold up in stressful situations. In addition, many clients report that the techniques result in speech that is limiting (or "robotic") or requires too much concentration (Conture, 1996; Kalinowski, Noble, Armson, & Stuart, 1994; Manning, 2001; Starkweather & Givens-Ackerman, 1997; Yaruss et al., 2002). They would rather take their chances with stuttering.

On the other end of the philosophical spectrum is **stuttering modification**, an approach based in large part on managing (as opposed to eliminating) stuttering while directly addressing the associated features (the secondary behaviors and negative emotions that develop with stuttering). Williams and Dugan (2002, p. 188) phrased their modification goals as "stuttering in a way you can manage," "talking without tricks or avoidances," and "taking charge of the stuttering, rather than letting it continue to run your life." The major goal of therapy was expressed as "saying whatever you want to say, whenever you want to say it, even if you sometimes stutter." These types of goals do not stress (or, for that matter, even mention) fluency, a drawback for some (Ryan, 2003; Shenker et al., 1998), but an omission that is quite intentional. Stuttering modification advocates assert that, because stuttering is not curable (Conture, 2001), it is best managed in a way that lifts the shame, embarrassment, and other barriers to effective communication. If clients are going to speak, the reasoning goes, they are going to stutter, and since they are going to stutter, they may as well confront this fact and assume some control over *how* they stutter. Thus, the hard and tense disfluencies characteristic of stuttering are replaced by easy repetitions and sound prolongations.

Recent survey data (McClure & Yaruss, 2003) lend support to advocates of this approach, indicating client satisfaction with common stuttering modification components such as changing speech-associated attitudes and, to a lesser extent, modifying disfluencies. Furthermore, stuttering may well decrease with the shedding of the fears associated with it (Sheehan, Williams, & Dugan, 2001; Van Riper, 1973). Where fluency-shaping therapists attempt to rid clients of emotional baggage by decreasing the stuttering, those administering stuttering modification try to do the opposite.

Despite the outward philosophical differences between the two approaches, both can be effectively merged into the same treatment plan (Dietrich, 2000; Gregory, 1991; Guitar, 1998; Latulas, Tetnowski, & Bathel, 2003; Ramig & Dodge, 2004). In fact, the fluency-shaping and stuttering modification camps are both spreading out so far from their bases that there is nearly as much overlap as there is segregation. For example, fluency-shaping techniques are now often part of "integrated" approaches that include goals addressing emotions and associated behaviors (Cooper, 1987; Dietrich, 2000;

THE CYCLE OF FEMALES TO IRONY

My downward slide started because of girls. I blame them to this day.

I was in high school, convinced that I was the only person in the known universe who stuttered. Unfortunately, I was equally convinced that it was time for me to date. First, however, I had to overcome some complications. For one, girls frightened me. Compounding this fear was the fact that, as someone who stuttered, I was afraid of placing telephone calls. Asking girls out over the phone was a terror beyond my comprehension.

All the other guys on the basketball team had girlfriends, based on locker room discussions (and we all know how honest those are). A few even paid attention to them. As I dwelled on these developments, a self-induced pressure began to build until it eventually outweighed my fear of girls. Even with this increase in courage, however, there was still that telephone thing.

My solution was to script calls. Reading my part of the conversation, I felt, would distract me from stuttering. I practiced with a tape recorder and found that when I played back my lines, they sounded ridiculous. This I resolved by scripting only the opening remarks, then conversing normally.

"Hello Debbie," I would say. "This is Blaise. I was just sitting here reading the paper and noticed that *Monty Python and the Holy Grail* is playing at the Dollar Theater, and I remembered that you liked Monty Python, and so I was just wondering if you'd be up for going to see it."

(Ok, it sounds dorky. But just imagine how bad it would have been off the cuff.)

In practicing my monologue, I realized the difficulty sounding casual while reading a transcript. I decided to shorten the opening.

"Hello Debbie. This is Blaise. I was wondering if you'd like to see *Monty Python and the Holy Grail.*"

The problem words were her name and mine. As I saw it, my options consisted of the following:

- Use interjections, such as "Hello, um, Debbie. This is, you know, Blaise." This might work, but the cost would be that she would wonder why I was uncertain about her name and, more important, why I had to think about my own.
- Word substitution, which would sound even dumber. "Hello you. This is, um, me."
- Faking distraction: "Hello—oh, just a minute! Anyway, this is—just a minute again!"

The last one would, of course, result in a mighty long phone call, but it did give me another idea. If I kept a rhythm—a normal sounding one as opposed to continually asking for another minute—I might be able to flow through the entire passage fluently. To sound more casual, I could shorten some of the sentences.

One day, my confidence swelled to a point at which I could dial the phone. As I listened to the ringing through the receiver, my stomach churned. I hung up after two rings and decided I would call back later.

I tried to watch television, but the churning refused to dissipate. Moreover, I was unable to concentrate on the professor's idea of how to get Gilligan and the others rescued from the island. I knew instinctively that there was only one solution. I grasped the phone and called again. This time someone answered before the second ring.

"Hello?"
"C-c-cuh …"
"Hello? Hello? Is anyone there?"
"C-could I please speak to Debbie?"
"This is Debbie."
"Hello D-debbie, this is B-b-blaise. I w-"
"Did you just call?"
"Huh?"
"Did you call a few minutes ago?"
"No," I could feel the heat of my face blushing.
"Because I picked it up and heard someone hang up."
"Wow. So anyway, I was wondering if you'd like to see the Holy Grail."
"How would I do that?"
"I mean the movie."
"Oh. OK."

I noticed the knot that was my stomach suddenly loosened. "Great. I'll come by around 7. I g-guess I'll see you then."

"Blaise?"
"Yes."
"Do you have to get off the phone so fast? I mean, we could talk a while."
"Oh. That's right. We can."

Although I had not scripted that last part, the resulting conversation was pleasant, albeit short in duration.

continued

Maybe, I thought, this dating thing was not going to be that difficult.

Unfortunately, subsequent phone calls did not always go as well. Occasionally, a parent would answer and hang up when I did not speak quickly enough. One mother misunderstood my stuttering and yelled something about hating crank calls. I waited a full day before redialing that number.

While I did date some, I did not have a steady girlfriend during high school. This affected my speech for two reasons. First, I developed a tendency to conceal my stuttering as much as possible early in a relationship. Second, I never progressed beyond the early stage of any relationship. Thus, avoidance of stuttering became a prevailing social behavior. I feigned accents, I yelled, and I pretended not to know things when I really did, among numerous other deceptions. When one trick stopped working, I would quickly find another. Sometimes, I just stopped talking. Even that was preferable to stuttering.

Based on trial and error, substituting easy words for those difficult to say became my primary strategy of evasion. I developed a notable ability to cogitate synonymous words and phrases so quickly that listeners were unable to detect the minuscule pauses in my speech (or at least I was convinced they couldn't). This led to some awkward phrasing, such as "a pair of eggs" used to avoid the word *two* or "this day" instead of *today*. Sometimes, the phrases were lengthy, as in "that city in Michigan where they make automobiles," which replaced *Detroit*. I once spelled out "G, A, R, Y, or maybe it's G, A, R, R, Y, I'm not sure," when I knew that the individual in question was named "Gary."

I scanned every utterance before producing it, searching specifically for words beginning with the letters t, d, p, b, k, and g. Because this included my name, I often gave myself nicknames when forced into introductions. I learned to eat French fries plain because I would not ask for *ketchup*. I told people I enjoyed "hoop" to avoid the word *basketball*. When forced into lengthy explanations, I withheld words, hoping that as I offered related points, listeners could fill in the gaps.

Constantly thinking ahead of my speech and then producing ungainly phrases was preferable to stuttering. This strategy was not without cost, however. It was mentally exhausting to always peruse my intended speech to form the proper substitutions. By the end of the day, I was weary. But, I was not overtly stuttering. In fact, by the time I was a high school senior, I stopped attending therapy, so certain was I that I had finally discovered the answer to stuttering. I was surprised, albeit ecstatic, that in the end it was such an easy condition to hide. Someday, I thought, I will write a book on how I conquered this disorder.

I continued to substitute words and avoid stuttering situations for close to five years. Many who knew me during that span of time, including all four of my college roommates, had no idea that I stuttered.

Then everything fell apart.

Although I did not know it at the time, the collapse started early, when the easy words that I was using as substitutions became hard to say. No problem—I just changed those also. The problem was that the third set also eventually induced stuttering. A bigger problem was that this pattern continued until I literally ran out of words. Then, I tried changing other aspects of speech—pitch, accent, loudness, and whatever else I could think of. But, all the fluency allowed by these behaviors also dissolved over time. Before long, I could not say anything without stuttering. Even worse, I was out of ideas. It was time for my last resort.

I returned to therapy.

One of the first things my SLP talked to me about was confronting my fears.

"Fears of what?" I asked.

"Words."

What I needed, she went on to explain, was to confront my speech-related anxieties to diminish their power. I had to be open with my speech, even the words I stuttered. "Get out of your comfort zone," was how she put it.

Quite honestly, this made no sense to me, but I was desperate enough to try anything.

We began by listing all of my feared sounds, words, and phrases. These fears could be unmasked, I learned over time, but not without effort. Each was a complex entity consisting of numerous intertwined variables—the word itself, syllabic stress, the rhythm of the utterance, and nearby sounds, to name but a few—that impacted fluency. For example, "Blaise Jackson" was easier to say than "Blaise," but more difficult than "My name is Blaise." Yet, in each case the feared word, my first name, was the same. The identical obstruction appeared very different as the language environment changed, a multicolored pattern placed in frames of varied hue. I had in the past perceived such differences but had never sought to comprehend them.

While understanding lessened the trepidation associated with stuttering, relief came only with improved speaking skills. Always good at predicting when I would stutter, I found I could use this

continued

ability to my advantage. On some occasions, I could prepare for the destined breakdown more productively. Other times, I could stutter on a different word, one easier to manage. Subsequent to doing so, the feared word no longer presented a problem. It was as if an established quantity of inevitable disfluencies was assigned to any spoken statement, but each did not necessarily have to materialize in its designated spot.

The resulting speech was not always fluent but was relatively tension free and flowed forward, an outcome unseen with the familiar hard sound repetitions. There were supplementary benefits as well. In comparison to speech revisions, modified stuttering was far less taxing on the brain. Rephrasing utterances and finding synonyms were, after all, mentally exhausting activities. My new speech was also easier on the listener, who was no longer asked to comprehend my awkward language forms. But, the most interesting gain was the feeling of actually stuttering less. In the end, the cruelest irony about stuttering was this: It did not decline until I stopped worrying about whether it would.

Gregory, 1991; Guitar, 1998; Latulas et al., 2003; Schwartz, 1999). Similarly, stuttering modification approaches utilize targets from fluency shaping (e.g., breathing and voicing techniques) to help manage disfluencies (Donaher, 2003; Ramig & Dodge, 2004; Sheehan et al., 2001).

This discussion of fluency shaping, stuttering modification, and integrated treatment approaches raises the question of which is best. The answer depends on the client. All have been successful with some clients, and all have failed with others.

Other Types of Management

In addition to traditional therapist-across-the-table-from-the-client therapy, there are other means by which people have tried to treat stuttering. Over the years, such attempts have included surgery, hypnosis, consumption of alcohol (really), and injecting botulinum toxin (the most poisonous compound known to humankind) into the vocal folds. More recently, much interest has been stirred up for both portable devices and pharmacological agents.

Portable Devices

During the past few decades, numerous portable electronic devices have been designed to reduce stuttering. The basic idea with all of them is to interfere with the user's auditory system. More specifically, they change whether or how the speaker hears him- or herself. The basis for this is research indicating that fluency often improves under conditions of

- delayed auditory feedback, or lengthening the time between the actual production of speech and when the speaker hears it,
- masking noise, which is essentially white noise that completely blocks out one's own voice (and everything else), and
- frequency-altered feedback, the electronic conversion of vocal frequencies to make a speaker's voice sound lower or higher in pitch (to the speaker, that is).

What electronic devices do is deliver these types of feedback during speech (Merson, 2003), thus allowing people who stutter to speak under conditions known to enhance fluency. Theoretically, then, electronic devices can afford people who stutter a solution that is both quick and enduring. Even so, however, most do not use them. The primary reasons for their relative scarcity are high cost, a lack of research demonstrating long-term effectiveness, and skepticism that they will work in the first place ("Results of Survey," 2004).

Those who do use electronic devices report varying success (Ramig, Ellis, Pollard, & Finan, 2010). In one survey, 38% indicated that their experience was not at all successful; 44% said their experience was somewhat successful; and 18% reported their experience was very successful. (Reeves, as cited in Kuster, 2004). While the exact reason or reasons for this discrepancy remain unclear, there are anecdotal reports that may cast some light on the issue. It appears that some users are simply less bothered by (or more willing to put up with) listening to masking noise or their own voices altered. In addition, background noise is an issue with some devices (Molt, 2002). Also, the effects of such devices wear off in some who stutter ("Devices Are," 2004). Finally, a number of those experiencing success used devices in conjunction with traditional therapy ("Results of Survey," 2004). As some undoubtedly have easier access to therapy than others, this might also account for some of the variability across users.

Given these factors, it appears that electronic devices can offer hope to some people who stutter. Issues of who will benefit and for how long remain unresolved.

Pharmacological Agents

For decades, people have been reporting on pharmacological agents and stuttering (Kent, 1963; Meduna, 1948; Molt, 1998). These reports have outlined the effects of such classes of agents as antipsychotics, neuroleptics, and sedatives (Molt, 1998). While recent research shows promise that some forms of stuttering may one day be treatable with medication (e.g., Maguire, Riley, Wu, Franklin, & Potkin, 1997), there are several points to keep in mind:

- Much of the research involved small sample sizes and soft science (Molt, 1998), making it difficult to know how far the results can be generalized. Stated differently, what works for one will not necessarily help another.
- Pharmacological agents can produce side effects, some more unpleasant than stuttering (Wells & Malcolm, 1971).
- While reductions have been noted (Brady, 1991), no agent has been found that eliminates stuttering in all test subjects (Molt, 1998).

In a sense, the topic of pharmacological agents is similar to that of electronic devices. No universal cure has been found, but it is nonetheless a potentially promising area of research.

☐ Synopsis

Fluency disorders can be difficult to identify and differentiate. Even stuttering, the most widely researched of these disorders, remains a mystery in many ways. Compounding the ambiguity are myths and outdated beliefs. Despite such concerns, however, SLPs can diagnose stuttering and other fluency disorders. Different treatment options exist as well, with new ideas being continually developed.

☐ Vocabulary

adaptation—tendency for stuttering to decrease over repeated readings of the same passage

cluttering—rare fluency disorder of likely neurological origin

direct therapy—treatment models in which the clinician provides open teaching and feedback

disfluencies—an interruption in the flow of speech sounds (Nicolosi et al., 1989)

environmental changes—altering the client's surroundings in a therapeutic manner

fluency shaping—stuttering intervention based on behavioral principles and designed to establish fluent speech by eliminating stuttering in a controlled-stimulus environment (Shapiro, 1999)

hesitations—cessation of sound

indirect therapy—implementation of therapy without any feedback (reinforcement or punishment) from the therapist

metalinguistic skills—ability to reflect language and to comment on it, as well as to produce and comprehend it (i.e., language about language) (Nicolosi et al., 1989)

modeling—emulation or following the example of another (Nicolosi et al., 1989)

neurogenic dysfluency—sometimes called *acquired stuttering*, is disordered fluency as a result of neurological damage

part-word repetitions—repetitions of sounds or syllables

prevalence—number of existing cases of a disease or condition within a population at any given time (Martin & Clark, 2006)

prolongations—audible extension of a sound

psychogenic dysfluency—disfluent speech in the absence of medical or developmental factors

repressed needs theories—hypotheses in which stuttering is viewed as the voluntary consequence of neuroses

secondary characteristics—behaviors performed to avoid or escape from instances of stuttering

speech-associated attitudes—belief system related to speaking; disposition to respond favorably or unfavorably to an object, person, institution, or event (Ajzen, 1988)

stuttering—speech characterized by abnormal hesitations, repetitions, and prolongations that may be accompanied by gestures, grimaces, or other bodily movements indicating a struggle to speak, blocking of speech, anxiety, or avoidance of speech (Nicolosi et al., 1989)

stuttering modification—a stuttering intervention process that seeks to reduce speech-related avoidance behaviors, fears, and negative attitudes, while modifying the form of stuttering (Shapiro, 1999)

☐ Discussion Questions

1. Do you view stuttering as a problem with speech, or do you feel there is more to it than that?
2. Taking into account your answer to the previous question, what do you feel are appropriate goals for stuttering therapy?
3. What do you think would be the most difficult fluency disorder to deal with? Why?
4. What, in your opinion, would be the worst age to stutter? Explain your answer.

5. What is the most interesting theory you ever heard about stuttering? Why do you think people believe or believed this? Why do you feel that weird beliefs about stuttering persist to this day?
6. Is there a problem with thinking that all breaks of speech are stuttering? Explain your answer.
7. Why do you think there is no known cause of stuttering?
8. Why do you think there is no cure?
9. What would you say is the difference between fluent speech and effective communication?
10. Do you agree that the "stutterer stereotype" affects people academically and professionally? Explain your answer.

☐ Note

1. This is based on an old joke often told to illustrate past (and sometimes present) stuttering theories: A woman notices a man on his hands and knees searching for something under a streetlight. "Excuse me," the woman says. "Do you need some help?" "I'm looking for my car keys," the man replies and gestures toward his idle car in the darkness half a block away. As she kneels down to assist, she asks, "Where exactly did you lose the keys?" "Over there by the car," he replies. She pauses, looking quizzical. "If you lost your keys over there, why are you looking here?" The man replies, "The light's better over here."

☐ Recommended Reading

Drayna, D. (2005). *New clues into stuttering may be found in genes.* Paper presented at International Stuttering Awareness Day Conference. Retrieved from http://www.mnsu.edu/comdis/isad8/papers/drayna8.html.
In this short essay, a researcher from the National Institutes of Health examines the nature side of the nature-nurture discussion.
Eldridge, K. (1997). A conversation with my stutter. Retrieved from the Stuttering home page at http://www.mnsu.edu/comdis/kuster/casestudy/eldridge.html.
An adult addresses his stuttering in a letter, and the result is an intensely personal and emotional invective. One of the most striking elements of this letter is that the author is knowledgeable about stuttering and his own speech and has, by any standard, achieved a level of acceptance for which many would strive. Hatred of stuttering clearly dies hard.
Hood, S. (2003). *Desirable outcomes from stuttering therapy.* Paper presented at International Stuttering Awareness Day Conference. Retrieved from http://www.mnsu.edu/comdis/isad6/papers/hood6.html.

This is a concise essay that covers a lot of ground: desirable outcomes, advice for achieving them, and examination of many contemporary issues surrounding treatment (e.g., fluency shaping vs. stuttering modification).

Jezer, M. (1997). *Stuttering: A life bound up in words*. New York: Basic Books.

This book thoroughly illustrates how stuttering impacts all phases of life.

Love, B. (1994). Keeping the dream alive. In J. Ahlbach & V. Benson (Eds.), *To say what is ours: The best of 13 years of letting go*. Anaheim Hills, CA: National Stuttering Project.

This entry contains excerpts from a speech delivered by former professional basketball great Bob Love. The idea of never giving up, even when life is at its darkest point, has never been illustrated better.

Murphy, B. (1994). Hello, fart face. In J. Ahlbach & V. Benson (Eds.), *To say what is ours: The best of 13 years of letting go*. Anaheim Hills, CA: National Stuttering Project.

If you ever need an example of how stuttering openly is preferable to using secondary behaviors, you will not find a better one than this humorous essay by Bill Murphy.

Murray, F. P., & Edwards, S. G. (1994). *A stutterer's story*. Memphis, TN: Stuttering Foundation of America.

An autobiographical account of Fred Murray, one of the foremost authorities the field has ever known, is a worthwhile read in its entirety.

Quesal, R. (2002). *Some people just don't get it*. Paper presented at International Stuttering Awareness Day Conference. Retrieved from http://www.mnsu.edu/comdis/isad5/papers/quesal5.html.

An "expert" in stuttering takes the author to task for not achieving a degree of fluency the so-called expert deems appropriate. While Dr. Quesal's response is thorough, direct, and a fast read, it is not for the faint of heart. It will unquestionably generate discussion about the purpose of therapy and what recovery really means.

Ramig, P. R. (1997). Various paths to long-term recovery from stuttering. Retrieved from the Stuttering home page at http://www.mnsu.edu/comdis/kuster/casestudy/path/pramig.html.

In this insightful piece, Dr. Ramig outlines specific factors responsible for the recovery he experienced.

Waggott, G. (2004). *Wall of silence: What your kids won't tell you about bullying*. Paper presented at International Stuttering Awareness Day Conference. Retrieved from http://www.mnsu.edu/comdis/isad7/papers/waggott7.html.

Bullying is described not as a subject of theory and research, but through the eyes of the victim. In an account that is both touching and disturbing, the experiences, the emotions, and the aftermath of bullying are related frankly and honestly.

Williams, D. F. (2006). *Stuttering recovery: Personal and empirical perspectives*. Mahwah, NJ: Erlbaum.

Hey, I have to cite my own book, right?

Voice and Resonance Disorders

Richard K. Adler and Dale F. Williams

Richard K. Adler, PhD, CCC, SLP, Fellow, ASHA, is a professor of speech-language hearing sciences at Minnesota State University Moorhead. His career has spanned over 40 years in all clinical settings, including private practice, public schools, hospitals, and university clinics. Dr. Adler primarily works with patients with voice disorders, traumatic brain injuries, and strokes. Within the area of voice, Dr. Adler has specialized in transgender voice and communication therapy. He has published two books—one on neurology for the speech-language pathologist with Wanda Webb—and was one of three coeditors and writers of the first book for working with transgender clients, titled *Voice and Communication Therapy for the Transgender/Transsexual Client: A Comprehensive Clinical Guide.*

Each individual is unique in many ways: hair color, eye color, height, weight, and even smell (we all know who these guys are). Any or all of these features make a person stand out from the crowd. One's voice is another indicator of individuality. We immediately recognize a friend or relative when we hear a familiar voice on the telephone. Listeners also hear differences within an individual voice, easily detecting when, for example, "something doesn't sound right."

Our voices tell a lot about us. They are capable of producing a large variety of tones and pitch levels to convey different emotions. People often identify mood simply by hearing someone's voice. And, when someone asks, "How does he or she sound?" about a speaker or a professor, what is really being asked is: How is that person's voice? Will we fall asleep during the lecture? Will the speaker spark my interest because of the way he or she sounds?

For someone who is speaking, of course, the voice is the outlet for communication. As such, we use it to convey not only content, but also the feelings behind it. For example, we scream when angry, we whisper to show someone we want to be quiet, and we soften our voices to express affection or extreme pleasure. Actors and actresses study ways to modify voice to play a variety of characters (A. Williams, 2007, personal correspondence). Colton and Casper (1996) wrote that a voice is a tool we use to deliver what we are thinking, and our voice helps to add meaning to our messages.

Those who have read Chapter 2 know that the voice being discussed to this point is a combination of phonation (or voicing) and resonance. In other words, what people usually think of as *voice* (the sound that comes out of your mouth when you speak) is the result of both processes. To help you to better understand this concept, we divide the processes here, starting with phonation.

☐ Structures of Phonation

In Chapter 2, the anatomy and physiology of speech was discussed. In this chapter, it would be beneficial to provide some additional information specific to voicing. The most important structure for this process is the **larynx**, which is illustrated in Figure 10.1. The larynx is located in the neck, above the **trachea** and below the **pharynx**. Several **cartilages** make up the primary structure of the larynx. These are the **epiglottis**, thyroid cartilage, arytenoid cartilages, and the cricoid cartilage. Primarily, the cartilages keep the larynx in place and help with the upward or downward movement of the structure. The cricoid cartilage is actually the uppermost ring of the trachea. The thyroid is the largest of all the laryngeal cartilages. The front part of the thyroid cartilage is also known as the Adam's apple, a structure more prominent in males than in females. The *cricothyroid joint* connects these two cartilages and aids in laryngeal movement.

The larynx functions biologically in several ways. It protects the trachea, keeping food particles and liquids from entering and falling into the lungs. In addition, it helps build up air pressure for basic functions such as body waste elimination, childbirth, coughing, throat clearing, and lifting.

The human body is nothing if not economical, however, and thus the same structure that exists for the most basic of needs—protection and bodily functions—is also used to produce speech. More specifically, portions of the aforementioned cartilages combine to form the **vocal folds** (often referred to as the *vocal cords*), giving the larynx a secondary function—phonation. It is the two arytenoid cartilages that are most important for phonation. The vocal folds are attached to the arytenoids. Moreover, the cricoarytenoid joint attaches to the arytenoid cartilages

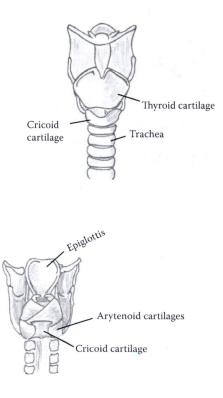

FIGURE 10.1   Anterior and posterior views of the larynx (Artwork by Barbara Fries, Ed.D).

(and to the cricoid, giving it its name). This joint is most important for ease of vocal fold movement.

Laryngeal Musculature

The larynx is made up of a series of **intrinsic** and **extrinsic muscles**. The *vocal folds* (often called the vocal cords) vibrate during sound production. These structures are primarily made up of a pair of thin muscles also known as the *thyroarytenoid muscles*. As the vocal folds vibrate, they also move closer to each other (adduct) and then separate (abduct). These adduction-abduction cycles are made possible by the **lateral cricoarytenoid** and **interarytenoid muscles** (for adduction) and the **posterior cricoarytenoid muscle** (abduction). Through the action of the cricothyroid muscle, attached to (as the name suggests) the cricoid and thyroid cartilages, the larynx and hence the vocal folds may be shortened or stretched to regulate pitch (just as with a stringed instrument, shorter folds mean higher pitch). For example, in **transgender voice therapy**, male-to-female (MtF) clients are taught to raise the position of the larynx to regulate and establish a new **optimum pitch** that matches the new gender.

Power Source for Voice

In Chapter 2, we learned that the lungs and the vocal folds serve as the power source for voice production. When we are not speaking but just silently breathing, the abduction and adduction of the vocal folds occur alternately and smoothly as air passes through the **glottis**. When we start to speak, however, we must vibrate our vocal folds to produce sound. The **myoelastic-aerodynamic theory of vocal fold vibration** explains this phenomenon. The vocal folds vibrate due to air pressure buildup, the force of the air expelled, and the **elastic** quality of the vocal folds.

When we inhale, the lungs fill with air, the **diaphragm** lowers, and we begin to build pressure that will help our vocal folds vibrate and allow us to be heard. During exhalation, the vocal folds close, effectively blocking the air from the lungs. This blockage results in increased pressure beneath the vocal folds. This buildup is known as **subglottal air pressure**, as it is below the glottis. This air pressure eventually causes the vocal folds to separate. As the air blasts through this area of the larynx, the folds are still somewhat constricted. The cycle of vibration that produces sound is in full swing now. As pressure decreases, the folds are brought together again, and then the subglottal air pressure begins to build up again, and the cycle repeats itself. It repeats often in fact: The opening and closing of the vocal folds occurs over 100 times per second. These abduction-adduction cycles help us to recognize certain qualities of a person's voice. The folds could vibrate slowly, for example, resulting in a deep voice. They could be irregular or incomplete, resulting in a voice that sounds hoarse (think Rod Stewart) or breathy (Marilyn Monroe).

Vocal Folds

Vocal folds must vibrate if they are to produce sound. Some voice disorders cause fatigue or paralysis of the folds, or growths on them, and thus they vibrate aperiodically and arhythmically. In addition, there are everyday factors that affect vocal fold vibration, including the tension and mass of the vocal muscles. The first of these, tension, affects the rate of vocal fold movement in that folds that are tense will vibrate faster than those that are relaxed. Mass, on the other hand, has an inverse relationship with vibration rate—the larger the mass, the less vibration that occurs. When vibration slows, the **fundamental frequency** (often abbreviated as *Fo*) lessens, and the voice is perceived to have a lower pitch. It is this reason, in fact, that adult males are perceived to have lower pitches than females.

☐ Parameters of Voice

In Chapter 2, we learned that the three parameters of voice are loudness, pitch, and quality. As you will read in this chapter, when assessing voice, it is important to examine these parameters and to evaluate the individual's resonance, rate, and intonation. When one of these last features is disordered, it can reflect (or help rule out) problems at the respiratory or vocal fold levels (see Table 10.1). Such problems may be due to either vocal abuse or misuse or specific acquired or congenital conditions that directly affect the voice.

☐ Voice Disorders

A voice is considered disordered when characterized by an abnormal pitch, loudness, or vocal quality. Voice disorders may range from a mild hoarseness to a complete loss of voice.

Voice disorders have historically been classified as organic and psychogenic or organic and functional (see Table 10.2). Current classification systems are more descriptive. Voice disorders are now categorized as deficits of phonation, resonance, loudness, or pitch, depending on the most prevalent characteristic of the voice disorder in question. Examples of disorders classified in this manner are listed in Table 10.2.

Disorders of loudness encompass pretty much what you would expect. Voices can be too loud or not loud enough. In addition, there can be abnormal variations or lack of variations (as seen in **monotone**).

As can be seen in Table 10.1, a quiet voice can often be traced back to insufficient respiratory effort. Three areas of our bodies aid us in breathing: the **abdomen** (used in diaphragmatic breathing), **thorax**, and **clavicle**. Overreliance on either of the last two can result in a shortage of air support for speech. Medical conditions can also affect loudness. For example, someone with an upper respiratory infection might have difficulty being heard by listeners.

As anyone who has been to a movie theater in south Florida knows, hearing loss is a common cause of loud voice. This is because the speaker

TABLE 10.1 Vocal Parameters

What Is Assessed	What Is Measured	Examples/Types	Notes
Pitch	Fundamental frequency (Fo)	Optimum pitch Habitual pitch Both measured in hertz (Hz)	The faster the vocal folds vibrate, the higher the pitch that is perceived
Volume	**Loudness** or amplitude	Determined by the intensity of the sound; controlled by breath support	The greater the amplitude, the louder the sound that is perceived
Quality	Harsh Breathy Hoarse	"Gravelly" sounding, strident, or harsh Air escapes when the vocal folds do not approximate fully From irregular vocal fold vibration cycles with random Fo	Poor quality is the earmark of a voice disorder; harsh, breathy, or hoarse voices are usually accompanied by an illness or disease process or a pathology of the vocal folds
Resonance	Vocal tone is modified by the oral, nasal, or pharyngeal area; does not produce sound but rather vibrates as sound comes through	Oral resonance Nasal resonance	Velopharyngeal insufficiency causes excessive nasal resonance; cleft palate may cause excessive nasality known as hypernasality; too little nasal resonance is hyponasal
Rate	Rate of speech production	Slow speech output Fast speech output due to lack of breath support for speech production	Rate is the parameter that is usually regulated by sufficient breath support

is unable to monitor his or her voice properly when speech is at a normal conversational level.

Similar to loudness, there are also a variety of ways in which pitch can sound abnormal. A speaker's pitch might habitually be too high or too low for his or her age and gender. Pitch may possess too little variation (monopitch). Conversely, too much variation can occur in the form of pitch breaks. Possible causes for pitch problems include growths on the vocal folds (which add weight and slow their movement, resulting in lower pitch); a hearing deficit, which makes the monitoring of pitch difficult; and psychological conditions, which are elaborated in this chapter.

Common (and previously mentioned) disorders of quality include voices that sound excessively hoarse or breathy. These conditions are caused by the person's vocal fold movement patterns. If the adduction-abduction cycles are less than periodic, the voice will sound rougher. If the folds do

TABLE 10.2 Voice Disorders

Classification Type	Definition	Example
Organic versus psychogenic	**Organic** may be due to a structural deviation, disease; **psychogenic** usually are emotionally based with no structural problem present	Organic: nodules, paralysis Psychogenic: hysterical aphonia
Organic versus functional	**Organic** may be due to physical etiologies such as tumor or cancer; **functional** disorders usually due to **phonotrauma** or misuse/abuse	

Examples of Voice Disorders by Parameter

Disorders of Phonation	Disorders of Loudness	Disorders of Pitch	Disorders of Resonance—Change to Quality
Aphonia	Monoloudness	Monopitch	**Cul de sac resonance**
Dysphonia	Variations of loudness	Pitch breaks	Excessive nasal resonance
		Inappropriate habitual pitch	Hypernasality or hyponasality

not come together completely, air gets through the resulting gap, resulting in a voice that is breathy.

Phonotrauma is often the cause of a quality disorder. Hoarseness is often related to inflammatory conditions of the voice mechanism. Often, when these conditions exist, the patient tries to overcompensate his or her voice and often ends up exacerbating the situation. For example, an individual might whisper to reduce the overt hoarseness. Unfortunately, however, whispering makes the hoarseness worse because the vocal folds actually vibrate more when whispering. This extra vibration may exacerbate the inflammation causing the hoarseness.

Other causes of disordered quality include chemical exposure; persistent, inappropriate, or violent coughing spells; disease; neurological conditions such as a stroke or degenerative diseases; growths on the folds; poor vocal habits (e.g., a lot of yelling and screaming, causing swelling); smoking; drinking; and psychological factors.

According to the National Institute on Deafness and Other Communication Disorders (2002), over 7 million people in the United States have a voice disorder. This includes anywhere from 3% to 23% of school-age children (Hooper, 2004) and 12% of the elderly population (Shindo & Hanson, 1990).

As noted by Ramig and Verdolini (1998), voice disorders limit more than just communication of everyday messages. It must be remembered that the voice is often a reflection of a person's emotions and personality, as well as the source of production for intelligible oral communication.

TABLE 10.3 Voice Disorders Classified by Specific Causes

I. Physical voice disorders
   A. Vocal fold paralysis (recurrent laryngeal nerve paralysis)
      1. Unilateral
      2. Bilateral
   B. Laryngeal webbing
   C. Laryngeal trauma
      1. Traumatic brain injury incident
      2. In pediatrics: swallowed foreign objects
   D. Papilloma
   E. Carcinoma of the larynx
      1. Laryngectomy
         a. Artificial larynx
         b. Esophageal speech
         c. Blom-Singer prosthesis
         d. Blom-Singer tracheoesophageal puncture
II. Disorders of phonotrauma (vocal abuse and misuse)
   A. Causes
      1. Excessive yelling, coughing, throat clearing
      2. Inappropriate pitch
      3. Excessive volume
      4. Excessive talking
   B. Types of problems
      1. Vocal nodules
      2. Vocal polyps
      3. Contact ulcers
      4. Thickened vocal folds
      5. Acute laryngitis
      6. Traumatic laryngitis
III. Disorders of hypoadduction
   A. Parkinson's disease (hypokinetic dysarthria)
   B. Paralysis of the folds
   C. Diplophonia
IV. Disorders of hyperadduction
   A. Pseudobulbar palsy
   B. Huntington's chorea (hyperkinetic dysarthria)
   C. Spastic dysphonia (spasmodic dysphonia)
V. Psychogenic voice disorders
   A. Hysterical dysphonia (conversion disorder)
   B. Hysterical aphonia (conversion disorder)

TABLE 10.4 Three Centers for Breathing for Speech Production

Type of Breathing	Results
Abdominal/diaphragmatic	Concentration is at the diaphragm; full breath support for speech sound production; most efficient way of breathing for speech; gives greatest control over breath cycles
Thoracic	Concentration is in the chest area with limited use of the diaphragm for breathing for efficient speech production; causes fatigue in some clients due to excessive overuse of muscles; limited support for speech sound production; often runs out of breath when speaking; requires more inhale/exhale cycles to complete a longer sentence
Clavicular	Concentration is on the shoulders; very poor usage of the diaphragm for breathing for speech sound production; usually a short choppy breathing pattern during speech production; often runs out of breath while speaking; complains of fatigue if having to speak a lot

An individual expresses his or her wants, desires, needs, and emotions through the voice. A disorder may have a devastating effect on that individual if these features are misunderstood by listeners. In such cases, the speaker could experience stress and frustration, develop a poor self-image, and even withdraw.

As noted, there is a variety of causes not only for disorders of quality but also for other parameters. Some of the specific conditions—physical, neurological, or psychogenic—associated with voice problems are outlined next.

Physical Voice Disorders

Vocal Fold Paralysis

The vocal folds are muscles and therefore, like other muscles, may become paralyzed if the **innervation** is interrupted. Trauma to the *recurrent laryngeal nerve* (RLN) is the main source of vocal fold paralysis. The RLN, a branch of the **vagus nerve**, courses throughout the neck area, supplying several of the laryngeal muscles. Because of its wide distribution, it is quite vulnerable to injury during both neck and chest surgeries. Other than surgeries, viral infections or traumatic injuries to the head, neck, or chest may also cause paralysis of this nerve and, in turn, to the vocal folds.

Vocal fold paralysis may be **unilateral** or **bilateral**. Unilateral paralysis causes one of the vocal folds to remain static while the other fold is capable of movement. In some unilateral cases (that is, when the paralyzed fold is relatively close to the midline of the glottis), the paralyzed fold may approximate the static fold. If this occurs, voicing is possible. If not, aphonia could occur, as the working fold would not reach the other to complete adduction. In other cases, there is voicing, but it is breathy and very weak.

Paralysis of both vocal folds (bilateral paralysis) can also cause aphonia when the two folds are paralyzed in an abducted position, thereby leaving the glottis wide open. If the vocal fold paralysis occurs when both are close to the adducted position, the patient may be able to produce enough muscle tension to generate voicing. However, this resulting voice is likely to be harsh or strained. Of course, if both folds are completely adducted, a medical emergency results, as the one pathway to and from the lungs becomes obstructed.

Laryngeal Webbing

Vocal folds are covered with a thin membranous material. Sometimes in children, the membrane grows across the two folds, and what occurs is known as **laryngeal webbing**. Sometimes, a web is noticed just after a baby is born, and in this case it would be considered a *congenital* laryngeal web. In cases of accidents or other laryngeal trauma, *acquired* webbing may occur. Surgery is usually the solution of choice with voice therapy follow-up.

Laryngeal Trauma

In some severe **traumatic brain injury** cases the patient's neck is injured. This often occurs from an accident—automobile, motorcycle, snowmobile, to name three relatively common examples. The result is **laryngeal trauma**. Other instances that may affect the patient's larynx include a bullet wound in the neck or a sports- (including extreme sports-) related accident that caused trauma to the larynx. Some hospitals have reported that a child's larynx was traumatized due to the child swallowing poisons, glass, or other sharp or dangerous objects.

Papilloma

Another, albeit less traumatic, type of physical voice disorder is a **papilloma**. This is a type of growth in the larynx that may occur on the vocal folds. Although not cancerous, a biopsy is often performed to determine that it is, in fact, not a more dangerous type of growth. More often than not, papillomas are caused by viruses.

Carcinoma of the Larynx: Laryngectomy

Some patients need to communicate *without* vocal folds. For example, those who undergo a procedure called a *laryngectomy* lose part or all of the larynx. I suppose the obvious question here is: If they lose a section of airway, how do they breathe? The answer is that a **stoma** is constructed in the neck to allow for air to enter and exit the trachea. While this allows the patient to live, he or she no longer has a larynx. And without a larynx, of course, there are no vocal folds and, therefore, no voice.

Laryngectomy surgery, although not common, is not exactly unheard of either. Something like 3,000 of these procedures are performed each year in the United States alone (Hadi, 1987; Waldrop & Gould, 1994), nearly always because of cancer, which in turn is nearly always because of smoking (American Academy of Otolaryngotomy, 2008). Laryngeal cancer takes a while to develop, as most **laryngectomees** are in their 50s and 60s at the time of onset (American Cancer Society, 2007). But, it is a nasty killer, claiming 3,670 lives every year (National Cancer Institute, 2008).

Removing the larynx is a delicate procedure, taking as long as 8 hours, most of which is spent just getting *to* the larynx (past numerous nerves positioned over it). The procedure involves not only removal of at least some of the larynx, but also turning the trachea sideways and suturing it to the neck (i.e., to form the aforementioned stoma). The patient is in the hospital for close to 2 weeks (barring complications), after which he or she breathes, coughs, and so on (and even, in some cases, continues to smoke) through the stoma.

Because the patient cannot produce a voice, at least not in the traditional way, he or she is left with three options:

- purchase an *artificial larynx* (or electrolarynx),
- learn *esophageal speech* (also known as alaryngeal speech), or
- (if he or she is willing to undergo a second surgery) learn *tracheoesophageal speech*.

Artificial larynges are usually introduced early to laryngectomees, as they are easy to use and can thus offer immediate communication, even for patients who will eventually discard them in favor of esophageal or tracheoesophageal speech. Essentially what these devices do is replace the usual speech system vibratory source (i.e., the air in the vocal tract) with an electromechanical vibration that can be heard as a tone. That is, an external source (from a reed placed in the mouth or a device held against the tissue of the neck) provides sound to the pharynx that the user can articulate into recognizable speech.

Although artificial larynges are easy to use and provide the laryngectomee with an instant form of communication, there are drawbacks as well. For one, the voice quality sounds mechanical, even robotic. Also, these devices require the use of a hand to communicate (to hold the device in place). Then, there is the high initial cost (in addition to possible repair costs later).

Esophageal speech does not require an external device, but it does entail more training than use of an artificial larynx. In essence, esophageal speakers learn to trap air in the esophagus (the **pharyngeoesophageal segment** actually), then expel it back out of the mouth. If this sounds like burping to you, then you are getting the idea. When little brother decides that it is funny to belch at the dinner table, trapping and expelling air is essentially what he is doing. In fact, that is often how the initial tone is taught. In time, people learn to continually take in air and release it in a controlled manner, resulting in a tone that can be used for running speech (Waldrop & Gould, 1994).

Not everyone can learn esophageal speech. Although success rates vary, most research indicates that less than half are able to utilize it functionally (e.g., Hotz, Baumann, Schaller, & Zbären, 2002). Even those who can produce the initial tone may not take the time needed (3–6 months) to learn how to use it in conversational speech.

In addition to the hard work involved in learning esophageal speech, another potential drawback is the speech itself: The pitch is lower than the usual range for humans, even adult males, and the intensity is poor. Combine these and the result is that the speaker is often not understood. On the other hand, in comparison to speech with an artificial larynx, esophageal speech is more natural sounding, as well as more convenient.

Tracheoesophageal speech makes use of a **tracheoesophageal puncture**, an idea first put forth by Blom and Singer (see Robbins, Fisher, Blom, & Singer, 1984). This is a puncture inside the stoma that serves as a *fistula* or tunnel between the trachea and the esophagus. As Figure 10.2 indicates, the smaller hole is high and in the back wall opposite the first.

Such a puncture can, of course, be quite dangerous to the subject. Should food or liquid go through it and fall into the lungs, **aspiration** can result, potentially resulting in pneumonia. This problem is taken care of with a **prosthesis** that serves as a one-way valve—it keeps food out and lets air from the trachea into the esophagus. Thus, if the individual occludes the stoma when talking (i.e., so air goes to the mouth and not out the neck), he or she can safely use air from the lungs to vibrate the pharynx. The greatly increased air supply also allows for better loudness, pitch range, and duration in comparison to esophageal speech. The comparative ease of production is an additional advantage.

Disadvantages include the following:

- It requires a secondary surgical procedure.
- The patient must deal with daily maintenance of the prosthesis.
- After a period of time, there may be recurrent leakage of the prosthesis.
- The costs of the initial prosthesis and the eventual replacement prostheses can be high.
- The fistula can close if something is not in it at all times.

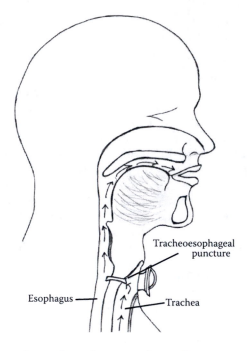

Tracheoesophageal
puncture

Esophagus

Trachea

FIGURE 10.2   Location of tracheoesophageal puncture (Artwork by Barbara Fries, Ed.D).

Another potential drawback is that laryngectomees might need to use a hand to occlude the stoma (so air goes to the mouth and not out the neck). However, special breathing valves are available to help with this particular inconvenience.

Whatever form of communication is used, the laryngectomee needs training with an SLP. Many also attend support groups, as the effects of such a traumatic experience are more than anatomical (see "Kate's Story"). Spouses are often active in such groups as well, given that their lives also change significantly, leading them to seek the aid and support of others in the same situation.

Voice Disorders Associated With Phonotrauma and Tension

Many individuals have a voice disorder due to either poor vocal habits, trauma to the vocal folds, or excessive vocal tension. The vocal folds and the surrounding tissues are made for normal usage, that is, conversational loudness and optimum pitch. Andrews (2007) described vocal behaviors as "misuse" when inappropriate pitch and loudness are present, whereas vocal

KATE'S STORY

Kate was a professional woman, one successful enough to own a business with her name on it. Nevertheless, she was worried. Not about the business, although that certainly contained its share of headaches. No, Kate was more concerned about how hoarse her voice was becoming. Along with this change, she had developed a cough that was not going away. To Kate, these happenings were more than nuisances. Five years earlier, she had undergone surgery to remove a polyp from her left vocal fold. Six weeks of radiation followed. Thus, any differences in the throat area were causes for great trepidation.

Visits to the doctor over the next 3 months brought the news Kate feared: She had cancer of the larynx. The disease was so widespread, in fact, that it required a laryngectomy. On hearing this, Kate described her reaction as "devastation." She sought out a surgeon as carefully as possible. Family concerns forced her to stay local, and she hoped she could find someone highly regarded.

The surgeries—a complete removal of the larynx, reconstruction of an esophagus damaged by previous radiation, and a tracheo-esophageal puncture—were successful, but Kate's mood did not improve. If anything, it worsened, as "shock and confusion" were added to her "continued devastation." It did not help that the subsequent chemotherapy and radiation treatments made her physically ill, or that the first SLP to see her recommended against hands-free communication, instructing her to occlude her stoma every time she wished to speak. For Kate, this difference was too much to deal with on top of everything else.

Kate did not talk "for months" following the surgery. She gave little information about this period, other than telling me that imagining no voice is nothing like actually living it. During that time, she did meet another laryngectomee, which helped some, but the frustration of communicating only through written notes was still overwhelming. No matter how much encouragement she received, she did not feel normal or even self-reliant.

Kate's husband, Jack, did not always read the notes intended for him. The reason for this was unclear, but seeing Kate in such a helpless situation, and being a part of it himself, was a difficult adjustment for him as well. He was not used to caring for her in quite the manner now required. Unfortunately, Jack never got to experience much of Kate's new voice, as he passed away shortly after she began her first attempts at producing esophageal speech.

There was some good news in Kate's life, in the form of a new granddaughter. Although she adored the baby, she again found herself focusing on differences, such as being unable to talk while feeding or changing the little one (because of the need to occlude her stoma while speaking).

Family members sought out a second opinion on Kate's behalf. A new SLP evaluated her 10 months after the laryngectomy. This SLP recommended hands-free communication in the form of a tracheostoma valve. It requires a lot of maintenance—it gets plugged, it needs to be glued in, and it can irritate the skin—but it gave Kate a voice the instant she tried it. This voice was inconsistent, and it took Kate several months to master speaking with the valve, but she persevered. Communication obviously outstrips any of the aforementioned disadvantages.

I asked Kate if she had been a smoker. She rolled her eyes before telling me that she had quit 25 years prior to her initial cancer diagnosis. When I inquired regarding why she reacted the way she had to my question, she explained that questions about smoking always come across as "you deserved this," like laryngectomees have only themselves to blame for their misery. In a sense, I was looking for a reason, something to explain why this all came about. And, I did zero in on a choice she had made. It was not my intent to dismiss her suffering, but I do understand the reaction.

Kate is now self-sufficient, as she takes care of her home and business. She regularly babysits her granddaughter when she is not traveling for work. And, she has a real appreciation that her situation was not worse than it was, as was the case for some with whom she shared the same diagnosis. There are, however, still problems to deal with:

- As her loudness is limited, Kate cannot be heard in some (noisier) social environments.
- She lost business because some older clients had trouble hearing her.
- Self-consciousness is still an issue as Kate wonders what others think about the comparatively frequent coughing she does, along with the gurgling noises and the actual presence of the stoma (which she often covers with turtlenecks).
- She cannot laugh out loud and therefore slaps her knee to show appreciation of humor.
- A protective guard is needed to shield the stoma from streaming water in the shower.
- Kate used to swim but no longer does. There are devices for laryngectomees who wish to do so, but, for Kate, that is "another life."

continued

Kate also reported that little boys are often afraid of her voice (more so than little girls, for reasons unknown). They sometimes ask her why she talks as she does (as if she could just turn it off). Reactions of adults are not always better. Some stare. Others are visibly uncomfortable and try to end conversations quickly. Listeners have expressed hope that her throat gets better and suggested cures such as lemon and hot water. Of course, there are also those who show no visible reaction and simply communicate as they would with anyone else.

Two people who do not care a bit about her new voice are Kate's granddaughters. To them, she is just Grandma, and they do not consider much beyond that important fact. The others in the laryngectomee self-help group are accepting as well. Still, Kate finds it difficult to open up much with either children or strangers.

Kate's advice for future SLPs is to take account of clients' entire situations (and not just their diagnoses). And, "if you don't know as much about an area of treatment as someone else does, please don't be afraid to refer."

"abuse" is behavior that is inappropriate and injurious to the vocal folds. When either happens, the vocal folds react in a phonotraumatic manner.[1]

Most commonly, phonotrauma may lead to the formation of **vocal nodules**, muscle tension **dysphonia**, or more seriously, damage to the vocal folds, larynx, or surrounding tissues due to serious trauma such as ingesting harmful chemicals, drug usage, excessive alcohol consumption, or delicate laryngeal or neck surgery. Table 10.5, adapted from Andrews (2007), lists some additional causes of phonotrauma and tension.

Sometimes, physicians prescribe medication to help the patient diagnosed with **gastroesophageal reflux disease (GERD)**. These medications may have a drying affect, which could cause phonotrauma to the folds. There are also less-common agents that can affect the performance of the larynx and vocal folds. These include both medications prescribed by physicians and illegal drugs. Table 10.6 describes many chemicals—legal and illegal—that affect the vocal folds.

Vocal nodules are small growths or nodes that develop on the vocal folds. Nodules may be unilateral or bilateral. With bilateral nodules, the nodes are on the same portion of the vocal folds, opposite each other at the junction of the anterior, middle third portion of the folds. As they increase in size, they cause progressively more problems with phonation. In some cases, the vocal folds thicken but never form a nodule. The thickening may cause breathiness (as complete adduction does not occur, allowing air to rush through the glottis along with phonation) and a lower habitual pitch

TABLE 10.5 Causes of Phonotrauma and Tension

- Hypertonic laryngeal muscles due to usual stress/tension
- Inappropriate elevation of the larynx
- Inhaling indoor or outdoor environmental irritants
- Excessive cheering or yelling (cheerleaders, sports fans)
- Inappropriate/excessive volume
- Excessive coughing or throat clearing
- Excessive singing without proper training in safe singing techniques
- Inappropriate pitch
- GERD (gastroesophageal reflux disease)
- Excessive talking or yelling

Source: Adapted from Andrews, M. *Manual of Voice Treatment*, 3rd edition. Clifton Park, NY: Delmar Cengage, 2007.

TABLE 10.6 Drugs and Their Effect the Voice Directly or Indirectly

Drug Name	Effect on Voice	Possible Results
Alcohol (A)	Drying effect to the vocal folds and surrounding laryngeal mucous membranes	Phonotrauma, including vocal nodules, polyps, or irritated larynx
Aspirin (O) (some patients are more sensitive to these)	May cause bleeding in the stomach or vocal folds/larynx	Phonotrauma, nodules
Antihistamines (P or O)	Excessive dryness of mucosal tissue	Nodules, muscle tension dysphonia
Cocaine (I)	Nasal irritation; phonotraumatic behaviors	Muscle tension dysphonia, polyps, bleeding
Diuretics (P)	Dryness, thickened secretions	Phonotrauma
Inhalers (P)	Infections of the larynx, dryness	Lower pitch, inappropriate pitch
Marijuana (I)	Irritation of the mucosal lining	Various vocal effects
Tobacco (O)	Respiratory disease, breathing difficulties, swelling, irritation	Polyps, cancer of the larynx, hoarseness

Source: Adapted from Andrews, M. *Manual of Voice Treatment*, 3rd edition. Clifton Park, NY: Delmar Cengage, 2007.
I, illegal; P, prescribed; A, abusive; O, over the counter.

(because the folds are thicker and, as a result, move slower). If nodules develop, hoarseness will almost surely be noted, as the periodicity of the abduction-adduction cycles will be affected.

Vocal polyps are also masses that grow on the vocal folds. Similar to nodules, they grow on the anterior to middle third of the folds. Polyps are softer than nodules and often contain fluid or blood. Most, but not all, of the time, polyps are unilateral. Common causes are smoking, phonotrauma, or vocal fold hemorrhaging. Large polyps will likely be removed by a surgeon through conventional or laser surgery. Sometimes, when the polyp is small enough, vocal therapy can eliminate it without invasive procedures.

Another type of vocal fold growth is a *contact ulcer*. These occur on the arytenoid cartilage and may be unilateral or bilateral. They are basically sores that develop on one or both sides of the vocal folds (Hegde, 1995) and occur most frequently in adult males, when they occur at all (they are the least occurring of all the vocal fold growths). The cause is usually hyperfunctional behaviors, often excessive talking. Symptoms are hoarseness and some pain. Medical attention is usually required, often coupled with voice therapy to help the patient change vocal practices.

A *granuloma* is a type of contact ulcer. These are caused by an inflammation of the tissues surrounding the larynx, in particular the glottis and vocal folds. The patient will likely present a breathy voice along with some hoarseness, low pitch, vocal fatigue, and excessive throat clearing. He or she may also complain that "something feels like it is in my throat."

Some patients are more prone to colds or allergies and therefore experience many bouts of **laryngitis**. When it is persistent and occurs often, the inflammation of the mucosal membranes of the larynx cause **acute laryngitis**. It is considered an infection and usually causes additional *edema* or swelling. This type of organic laryngitis usually is cleared with some medications and mostly with vocal rest. However, **traumatic laryngitis** will occur with continual vocally abusive or phonotraumatic behaviors. An individual may experience bouts of excessive yelling, coughing, crying, throat clearing, or loud, boisterous laughing. These cause irritation to the larynx and its structures, which causes them to swell. The voice becomes hoarse, and voice therapy is usually ordered to include vocal rest and techniques to alleviate the phonotraumatic or abusive behaviors.

Voice Disorders of Hypoadduction

Patients who are diagnosed with **Parkinson's disease** experience **hypokinetic dysarthria**. This was discussed in Chapter 7. The client's voice becomes very weak due to **basal ganglia** damage and the reduced production of the neurotransmitter **dopamine**. As the vocal folds are muscles, they have a more difficult time abducting and adducting to produce sound as the Parkinson's progresses. If the folds do not adduct fully, the voice becomes breathy with little volume and is most difficult to understand. The Parkinson's patient's voice characteristics include breathiness, hoarseness, pitch breaks, and vocal tremor.

Vocal fold paralysis also is a culprit in causing incomplete abduction and adduction of the folds. According to Andrews (2007), about 10% of laryngeal problems are caused by paralysis. Paralysis of the vocal folds may be unilateral or bilateral, as discussed previously in this chapter. It is worth noting here that even when the unaffected fold can move to the paralyzed vocal fold, there is still hypoadduction. Of course, during bilateral paralysis of the vocal folds, the glottis may be wide open, and therefore no voice is produced (i.e., aphonia).

Some individuals seem to produce two different tones when phonating. This is usually due to both the true vocal folds and **false vocal folds** vibrating at the same time, thus producing the different simultaneous frequencies (Andrews, 2007), or when the true folds have different degrees of tension or mass and vibrate separately (Colton, Casper, & Leonard, 2006). The word *diplophonia* itself means "double voice" (Colton et al., 2006). This condition does not seem to be a consequence of a vocal pathology.

Voice Disorders of Hyperadduction

Huntington's chorea, a progressive neurological disorder discussed in Chapter 7, is usually characterized by *hyperkinetic dysarthria*. This condition is caused by an excessive production of a **neurotransmitter** called *acetylcholine*. When this occurs, there is notable malfunction of the basal ganglia along with **extrapyramidal tract** damage. The result is hyperkinetic dysarthria with prolongation of sounds, along with short vocal bursts and excessive facial and tongue movements.

Pseudobulbar palsy, also known as supranuclear bulbar paralysis, is due to bilateral damage of the **corticobulbar tract**. Noted characteristics include **spasticity**, muscle weakness, limited **range of motion**, bouts of **emotional lability**, and difficulty with both swallowing and speaking. Notable voice characteristics include pitch breaks, hoarseness, and a strained, almost strangled, voice caused by the vocal fold **hyperadduction**.

Spasmodic dysphonia is characterized by momentary interruptions of voicing, usually resulting from tight closure and spasm of folds (although these interruptions can also occur when the folds suddenly burst open during speech). As might be expected, the resulting voice lacks flow, so much so that this disorder is sometimes mistaken for a fluency deficit.

Spasmodic dysphonia was for a long time thought to be a psychogenic disorder of voice. This was when the disorder was known primarily as *spastic dysphonia*. Today, most researchers and clinicians do not accept the notion that the disorder is purely psychogenic but, rather, agree that it could be of neurologic or even **idiopathic** origin. Often, clients who are diagnosed with spasmodic dysphonia report a previous upper respiratory infection, severe emotional trauma, or stress when required to use their voices at work or social events. Three types of spasmodic dysphonia are recognized: adductor type, abductor type, and mixed.

Adductor spasmodic dysphonia is usually strained, effortful phonation and voice stoppages (Andrews, 2007). Patients complain of vocal fatigue, and

BOTULINUM TOXIN

Botulinum toxins are the most poisonous compounds known (Jankovic, 2004). A fair question, then, is why people would inject it into their vocal folds. The reason is that one form of botulinum has been found to relax (actually, it induces temporary paralysis in) muscles that contract excessively or inappropriately (Blitzer & Sulica, 2001). For this reason, botulinum injections have been used to treat a variety of conditions, including tics (Jankovic, 1994), migraines (Blitzer & Sulica, 2001), and stuttering (Ludlow, 1990). It has also been used effectively with spasmodic dysphonia (Ludlow, 1990), with few side effects and no loss of effectiveness with repeated injections.

vocal tremor is usually present. Swallowing problems often accompany this disorder. Most patients are women. In some mild cases, voice is produced intermittently, but the usual recommendation is **Botox** injections.

Abductor spasmodic dysphonia is less common than the adductor type. A sometimes-normal and sometimes-strained voice is interspersed with breathiness. It can be caused by psychogenic, neurologic, or idiopathic factors (Aronson, 1990). As with the adductor type, onset is gradual.

In rare cases, the vocal folds can suddenly adduct and, at other times, abduct during speech. This is known as *mixed spasmodic dysphonia.*

Psychogenic Voice Disorders

Some voice disorders are caused by psychological trauma. Some aphonias and dysphonias in particular are behavioral responses to emotional distress, social pressures, or on-the-job stress. These are usually known as *conversion disorders.* With these conditions, an individual's severe psychological trauma causes a loss of voice or at least a disturbing quality and pitch to the usually normal voice. Psychologists have noted that this is likely an unconscious attempt to avoid dealing with the stressors in one's life.

Hysterical aphonia, or conversion aphonia, is the term used to describe such a psychological loss of voice. In the film *The Spiral Staircase* (1946), the main character "loses" her voice as a child when she sees her parents die in a fire. As happens with conversion aphonia, the girl converts her emotional trauma into a loss of voice. She remains mute until, in the grand tradition of Hollywood (see every movie ever made about amnesia), a second trauma allows her to regain phonation.

A similar disorder is *hysterical* or *conversion dysphonia.* The mechanism (conversion of an emotional disorder to a physical one, despite the absence of neurological or anatomical trauma) is the same, but the disorder is characterized by only a partial loss of voice.

Mutational falsetto is another conversion disorder in which there is an absence of physical factors. It is characterized by pitch that is excessively high for the speaker's age and gender. The role of the communication sciences and disorders (CSD) professional may well include convincing the client that a lower pitch sounds appropriate. Additional help, in the form of psychoanalysis, might also be required.

Voice Difference vs. Voice Disorders

There is a fairly new area of voice that is becoming more apparent, with more people seeking help. The controversy, among others, is whether to consider transsexual/transgender voice a disorder or a difference. To some clients, their voices are disordered because they do not match their outward or even inward personality and physical statute. To most SLPs, however, these clients' voices are not disordered but, rather, different from the clients' preferences.

An MtF (male-to-female) or FtM (female-to-male) patient often seeks voice therapy to learn techniques that will make the voice sound more feminine or more masculine. It is worth noting that the "voice" they are seeking does not necessarily mean only sound production and pitch, but also includes resonance, volume, rate, intonation, vocabulary, syntax, articulation, and nonverbal communication. Adler, Hirsch, and Mordaunt (2006) outlined a vocal health program for the MtF and the FtM transsexual patient to protect and nurture the changing voice.

An evaluation of a transsexual patient does not aim at finding a solution to the problem but rather aims at modifying the voice accordingly. Analysis of the pitch, volume, rate, resonance, intonation, and other parameters will allow the client and the clinician to learn how much modification is necessary for the individual to feel comfortable passing in the new gender.

☐ Evaluation of the Voice for Differential Diagnosis

Because of the variety of causal factors associated with voice disorders, other professionals may also be involved in the diagnosis. Possible team members, aside from the SLP and audiologist (to evaluate hearing, a possible cause of pitch, loudness, and quality disorders), include a

physician to assess overall health, a pathologist to report on tissue samples, a psychologist or psychiatrist, a neurologist, and of course, family
members. The role of the SLP is outlined as follows:

I. Assessment
   A. Case history and background information
      1. Inquire about onset of the voice problem
      2. Obtain a history of illnesses; medical profile with conditions
         relevant to voice problems
      3. Observe tension in the larynx, shoulders, neck
      4. Be aware of any visible or audible vocally abusive or phono-
         traumatic behaviors such as yelling, excessive talking, cough-
         ing, throat clearing
      5. Notice tremors of the face or hands, other physical character-
         istics that would lead to a suspected voice disorder
      6. Discern a typical day for this person; note tension-causing
         situations or stresses
      7. Find what the patient eats, drinks, and how much sleep is usual
         each night
      8. Discuss any sudden physical traumas, strokes, head injuries,
         conversion reactions, psychological traumas, allergies, GERD
      9. Inquire about intake of citrus juices
      10. Inquire about intake of soda pop, alcohol, or other irritant
          liquids
      11. Obtain a history of smoking or secondhand smoke
      12. Obtain a history of drug usage
      13. Find out when are the vocal behaviors are best, worst
      14. Elucidate consistency of these symptoms or if they intermittent
   B. Evaluate breathing style and strength of inhalation/exhalation
   C. Evaluate maximum phonation time (MPT): a measure of phona-
      tory ability during exhalation.
      1. Patient inhales a sufficient breath and exhales while saying the
         vowel /ah/.
         a. Adults: 15–20 seconds in length before running out of
            breath
         b. Children: 10 seconds in length
         c. Three trials are made and an average is noted.
   D. S/Z ratio
      1. Measures respiratory and phonatory efficiency
         a. /s/ is a voiceless consonant and therefore will measure
            the length of the exhalation phase of breathing cycles.
         b. /z/ is voiced and therefore will measure the length of
            phonation possible based on breathing efficiency.

1) When /z/ is prolonged, we can see if the vibratory pattern of the vocal folds can be sustained as long as the exhalation phase of breathing when measuring the/s/ sound. It should be for the same amount of time, thus producing an S/Z ratio of 1:1.
2) If /z/ is sustained for a shorter period than /s/, there would be poor laryngeal control or a physical (lesion) problem of the vocal folds.
3) Three trials are completed and averaged.

E. Laryngeal imaging
1. Fiberoptic rigid endoscopy: a rigid tube is inserted into the oral cavity; provides a view of the larynx
2. Fiberoptic flexible nasendoscopy: flexible tube inserted into the nasal passage, and a light illuminates the structures
3. Laryngoscopy: views the larynx
4. Stroboscopy: video to observe the movement of the vocal folds and larynx using phonation and nonphonation

F. Acoustic analysis of the voice (Kay Elemetrics Visipitch)
1. Fundamental frequency (*Fo*)
2. Range of frequency
3. Average fundamental frequency
4. *Jitter* measurement: Since the vocal folds do not vibrate periodically, there are fluctuations in the frequency and amplitude of the vibrations. This variation is called *frequency perturbation* or jitter. The patient sustains a vowel while producing a steady pitch level using a Visipitch.
5. *Shimmer* measurement: Variations in the vibratory cycles is known as *amplitude perturbation* or shimmer. On the Visipitch, the patient sustains a vowel while producing a steady pitch.

There are several vocal perceptual measures that are completed by the patient, by the clinician, or both. These will assess the patient's vocal abilities, psychological effects on the voice, as well as how the patient views quality of life based on the voice problem or modification.

The *Voice Handicap Index* (VHI) (Jacobson et al., 1997) aims at assessing the psychological ramifications of the voice as seen from the patient's viewpoint. In many cases, the patient perceives the voice to be either more or less severe than what the SLP thinks. The clinician is able to determine the mild, moderate, or severe effects that the voice has on the patient's thoughts and whether it is an impairment to that patient.

The *Voice-Related Quality of Life* (V-RQOL) (Hogikyan & Sethuraman, 1999) is a psychometric measure of four quality-of-life parameters of voice disorders. It gives the patient and the clinician an idea of how the voice in question affects the everyday life of the patient.

In 2002, the *Consensus Auditory-Perceptual Evaluation of Voice* (CAPE-V) was developed through Division 3, Voice and Voice Disorders, of the American Speech-Language-Hearing Association (ASHA) in conjunction with the University of Pittsburgh. Voice scientists, SLPs, and other research scientists met to determine a perceptual rating system for disordered voices. The group wanted to develop a standardized rating protocol, determine which parameters of voice should be rated, and finally recommend such a system be developed. The CAPE-V has been tested and trialed extensively since that first meeting. The basic premise is that six parameters are measured:

1. Overall severity of voice
2. Roughness
3. Breathiness
4. Vocal strain
5. Pitch
6. Loudness

Instructions for rating and summarizing the measures are included, as is a rating form with a place to write notes as the evaluation proceeds. In this way, all relevant factors—objective and subjective—are addressed, and an overall assessment is made of the individual client.

☐ Voice Therapy

As with evaluations, input regarding therapy will likely also come from a variety of sources. If nothing else, prior to therapy with an SLP, the client must be assessed by a physician. The purposes of this assessment are to help identify the cause of the disorder and to produce information about vocal fold function.

Choosing a voice therapy solution can be daunting, especially for the inexperienced clinician. There are a variety of therapy protocols available, but teaching a patient about good vocal health is always a good first step when devising a treatment plan. Many voice disorders occur because the patient is not using his or her voice safely and efficiently. Even if the cause of the disorder is neurological or physical (e.g., stroke, traumatic brain injury, or even smoking or drug abuse), a vocal health program will help the patient learn new vocal habits and better understand how to take care of the voice. In cases of phonotrauma, this type of intervention will help ensure that the disorder (nodules, for example) does not recur.

TABLE 10.7 Some Suggested Elements of a Vocal Health Protocol

• Marked periods of vocal rest	• Reduce volume
• Limit intake of carbonation	• Abdominal breathing
• Limit intake of citrus juices	• Avoid smoking or secondhand smoke
• 8 hours of sleep each night	• Avoid yelling
• Learn safe coughing techniques	• Make sure you are hydrated
• Limit intake of spicy foods	• Drink water and herbal or green tea with honey
• Learn safe throat clearing	• Avoid antihistamines as they are drying agents
• Keep a daily journal to track your good and poor vocal usage	• Avoid alcohol

---

Andrews (2007), Adler et al. (2006), and others emphasized the importance of the vocal health program. For the patient to learn new techniques, the protocol in Table 10.7 is helpful to implement. Not every patient will need all of these elements, but it will give the clinician some guidance about what can be included in an individual vocal health program.

Ramig and Verdolini (1998) explained that appropriate treatment of the disordered voice plays a central role in preserving an individual's quality of life. The primary goal of voice therapy is to enable the clients to obtain a voice that satisfies their needs while considering any structural and functional limitations of the vocal mechanism. Hillman, Gress, Hargrave, Walsh, and Bunting (1990) stated that the role of the SLP is comprised of five basic elements:

1. Evaluation
2. Remediation of the faulty functioning of the voice
3. Teaching compensation for deficits of the vocal mechanism
4. Replacement of the voicing source
5. Modification of the use and care of the vocal mechanism[2]

Ramig and Verdolini (1998) gave four main reasons for **behavioral voice treatment**:

1. It is the preferred treatment of choice to resolve a voice disorder when medical or surgical treatments are not recommended.
2. This type of treatment may be used during the initial treatment period when medical treatment is expected. The voice therapy success may then either require medical treatment or dismiss that need.
3. Behavioral voice treatment is used before and after laryngeal surgery to ensure a more successful postsurgery voice.
4. Behavioral voice treatments are often used as a preventive treatment to preserve vocal health.

Each client is evaluated carefully to determine which behavioral voice therapy protocol would work for the particular need of that individual. There are many techniques that the SLP will choose from, including

- Chewing approach
- Open-mouth approach
- Pushing approach
- Respiratory training
- Yawn-sigh technique
- Relaxation training
- Half-swallow boom method

Chewing Approach

Developed by Froeschels (1952), the chewing approach is used primarily with clients exhibiting reduced mandibular restriction associated with a hyperfunctional voice (Boone & McFarlane, 1994). In short, the patient practices the motion of chewing in an exaggerated manner and, over time, adds voicing, random sounds, words, phrases, sentences, and finally, conversation. This method helps to eliminate hard glottal attacks on the initiation of voice.

Open-Mouth Approach

The open-mouth approach requires the patient to open the mouth more than usual while speaking. This positioning change results in less phonatory effort and strain (Boone & McFarlane, 1994) and, as a result, helps decrease problems with quality, pitch, and volume. In addition, oral resonance and overall quality are likely to improve. The open-mouth approach may be effective with a client who exhibits hypernasality, which is often produced, assuming no pathology, by a restriction of the oral cavity.

Pushing Approach

The aptly named pushing approach includes activities such as pushing down on a chair, pushing against a wall, or placing the palms together at the level of one's chest and pressing them together. Whatever is being pushed, the client phonates at the point of maximum push. The phonation will sound like a forceful grunt; it forces a temporary hyperfunction of the voice. The approach is used to increase glottal closure and reduce glottal insufficiency (Colton et al., 2006; Pannbacker, 1998). It is also likely to facilitate lowered pitch (Colton et al., 2006). It is used often with patients with unilateral vocal fold paralysis or puberphonia and some patients with psychogenic aphonia.

Respiratory Training

Many clients with voice disorders need to modify their functional respiratory (breathing) habits. Some continue to talk once their expiratory air is depleted, often causing undue tension and stress on the larynx and in particular the vocal folds.

Many clinicians (e.g., Case, 2002) pointed out signs that patients are using inadequate breath support for speech production:

1. Voicing is attempted before inspiration.
2. Voice is begun after most of the expiratory air is depleted, and the patient then attempts to speak on residual pulmonary air.
3. Poor coordination of the muscle of inspiration with the muscle of expiration.

Respiratory training is helpful for patients exhibiting such characteristics. It has been found to be particularly useful for those with vocal nodules or contact ulcers. In addition, such training can help people who have difficulty projecting their voices (or other loudness issues).

Yawn-Sigh Technique

One way to relax phonation is to simulate (or actually trigger) a yawn, then end the yawn with an audible sigh. This can be a helpful means toward reducing hyperfunction because the physiology of the yawn is incompatible with the excessive tension that a hyperfunctional larynx produces. In other words, it is impossible to be tense while yawning. The yawn-sigh can be used to produce words, phrases, and sentences. Over time, the yawn is gradually eliminated, leaving a relaxed speaking pattern. A disadvantage is that many patients are reticent to try this method because society has taught them to stifle (or at least hide) yawns (Colton et al., 2006).

Relaxation Training

In addition to the yawn-sigh, there are other means of reducing tension. For example, the CSD professional can instruct the client to contract and loosen different muscle groups as a way of helping him or her discriminate the feelings of tension and relaxation. Hyperfunctional voice disorders can be helped when the client becomes aware of and then voluntarily reduces tension in the neck, laryngeal area, and shoulders.

Half-Swallow Boom Technique

For patients suffering from unilateral vocal fold paralysis, bowing of the vocal folds, or falsetto voice, Boone and McFarlane (1994) developed the half-swallow boom technique. Designed to maximize closure of the larynx, this procedure involves swallowing and saying the word *boom* as the swallow is in progress. The word *boom* is produced in a low-pitched voice.

Once this is accomplished, the patient is instructed to say the word *boom* louder and with less breathiness. It helps for the patient to turn his or her head to one side before saying the word, then turning to the other side to say boom again. From there, the patient adds other sounds while still turning his or her head from one side to the next: "boom … one," "boom … two," and so on. Eventually, the patient adds phrases and sentences to the word *boom*. Over time, the boom-and-swallow trigger is faded out.

Why, of all possible words, do clinicians use *boom*? This is because it is a word composed of sounds that can all be produced as the air is released from the contracted larynx. The oral opening of this word is minimal, which produces back pressure on the larynx (Boone & McFarlane, 1994).

There are many other techniques that clinicians have developed on their own and that work for their patients. As Ramig and Verdolini (1998) suggested, voice therapy has a general effectiveness but do advocate for further research regarding the efficacy of these and other techniques.

☐ Resonance Disorders

As noted in this chapter and elsewhere, **resonance** is how the tone coming off the vocal folds is shaped into what we hear as recognizable voice. The term *resonance disorders*, then, refers to any disruption of the vocal tone above the folds. Again, there are three primary resonance disorders. *Hypernasality*, or excessive nasal cavity resonance, is often the result of the soft palate not reaching the back wall of the pharynx, thereby allowing more sound than usual to pass through the nasal chamber. Hypernasality can also occur as a result of a cleft palate. In this case, the oral and nasal cavities are not properly divided, a circumstance that allows sound to pass into and through the nose. The resulting sound is distinctive to the listener. Simply put, the speaker sounds as if he is talking through his nose.

Hyponasality, a condition of limited nasal resonance, is due to blockage of the nasal cavity. This is probably more familiar to most listeners.

This is because a person often sounds hyponasal when suffering from a cold. This condition can also be created by pinching closed one's nose and speaking. In terms of speech output, hyponasality is essentially the opposite of hypernasality. That is, the voice does not move through the nasal cavity at times when it should. Sounds that normally depend on nasal cavity resonance are changed. For example, /m/ sounds more like /b/, and /n/ becomes /d/.

With the third resonance disorder, *cul-de-sac resonance*, full resonance cannot occur. The resulting vocal sound is often described as sounding hollow. This is due either to an obstruction in the front of the nasal cavity or from having the tongue positioned too far back in the oral cavity. Cul-de-sac resonance affects sounds that would normally be resonated nasally. For this reason, it is often confused with hyponasality.

As is the case with voice disorders, treatment of resonance may well involve a team approach. The classroom teacher could be called on to monitor resonance as well as associated communication problems, should any exist. Input from an audiologist is also needed, given that hearing loss is a possible causal factor. If resonance imbalance is due to a cleft palate, a plastic surgeon and dentist, among others, will be included on the team.

In addition to the professionals noted, the SLP is, of course, necessary in the evaluation and treatment of resonance disorders. The SLP can help the child improve not only his or her resonance but also any associated deficits of respiration, voice quality, loudness, or articulation.

Because improving resonance may involve increases in respiratory effort and muscle tension, the plan of therapy, as with most of the voice disorders already discussed, usually begins with short utterances and progresses to longer strings of speech. If there are associated deficits, the therapist will address these directly.

Also, there is equipment available to measure nasal and oral sound energy and provide visual feedback. Other items that can be used in the diagnosis and treatment of resonance disorders include mirrors to detect excessive airflow through the nose and *videofluoroscopy*, which is a motion X-ray on videotape. In some cases, fixed or removable prosthetic appliances may be necessary because the existing structures cannot close off the nasal cavity during speech.

Cleft Palate

As previously noted, resonance is disordered (and hypernasality often results) when an individual suffers a cleft palate. Clefts occur in the first trimester when facial bones of a fetus do not fuse properly. Because such fusions occur front to back, clefting occurs back to front. That is, one cannot have a congenital cleft anterior to a closed section of the palate.

Why clefts occur every 700 to 750 live births[3] is unclear, but likely reasons include genetic predispositions, the uterine environment (e.g., decreased oxygen in the blood, even for a short time), infections, and diseases. Contrary to old wives' tales, season or manner of conception are not included in these reasons.

Surgical management (to close the gap and rebuild the palate) starts early, often when the child is only 10–12 weeks of age. Depending on the severity of the cleft, additional surgeries (by different specialists) may well follow. Surgeons are most interested in restoring the symmetry of facial features, hoping for adequate muscle movement in the process.

Cleft palates can occur along with clefts of the lips. In many cases, the disfigurement affects basic functions, such as hearing and eating. Articulation may be affected as much as resonance if the speech structures are deformed. It is also worth noting that, in many cases, the development of articulation may be slowed by deformities. Because air for speech production is escaping through the opening, the voice may sound weak (in addition to being hypernasal). If the client tries to compensate by increasing airflow or tension of the speech structures, hyperfunctional pathologies can result.

Because of the number of issues involved, cleft palate teams are common in the diagnosis and treatment of children with clefts. Team members might include a(n)

- speech-language pathologist
- audiologist
- plastic surgeon
- otolaryngologist (also known as an ear, nose, and throat [ENT] physician)
- oral surgeon
- orthodontist
- dentist
- psychologist or counselor
- social worker to help with funding issues

The team exists to oversee the entire client, assessing such areas as speech production, hearing, appearance and function of the facial structures, nutrition, emotional well-being, and funding for necessary treatments.

☐ Synopsis

Disorders of voice can affect any of its parameters—loudness, pitch, or quality. Causes can be organic, psychological, or functional and thus often

PAT'S STORY

Pat was born with a bilateral cleft of the lip and a complete cleft of the palate. She was also born without parents. Pat was, in other words, a ward of the state who would need a lot of attention—surgical and otherwise. The clefts were repaired early—too early as it turned out, because the palate reopened as baby Pat's face grew and expanded. This opening was never reclosed.

Until the age of 6, it was up to various foster parents to get Pat to the Cleft Palate Clinic once a year and to speech therapy as often as it was scheduled. When Pat began school, speech treatment was the highlight of her week, mostly because it took her out of her sweatbox of a school and onto an air-conditioned bus.

Pat's life gained some measure of permanence at the age of 6, as she moved in with the foster family she would be with for the next 9 years. Speech therapy continued for much of that time. In addition, there were more surgeries, sometimes only months apart. Surgeons worked on her lips, ears, and teeth, attempting to help her toward a normal appearance and normal functioning (eating, speaking, and other basic tasks).

Cosmetically, it is the teeth that conjure the most memories. Many of the ones in front were either missing or came in small and inverted. The result was a smile with few discernible teeth, which led to some particularly nasty teasing from classmates. As much of her speech escaped into and out her nose, Pat's voice sounded quite hypernasal, another feature mimicked by cohorts.

Home offered little relief from the prodding doctors and teasing peers that made up Pat's life. Although she appreciates the fact that her foster parents took her in despite all of her special needs, they were in many ways distant from Pat. For one thing, they dismissed her concerns about classmates, stating that bullies only tease those they like. Her foster mother and Pat did not see eye to eye on clothing either, and Mom saw no reason to allow her foster daughter to wear the latest fashions.

Mom would ask, "If everybody else was jumping off a bridge would you jump, too?"

And Pat would think, "Yes, I would," so desperate was she to fit in.

The good news was that her foster dad was a little more nurturing. The bad news was that he rarely spoke during the arguments. Even worse, he was out of the picture by the time Pat was 10.

continued

The result of her foster parents' divorce was a move across country for Pat, her mother, and her new stepfather, a man with whom she did not get along. On top of all that, she had just received an appliance to cover the opening in her palate and was still adjusting to this difference.

This move turned out to be one of many, a situation that forced Pat to continually start over in her attempts to fit in. Thus, not only was family life unhappy, but also she was unable to make lasting friendships. Teachers also gave her the impression that they did not expect much from her. Pat eventually even turned on herself, deciding she was unlikable.

At age 15, Pat left her household and returned to foster care. Although this was a difficult decision to make, it was the start of a happier period for Pat. Her teeth grew in normally (for the most part), and boys began to notice her. She began dating. Academically, there was improvement as well, as Pat's high school grades were good enough to get her into college.

Pat left college after a year, however. Well, she sort of did, anyway. She got a job, got married, and had kids, but through it all kept returning to take more classes. Finally, 20 years after dropping out, Pat enrolled full time again. Four years later, she graduated with honors, earning a bachelor of science in CSD. Her fond memories of therapy were a big factor in choosing her major and, subsequently, in pursuing a graduate CSD degree.

Now a fully certified and licensed SLP, Pat is, as you might expect, heavily involved with children with cleft palates. She works on a diagnostic/treatment team of professionals to ensure that children get the best care available. In addition, Pat serves as an advocate for the families, important work and also uniquely interesting to Pat, as she has the opportunity to view her former situation from the other side.

She has learned, among other things, that she was not as alone as she thought when suffering the wrath of peers. Teasing of those with clefts is actually quite common. In fact, it is a primary reason why there is a social worker on the cleft palate team.

In Pat's opinion, teasing is based on ignorance, and it is therefore important to educate all kids about clefts. She added, "The general population has no idea what the heck a cleft of any kind is." This ignorance is often manifested in remarks that are clueless or just plain rude.

The following are other insights she would like to pass along to new SLPs:

- Parents are an important component of this whole process. They not only need to be involved but also to be educated so that they can understand as much of the experience as possible. Parents also need to advocate for their children (e.g., tell the teacher the kid is not slow, he or she just looks and sounds different) and find proper counseling for their children if and when this is needed.
- SLPs can advocate as well. In her early school years, Pat had an SLP who did so, and this helped her to cope.
- Understand that a cleft palate is a diagnosis, but those who have them are *people*, and as such, they cannot just ignore teasing, not fitting in, and so on. With girls, for example, TV commercials and print ads emphasize a form of beauty difficult to achieve with malformations of the teeth or jaw. For Pat and others, falling short of this standard is a huge emotional hurdle.
- Know the basics with respect to clefts: the types, anatomy, physiology, and compensatory strategies (e.g., making sounds deep in the glottis because the oral cavity is malformed). By being on firm ground with the relevant information, SLPs are better able to diagnose, make treatment recommendations, and just as important, know when treatment is not the best option (if the structures simply cannot move in ways that allow for normal speech).

require the services of more than one professional. Similarly, disorders of resonance may require a team approach, particularly in instances of structural differences, such as a cleft palate.

☐ Vocabulary

abdomen—the part of the trunk that lies between the thorax and the pelvis (*Stedman's Medical Dictionary*, 2000)

acute laryngitis—may accompany any form of upper respiratory tract infection. The main symptom is of hoarseness and often pain in the throat. Swelling of the cords may occur; the voice becomes husky, or it may be lost (Marcovitch, 2006).

aphonia—absence of voice

aspiration—fluid or other foreign material entering the airways

basal ganglia—the caudate and lentiform nuclei and associated areas

behavioral voice treatment—changing the biomechanics of voice production by using a "behavior modification" type of protocol to implement vocal health programs, breathing for speech protocols, or vocalizing warmup and cool-down exercises for increasing adequate, proper, and safe vocal productions

bilateral—affecting both of two sides

Botox—an extremely neurotoxic protein, usually administered via injection, that relaxes muscles; often used to relax a paralyzed vocal fold in the case of spasmodic dysphonia or partial paralysis of the vocal folds

cartilage—connective tissue characterized by its firm consistency (*Stedman's Medical Dictionary*, 2000)

clavicle—a doubly curved long bone that forms part of the shoulder girdle; the collar bone (*Stedman's Medical Dictionary*, 2000)

corticobulbar tract—fibers that innervate the motor nuclei of the trigeminal, facial, and hypoglossal nerves

cul de sac (resonance)—the voice resonates in the throat or nose (as opposed to head or chest) and is often trapped in the throat or nose without a solution to change that; Oftentimes, speech sounds are muffled and most clients are accused of mumbling or not speaking up so they can be heard. Usually an area in the throat or nose is blocked that causes this type of resonance

diaphragm—the musculomembranous partition between the abdominal and thoracic cavities (*Stedman's Medical Dictionary*, 2000)

dopamine—a neurotransmitter related to normal functioning of the central nervous system

dysphonia—disordered phonation

elastic—flexible; returns quickly to its original shape

emotional lability—uncontrolled affect or expression of emotions

epiglottis—a leaf-shaped plate of elastic cartilage at the root of the tongue; serves as a diverter valve during the act of swallowing, keeping food and liquids from entering the trachea (*Stedman's Medical Dictionary*, 2000)

extrapyramidal tract—portion of the nervous system that includes the brainstem and cerebellum

extrinsic muscles—muscles arising outside of, but that act on, a structure

false vocal folds—muscle folds in the larynx separating the ventricle and vestibule of the larynx

functional—voice problems related to abuse or misuse of the vocal mechanism that are not related to a neurological or organic cause. The voice mechanism is structurally sound

fundamental frequency—the lowest frequency of vibration in a complex wave; in voicing, determined by the number of times the vocal folds open and close per second

gastroesophogeal reflux disease (GERD)—the backward flow of stomach acid up through the lower esophageal sphincter and into the lower esophagus (Thibodeau, 2003)

glottis—the vocal folds and the space between them

hyperadduction—increased vocal cord adduction (coming together) (Owens, Metz, & Haas, 2007)

hypoadduction—reduced vocal cord adduction (coming together) (Owens et al., 2007)

hypokinetic dysarthria—results from disorders of the extrapyramidal system (e.g. Parkinsonism); associated with frequent respirations with shallow inspiratory phases and lack of expiratory control; a harsh, tremorous voice with reduced pitch and loudness levels; normal resonation; and fluctuating imprecise articulation, articulatory bursts, and low intelligibility (Bauman-Waengler, 2008)

idiopathic—unknown origin

innervation—stimulation by means of a nerve (Saladin, 2005)

interarytenoid muscle—muscle that glides the arytenoid cartilages together

intrinsic muscles—muscles fully contained within a structure

laryngeal trauma—an injury relating in any way to the larynx (Medical Economics Staff, 2000)

laryngeal webbing—congenital anomaly consisting of connective tissue between the vocal cords; causes airway obstruction and hoarseness (Medical Economics Staff, 2000)

laryngectomee—one who has undergone a laryngectomy

laryngitis—inflammation of the mucous membrane of the larynx and vocal cords; may be acute or chronic. The cause is usually an infection, most commonly viral, although it may be the result of secondary bacterial infection, voice abuse, or irritation by gases or chemicals (Marcovitch, 2006).

larynx—the organ of voice production; the part of the respiratory tract between the pharynx and the trachea; consists of a framework of cartilages and elastic membranes housing the vocal folds and the muscles that control the position and tension of these elements (*Stedman's Medical Dictionary*, 2000)

lateral cricoarytenoid muscles—muscles that close and medially rotate the arytenoid cartilage

loudness—the amount of sound the listener perceives

monotone—voice produced with little variation in loudness

myoelastic-aerodynamic theory of vocal fold vibration—compressed air exerts pressure under the closed vocal folds to cause the folds to open; elasticity of displaced tissue (along with the Bernoulli effect) causes the vocal folds to snap shut, resulting in sound

neurotransmitters—chemicals in the brain that allow neural signals or "messages" to be transferred between neurons, as well as to muscle fibers and other tissues, thus keeping the synapse process alive

optimum pitch—or optimal pitch, the most efficient frequency of vibration of the vocal folds

organic—there are two groups of organic voice disorders; one is structural and one is neurological: Structural causes involve something that is physically wrong with the voice mechanism usually involving tissue or fluids of the vocal folds; neurological causes come from an interruption in the nervous system (i.e., vagus nerve, etc.)

papilloma—benign tumor projecting from the surrounding surface

Parkinson's disease—central nervous system disease that results in vocal fold hypoadduction. Muscle rigidity, tremor, and an overall slowness of movement, or hypokinesia, are characteristics of the disease. Facial appearance is unemotional and sometimes referred to as mask-like. The voice symptoms associated with Parkinson's disease include monopitch, monoloudness, harshness, and breathiness (Owens et al., 2007).

pharyngeoesophageal segment—sphincter-like muscle located between the laryngopharynx and the esophagus (Nicolosi et al., 2004)

pharynx—the upper expanded portion of the digestive tube, between the esophagus below and the mouth and nasal cavities above and in front; distinct from the rest of the digestive tube in that it is composed exclusively of skeletal muscle arranged in outer circular and inner longitudinal layers; the throat (*Stedman's Medical Dictionary*, 2000)

phonotrauma—the accumulated stress from voicing

pitch—the subjective quality that listeners use to order tones from low to high; a perception based on *frequency*, or vocal fold vibration rate

posterior cricoarytenoid muscle—intrinsic muscle of the larynx that widens the glottis

prosthesis—fabricated substitute for a damaged or missing part of the body (*Stedman's Medical Dictionary*, 2000)

psychogenic—usually manifested by a poor voice quality that is the overt manifestation of a psychological or emotional problem

quality—the perception of how the patterns of loudness and pitch combine to make a person's voice recognizable

range of motion—distance and direction of a movement

resonance—the process by which sound emitted by the vocal folds is changed before being heard by a listener

spasticity—condition in which certain muscles are continuously contracted. This contraction causes stiffness or tightness of the muscles and may interfere with movement, speech, and manner of walking (National Institute of Neurological Disorders and Stroke, 2009b).

stoma—an opening in the body

subglottal air pressure—air pressure beneath the level of the vocal folds

thorax—the upper portion of the trunk between the neck and the abdomen; formed by the 12 thoracic vertebrae, the 12 pairs of ribs, the sternum, and the muscles and fasciae attached to these; below, separated by the diaphragm; contains the chief organs of the circulatory and respiratory systems (*Stedman's Medical Dictionary*, 2000)

trachea—the windpipe; the tube from the larynx to the main bronchi that allows the passage of air to the lungs

tracheoesophageal puncture—a procedure by which a fistula (passage) is formed between the trachea and esophagus through which air is directed by means of a prosthetic device to generate esophageal speech (Nicolosi et al., 2004)

tracheostoma breathing valve—a valved device placed in the stoma that enhances breathing ability for implementing an inhalation/exhalation cycle. The valve remains open during breathing but will close with increased expiration of air, allowing the air to be directed into the pharynx to produce speech.

transgender voice therapy—speech therapy to change both the pitch and quality of an individual who desires development of a voice consistent with the new sex role (Nicolosi et al., 2004)

traumatic brain injury—also called acquired brain injury (or just head injury); involves sudden trauma that causes damage to the brain

traumatic laryngitis—commonly caused by vocal abuse, but can result from persistent coughing, muscle tension dysphonia, or direct endolaryngeal injury. This form of laryngitis is self-limited and subsides within a few days when treated with voice conservation and humidification (Bailey, Johnson, & Newlands, 2006).

unilateral—one sided

vagus nerve—cranial nerve X; the vagus nerve contains both sensory and motor fibers. The name *vagus* means "wanderer" and aptly describes this nerve with many widely distributed branches. Its sensory fibers supply the pharynx, larynx, trachea, heart, carotid body, lungs, bronchi, esophagus, stomach, small intestine, and gallbladder (Thibodeau & Patton, 2003).

vocal folds—twin pliable tissue structures involved in breathing, protection of the airway, and producing voice

vocal nodules—tissue masses that grow on the vocal folds

☐ Discussion Questions

1. What parameters of voice are affected by cultural rules or boundaries?
2. What are the aspects of voice that are gender specific? Nongender specific?
3. What physiological characteristics of voice change if someone is ill? Does the particular reason for the illness make any difference?
4. How does one distinguish a male voice from a female voice? A child from an adult?
5. If you were a prominent political figure, how would the resonance and pitch of your voice affect your credibility with the public you serve?
6. You are going to have surgery on your thyroid. How might that surgery affect your voice during your recovery?
7. Why is it that athletes (weight lifters or runners, for example) often complain of difficult breathing while running or lifting?
8. What would be a reason why a boy would want to maintain a falsetto voice even after the age of 14–16?
9. Think about a favorite professor or two you have had in some of your courses. You liked that professor, but it was not just because he or she was an easy grader. What about that professor's voice affected your thoughts and perception of that professor?
10. What is or are the key element(s) of voice that you would have to be aware of that would allow you to be heard in the back of a large auditorium?

☐ Notes

1. Currently, best practices in vocal diagnostics and therapy methods use descriptive terms such as phonotrauma (consensus approval from the Voice and Voice Disorder Special Interest Division 3, ASHA), but it may also be described as vocal hyperfunction or functional dysphonia. These have become good descriptions of stressful and inappropriate laryngeal muscle activity.
2. A vocal health program sets up parameters for the SLP to present to a client/patient. Although the ENT, other surgeon, medical doctor, and so on might prescribe medications or order surgical intervention or laser treatment to remove growths such as nodules or polyps, it is the SLP who teaches the patient how to care for the voice before, during, and after medical, pharmaceutical, or surgical treatments. Behavioral therapy, as mentioned by Ramig and Verdolini, is what the SLP does. It is the "type" of therapy that is done by the SLP, in contrast to a physician's surgical treatment, laser treatment, other medical treatments, or prescription medicines (GERD is often present with voice disorders, and it seems to be the "diagnosis du jour" for all of my

voice patients. They always come to me for therapy after they have seen their doctor and tell me that they are on Prilosec or some other brand of GERD medication). So, vocal health is only one part of behavioral intervention done by the SLP. We "intervene" by analyzing the current vocal behaviors used by our clients and then prescribe a treatment plan as a behavioral intervention to teach new, safe, and often more appropriate use of the voice.

3. Clefts are racially affected, occurring more often with Native Americans and individuals of Asian descent than for Caucasians and less still for African Americans. Gender effects have been noted as well: Males are twice as likely as females to present cleft lip with or without cleft palate; females present cleft palate only at a ratio of about 3:2 in comparison to males.

☐ Recommended Reading

Andrews, M. (2007). *Manual of voice treatment* (3rd ed.). Clifton Park, NY: Delmar Cengage. This text outlines an extensive variety of voice disorder recommendations for treatment.

The text provides a multidisciplinary approach to the clinical treatment of voice disorders as they occur in pediatric through geriatric populations and includes intervention selection suggestions as well as treatment approaches.

Case, J. (2002). *Clinical management of voice disorders* (4th ed.). San Antonio, TX: ProEd.

This text includes a summary of the anatomy and physiology of phonation, including medical aspects of voice disorders. The evaluation and management of a variety of voice disorders includes diagnostic techniques and therapy suggestions.

Colton, R. H., Casper, J. K., & Leonard, R. (2011). *Understanding voice problems: A physiological perspective for diagnosis and treatment*. Philadelphia: Lippincott, Williams, & Wilkins.

This comprehensive text emphasizes the physiological aspects of voice disorders but also includes the usual discussions about the emotional and behavioral aspects of the treatment and management of a variety of voice disorders and what influences the voice changes that occur due to these aspects. The text stresses the analysis and synthesis of information to determine the diagnosis and treatment plan for each disorder.

Gallena, S. K. (2007). *Voice and laryngeal disorders*. St. Louis, MO: Elsevier Mosby. This is an interactive text written in workbook style; it includes highlights of relevant concepts that are needed to use effective evaluation and treatment techniques for voice and laryngeal disorders. It includes numerous case studies as well as audio samples of voice disorders and differences.

Stemple, J. (2000). *Voice therapy clinical studies*. Clifton Park, NY: Delmar Cengage. This text provides a case history/case study approach to evaluation and treatment of voice disorders, including vocal hypofunction, vocal hyperfunction, and functional voice disorders, laryngeal disorders, and spasmodic dysphonia. Management of the professional voice is an added feature to this text.

CHAPTER

The Auditory System

Richard Saul, Ali A. Danesh, and Dale F. Williams

Richard Saul, PhD, is associate professor of audiology at Nova Southeastern University. His specialties and research interests include diagnosis and treatment of auditory processing and dizziness and balance disorders. In addition, Dr. Saul serves as adjunct faculty at Florida Atlantic University and clinical associate at Labyrinth Audiology Incorporated of Boca Raton, Florida.

Ali A. Danesh, PhD, is associate professor in the Department of Communication Sciences and Disorders at Florida Atlantic University. His academic background is concentrated in audiology and auditory electrophysiology. Dr. Danesh teaches courses in audiology, anatomy and physiology of the human communication system, and genetics. His research interests are on auditory evoked potentials and tinnitus.

We may be going out on a limb here, but we feel strongly that, for many, the anatomical structure most closely associated with hearing is the ear.

There. We said it.

Although you might think of the ear as the part of the head that is difficult to sunscreen, this apparatus performs a function that is truly extraordinary: It takes mechanical sound vibrations from the air and turns them into meaningful units of information for the brain.

Think about that for a moment.

Sound waves—molecules of air moving through space—are collected and converted to words, warnings, your roommate's armpit noises, or any

A BIT ABOUT BALANCE

It seems so easy to stay upright, without falling. Our balance mechanism is actually a complex group of systems, it is the means by which we relate to our environmental space and maintain our posture. Signals from the inner ear, our eyes, the sensation of touch (primarily in the soles of our feet), and in our joints combine to provide us with the information we need for efficient balance. The **vestibular system**, a major part of our sense of balance, is located near our hearing mechanism. Fibers from the inner ear come together to form the eighth cranial nerve. That is one of the reasons that problems affecting hearing can also have an impact on balance. Fluid-filled structures within the vestibular system detect the position and motion of the head in space. **Semicircular canals**, representing each direction (up and down, forward and back, and laterally) sense circular or angular movement of the head (anything from nodding yes or no to performing ballet). Two other small sacs, the utricle and saccule, sense linear movement (like going up and down in an elevator). Sensory cells in each of these structures respond to the movement of the fluid—which moves when our head moves—and provide neural information needed by the brain to interpret our body's spatial relationship to our environment, keep our eyes steady when we move our head, and help maintain body posture.

Therefore, you can see how difficult it is to describe dizziness. The condition may result from problems with structures of the inner ear, the eyes, the feet, or the various neural connections and tracts. That is why dizziness is described in so many different ways: from lightheadedness to unsteadiness, to a feeling of rotating or spinning. Treatment options are readily available to lessen dizziness and improve balance. These include various medical and surgical procedures, as well as vestibular and balance rehabilitation.

of a million other recognizable sounds to which we can appropriately respond (with, respectively, language, flight, and either revulsion or a high five).

Here is further evidence of the ear's greatness:

- It allows you to detect even the softest sounds, ones that barely vibrate the eardrum.
- The positioning of our two ears (one on each side of our head, for you beginners) helps you to accurately **localize** the direction of sound.
- The neural fibers of this finely tuned sensory organ ascend the nervous system, allowing you to hear and make sense of complex

speech sounds, even in relatively high levels of distracting background noise.

- The human ear is responsible for not only hearing, but also balance—our ability to literally "know where we are" and maintain
our position in space.

So, you can see that the ear, with all its components, is a remarkable structure. When something goes wrong with it, it can affect hearing and balance,
among other functions. The study of such disorders is called *audiology*.

The auditory system (from the ear capturing sound to the ability of the
brain to interpret it) is one of the primary body senses connecting us with the
outside world. Think about how isolated you would feel if you were no longer
aware of the wind, approaching footsteps, background music, traffic noises,
human conversation, the hum of common household appliances, and the
like. Helen Keller, a writer and activist who was deaf and blind for almost
all of her life, argued that such detachment is worse than losing one's sight
(Meador & Zazove, 2005). Keep in mind also that being born without the
sense of hearing is a major obstacle to efficient learning of spoken language.

Auditory system breakdowns rarely lead to a complete loss of hearing.
But, even partial hearing loss can be pretty bad, resulting in deficits such
as a decreased ability to detect specific sounds, difficulty localizing the
source of a sound, problems hearing in noisy environments, and trouble
learning through the auditory channel. Disordered communication can
also result, given that the auditory system is a major conduit for speech
and language.

On the surface, the auditory system appears simple enough; it is made
up of the outer, middle, and inner ears (see Figure 11.1). However, as we
dig deeper (figuratively, of course), we see that regions of the auditory
nervous system, including these peripheral portions of the ear and many

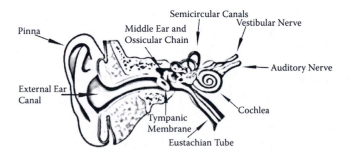

FIGURE 11.1 Structure of the ear showing the outer, middle, and inner
ears (Artwork by Maryam Kaveh, BFA).

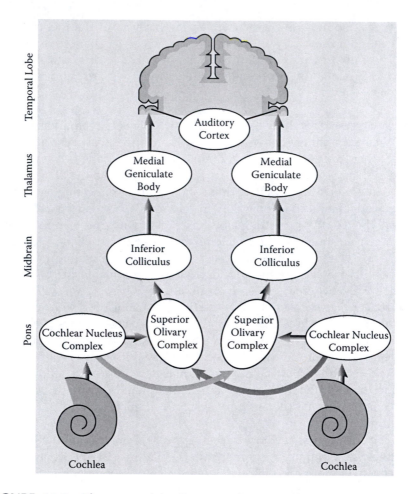

FIGURE 11.2   The central auditory pathway and its different nuclei (Artwork by Maryam Kaveh, BFA).

parts of the brain and brainstem, work together to provide us with auditory input and interpretation (see Figure 11.2). In other words, it is a complex system that affords all of us the common hearing functions (e.g., a chance to understand language, knowing where a sound came from) that seem so routine.

The auditory system progresses from the *auricle*, the outer ear portion on the side of the head (also called the *pinna*)—the thing you hang earrings on and Van Gogh gives to people—all the way to the cortex of the brain. While traveling this route, the physical attributes of sound—**frequency** (which our brain interprets as **pitch**), **intensity** (perceived as **loudness**), and time—are turned into neural information that the brain can understand. In fact, as a signal (i.e., tones, noise, or speech) travels to the brain, it is constantly refined along the way. In essence, the signal is being prepared for processing and then is actually processed by the brain. Problems at different points along this journey may cause distinct effects on hearing and auditory function, ranging from hearing loss to problems combining heard sounds into words.

We can conceive of this system as one continuous nervous system function from the outer ear to the brain. As with any nervous system, its major function is to communicate with the external and internal environments of the body. That is, it takes in information from the sense organs (in this case those for hearing) and sends out signals to the body so it may respond appropriately to different situations (for example, with speech). The **auditory nervous system** can be seen as performing the task of receiving and interpreting auditory input from the outside world. A sound is made, the ear collects it, and the brain makes sense of it (provided, of course, that it makes sense).

The anatomy of the auditory system includes the aforementioned outer and middle ears, the auditory portion of the inner ear or **cochlea**, the **auditory nerve**, structures within the brain stem, and areas deep within the brain (around a neural structure called the *thalamus*), as well as portions of the **cerebral cortex**. Let us divide the auditory system piece by piece and explore how each part contributes to hearing and processing.

As noted, the actual sound, or mechanical vibrations, entering the ear cannot be understood directly by the brain; thus, they must be changed into neural impulses, or language (i.e., neural coding), that the brain can understand. The various structures ascending the auditory system each play a role in translating information into signals that can be processed by the cortex. This translation is accomplished first by converting the sound from **mechanical energy** (vibrations in the outer ear and middle ear) into **hydraulic energy** (vibrations in the fluid of the cochlea), then into *mechanoelectric energy* (produced by the cells within the cochlea), and finally, into **neural or bioelectric signals** that can be interpreted by the auditory cortex.

☐ Hearing and Auditory Impairment

The various structures of the auditory system affect the perception of sound in different ways. That is, each structure has a unique influence on hearing sensitivity, speech clarity, the ability to localize the source of a sound in space, and the perception of complex auditory input. Because of this uniqueness, the type and extent of deficits are different with different malfunctions along the pathway from the outer ear to the cortex. For example, an infection of the middle ear would likely result in hearing loss because it impedes the mechanical transmission of sound through the ear. Yet, if the sound is intense (loud) enough (i.e., the intensity is sufficient to overcome the loss), it will be perceived clearly because the electrical or neural activity needed for perception is not significantly affected by the obstruction of the flow of energy from the outside. A case such as this would be considered a loss of **hearing sensitivity**. On the other hand, a disorder at higher levels of the auditory system, such as the upper brain stem or cortex, would not result in significant sensitivity loss, but rather in difficulty interpreting complex auditory information. In this case, the individual may complain of an inability to hear speech clearly when there is background noise or perhaps report being unable to accurately distinguish complex speech sounds.

When discussing a hearing sensitivity loss, it is important to remember that all speech sounds are not created equal. This is because of differences in how they are produced in the **vocal tract**. Those produced using the energy from vocal fold vibrations (e.g., voiced sounds such as vowels) have more speech power than sounds produced by constricting the outward flow of air (for example, /s/ or /f/). Therefore, individuals with loss of hearing sensitivity may hear some parts of the conversation better than others.

Losses of sensitivity can take different forms. When sounds are poorly conducted through the outer or middle ear, the result is a **conductive hearing loss**. For example, wax totally blocking the ear canal (or the aforementioned middle ear infection) could cause a conductive hearing loss because sound does not reach the inner ear at sufficient intensity. On the other hand, disorders of the cochlea (or, more specifically, its sensory cells) or the eighth cranial (i.e., the auditory branch) nerve result in **sensorineural hearing loss**. Causes of sensorineural hearing loss include excessive or prolonged noise exposure, various systemic disease processes, and aging. A combination of conductive hearing loss and sensorineural hearing loss is referred to as **mixed hearing loss** (see Figure 11.8 for an illustration). Table 11.1 describes the three major types of hearing losses and their audiometric characteristics.

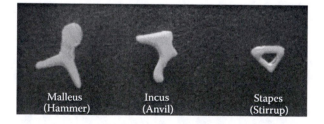

FIGURE 11.3 The ossicles of the human middle ear.

TABLE 11.1 Different Types of Hearing Loss and Their Audiometric Features

Type of Hearing Loss	Site of Lesion (Where the Problem Is)	Air Conduction (AC) Hearing Sensitivity	Bone Conduction (BC) Hearing Sensitivity
CHL	Middle and external ears or both	Abnormal	Normal
SNHL	Inner ear or hearing nerve or both	Abnormal but equal to BC	Abnormal but equal to AC
MHL	Combination of the lesions above	Abnormal	Abnormal but better than AC

CHL, conductive hearing loss; SNHL, sensorineural hearing loss; MHL, mixed hearing loss.

In addition to a loss of hearing sensitivity, disorders can occur at higher levels of the auditory nervous system, from the upper brainstem to the cortex. This type of dysfunction is referred to as *central auditory disorder* and does not typically result in significant sensitivity loss, but rather in difficulty interpreting complex auditory information. The sound gets in, but the brain has difficulty interpreting it. It is sort of like constantly listening to a foreign language or a political debate. Clients with central auditory impairments may well have particular difficulty when there is background noise. They also often report being unable to accurately distinguish complex speech sounds.

☐ Function of the Outer Ear

As noted, the part of the ear that we all see on the side of the head (what most of us actually call "the ear") is referred to as the *auricle* or *pinna*. This structure joins the ear canal, or *external auditory meatus*, to make up the *outer ear*. Its job is to gather sound from the outside world and funnel it to the middle ear, the cochlea, the brain stem, and beyond (well, to the brain). Interestingly, at this point in the evolution of the ear, the auricle even helps to amplify sound just a bit. In other words, if sounds were to travel directly into the ear through the ear canal (as though we did not have an auricle), a small amount of sound energy would be lost.

Because the outer ears are paired, they also allow us to effectively localize the source of a sound. The brain knows (as it were) when and at what intensity a sound arrives at each ear and uses this information to more accurately ascertain the direction of the source.

THE AUDIOGRAM:
A PICTURE OF HEARING AND HEARING LOSS

The audiogram is a graph of hearing ability. More specifically, it is a representation of the softest sounds that we can hear at different frequencies. Audiologists use various test procedures to find this softest sound or threshold. We measure hearing through air conduction as well as bone conduction. Air conduction is essentially testing through the ear canal using earphones or ear insert phones. This helps us determine the extent of hearing loss. Testing directly through the bones of the skull, using a bone oscillator (i.e., by bone conduction), tells us more about the type of hearing loss. How does testing both air and bone conduction tell us about the type of hearing loss (conductive or sensorineural)? When you test by air conduction through earphones, you are testing the entire system beginning at the outer ear. When testing by bone conduction, the tones are presented or transduced through a vibrator placed against the skull. This bone-conducted signal travels through the skull directly to the inner ear. This way, you can compare thresholds by air—including the middle ear—with bone-conducted thresholds that bypass the middle ear. A comparison of air-conducted and bone-conducted thresholds tells us about the extent of middle ear involvement as compared with the rest of the auditory system. Figure 11.4, shows normal hearing sensitivity for a 22-year-old woman. In addition, Figure 11.5 represents a conductive hearing loss, and Figures 11.6 and 11.7 depict two

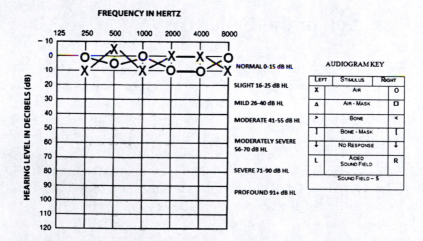

FIGURE 11.4   Bilateral normal hearing sensitivity in a 22-year-old female college student.

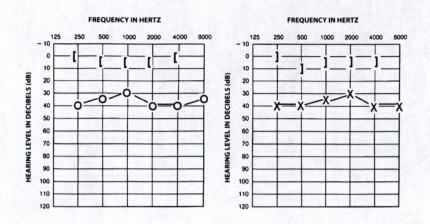

FIGURE 11.5 Bilateral conductive hearing loss in a 7-year-old child with serous otitis media.

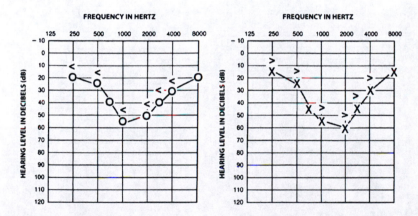

FIGURE 11.6 Bilateral *cookie-bite* audiogram due to rubella in early childhood resulting in moderate sensorineural hearing loss in a 17-year-old adolescent.

different versions of sensorineural hearing losses. Finally, Figure 11.8 illustrates an audiogram of a patient with mixed hearing loss.

Each of the tones tested represents the frequencies considered important for communication ability. We generally test at octave intervals to sample a range of frequencies for which the ear is sensitive. Thus, the frequencies 250, 500, 1,000, 2,000, 4,000, and 8,000 Hz (**hertz**) are commonly tested. For even more detailed information, we may test at interoctave frequencies (e.g., 750, 3,000, and 6,000 Hz).

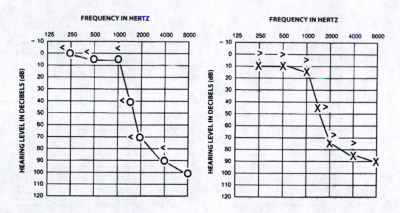

FIGURE 11.7 Bilateral sloping sensorineural hearing loss in a 50-year-old male due to long-term industrial noise exposure over a 30-year period.

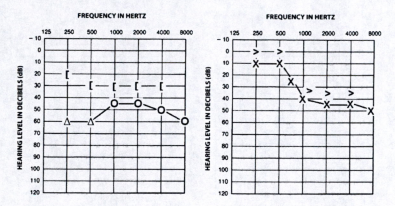

FIGURE 11.8 Mixed hearing loss (combination of conductive hearing loss and sensorineural hearing loss) for the right ear in a 70-year-old female with presbycusis as well as otitis media. Note that the left ear shows the existing sensorineural hearing loss.

We plot the threshold at each of the frequencies to create this graph. The configuration of the graph can provide valuable clues about the nature of the disorder.

☐ What Is Normal Hearing?

If you take a whole bunch of young adults, without any hearing or auditory problems, and determine their average hearing for a particular tone,

THE DECIBEL

The ear is an amazingly sensitive mechanism. It is sensitive to very soft sounds. The greater the sound pressure applied to it, the greater the response of the auditory system. The magnitude of the response between the softest sound the ear can detect and a sound that is sufficiently intense to cause discomfort is really large—like 10 million to 1. So, we use a scale called the *decibel* (named after Alexander Graham Bell), which is a ratio based on a reference to a very soft sound. This way, we can reduce the range of these really big numbers such that 10 million to 1 would range from 0 to 140 dB.

you will have a reasonable threshold for that tone (i.e., the lowest intensity level at which it can be heard). This can be done for all frequencies of interest as our hearing ability is not the same for each frequency. You can then assign a value of 0 dB (decibel) hearing level (HL) to each of these average thresholds. That will be your starting point. Normal audiometric hearing is about 0dB HL, with a range to about 25dB HL. That is not an absolute. There are still varied opinions about what is normal hearing; for example, a young child learning language may be affected by hearing loss as low as 15 dBHL.

☐ A Note About Our Description of Hearing Levels

The scale used by hearing scientists (those involved in the science of sound) to measure hearing is called *sound pressure level* or SPL. This is based on a reference point with which other levels may be compared. It is expressed in decibel sound pressure level (dB SPL). Audiologists have modified this scale to represent hearing sensitivity. This modification is expressed in decibel hearing level (dB HL).

Here is an amazing caveat to the function of the outer ear: as does any cavity, the ear canal resonates. *Resonance* is the process by which air molecules vibrate the most at certain frequencies. Every substance has a **resonant frequency** (it is the reason opera singers can vibrate glass or, as in the case of one TV ad, glass beer bottles). As it turns out, the resonant frequency of the ear canal is around 3,000 Hz. Thus, parts of incoming sound are amplified around this frequency. This helps us a great deal in our daily lives because several harder-to-hear consonant sounds, such as the /th/ in *thin* or the /f/ in *fast*, come into the system at frequencies close to 3,000 Hz.

NONORGANIC HEARING LOSS
(ALSO CALLED PSEUDOHYPACUSIS)

From time to time, finding threshold is not so easy. A small number of the patients seen in audiology clinics will pretend to have hearing loss or exaggerate an existing hearing loss. They may do this for a variety of reasons, such as financial gain, avoidance of obligations, or perhaps to seek attention. The term *nonorganic* tells us that the observed hearing thresholds are not true or "organic" thresholds. There are a number of audiometric tests that provide information or clues regarding response inconsistencies. One of the significant contributions of audiology is to identify nonorganic hearing loss (pseudohypacusis) and obtain a valid hearing test for diagnostic as well as for medicolegal purposes.

As audiologists, our position is not to judge the reason for nonorganicity. We do not assess the motivation or underlying reason for the problem. It may be an underlying psychological or emotional involvement. We can however try to ascertain the true organic hearing ability.

In current audiological practice, we not only have sensitized behavioral tests to look for inconsistencies (such as comparing speech and tones for accuracy), but also we have electrophysiological measures such as the auditory brain stem response (ABR), otoacoustic emissions (OAEs), and acoustic reflex measures (see discussion of electrophysiological measures). These tests can help estimate hearing ability without a patient's active participation.

If we think of the 1-inch long (or so) ear canal as the pathway for outside sound to get to the eardrum, it follows that a clear ear canal is needed to hear well. In fact, because of the need for an unobstructed pathway, glands in the outer third of the ear canal produce *cerumen* (or earwax) to safeguard this pathway. From our perspective, then, earwax is a good thing, and not only because you can mold it into little bunnies or snowmen. Earwax also keeps the canal moist and protects it from invading insects, little brother's spitballs, or anything else that might inappropriately find its way into the ear. And, in addition to being blessed with earwax, the canal is also lined with little hairs, or *cilia*, that help keep the ear fresh and clean. They are so good at this in fact, that there is typically no need to clean inside the ear canal (i.e., save the Q-tips for the auricle or, for that matter, for putting on eye shadow). As a side note, there is a branch of the vagus nerve (cranial nerve X) that travels near the surface of the ear canal. This nerve is associated with the "cough reflex." So, next time you are sticking something inside your ear canal and you notice the initiation of coughing, you will know why this happens. Then, stop putting stuff in there; you could hurt your eardrum.

An outer ear problem may or may not affect hearing ability. This would depend on the type and location of the problem. For example, *otitis externa*, usually caused by a bacterial infection, can cause a great deal of discomfort, but usually not hearing loss. This condition has most often been associated with heat and moisture from swimming or similar activities that can create a perfect setting for bacteria, fungi, or viruses. If the condition results in significant swelling that subsequently obstructs the ear canal, a loss of hearing may result. The auricle, because it is the most exposed portion of the ear, may show signs of skin disorder and infection. Those of us who like to scratch our ears incessantly often create a path for bacteria or virus. An infection of the cartilage of the auricle is called *chondritis*. Likewise, *microtia*, a congenital malformation of one or more parts of the outer ear present at birth, would not result in any real hearing loss if the ear canal is unaffected and sound is allowed to pass through. However, if the malformation involves the ear canal, such as *atresia*, blocking sound from flowing to the eardrum, impaired hearing results. A *stenosis*, or narrowing of the ear canal, does not cause significant hearing loss as the canal is not completely occluded.

Other conditions are better bets for creating hearing loss. For example, excessive amounts of cerumen, if impacted, would create a complete or near-complete barrier to the flow of sound, obviously a significant interference to hearing it. Hearing loss may also occur from obstruction by other foreign material, but again, these materials would have to occlude the ear canal completely or near completely. We have seen cases in which pencil erasers, marbles, or beans have been stuffed into the ear, effectively impeding the flow of sound and causing hearing loss. Here, we recommend a two-step treatment: (1) take them out and (2) keep them out.

☐ The Middle Ear Transformer Mechanism

The great thing about having a middle ear is that it acts as a matching device between the outside world and the inner ear. What does it match, you ask? Well, it allows sound molecules floating around in air from the outside world to match the more tightly packed molecules in the fluid of the inner ear. Why is this important? Read on.

Air molecules cannot move very far. When pressure is applied from, let us say, the force of your voice, sound waves bump into the air molecules, which in turn bump into other molecules. That is the continuation of sound wave movement in air.

However, this kind of movement is not possible in the inner ear. That is because the density of fluid molecules is greater than that of air molecules. Sound flows more easily in inner ear fluid than in air. It is rather like the difference between moving your hand through air as compared to moving it through sand (although the sound actually travels *slower* in air than in the densely-packed fluid). The difference in densities is called an *impedance mismatch*. But as we know, sound moving through air must eventually enter the inner ear for analysis. The problem is that there would be a significant loss of energy in changing from one medium to another, that is, air to inner ear fluid. We have to somehow recover this energy loss.

There are two main mechanisms that help to amplify airborne sound moving to the fluid-filled cochlea: the condensation effect and the lever action of the ossicles. The eardrum attaches to the ear canal by a cartilaginous ring called the *annulus* and seals off the middle ear from the ear canal. The eardrum is flexible and very strong. If you could shrink yourself, then run through the ear canal and smack right into the eardrum, you would bounce off, as if it were a trampoline (trust us on this). This resilient membrane is made up of three layers: an outer epithelial or skin-like layer, a strong fibrous middle layer, and an inner membrane continuous with the mucous lining of the middle ear space.

Sound is funneled through the middle ear from the larger eardrum at one end to the much smaller (about 1/17th the area) membrane at the entrance to the inner ear, the *oval window*. How does the eardrum connect through the middle ear to the oval window? This gap is traversed by three tiny bones collectively known as the *ossicular chain* (for those needing a fast fact for cocktail parties, these are the smallest bones in the human body, and as a unit, they can almost fit onto a dime) (Figure 11.3). The first of these bones is the *malleus*, which is partially embedded in the eardrum at one end and connects with another bone, the *incus*. The incus also connects with the neck of the *stapes* at the entrance to the inner ear. The footplate or base of the stapes (the smallest of these tiny bones) sits in the oval window—transferring the mechanical vibrations to the fluid of the inner ear. And that is pretty much it. The large size of the eardrum funneling sound vibrations to the smaller oval window creates an increase in sound pressure that compensates for the mismatch between air and fluid.[1]

Another important middle ear landmark is the *Eustachian tube*, a narrow channel that runs from the nasopharynx (essentially the part of your throat at the back of the nose) to the middle ear. This tube is normally closed (at the soft tissue entrance at the throat). Its major function is to equalize the pressure between the outside world and the middle ear space. This is a worthwhile function to say the least, given that the middle ear is a closed space, and the only way to get fresh air into it is through this tube. When your ears "pop" (think airline travel), that is the Eustachian tube opening and equalizing pressure. If pressure does not equalize, the middle ear will further absorb oxygen, resulting in lowered air pressure within the middle ear space. If you then look into the ear canal, you can see the eardrum being sucked in a bit. This results from the higher outside air pressure. You can force the muscles around the tube to open it by yawning, swallowing, or even chewing. It is important for the tube to work properly because a well-aerated middle ear, in which the pressure within its space is the same as the pressure in the outside atmosphere, makes for a healthy and happy middle ear.

Because of its location, the Eustachian tube is ripe for spreading infection. This is particularly true for children because the tube is shorter, wider, and oriented more horizontally than that of an adult. This makes it easier for infection to travel through the tube from the back portion of the throat. Being that the middle ear is indirectly connected, by way of the Eustachian tube, all the way to the membranes of the lungs, you can see how infection can easily move from areas of the respiratory system to the ears.

An infection of the middle ear, or *otitis media,* may be caused by reduced ventilation of the middle ear resulting from poor Eustachian tube function. In fact, as mentioned, when the middle ear pressure is lowered, creating a partial vacuum, a clear fluid may be secreted. This would be an otitis media *with fluid,* or *serous otitis media* (SOM). This condition causes conductive-type hearing loss. If left untreated, the infection can get *really* serous (sorry about that), spreading to the air cells of the surrounding mastoid bone. When this occurs, the condition is called *mastoiditis.* This is potentially dangerous, given that the ear is quite close to the brain, and for reasons you can probably guess yourselves, you do not want an infection near the brain.

Other possible middle ear problems include *cholesteotoma* and *otosclerosis.* The former consists of a cyst-like growth that begins in the top portion of the middle ear near the eardrum and, in time, may extend far into the ear canal—even wearing away the bone separating the ear and the brain. The associated conductive hearing loss can be anywhere from mild to severe depending on the extent of the growth. With otosclerosis, bone tissue surrounding the stapes footplate grows around it and restricts its movement. You will surely recall our explanation of how the middle ear bones, or ossicles, transfer vibrations from the eardrum to the inner ear through the middle ear space. With that in mind, you can see how any restriction in that movement can cause conductive-type hearing loss. For reasons that are not entirely clear, women are more susceptible to this condition than are men (Sakihara & Parving, 1999).

There are other disorders (many, in fact) that affect the middle ear. The common feature across them is that the flow of energy is reduced through the middle ear system, resulting in a loss of signal and, in turn, decreased hearing sensitivity.

☐ The Sensory Mechanism of Hearing: The Cochlea

The hearing portion of the inner ear, or *cochlea*, is one of the most complex structures of the body. Early anatomists saw this formation as a maze of channels, referring to it as the *labyrinth* (*mazelike* in Ancient Greek). It is the site at which frequency and intensity information are separated and then recombined for higher levels of auditory analysis.

Within the cochlea, tiny hair strands, or *cilia*, send information on a given sound to the brain. Exactly what is passed on by a given cell depends on where it is located along the *basilar membrane* within the cochlea. Across the length of this membrane, the high frequencies are coded at the entrance and low frequencies at the farthest section. This is referred to as *tonotopic organization*. Remember it this way: The high frequencies are coded at the low end, low frequencies at the high end. (Come to think of it, never mind.) In any case, depending on the specific frequency of the sound going in, there will be displacement at a corresponding point along the membrane—much like the strings of a piano or harp (yes, the keys are connected to the strings of the piano). Differences in width and thickness of this basilar membrane create a variety of resonances along its length (resulting in different areas of maximum frequency stimulation). The amount of displacement at any one point depends on the intensity of the sound. The more intense the sound, the greater the displacement. And, the greater the displacement is, the more robust is the perception.

The tiny sensory hair cells are many (about 15,000 of them; one inner row of approximately 3,000 cells and about three outer rows totaling about 12,000). They detect the motion of vibrations in air (coming from the outer and middle ear via the fluid movements of the inner ear) within a frequency range of about 20 to 20,000 Hz. This range of sensitivity is, at the very least, adequate for the needs of human survival. It allows us to hear much, but not all, of the sound around us. Other species are sensitive to different ranges of sound frequencies that more closely meet their survival and communicative needs. A dog, for example, has similar hearing to humans at the low-frequency end, but somewhat better hearing in the high frequencies—up to about 40,000 Hz. This gives our canine friends the awareness of particular sounds necessary for their survival—like the squeaks of small animals (although our domestic dogs' survival depends mainly on hearing food being poured into their supper

AUDITORY ELECTROPHYSIOLOGY: AN AID TO DIAGNOSIS

Diagnostic audiology has come a long way—from simple evaluations of hearing a whispered voice, tuning fork tests, to well-designed behavioral procedures using tones of specific frequencies. In addition, more specialized tests of speech sound recognition helped us understand how individuals perceived the auditory world around them. With increasing technology came the addition of efficient electrophysiological and electroacoustic equipment specially designed to evaluate the status of the middle ear, inner ear, and auditory pathways through the brainstem and brain. We mention three of the most widely used procedures.

IMMITTANCE MEASURES

Immittance measure procedures involve measuring the movement of the eardrum in response to pressure changes in the ear canal. In this way, we can assess the integrity of the middle ear system. Ear infections and other middle ear disorders affect the results in predictable ways. Part of the immittance battery is to measure the pressure changes in the ear canal resulting from middle ear muscle reflexes elicited by intense sound introduced into the ears via earphones. These reflexes arise from a connection between the auditory and facial cranial nerves. The information is valuable in providing information about the type of hearing loss and the integrity of the neural pathways in the brainstem.

OTOACOUSTIC EMISSIONS

One of the more important advances in diagnostic audiology has been the clinical use of otoacoustic emissions (OAEs), a low-level acoustic signal likely generated by small changes in the movement of the cochlear outer hair cells. Using ultrasensitive microphones inserted into the ear canal, these inner ear sound responses can be recorded and analyzed. Audiology has been able to use this phenomenon to study the function of the auditory system, specifically at the cochlea. OAEs can help to determine the site of auditory dysfunction and monitor medications that are toxic to the ear. The presence of OAEs indicates normal cochlear function. OAEs are commonly used in neonatal hearing screening and are mandated in more than 40 states as a routine procedure prior to newborn discharge from the hospital. OAEs are also useful in distinguishing different types of sensorineural hearing loss.

continued

THE AUDITORY BRAINSTEM RESPONSE

In addition to testing the integrity of the middle and inner ear, we can use specialized computer equipment to average the very small electrical responses from the brain stem in response to sounds such as clicks presented to the ears through earphones. The electrical activity is measured through surface electrodes placed on the scalp and areas near the ears. The auditory brain stem response (ABR) is not a test of structure—like computed tomography (the CT scan) or magnetic resonance imaging (MRI). It is a test of function—how the system responds synchronously to sound. This procedure has been helpful in estimating hearing sensitivity for individuals who cannot respond behaviorally and in identifying many types of disorders along the auditory nerve and brain stem neural pathways. The ABR has also been used with success in neonatal hearing screening programs. When we combine the results of these electrophysiological test procedures, we have a unique opportunity to assess the auditory system at diverse levels: middle ear, auditory nerve, and auditory brain stem pathways. A disorder called *auditory neuropathy/auditory dyssynchrony* occurs when the outer hair cells of the cochlea are normal, yet there is reduced function at the brainstem level. In this case, there is poor transmission of auditory information from the cochlea to the brain. Inner hair cells are likely involved. Hearing sensitivity can be anywhere from normal to profound. Hearing loss is often progressive. The condition is diagnosed primarily by the following results on the tests described: The ABR shows poor auditory neural function, middle ear muscle reflexes are absent, and the OAEs show normal-cochlear (outer hair cell) function. Individuals with this condition have difficulty hearing speech clearly and consistently. Speech and language are often affected. Speech and language therapy is indicated, and some individuals with more severe hearing loss may benefit from cochlear implants.

dishes). Small animals, vulnerable to a wide range of predators, may have extended high-frequency hearing so that they may hear the quick, sharp sounds that can alert them to danger. The mouse, for example, can have a high-frequency hearing range up to 90,000 Hz. And try talking to a bat sometime. They may well not understand a thing you say because they have poor low-frequency hearing (not to mention their poor understanding of human language). Still, they are well aware of what is going on around them and can locate objects by sending and receiving sound up to or even greater than 100,000 Hz. They need this sensitivity for high frequencies because, well, they are blind as bats.

But, back to humans. The hearing loss that we experience with inner ear damage is the sensorineural type and can be related to many factors, including trauma, excessive noise (see Figure 11.7), chemical exposure, certain drugs, aging, metabolic disturbances, childhood diseases, and genetic abnormalities. Thus, sensorineural hearing loss can occur at any age. One common example, noise-induced hearing loss, usually occurs gradually over time, initially affecting the higher frequencies. The first noticeable effect is often difficulty clearly hearing the sounds with higher-frequency energy, such as /s/, /t/, /f/, /θ/ (the th in "think"), and /ʃ/ (the first sound of "shoe").

□ Function of the Eighth Cranial Nerve and Auditory Brainstem

As mentioned, the cochlea is the first place where simple elements of frequency and time of auditory signals are processed. Should a disorder occur at this level, a distorted response will ascend to higher levels of the brainstem and brain, influencing the final perception of sound. Therefore, an impaired cochlea not only may complicate hearing simple sounds and speech, but also can affect the processing of complex auditory stimuli.

Past the cochlea, fibers from the auditory (eighth cranial) nerve enter the brain stem, forming the early auditory cell networks as they go. Within these networks, aspects of frequency, intensity, and time are further analyzed, as numerous ascending fibers (or *fiber tracts*) carry auditory information to the cortex of the brain. In essence, the fibers act as an elevator from the ear to the brain. As the signal rides to the top, it stops at different levels (the nuclei comprised of groupings of cell bodies) (see Figure 11.2). Each of these levels serves to further refine auditory information.

As the fibers continue up the stem, fiber networks from the right side interact with networks from the left side at the midlevel of the brain stem. In this manner, a highly sophisticated capacity is achieved to help localize the source of a sound in space. As noted, depending on the angle of incoming sound, the brain figures out when a sound hits each ear (there is a delay between a sound reaching the near ear and when it reaches the far ear). The brain analyzes the differences in intensity between the near and far ears. Well, truthfully, it is not actually the brain that first analyzes the differences. The differences in time and intensity are, in large part, analyzed and calculated at the mid-brain stem level—at nuclei called the *superior olive*. This group of cells provides a crossover point, a place where fibers switch sides while continuing their ascent (see Figure 11.2). The nuclei, at this point, are **innervated** from each ear, and the information (from the ears) is combined as it travels to the brain. This process—getting information from both ears—is one of the most important auditory features of the brainstem as it provides us with the ability to know where a sound of interest is originating in the world around us. Simply put, the brain determines which ear heard the sound first and loudest (and the differences in time and intensity of the perception of the second ear), allowing us to ascertain where the sound came from.

At higher levels of the brainstem, cellular networks increase their analyzing capacity to prepare auditory information for processing at cortical levels. Increasing anatomical redundancy (i.e., going up and down, left and right as they ascend) allows for overlapping functions at each of these levels. What this means is that fibers go up one side while traveling to the other side—allowing the same information to take different pathways to the brain. In fact, one outstanding feature of the auditory system is that information can be processed simultaneously at each level. Hence, the brain receives the same information from different processing centers. This is particularly helpful when hearing is difficult. For example, anyone attempting to hear a cell phone call in a football stadium after the home team scores would miss much of the message without multiple providers. Also, this design allows individuals with neurological **lesions** (abnormal tissue that would otherwise block the signals) extra pathways to receive the auditory information.

Lesions in the auditory system can result in disorders of the hearing nerve and auditory brainstem. One major type of lesion is a tumor arising from the eighth cranial nerve. This is a benign lesion on the vestibular branch of the nerve that, eventually, may expand to the auditory branch. This tumor may be associated with tinnitus, dizziness, and often poor speech understanding on the affected side.

In addition to tumors, other problems can also affect the auditory nerve and brainstem pathways. These include disease, trauma, or growths on the auditory nerve or within the brainstem. It is important to remember that as auditory information ascends from the ear to the brain, the resulting auditory effects become subtler because the structures are refining in addition to performing new functions. Also, there is more than a single route that auditory information can use to reach the brain. At the level of the auditory nerve and low brain stem, the auditory effects of damage can be quite dramatic—causing significant hearing loss, tinnitus, and reduced speech clarity on the affected side. If the system were a bottle, the auditory nerve would be the bottleneck through which all information must pass. This is quite a responsibility for a small nerve. So, as you can imagine, disorders of the eighth nerve can result in dramatic effects on hearing and understanding speech clearly. The same types of disorders may also manifest themselves at higher levels of the brain stem, but would likely be less dramatic—showing variable, if any, hearing loss. As it turns out, the

NOISE IN THE EARS: TINNITUS

Tinnitus (ti.ni.tus or ti.nigh.tus) is the perception of ringing, noise, or other sounds in the ear(s) or head without an external source. The sound is often described as a hissing or roaring sound; some older patients say that it sounds like a steam radiator.

Approximately 10% of the population has reported some sort of tinnitus in one or both ears. Tinnitus can be a result of many conditions, such as excessive noise exposure (which, by the way, can include loud music), ear infections, or damage anywhere along the auditory pathway from the outer ear to the brain. It can occur with or without a hearing loss and frequently affects concentration and, not incidentally, sleep. Although many affected individuals are being told that there is no cure for it, tinnitus is manageable, and many report relief after proper intervention.

Managing tinnitus can be difficult. However, we are seeing more success in recent years. If a hearing loss is present, hearing aids may serve to mask the tinnitus. That is, they can raise the intensity of background noise to hide the ringing. Also, wearable tinnitus maskers and sound generators have been used with some success. These units produce a noise that acts to inhibit the tinnitus and helps to make the individual habituate. Other treatments include various drugs and surgeries.

Some years ago, when patients reported difficulty sleeping, we had suggested keeping a radio or noise generator in the background. With current technological advances, therapeutic sound therapies are available—these are even downloadable to their MP3 players or iPods.

Sound therapies for tinnitus include a variety of sound stimuli, such as music and acoustically engineered noise, and have been used to desensitize and retrain the brain to better cope with tinnitus. In many cases, the combination of sound therapy and planned education and counseling serve to minimize the emotional and psychological effects of tinnitus on a patient's daily life.

lower portion of the brain stem, around the area called the *cochlear nucleus*, is the last point at which fibers ascending the brain stem are on the same side of the ear from which they receive information. After that, a sound presented to one ear travels along fibers to both sides of the brain. And as you get to higher levels, more fibers cross than stay on the same side. Therefore, disorders at the higher portions of the brainstem often show contralateral auditory effects; that is, they affect the ear opposite the side of the lesion (Katz, 1970).

☐ Cortical-Level Processing

By this point, you can see that the act of hearing is much more than simple physical analysis of the acoustic waveform. Many brain mechanisms are involved in decoding, remembering, and interpreting auditory signals. The individual parts that comprise the auditory nervous system each play a vital role in the final processing of acoustic information. We tend to think of hearing in terms of a sound being *loud enough* to detect, but in addition to intensity, our system has to be able to resolve detailed information in the duration and frequency domains (what we think of as time and pitch), further refining those aspects that are analyzed at lower levels.

As explained, auditory information from both ears travels to the brain for processing. And, the brain interprets the auditory signals that it receives.

Clearly, it is possible to have auditory problems without a hearing loss. In fact, standard hearing tests are not sensitive to higher levels of auditory dysfunction. Individuals with such deficits may report difficulty hearing speech clearly in groups or even in low levels of background noise (and might thus turn up the TV). They may have a hard time understanding rapid speech, putting certain sounds together into words, or remembering what they hear. Some even report difficulty localizing the source of a sound.

What can cause these types of auditory problems? Various disease processes, damage caused by trauma or stroke, or various types of brain dysfunction are possibilities. Such lesions at this level primarily affect perception in the opposite ear. Although rare, **cortical deafness** can occur if the disorder is bilateral (i.e., if both sides of the temporal lobe are affected).

☐ A Bit More About Hearing and the Aging Process

Structural and functional changes in hearing and auditory processing due to aging is called *presbycusis*. This process results in a decline in peripheral hearing, higher-level auditory function, or both. As it is a function of growing older, most people will eventually experience presbycusis to some degree. What makes this process particularly challenging is that the hearing problem is often a combination of peripheral and central auditory system effects. Degeneration of the structures of the outer, middle, and inner ear, in addition to changes in the auditory nerve, brain stem, and brain may produce a combination of reduced hearing sensitivity, distorted perception of speech sounds, and an array of other perceptual effects, such as difficulties integrating and separating auditory information, interpreting speech sounds effectively, and even remembering and sequencing speech and nonspeech sounds.

Considering that the central auditory components of the dysfunction involve higher-order functions of perception, the effectiveness of hearing aids, for some individuals, may be limited. Hearing aids, which serve as frequency selective amplifiers, provide better clarity from the periphery and can also help provide a foundation for effective management of auditory processing disorders. Audiologists can carefully define the contributions of peripheral and central auditory effects of the impairment through sensitized diagnostic procedures, then provide realistic counseling regarding the benefits and limitations of amplification as well as begin direct treatment such as audiologic rehabilitation.

☐ Audiologic Rehabilitation

When you get right down to it, the audiologist's work is comprised of two major purposes: diagnosis and rehabilitation of auditory disorders. Diagnostic audiology includes identification and, as the name suggests, diagnosis. AR consists of management and treatment.

The *identification* part of diagnostic audiology involves detecting hearing loss using screening techniques routinely carried out at hospitals, schools, and clinics. *Diagnosis* refers to evaluating the auditory system to measure the extent and type of hearing loss. Following these procedures, management can include various recommendations, such as referrals to other specialists, continued monitoring of hearing, and direct treatment, which may consist of auditory training, use of amplification, or speechreading. Treatment is initiated for those with hearing loss or those with auditory processing disorders.

Audiologic rehabilitation (AR) refers to techniques and strategies that help individuals approximate the hearing capacities they enjoyed before they were lost. *Audiologic habilitation* (AH; i.e., without the re- prefix), on the other hand, is the management of children born with hearing loss. The techniques used in AR or AH include auditory training, speechreading, and communication modes. A summary of each follows.

- *Auditory training* is comprised of various tasks designed to develop the hearing and listening capabilities of patients with hearing loss. These tasks are designed to improve the person's communication in noisy environments, enhance localization ability, and maximize benefits derived from amplification.

SOME IMPORTANT TERMS IN AURAL REHABILITATION

assistive listening device—instruments designed to assist hearing impaired

audiologic/aural rehabilitation—intervention for individuals who have not developed normal communication skills such as speech, language, and hearing

auditory training—techniques and interventions designed for individuals with hearing loss to maximize the use of their residual hearing

cochlear implant—an electronic device that is partially implanted in the skull and provides auditory stimulation to individuals with profound or total hearing loss

habilitation—process or intervention targeted at developing skills and abilities

hearing aids—electronic amplification devices that are employed to increase hearing sensitivity of individuals with impaired hearing

rehabilitation—process or intervention planned for reteaching lost skills

sign language—a type of manual communication in which hand positions and movements are employed to represent linguistic information

speechreading—recognition of speech with the use of auditory and visual cues

tinnitus—perception of ringing or noise in the ear(s) or head without any external source

- *Speechreading*, often referred to by the general public as *lip reading*, is the ability to comprehend oral communication with clues from lip movements, facial expression, and hand or body gestures. Speechreading enables the hearing-impaired individual to communicate more effectively with the use of visual information and, as such, requires sufficient illumination in the environment.

- *Modes of communication* are methods employed to help hearing-impaired individuals interact with others. Two major modes are *oral/aural communication* and *manual communication*. Each of these modes has subcategories. With oral/aural communication, emphasis is given to the use of auditory and visual channels. On the other hand, with manual communication, techniques such as finger spelling and sign language are employed as the means of communication. A combination of these modes is referred to as global or *total communication*. As far as we remember, there has been a long-standing controversy among the schools of thought in the education of the hearing impaired about the preferred mode of communication (e.g., see Eleweke & Rodda, 2000).

American Sign Language (ASL) is one of the widespread methods of manual communication. It is a complete language system, encompassing a structured grammar system that is quite natural for those without hearing.

☐ Hearing Aids, Assistive Listening Devices, and Cochlear Implants

We begin this section with what you probably already know about hearing aids. They are electronic devices that can amplify sounds to a desired level, designed to allow a hearing-impaired individual to hear and understand normal conversational speech.

Over the years, hearing aids have come a long way. The original electronic aids from the early 1900s were so heavy that users had to carry them with forklifts. Okay, we made that up, but they did require backpacks. Now, hearing aids are miniaturized to a point where they can be

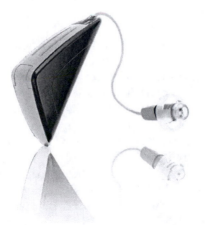

FIGURE 11.9   A contemporary hearing aid. (Courtesy of Oticon USA.)

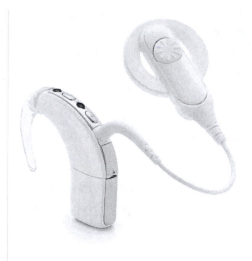

FIGURE 11.10 A cochlear implant device. (Courtesy of Cochlear Americas.)

inserted deep in the ear canal or worn behind the ear (see Figure 11.9). The majority of contemporary hearing aids are digital. These devices are capable of calculating the hearing needs of users in a variety of acoustical environments. Still, they are not perfect. While glasses restore vision to 20–20, hearing aids are a bit like going to 20–40 for this sense. That is just an analogy (i.e., it is not precise), but you get the idea.

Because hearing aids cannot do it all, additional tools have been developed to ease the process of communication in difficult listening situations. These are designed to reduce the effects of distance, background noise, and acoustical reverberation. Some examples include infrared transmitters for TV and telephones. There are also new devices with remote microphones that beam a clear signal to the hearing aid. Finally, there are wireless links that allow cell phone users to better hear calls.

Sometimes, the degree of hearing loss is so profound that a hearing aid cannot provide sufficient benefit for the user. In these cases, the patient is a candidate for a surgical and rehabilitation procedure that is referred to as *cochlear implantation*. If the inner ear is so damaged that it cannot create nerve impulses, this procedure provides another way to make the nerves fire. A series of tiny electrodes is placed in the inner ear. These electrodes are connected to a speech processor behind the auricle. Their function is to change sound into electrical impulses. The impulses travel through the electrodes to stimulate the fibers of the auditory nerve. Then, they travel up to the brain for perception. Cochlear implant technology is one of the most advanced methods to help those with "unaidable" hearing loss. Figure 11.10 shows this elegant instrument.

TREATMENT FOR AUDITORY PROCESSING DISORDERS

In addition to the varied treatment protocols for hearing loss, direct treatment approaches have been developed to address auditory processing disorders, which can exist with or without the presence of hearing loss. In this chapter, we have discussed auditory processing in terms of what the brain does with the information that it receives—it separates, integrates, and remembers it. Also noted was that auditory information is constantly being refined as it ascends the auditory nervous system from the cochlea to the cortex. Now, consider that neural information also descends to inhibit or suppress some neural information. This provides a filtering of sorts, which limits overload (the **efferent auditory system**).

Impaired function to the auditory nervous system may occur from various neurological and neurobiological conditions, such as stroke, head trauma, and central processing disorders of unknown etiology that may have arisen from prenatal, perinatal, postnatal, or adult-onset conditions. Individuals with auditory processing disorders often exhibit patterns of auditory behavior that can be categorized for more efficient diagnosis and treatment (Katz, 1992; Tillery, 2009):

Decoding: Although hearing may be normal, information is not clearly "coded" by the brain; speech sounds are often not readily recognized; the patient has difficulty matching sounds and letters; he or she may exhibit poor phonic ability.

Tolerance fading memory: The individual presents poor ability to hear speech in noise, decreased (recent) auditory memory, and usually, poor reading comprehension and expressive language.

Integration problems: There is difficulty synthesizing auditory information from the two ears and synthesizing auditory and visual information. The patient has delayed responses and severe reading and spelling errors.

Organization: Difficulties with sequencing and, yes, organization of auditory information.

MANAGEMENT STRATEGIES

Environmental modifications: Modifying the environment to improve auditory ability can include preferential seating; improved line of vision/decreased distance (e.g., in the classroom); noise-reducing, sound-absorbing materials; acoustic tile; window treatments.

continued

Use of technology: Technology can include personal FM amplification, large-area systems, and classroom systems.

Compensatory strategies: These strategies include **chunking** and verbal rehearsal; rephrase to add additional redundancy; providing preinformation (instructions for written and verbal assignments).

Direct treatment:

Phonemic synthesis: Work on putting together sounds into words

Speech in noise: Desensitizing the individual to background noise; relates to life situations

Localization: Improving the ability to localize the source of a sound

Memory: Increasing short- and longer-term memory through sequencing and increasing unit span

Dichotic therapy: Improving the ability to synthesize information arriving at the two ears simultaneously

☐ Synopsis

Getting from sound perception to information processing involves numerous systems and pathways between the outer ear and the brain. Because it deals with such complexities, the field of audiology has become increasingly more sophisticated over the years. By combining a range of behavioral and electrophysiological techniques, audiologists can more effectively evaluate and (re)habilitate those with hearing loss, auditory processing disorders, and balance dysfunction.

☐ Vocabulary

auditory nerve—cranial nerve VIII, which comprises auditory and vestibular branches, passing from the inner ear to the brain stem

auditory nervous system—nervous system pertaining to the sense of hearing or to the system serving hearing (Stedman, 2006)

cerebral cortex—the convoluted surface layer of gray matter of the cerebrum that functions chiefly in coordination of sensory and motor information (Merriam-Webster, 2007)

TREATMENT VIGNETTE 11.1   CENTRAL AUDITORY PROCESSING DISORDERED ADULT, NO HEARING LOSS

As noted in this chapter, presbycusis is a decline in hearing or auditory function related to the aging process. This decline in hearing is often a combination of peripheral hearing loss and a decline in central auditory function. In this case, though, the patient had normal hearing ability.

Mr. J was a 65-year-old gentleman in good health. All medical tests were negative. However, Mr. J had difficulties hearing in background noise, understanding speech when more than one person was talking, remembering what he heard, and identifying the direction from which a sound originated. He told us that his problems had impacted his work in insurance sales. Evaluation showed an auditory processing disorder with left ear deficit. Mr. J began an aural rehabilitation treatment program focused on listening strategies, specifically targeting the auditory processing deficit of speech discrimination in noise (via noise desensitization strategies). He also received binaural auditory treatment (different speech material presented to both ears simultaneously and varying the intensity to improve performance of the poorer ear) (see the treatment approaches discussion). Six months later, he reported significant benefit from the intervention provided.

This example illustrates the difficulty with auditory processing rather than peripheral hearing loss. It also shows why it is so important to check for auditory difficulties at both the peripheral (hearing) and central (processing) levels of auditory function.

cochlea—a cavity in the inner ear resembling a snail shell and responsible for converting sound waves into an electrochemical signal that can be sent to the brain for interpretation (Martin & Clark, 2006)

conductive hearing loss—breakdown in transferring sound from the outside world to the inner ear

cortical deafness—deafness resulting from bilateral lesions of the primary receptive area of the temporal lobe (Stedman, 2006)

efferent auditory system—pathway from the auditory cortex to the cochlea that parallels the afferent system; includes both excitatory and inhibitory activity and has significant implications for function such as detection of a signal in background noise (Mendel, Danhauer, & Singh, 1999)

TREATMENT VIGNETTE 11.2
5-YEAR-OLD WITH CONDUCTIVE HEARING LOSS

Serous otitis media (SOM) is the accumulation of a bacteria-free fluid inside the middle ear. Children with poorly ventilated middle ears, very likely due to decreased function of the Eustachian tube or enlarged adenoids, may develop SOM, which can result in a mild conductive hearing loss. Failure to treat this condition will often result in more advanced hearing losses, delays in speech and language development, and even damage to the structures of the middle ear.

Johnny was a 5-year-old kindergarten student. His parents reported that he snored at night and slept with his mouth open. They also noticed that Johnny tended to increase the TV volume. His kindergarten teacher reported that Johnny did not pay attention to her instructions. Audiological evaluation revealed that Johnny had a bilateral mild-to-moderate conductive hearing loss. Tests of his middle ear function indicated that there was not appropriate middle ear movement, which suggested the presence of fluid. Johnny was referred to a pediatric otolaryngologist (a physician who specializes in children's ear, nose, and throat diseases). The physician put Johnny under antibiotic treatment and stated that she would put small tubes (also known as ventilation tubes) in Johnny's ears if he did not respond to medications. Three months after his initial visit, Johnny had tubes on his eardrums. His hearing returned to normal, and it is expected that the ventilation tubes will be removed in just a few months.

TREATMENT VIGNETTE 11.3
MODERATE SENSORINEURAL HEARING LOSS: CHILD

Matt was a fourth-grade student at a local school. He failed a hearing screening at the school and was referred to the audiology clinic for a complete hearing evaluation. Mat had a severe fever when he was 6 years old and was hospitalized for 3 days. Audiological evaluation revealed that Mat had a moderate bilateral *cookie-bite* sensorineural hearing loss (so named because the audiogram looks like a piece was bitten out of it; see Figure 11.6). Although young, he was a candidate for a pair of hearing aids.

TREATMENT VIGNETTE 11.4
PROFOUND SENSORINEURAL HEARING LOSS: CHILD

Sarah was a lively and playful 12-month-old child when she was first seen at the audiology clinic last year. Her parents reported that she had some complications during birth. They indicated that Sarah did not say any words and hardly responded to loud noises. There was a history of hearing loss on the father's side. Audiological evaluations using sound field audiometry, OAEs, and ABR revealed that Sarah had a profound bilateral sensorineural hearing loss. Sarah's residual hearing was not at a level that could be compensated with conventional hearing aids. The idea of a cochlear implantation surgical procedure was shared with her parents. It was explained that Sarah could benefit from insertion of an electronic device to her inner ear that could directly stimulate the hearing nerve. Sarah's parents were able to observe other children with cochlear implants and were surprised how these devices facilitated the acquisition of speech and language in these profoundly hearing-impaired children. Sarah was scheduled for a cochlear implantation by a neurotologist (a surgeon who specializes in inner ear and hearing nerve disorders). Approximately 12 months after the surgery, Sarah started to articulate some words. It is anticipated that she will be able to attend school with her normal-hearing peers.

frequency—the number of complete oscillations (complete movements forward and backward) of a vibrating body per unit of time (Martin & Clark, 2006)

hearing sensitivity—capacity of the auditory system to detect a stimulus, most often described by audiometric pure-tone thresholds (Stach, 2003)

Hertz—the unit of frequency of a sound; cycles per second (Mendel, Danhauer, & Singh, 1999)

hydraulic energy—power created by the compressive force or movement of a liquid in a confined area

innervated—stimulated by means of a nerve (Seikel, King, & Drumright, 2010)

intensity—the amount of sound energy per unit of area (Martin & Clark, 2006)

lesion—zone of tissue injury (Saladin, 2005)

localization—the determination by a subject of the apparent direction or distance of a sound source presented in a sound field (Mendel, Danhauer, & Singh, 1999).

loudness—the psychological correlate of intensity: the subjective impression of how loud a sound is

mechanical energy—refers to an object that is doing work by being in motion.

mixed hearing loss—a combination of conductive and sensori-neural hearing loss

neural signals—nervous system impulses transmitted with the help of chemical substances

pitch—the psychological correlate of frequency; the subjective impression of highness or lowness of a sound (Martin & Clark, 2006)

resonance frequency—the frequency at which a mass vibrates with the least amount of external force; the natural frequency of vibration of a mass (Martin & Clark, 2006)

semicircular canals—three canals of the vestibular system (lateral, superior, and posterior) responsible for sensation of movement (angular motion) of the head in space; the membranous semicircular canals are housed within the bony semicircular canals (Mendel, Danhauer, & Singh, 1999)

sensorineural hearing loss—hearing impairment due to damage to the inner ear or the auditory nerve

vestibular system—a sophisticated organ in the inner ear mediating sensations of balance, orientation, and movement

vocal tract—the airway used in the production of speech; made up of the oral cavity, the nasal cavity, and the pharynx (Seikel et al., 2010)

☐ Discussion Questions

1. What are the different structures that make up the peripheral and central parts of the auditory system?
2. What are the two major factors in middle ear physiology?
3. What is the name of the smallest bone in the middle ear?
4. What is the difference between a conductive hearing loss and a sensorineural hearing loss?
5. What is presbycusis?
6. Is there such a hearing problem as nonorganic hearing loss?
7. Do hearing aids and cochlear implants provide the same results?
8. Who is a candidate for a cochlear implant?
9. Can someone with normal hearing suffer from a balance problem?
10. How do the assistive listening devices help us hear in difficult listening situations?

☐ Note

1. This condensation process is helped some by the fact that the ossicles act as a lever, which adds a small bit of amplification to the sound as well. (You know about the lever action; just think of a seesaw. If you change the pivot point, you can change the respective force on each side.)

☐ Recommended Reading

Lass, N., & Woodford, C. (2007). *Hearing science: Fundamentals.* Philadelphia: Mosby/Elsevier.
 A readable introductory treatment of science of hearing and hearing disorders. Topics range from basic acoustics and psychoacoustics to anatomy, physiology, and disorders of hearing.
Yost, W. A. (2006). *Fundamentals of hearing: An introduction* (5th ed.). San Diego, CA: Emerald Group.
 A clearly written introduction to hearing physiology, acoustics, and psychacoustics.

☐ Web Sites of Interest

American Academy of Audiology: http://www.audiology.org
American Auditory Society: http://www.amauditorysoc.org
American Speech-Language-Hearing Association: http://www.asha.org
American Tinnitus Association: http://www.ata.org
Vestibular Disorders Association: http://www.vestibular.org

Augmentative and Alternative Communication

Filip Loncke, Pei-Lin Weng, Barbara Fries,
and Dale F. Williams

Filip Loncke, PhD, is a native of Belgium. He obtained his PhD from the University of Brussels. He is an associate professor at the Curry School of Education of the University of Virginia. For more than 20 years, he has practiced and conducted research in atypical communication, manual signing, and the processes underlying the use of augmentative and alternative communication (AAC). He has previously worked in service and research centers in Europe and lectured in five continents. He is a past president of the International Society for Augmentative and Alternative Communication.

Pei-Lin Weng, MA, CCC-SLP, is a native of Taiwan and a doctoral student at Purdue University. She obtained her master's degree in speech-language pathology from Michigan State University. While at the University of Virginia, she conducted research into multimodality information processing. Her current research interests include AAC applications for individuals with autism spectrum disorders and information processing in individuals with sensory impairments.

Barbara Fries, EdD, CCC-SLP, is an instructor at Florida Atlantic University in the Department of Communication Sciences and Disorders. Specific interests include language development and disorders, mental disabilities, and early intervention of multiply impaired infants and toddlers, specifically sensory integration, feeding, and communication.

275

☐ What Is Augmentative and Alternative Communication?

Augmentative and alternative communication (AAC) is the term used to describe the practice of using nonstandard forms of communication as a support or a substitute for natural speech. In most cases, AAC is used with direct face-to-face communication. The nonstandard form that substitutes for speech can be as simple as inscribing a message on a writing pad and showing it to the interlocutor. It can consist of manual signing (often derived from the sign languages of deaf communities), the use of graphic symbols, or the use of a speech-generating device. The field of AAC is fascinating because it explores the potential of individuals to adapt alternatives for typical communication. Since the 1990s, the practice and theory of AAC rapidly developed as a result of advances in assistive technology as well as progress in our understanding of language and communicative processing. AAC research is focused on clinical and educational efficacy, as well as social and emotional factors that influence the success and outcomes of its use.

☐ History and Developments of Augmentative and Alternative Communication

Although AAC is generally considered to be a recent development within the field of communication disorders, it has its roots in long traditions. Zangari, Lloyd, and Vicker (1994) noted that for thousands of years nonspeech communication has been a compensatory strategy in cross-cultural communication. Intuitively, individuals with severe speech limitations and their partners and caregivers have explored pantomime, picture communication, and other behaviors to complement or compensate for missing speech. Similarly, the use of manual sign languages must have existed ever since deaf communities have developed (Armstrong & Wilcox, 2005).

Since the 1960s, major factors that have led to the early development of AAC are (1) the discovery of the potential of nonspeech communication (including the linguistic status of sign languages of deaf communities), (2) the study of children's prelinguistic stages and developmental precursors to language, and (3) technological developments, including the possibilities of speech synthesis.

The potential of nonspeech communication drew a lot of attention with the discovery in the 1960s and 1970s that the sign communication systems used by deaf communities are full-fledged languages (Klima & Bellugi, 1979; Stokoe, 1980). While traditionally "nonverbal" communication tends to be equated with "nonlinguistic" communication, the study of sign languages demonstrates that nonspeech modalities can assume full linguistic value. AAC exploits the principle that one can "upgrade" almost any behavior into communicative, symbolic, and even linguistic expressive forms.

The study of children's prelinguistic stages and developmental precursors to language has revealed that typically developing children reach a level of symbolic and linguistic behavior after a "prelinguistic" period of increasingly effective nonsymbolic communicative behaviors. In an overview of their own and others' research, Iverson and Goldin-Meadow (2005) concluded that gesture use reflects a developing child's future emerging symbolic and linguistic potential, and that gesture facilitates transition from prelinguistic to linguistic functioning. Similarly, AAC includes strategies and techniques that systematically lead the individual from nonsymbolic less-effective communication forms toward symbolic and more effective linguistic communication.

Technological developments, including the use of speech synthesis and switch technology, have allowed for substitution of some components of natural speech production with artificial processes. The most common substitution is device-generated speech. This has certainly permitted an increasing number of individuals with intact linguistic potential but severe forms of speech articulation disorders to produce understandable, intelligent speech. However, other components of natural speech production can also be facilitated through technology, from **lexical decision** (crucial in word finding)—being helped through picture-word associations—to the fundamental process of sentence planning, potentially aided via brain-computer interfacing. AAC explores the most effective ways to integrate technology into the natural processes of speech production and functional communication.

☐ Augmentative and Alternative Communication Classifications and Taxonomy

The communication process is often described as consisting of a sender, a message transmission, and a receiver component. AAC intervention can target each (or all) of these components.

The Sender

Most, but not all, AAC interventions appear to be focused on facilitating the sender. That is, they attempt to facilitate the process from intention of a message to a physically observable articulation. The adaptations provided by AAC are (1) accessibility of communicative symbols and (2) behavioral substitution of natural speech output.

Accessibility of Communicative Symbols

Accessibility of communicative symbols is often achieved using graphic symbols. Briefly stated, symbols that are expressed and perceived in a nonspoken modality are considered to enhance understanding and processing. The visual and tactile modalities are easier to learn than the auditory modalities. In most interventions, the former modalities are used in an augmentative way. In other words, they are produced along with typical (mostly spoken) communication.

AAC researchers have focused on attempting to determine which types of graphic symbols are the most effective. Lloyd and his colleagues (Fuller, Lloyd, & Schlosser, 1992; Lloyd & Fuller, 1986) have proposed a taxonomy that has explanatory power concerning how symbols support communicative processes. The taxonomy consists of four levels of categories to describe the use of AAC aids. These four levels are *aided/unaided, static/dynamic, iconic/opaque,* and *set/system.* It is important to note that these levels were based on a logical flow from Level 1 to Level 4 and not on the relative importance of one level over another.

Aided communication (Level 1 distinction) refers to the requirement of external assistance to present symbols; on the other hand, unaided communication does not require such assistance. The use of symbols or devices external to the person's own physical articulators (mouth, hands) is an important modification of typical and natural communication.

Level 2 is the *static/dynamic dichotomy.* Vanderheiden and Lloyd (1986) defined static symbols as "permanent and enduring." In contrast, dynamic symbols require movement, change, or transitions to convey meaning. Entire sets or systems (see Level 4) can be classified as either predominantly static or predominantly dynamic. For example, American finger spelling is predominantly static because only 2 of 26 English letters (J and Z) require movement.

Iconic, a Level 3 term, is used to describe symbol set/systems that appear relatively conventional in nature, whereas *opaque* describes those that are arbitrary. For instance, a picture of *girl* is considered iconic transparent, whereas the written word *girl* is opaque. It is important that this level is viewed as a continuum rather than a dichotomy. Fuller and Lloyd (1991) noted that transparent symbols are at one end of the iconicity continuum, whereas completely opaque symbols are at the other end. Between the two extremes are various levels of translucent symbols. Therefore, the iconicity of a symbol set/system could be described as either entirely transparent or relatively translucent according to the relationship between the symbols and the referent.

The fourth and final level is named for two terms, *symbol set* and *symbol system*, which have been used extensively in the AAC field. Vanderheiden and Lloyd (1986) defined a *symbol set* as "closed in nature," which allows for expansion without clearly defined rules. Basically, a set is a collection of symbols that might each have been extracted from different formational contexts. In contrast, a *symbol system* refers to "a set of symbols specifically designed to work together to allow maximum communication" (Vanderheiden & Lloyd, 1986, p. 316). In other words, a symbol system has internal principles of symbol formation and combination. The phonological and morphological rules of word formation and the syntactic rules of sentence formation make words of languages more system-based than most available AAC systems.

One distinction that is not reflected in the four-level taxonomy is that of **linguistic-based symbols** versus **nonlinguistic based symbols**. Some of the symbols used in AAC systems are derived from a language, while others are not. If manual signs are used, they are most often selected from the languages used in the deaf communities. Often, printed words or messages are used on cards, screens, and boards. Therefore, graphic symbols are often a combination of linguistic and nonlinguistic information. However, there is little information on how and how much AAC users actually process and combine linguistic and nonlinguistic information.

Behavioral Substitution of Natural Speech Output

Behavioral substitution of natural speech output (such as manual signs or speech output communication devices) is another necessary adaptation. AAC is probably best known for its function of substituting overt natural speech through an alternative form of communicative output. Instead of (or in addition to) natural speech, the AAC user may point to a graphic symbol, perform a gesture or manual sign, activate a speech-generating device, scan a bar code, or perform another type of behavior that has an agreed-on communicative meaning.

Message Transmission

AAC, like any form of communication, involves transmitting messages. A major principle in reinforcing message transition is the enhanced use of **multimodality**. The multimodality principle refers to the tendency of users to seek redundant and complementary information in more than one representational channel. In typical communication, information from speech is combined with nonverbal data to represent meaning. Spoken communication contains most of the linguistic message (words and sentences), while the nonspeech channel carries additional **paralinguistic** information. In AAC, the nonspeech channel will often be used for linguistic units such as manual signs (pertaining to a sign language), printed words, or graphic symbols with a conventionalized explicit meaning.

Receiver Components

Many of the characteristics that are considered beneficial for production will be helpful for reception. For example, the iconicity that has helped the sender in accessing symbols also aids the receiver in identifying the meaning of the perceived message.

☐ AAC and Language Development

One of the interesting questions is how AAC influences development of language. In its early years, practitioners often waited to introduce AAC in the hope that natural speech would still develop. The thinking was that the introduction of AAC would somehow impede language and speech development. In an early case description, however, Goossens (1989) discussed the development of a girl who was diagnosed as severely developmentally disabled. When AAC was finally introduced, she was unexpectedly found to possess normal intelligence. Because she was unable to communicate, she had been unable to show it.

Although AAC was initially introduced as a "last-resort" approach, it has increasingly become recognized that early introduction of AAC will facilitate general development. In the first place, early AAC use targets the development of symbol awareness and the transition from nonsymbolic communication to symbolic communication and to the use of language. Second, providing AAC increases the amount of communicative and linguistic experience of a developing child. One of the developmental challenges for children with severe communicative limitations is the fact that infrequent speech leads to infrequent feedback. To put it in simple terms, a child who does not speak will also receive less response. Hence, a limitation in natural speech tends to decrease the amount of language to which the children are exposed, depriving them of learning opportunities. Finally, AAC intervention lends itself to clinical and

TOMMY

When Tommy was a 5-year-old child, he was diagnosed with severe autism. Speech was limited to five single-word utterances: "More," "Come," "Mom," "There," and "Buster" (the name of his dog). All were barely intelligible to listeners who were not familiar with him.

Tommy essentially functioned at the preverbal communication level. Would AAC help him progress toward verbal or linguistic communication? The parents and educators sat together to discuss an implementation plan. The SLP suggested the use of picture communication. Initially, Tommy was encouraged to use pictures to request items for which he had a strong motivation. He was rewarded if he formulated the request by showing the appropriate picture card.

The team began with a simple request for candy. Tommy quickly learned that showing the card elicited a consistent response from his caregivers: the piece of candy. In this way, he felt, for the first time, the sensation of obtaining control over his environment. He also experienced the rudiments of communication, that is, passing on a message to a receiver.

The next step for Tommy was to learn to reject. When he became frustrated, he started to kick and scream. The parents and educators decided to teach him a manual sign for STOP, to indicate that he can no longer handle an ongoing situation. Upon seeing this sign, caregivers left him alone. It took weeks of training before Tommy consistently used the sign, but he eventually did, and it became a powerful tool for him.

Gradually more requests and messages were taught, some through pictures and some through manual signs. One year after the intervention was started, the team and Tommy are exploring the use of a simple eight-message speech-generating device. If he can learn to use this AAC system successfully, the road to more communication and more interaction with his environment will be opened.

The ultimate goal of the parents and educators is that Tommy will understand the use of symbols. The use of symbols implies that he has an internal representation of something. It can be a transition toward language communication.

educational applications that go beyond direct communication. While the earliest forms of AAC were mainly targeted at providing a means to express direct needs, AAC methods are increasingly used for educational and clinical language stimulation and literacy enhancement (Smith, 2005).

☐ Adult Users of AAC

In its early years, AAC was strongly focused on its potential to enhance development in children with limitations. While AAC for adults has always existed, since the 1990s there has been a tremendous increase in interest, research, and applications for older populations, especially for those with **acquired communication disorders**.

AAC users with acquired disorders (e.g., traumatic brain injury) are different from their counterparts with developmental communication disorders (such as cerebral palsy). The former group has already developed speech-language skills. Thus, the sudden onset of a communication disorder requires new ways to communicate (and to cope with the loss of established skills).

Although AAC has the potential to meet some of the needs of people with acquired disorders, acceptance of a new way of communicating is often difficult. There is a wide range of reasons for this difficulty. Some may fear that AAC will hinder future speech improvement and insist on using their natural speech alone (actually current research indicates opposite outcomes). Others might refuse to accept their current limitations or become frustrated with the AAC learning process. Whatever the reason, it is important for the AAC specialist to take account of these users' considerations or assist them and their communication partners to adapt to the new means of communication.

Adult AAC users with acquired language disorders often encounter serious changes in lifestyle, communication, family role, and vocational position, among other changes. These may cause tremendous stress. Therefore, in addition to monitoring the AAC user's physical capacity for an AAC system, specialists need to keep a close eye on whether the use of the system actually contributes to the person's well-being.

☐ Social Aspects of AAC

The effects of AAC go beyond improvement in exchange of information. Effective AAC can influence social factors such as (1) a person's participation in the community and (2) the development of social and pragmatic skills.

AAC and Social Participation

Blackstone and Hunt Berg (2003) have proposed a model that allows describing and evaluating the social participation of an AAC user with

DIANE

Diane is a 45-year-old teacher who lost major speech and language functioning as a result of a stroke 2 years ago. Specifically, she presented extreme nonfluent aphasia with anomia (word-finding problems). During the first year postonset, speech and language intervention was focused on training word finding and regaining automatic speech control. Her progress reached a plateau at a level where she could answer simple questions but not initiate speech. Together with her spouse, it was decided to introduce a small hand-held speech-generating device that records messages on bar codes. Diane's home environment is now "bar coded": little bar-code stickers have been placed on the refrigerator, kitchen cabinet, bathroom wall, and elsewhere. These codes allow the device to produce spoken messages, such as "I need help with something," or "Are there things I need to get from the grocery store?" among others. Bar codes are added as Diane and her spouse decide they are needed. Both of them are relearning communication interaction. The repertoire of messages grows, and they learn to use strategies such as asking yes-no questions (by the spouse) and multimodal communication (combining gestures with natural speech, device speech, and sometimes drawings).

Diane's progress shows that much is dependent on collaboration and support in the environment. If the communication partners do not want or are unable to renegotiate communication, the AAC user is unlikely to succeed. One of the common misconceptions is that it is the user only who has to relearn and adapt. The partners need to learn to pace themselves (because augmentative communication is typically much slower than normal communication) and to encourage the user to take an active role in communication. Frustration with waiting for message construction by communication partners and lack of encouragement to construct the messages can lead to device abandonment by the user when the efforts and the time to construct communication messages do not match the perceived results.

Fortunately, this has not been the case with Diane. Thanks to a supportive environment, Diane is now able to resume a social life. She uses her speech-generating bar-code reader for phone conversations that she prepares by having typical phrases stored in bar codes on a sheet next to the phone. She goes to the restaurant and the movies with her friends. Her device helps her in ordering her meal, buying her movie ticket, and most of all, in talking and gossiping with her friends.

different communication partners. The *circle of communication partner model* categorized AAC users' communication partners into five levels, based on frequency of social interaction, degree of closeness, and familiarity. It is important for AAC specialists to consider both users and the communication partners addressed in this five-circle model during the process of evaluation, intervention, and ongoing assessment.

- The first concentric circle includes AAC users' lifelong communication partners with whom they reside, such as a family member or a domestic partner in a group home.
- The second circle represents those who spend regular leisure time with the user, such as friends or relatives.
- The third level is for acquaintances with whom the AAC users interact less frequently, for instance, neighbors, colleagues, community helpers.
- The fourth level includes the people who are paid during the times of interaction with the AAC users. Examples include therapists, teachers, and personal assistants.
- The final circle symbolizes unfamiliar partners to the AAC users, such as waiters or public transportation workers. Effectively including communication partners in the fifth circle becomes important in terms of fostering lifelong independence.

As compared to familiar communication partners of AAC users, unfamiliar listeners may be less likely to understand the challenges these individuals encounter. As a result, these listeners may well lack effective strategies to communicate with them.

AAC and Classroom Inclusion

Another specific topic related to social participation is the issue of how developing AAC users and their nondisabled peers can benefit from an inclusive classroom. Soto and her colleagues (Soto, 1994; Soto, Muller, Hunt, & Goetz, 2001) have studied how an inclusive classroom provides young AAC users significant social interactions with their typically developing peers. The experiences AAC users encounter in the inclusive environment definitely have an important impact on the development of social and pragmatic skills. However, inclusion has disadvantages as well. If not well managed, the AAC user may not get the individual attention and stimulus that is needed, or the nondisabled peers may experience insufficient learning challenges. The AAC specialist's role is to maximize the advantages and minimize the disadvantages in a general education setting. Soto et al. (2001) interviewed five focus groups (i.e., speech-language pathologists [SLPs] who are AAC specialists, parents, classroom teacher, inclusion support teachers, and instructional assistants) whose roles were to facilitate the use of AAC with children. Information obtained from this qualitative research provides SLPs with guidance on how to address AAC in inclusive classrooms. Important principles include (1) maximizing the AAC user's social and academic participation in the classroom and (2) developing a flexible team approach.

AAC and Employment

Although employment remains a challenge for most AAC users, economic participation through work constitutes a high and very satisfying level of self-realization. However, an increasing number of studies (e.g., McNaughton & Bryen, 2007) revealed that employment success is highly dependent on attitude factors and the ability to eliminate societal barriers.

AAC and Social and Pragmatic Skills

By definition, the use of AAC affects the pragmatic dynamics of communication. This is an issue that needs to be addressed as part of the intervention for each individual AAC user and for his or her communication partners. Todman and Alm (2003) identified the following pragmatic features of natural conversations that are significant for AAC users and their communication partners:

1. Appropriateness of contributions
2. Speed of responding
3. Maintaining conversational flow
4. Share in control (leading and following the other speaker)
5. Uniqueness of content
6. Coping with the unexpected
7. Feedback
8. Repair (of misunderstandings)

Among these, speed of responding might be the most crucial pragmatic factor that affects AAC users' communication exchanges and social participation, as well as others perceptions of these users (Hoag, Bedrosian, McCoy, & Johnson, 2004; Todman & Alm, 2003). Although the issue of generated speech rate has been facilitated by the development of utterance-based systems—in which the AAC users prestore utterances/sentences based on the anticipated conversation situations—it is not uncommon that the pragmatic mismatch will occur during conversations. In other words, even preplanned responses can be misused in actual conversation.

EVELYN

Evelyn is an 11-year-old girl with cerebral palsy. Her need for AAC became apparent early in life. When she was 1 year old, it was clear that natural speech would remain limited for her. Evelyn's parents and educator started with a low-tech signaling system by which she learned to produce words or other spoken (or nonspoken responses) by using a one-message button. It was a very successful way to let Evelyn discover that she could control her environment. The one-button communication was soon insufficient, and Evelyn moved toward more advanced and complicated devices. At the age of 7, she successfully operated a device with hundreds of symbols and several theme pages (e.g., for school, home, play, etc.). Evelyn was a master in navigating through the pages. Although communication remains slow, she has been able to make friends at school by initiating contacts. Her peers like her because she is able to display her wit and interest in a variety of topics. She knows more about popular music and its stars than anybody at school.

As an AAC user, Evelyn had to learn not only how to generate messages, but also how to master a conversation. She learned how to initiate and maintain topics and to monitor the communication partner's involvement. These are difficult skills to learn as there is almost never anybody around her who can serve as a model. At the same time, her communication partners—her peers—also needed to learn to adjust their rate of speaking, to give sufficient time to Evelyn to respond and take her turn, and to focus on the content of the message and not on the artificial speech.

One of the biggest challenges in the past 2 years was Evelyn's literacy skills. For years, most of the efforts by her educators were focused on ensuring that she learns to communicate directly. However, a schoolchild's ability to function in the world depends largely on the ability to read and write. Maybe even more than typical children, AAC users benefit from good literacy skills (to make up for their lack of direct communication and information). Appropriate literacy teaching methods are required for nonspeaking children, as they often cannot "sound out" what they read or want to write. Fortunately, Evelyn's latest developments and progress show her to be well under way toward developing excellent literacy skills.

☐ Explanatory Models of AAC: Why Does AAC Work?

Since the 1990s, increased attention has been focused on identifying AAC interventions with high efficacy (e.g., Schlosser, 2003). This focus includes not only whether a particular system works, but also *why* it does. But how do we determine why AAC works? Why is an alternative mode of communication more effective for some users than the standard mode?

One explanatory framework is related to multimodality. *Multimodality* refers to the ideas that:

1. People process and store information in different modes (images, phonological encodings),
2. They access and produce this information via different channels (auditory, visual, tactile, and psychomotor), and
3. There is a distribution of type of information over the different channels and modes (Loncke, Campbell, England, & Haley, 2006).

In typical spoken communication, the spoken words contain the explicit linguistic information, while gestures contain more **imagistic elements** (McNeill, 1985). In sign languages, there is a shift toward increased linguistic investment in gestures, as manual signs become the linguistic equivalents of spoken words. AAC capitalizes on the fact that individuals can rearrange where they invest linguistic, **conventionalized**, and **explicit information**. In typical communication, gestures function as background information with limited conventions. AAC intervention can "upgrade" gestures into meaning-specific symbols. The same is the case for the use of graphic symbols that will replace or reinforce spoken words or messages.

This explanation of why AAC works relates to the thesis that individuals have multiple ways of expression, related to internal networks of multimodal representations. AAC intervention is essentially based on searching for the right configuration of expressive modes to use in a given situation.

Interestingly, this explanation goes against the *incompatibility hypothesis*. This hypothesis, which has been powerful in the history of speech-language pathology and special education, states that expressive modalities are in mutual competition. The hypothesis and fear exists that training a person in the use of one modality will decrease the strength in another modality. Will the use of an alternative of speech prevent the development of speaking skills? Or, will the alternatives promote the development? This issue, which can be called the *(in-)compatibility of expressive modalities*, has been the topic of discussion for centuries. The debate was already present in the early days of deaf education at the end of the 18th century (Savage, Evans, & Savage, 1981).

Millar, Light, and Schlosser (2006) conducted a **meta-analysis** of 23 studies that examined the effects of AAC intervention on speech. The authors' general impression was that evidence supports the hypothesis that the modalities such as speech, manual signing, and graphic symbol use are mutually reinforcing. This corroborates the theory that lexical representations can be multimodal and internally connected (Loncke et al., 2006). As more studies become available, practitioners will find it easier to determine how to reconcile multimodal goals. At any rate, since the turn of the century, the fear of incompatibility of AAC with natural speech has diminished among clinicians, which has led to earlier and combined use of AAC with traditional speech therapy.

☐ Assessment and AAC

With individuals presenting no functional speech, as one might imagine, assessment of AAC needs is a difficult task. Often, the client has not had much experience with any device or communication tool, which makes it difficult to assess his or her potential for learning. For this reason, it is useful to have tools that allow the examiner to conduct **dynamic assessment**.

The use of AAC relies on multiple skills. Although our body of knowledge is still limited, research studies and clinical (and educational) experience have identified a number of skills that may be critical for the use of communication devices. These skills include (but are not limited to) **symbol awareness, choice making, short-term visual memory, auditory memory**, and **combinatorial capacity** (to form sentences).

We presently lack a protocol or a formal test procedure that allows the examiner to proceed from one domain of testing to another. In the future, assessment will need to include a greater focus on validity (What is it that we are actually measuring? Are we measuring what we intended to?), including *predictive validity* measures (i.e., How do we know future successful use of the AAC instrument?).

☐ The Future of AAC

Since the 1980s, AAC has developed from a marginal phenomenon to an approach that has pervaded many of the domains of communication disorders, including childhood developmental and acquired language disorders. It is expected that AAC will continue to develop as both a separate subdiscipline within CSD and as an integrated part of the repertoire of interventions for the wide range of clients seen by SLPs.

At the same time, it is expected that AAC will one day not be the exclusive domain of speech-language pathology but will rather become part of rehabilitation disciplines and special education. AAC techniques can be utilized for word learning, evoked response technology, psycholinguistics, and the growing field of brain-computer interaction. Furthermore, AAC techniques will find applications within second-language learning, adult teaching (for migrant populations), and literacy education. Finally, AAC will become a clear factor in social inclusion and social participation and in enhancing and preserving a person's personal well-being and mental health.

☐ Synopsis

AAC is an area of study exploring both the boundaries of human communication and the flexibility of humans to adapt and find new solutions. Although still a young discipline within the study of interventions for communication disorders, AAC is one of the fastest-growing and most promising domains. The number of individuals who can benefit from AAC intervention is steadily growing as a result of such developments as the aging of the population, better identification of where AAC can benefit people, increased availability of technology, and improved intervention services.

☐ Vocabulary

acquired communication disorders—communication disorders not present during the period of normal acquisition of language. They developed as a result of damaging or traumatic developmental, traumatic, or neurological conditions.

auditory memory—capacity to retain auditory information. Auditory memory is crucial in auditory information processing such as understanding speech (especially messages with a long string of words).

choice making—ability to select from two or more options. Presenting two objects as choices to a person is a strategy often used with emerging communicators.

combinatorial capacity—ability to combine two or more elements in a sequence to express an action or a relationship (e.g., a possession) between them. Combinatorial capacity is one of the bases of syntax use.

conventionalized information—information that is represented through symbols whose meaning is shared by a group of people. Words have a conventionalized meaning for language users. Graphic symbols can have a conventionalized meaning if several people agree on what they represent.

dynamic assessment—assessment focused on the learning potential of the learner, rather than on the actual level of knowledge or skill

explicit information—unambiguous information, with clear reference to its meaning

imagistic elements—elements in communication production that are driven by an internal image representation. Visual communication through gestures or pictures tends to contain more imagistic elements than auditory/spoken communication.

lexical decision—process in which a language user identifies a word within the internal lexicon either through (1) recognition (when the language user is listening or reading) or through (2) active selection (when the language user "decides" to use a word in an utterance)

linguistic-based symbols—symbols that are taken from a language (e.g., spoken or written words) or manual signs

meta-analysis—an analysis of the combined information of multiple studies focused on (different aspects) of a related research question

multimodality—refers to (1) the fact that utterances can be expressed in more than one modality (e.g., spoken and signed modalities); (2) the fact that utterances can present as a simultaneous combination of modalities (e.g., a word and a sign at the same time, having the same meaning); (3) the fact that utterances can be a combination of different modalities (e.g., one word in speech, two words produced by a speech-generating device, and one word in manual sign); and (4) the hypothesis that modalities correspond to an internally connected network of interconnected mental representations

nonlinguistic-based symbols—symbols that do not originate in a language system, such as pictures or gestures that are not part of a sign language

paralinguistic—is the term used for features of behaviors that are produced parallel with speech or manual signing. They can include gestures, facial expressions, and speech tone variation.

short-term visual memory—capacity to retain visual information during a short time span. This skill is important in not only visual language information processing such as reading but also the use of graphic communication symbols.

symbol awareness—the understanding the words, pictures, manual signs, or other objects and behaviors can have an agreed-on referential relation with another object, person, action, or concept

☐ Discussion Questions

1. What skills would be necessary for the AAC specialist? Should the AAC specialist be focused on assistive technology, or is there also an understanding required of the social, psychological, and developmental aspects of AAC?
2. A well-meaning teacher decides to turn off the device of a young AAC user in the classroom because his use of the device is disrupting the class. Is this an appropriate reaction of the teacher? What kind of solutions does the teacher have instead?
3. Put yourself in the position of a new AAC user. What barriers to AAC would there be in your own life?
4. How do you explain device abandonment? Why is it that sometimes individuals for whom a device has been carefully selected still will not use it (or give up using it after a relatively short time)?

☐ Recommended Reading

The journal *Augmentative and Alternative Communication* has been published since 1985.

It contains excellent research articles as well as thought provoking reports and editorials. It is a must for everyone with a more-than-superficial interest in AAC.

Beukelman, D., Garrett, K., & Yorkston, K. (2007). *Augmentative communication strategies for adults with acute medical conditions.* Baltimore: Brookes.

This book contains a collection of chapters describing how clinicians and caregivers, together with their clients and patients, can find ways to prevent communication deterioration and to improve quality of life, primarily for individuals who have lost speech as a consequence of a medical condition in adult life.

Beukelman, D., & Mirenda, P. (2005). *Augmentative and alternative communication. Supporting children and adults with complex communication needs* (3rd ed.). Baltimore: Brookes.

This textbook provides an excellent overview of the field of AAC together with practices for clinical and educational use.

Schlosser, R. W. (2003). *The efficacy of augmentative and alternative communication: Toward evidence-based practice.* San Diego, CA: Academic Press.

This book focuses on the evidence that underlies the practices of augmentative and alternative communication. Which strategies work best? The book also provides an excellent introduction into research design applicable to the field.

13
CHAPTER

Swallowing Disorders

Connie Keintz and Dale F. Williams

Connie Keintz, PhD, CCC-SLP, is associate professor in the Department of Communication Sciences and Disorders at Florida Atlantic University. She has worked clinically in medical settings for over 20 years. She teaches courses in neurogenic disorders, including dysphagia and motor speech disorders. Dr. Keintz has published articles related to these areas and is a frequent presenter at state and national conferences.

You can't swallow.

Think about that for a moment.

No eating. No drinking. Nutrition and hydration by tube. Probable loss of weight and strength. On top of all that, your social life suffers. After all, we plan meetings, dates, and family gatherings around meals or coffee breaks. These activities would no longer be enjoyable for you. In fact, they would likely become so stressful that you would avoid them altogether.

Unfortunately, this scenario is reality for the many people who suffer from **dysphagia** (dis-fay-ja), or disordered swallowing. Swallowing can be disrupted when the muscles of the mouth or throat become weak or when movements of these structures become uncoordinated.

For most of us, swallowing is so routine that we do not even realize we are doing it. Although it is a complex process, we do not really give it any thought because it is so automatic. In fact, you will probably be surprised to learn that we swallow over 500 times a day (Roueche, 1980). Obviously, much of this is done during meals, but we also swallow at other times (including while sleeping) to clear saliva from our mouths.

Given how important swallowing is, it is not surprising that people take immediate notice when something goes wrong. And, that is when speech-language pathologists (SLPs) get involved.

This raises a question: If SLPs are communication specialists, why are they involved with swallowing?

The question of whether SLPs *should* treat swallowing disorders is debated in Chapter 17. For the more central issue of *why* they do, let us start with the fact that their national organization, the American Speech-Language-Hearing Association (ASHA), designates that SLPs are responsible for identifying, evaluating, and treating anyone from infancy to old age who is experiencing dysphagia (ASHA, 1997).

If you are wondering how SLPs ever became involved with this disorder, the history goes back many decades. In the 1930s, SLPs began performing feeding treatment with children with cerebral palsy (Miller & Groher, 1993). SLPs working in medical settings started treating dysphagia in the 1970s. Physicians and nurses valued the training that these professionals had with respect to the anatomy and physiology of the mouth and throat and were therefore comfortable referring dysphagia clients to them.

Since that time, dysphagia as a field of study has grown to the point at which course work in this area is now required for a master's degree in speech-language pathology (ASHA, 1997). According to the 1995 ASHA Omnibus Survey, approximately 52% of practicing SLPs are involved in the management of dysphagia. Much of this management takes place in medical settings, such as hospitals, nursing homes, and rehabilitation centers. However, dysphagia remediation is getting more common in schools and preschools as well, as greater numbers of children with disabilities are mainstreamed into regular classrooms and schools.

☐ Normal Swallowing

To understand what goes wrong with the swallowing process, we must know how it is supposed to work. As previously noted, swallowing is both frequent and automatic. So much so, in fact, that most people do not think about it as a complex process. We simply put food into our mouths, chew, and swallow. In reality, of course, there is much more to it than that. Every normal swallow has four separate stages, beginning with the preparation of the oral cavity (see Figure 13.1).

Oral Preparatory Phase

One of the more interesting questions about the normal swallow is: When does it begin? Is it when we are chewing? When we are pushing food

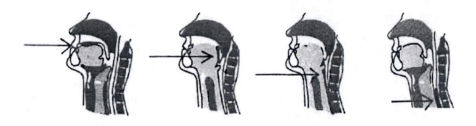

FIGURE 13.1 The stages of the normal swallow: Oral preparatory stage—the bolus is formed in the oral cavity; oral transport stage, the bolus is moved to the back of the oral cavity; pharyngeal stage, the bolus is propelled through the pharynx while various structures move to keep the bolus from entering the entrance of the airway; esophageal stage, gravity and muscular contractions move the bolus through the esophagus to the stomach. *Note:* The arrow indicates the position of the bolus.

toward the back of our mouth? Or, is it before the food is even served? Surprisingly, it is often the last. Seeing or smelling say, pizza, will make a lot of us salivate. This is the mouth's way of getting ready to eat, as it is helpful to have a moist oral cavity (to slide the food around in preparation of swallowing it). When food goes into the mouth, the lips close and chewing begins. Chewing, along with movements of the jaw and tongue, helps to form the food and saliva into a **bolus**, which is a fancy term for the wad of spit and food chunks that eventually makes it to the stomach. A bolus is also formed when swallowing liquids, as the tongue forms a rounded, cupped shape to hold the saliva and liquid combination.

Oral Transport Stage

In the oral transport stage, the bolus moves from the front or middle of the mouth to the back. It is coated with saliva, which helps reposition it and provides the bolus with chemicals to soften the food to make it easier to digest. The transport happens when the tip of the tongue pushes the bolus up against the roof of your mouth. The bolus is then "stripped" back into the pharynx, as the tongue sequentially squeezes the bolus against the hard palate (Dobie, 1978). Foods with thicker consistencies require more work during this stage than do liquids or soft, squishy foods such as Jell-O. Oral transport usually takes about 1 to 1.5 seconds to complete. It is considered a voluntary portion of the swallow in that the individual can stop it if he or she desires. Even so, the amount of attention required for this stage is minimal (Roueche, 1980).

Pharyngeal Stage

The pharyngeal stage begins when the bolus reaches the pharynx and triggers a swallowing response. Once this occurs, the food could travel any one of four routes. Three of them—down the trachea, up through the nose, and back into the mouth—are, respectively, dangerous, embarrassing, and disgusting. And none of them is helpful to nutrition. Therefore, these three routes must be closed off so that the food passes into the remaining one, the esophagus. A series of maneuvers is needed to direct the bolus along the proper path.

Muscles in the base of the tongue and the pharynx contract, which propels the bolus through the pharynx (see Figure 13.1). At the same time, the tongue raises to touch the hard palate, closing off the exit back to the oral cavity. The soft palate rises, and the rear wall of the pharynx moves forward, a combination of movements that keeps the bolus from going into the nasal cavity. The hyoid bone lifts, elevating the larynx and moving it forward (you can see this upward movement if you look at your Adam's apple in a mirror while swallowing). This elevation closes off the trachea and keeps food and liquid from entering the lungs. Finally, muscles at the top of the esophagus relax, which allows the bolus to enter the esophagus. All of the movements that take place in the pharyngeal stage do so in less than 1 second during a normal swallow.

Esophageal Stage

The last stage in a swallow takes place as the bolus is transported by the esophagus to the stomach. The esophagus uses rhythmic muscular contractions called **peristaltic contractions** to move the bolus toward the stomach. That is, a series of small spasms pushes the bolus sequentially along the length of the esophagus. Gravity also assists with pulling the bolus down. This stage typically lasts from 8 to 20 seconds.

☐ Disordered Swallowing

Disordered swallowing can occur during any or all of the aforementioned stages. In this next section, problems that can arise at each stage are discussed. How such problems are evaluated and, in some cases, treated are also outlined.

Oral Preparatory Stage

There are several possible problems that can occur during the oral preparatory stage of a swallow. In preparing to swallow, it is important that the person is able to recognize food and liquids that are appropriate to ingest. Some cognitively impaired individuals lose the ability to recognize food as something to eat. This is called **food agnosia**, and it can actually impede the preparation of a swallow. Salivation does not occur, which hinders the ability to form a bolus.

Other impairments can also affect oral preparation:

- If the lips do not seal properly and remain sealed during chewing and bolus formation, food or liquid will be drooled from a person's mouth.
- Weakness or incoordination of the tongue and jaw can result in difficulty chewing.
- A person experiencing sensory deprivation may not have information sent from his or her body to the brain regarding taste, smell, or the feel of food, thus making it difficult to form and manipulate a bolus.

Dysphagia difficulties noted in the oral preparatory stage are usually diagnosed by observing the patient eating and drinking. When problems are suspected, the likely first step is a dysphagia screening. As with all screenings, this usually consists of quickly administered tasks designed to determine whether further evaluation is needed. With a swallowing screen, the patient should be observed eating and drinking in a natural environment with their normal diet. In looking for oral preparatory difficulties, the SLP can observe whether drooling is taking place and if the patient is able to form and manage a bolus. If the screening indicates problems, the SLP will then complete a bedside swallowing evaluation (with dysphagia, the bed the SLP is beside is usually in a hospital room). During the evaluation, the SLP would observe the patient consume various amounts and consistencies of food and liquid. It is important to learn which foods are difficult for the patient and to observe which solids and liquids can be safely handled. Depending on the problems experienced by the patient, the SLP might recommend some or all of the following options:

- To help with chewing, replace ill-fitting dentures or bridges.
- Change the diet to soft foods if chewing is problematic.
- Recommend thicker liquids with meals if thin liquids are difficult to manage.
- Crush pills and medications before taking.
- Use small bites and small sips with all meals.

Oral Transport Stage

As previously noted, lack of saliva or a weakness in oral structures can result in difficulty transporting the bolus to the back of the mouth. When this occurs, the person may have food that pockets in the areas between the teeth and gums. This can be dangerous if the person falls asleep and the food becomes dislodged and blocks the airway.

Just as with oral preparation, the screening and bedside evaluation can be used to assess a patient's oral transport stage. The SLP will look for pocketed food. Dietary changes, such as softer foods (which are easier to chew and move within the mouth) and thicker liquids (less likely to immediately go where gravity takes them) might be helpful for patients who have difficulties transporting the bolus.

The SLP may also use instrumentation to study the patient's swallow. During a *flexible endoscopic examination of swallowing* (FEES) study, a small flexible tube with a camera is utilized to view the pharynx. This procedure can be completed by an otolaryngologist (ear, nose, and throat [ENT] physician) or an SLP with proper training. Either way, the qualified professional inserts the tube through the patient's nose and into the pharynx. The SLP then presents the materials to be swallowed. Food and liquid are often dyed a bright color so that their paths can be tracked by the camera. This allows the SLP to observe how the patient transports a bolus. For example, if the patient is not managing food in his or her mouth properly, it may spill over into the pharynx before the patient actually triggers the pharyngeal stage of the swallow. In such a case, the spilled food would be easily viewed by the camera.

Another type of procedure used for evaluation is a *modified barium swallow* (MBS) study. The SLP presents food and liquid mixed with barium (a radiopaque material that shows up on X-rays). The radiologist then takes an X-ray of the person's swallow. This procedure can detect difficulty moving the bolus backward in the mouth and spillage into the pharynx. In fact, an MBS shows the oral, pharyngeal, and esophageal stages of the swallow.

Pharyngeal Stage

There may be grave medical consequences if problems occur during the pharyngeal stage of the swallow. Remember that much of what happens in this stage is designed to protect the airway from food or liquid. If the swallow is delayed or not triggered at all, the bolus may enter the trachea and, even worse, the lungs. This circumstance is known as **aspiration**, and it can lead to very serious, even life-threatening, conditions, including

aspiration pneumonia. For clients who cannot seal off the trachea when swallowing, liquids are of greater concern than solids, as they can more quickly flow into the lungs. SLPs, and indeed all professionals caring for the patient, have to be alert to this fact. A patient's seemingly innocent request for a drink of water could result in a dangerous circumstance.

In some cases, the trachea is closed off, but other pathways are not. If the nasal cavity remains open, food or liquid can enter it, which is uncomfortable, unattractive, and obviously not helpful to the patient's nutritional needs. And, if the pharyngeal pressure is insufficient to move the bolus, it may go back into the oral cavity or fail to reach the esophagus. Either way, the swallowing process is clearly compromised.

The bedside evaluation can be helpful when attempting to determine difficulties with the pharyngeal stage. When aspiration occurs, most patients cough, a protective measure utilized by the body to protect the airway (by launching foreign matter out of it). An individual who demonstrates coughing or a wet gurgly voice during or following meals would likely be a good candidate for an MBS study, which can determine if a bolus is entering the airway and, if so, why this is occurring.

Unfortunately, not all patients who aspirate will cough. Patients suffering from **silent aspiration** are often in severe danger because the airway is not protected, and the aspiration may not be evident until it has been going on a while. MBS or FEES can be used to visualize this and other pharyngeal stage problems. During these procedures, the SLP would likely present food and liquids of different textures, amounts, and consistencies to determine which can be safely tolerated by the patient. In addition, postural changes, such as turning the head or tucking the chin during a swallow, or even changing the way the patient is sitting, can be attempted so that the SLP can determine what positions are most helpful to the patient. Such techniques are often utilized because they allow improved movements of the structures involved in swallowing and protection of the airway. For example, if the right side of the esophagus is impaired, turning the head to the right might force the bolus down the better-working left side.

Management for pharyngeal-stage difficulties may include diet modification or appropriate positioning during meals. In some cases, patients are not able to safely swallow any substances without aspiration. The patient's doctor would be advised by the SLP to order that patient to be "NPO," which means that the patient cannot eat or drink anything (in Latin, *non per os* means nothing by mouth). In these instances, other forms of nutrition and hydration, such as feeding tubes and intravenous treatment, would be necessary.

Esophageal Stage

If the peristaltic contractions that bring food to the stomach are weak or slow, the bolus may not be completely transported. Residue left on the pharyngeal walls can result in infection. Also, **gastroesophageal reflux disease (GERD)** can work against this portion of the swallow if patients are unable to keep food in their stomachs. This condition may result in pain during or after swallowing or a sensation of food getting stuck in the throat.

Problems in the esophageal stage are often reported by the patient. This is fortunate in the sense that they must be found, and it is not possible to observe them during a bedside evaluation. A barium swallow study can be performed to view the esophagus during the swallow, and the radiologist or gastroenterologist can assess any observed difficulties. Medications and sometimes surgeries are typical recommendations for problems with the esophageal stage. Still, it is important for SLPs to know about disorders of the esophageal stage of swallowing and how they are treated. After all, the SLP is often the first person to see patients with esophageal disorders. The SLP can carefully question the patient to help determine if he or she needs attention—medical or otherwise.

☐ Populations Affected by Dysphagia

Dysphagia can be experienced by individuals of all ages, from infants to the elderly. It can result from damage to any of the numerous structures involved in swallowing, the muscles that move them, or the central and peripheral nervous system components that supply the muscles or affect the timing and coordination of these movements.

There are many types of illness, injury, or trauma that can affect the ability to swallow. Patients of all ages who experience neurologic trauma often present with dysphagia. Individuals who have a stroke commonly report at least mild swallowing problems. Sometimes, these problems are temporary, but other times they impair swallowing for longer periods of time. A head or spinal cord injury may also result in dysphagia. In addition, neurogenic diseases can affect a person's ability to swallow. These include Parkinson's disease, amyotrophic lateral sclerosis (ALS or Lou Gehrig's disease), and multiple sclerosis. Patients who undergo surgery and radiation for head and neck cancer often experience dysphagia before and after treatment.

In infants, cerebral palsy is a very common reason for swallowing difficulty. Cerebral palsy occurs when an infant experiences damage to the

DYSPHAGIA CASE STUDY

Mrs. Smith, a 79-year-old woman, suffered a stroke that affected her tongue and lip movements. Family members reported that her speech was difficult to understand and that she was not able to eat effectively. One major problem was that food and liquids spilled out of her mouth because her lips were too weak to keep them in. Also, it was difficult for Mrs. Smith to form a bolus because of weak and uncoordinated tongue movements. After swallowing, it was noted that some food remained in her mouth.

During breakfast one morning, Mrs. Smith was seen by an SLP for a bedside evaluation. She was given a tray of "regular" foods, including scrambled eggs, toast, oatmeal, and juice. The SLP noted that the thicker foods tended to be pocketed in her cheeks and not swallowed. When this was pointed out to her, Mrs. Smith was able to use her tongue to clear the bolus and then swallow it. Drooling was noted with all foods, especially the juice.

A FEES was performed so that Mrs. Smith's pharynx could be viewed while she swallowed different consistencies of foods and drinks. When given reminders to use her tongue to clear the pocketed food, Mrs. Smith was able to swallow applesauce and small bites of cracker without difficulty. A small amount of juice was also presented. The FEES clearly showed that this juice ran into Mrs. Smith's pharynx before she actually began to swallow. It also spilled out of her lips. The juice was thickened to a consistency more like nectar and presented again. Mrs. Smith was able to swallow the thicker juice without problems.

In summary, despite the potential seriousness of Mrs. Smith's swallowing problems, two relatively simple adjustments (occasional reminders and thickened liquids) allowed for proper and safe nourishment.

It was recommended by the SLP that Mrs. Smith have a diet of mechanical soft foods, which would require less-vigorous chewing and manipulation than a regular diet. An order was also written for all liquids to be thickened to a nectar consistency to prevent her inability to control thin liquids. Family members and nursing staff were trained to give her verbal cues to remind her to clear her oral cavity, and good oral care was to be provided several times per day. Mrs. Smith remained in the hospital for 5 days and, by the end of that period, had recovered enough to return to a normal diet when she was discharged to her home.

neural system before, during, or shortly after birth. While there is a wide range of symptoms, most individuals experience dysfunction of their neuro-motor system, which has an impact on movement and sensory abilities. In some cases, the diagnosis of cerebral palsy is made in large part because the infant is experiencing difficulty with the feeding or swallowing process.

Finally, infants born with cleft lip and palate often require special techniques and equipment to help them with nourishment. SLPs work closely with parents of infants and children to improve their feeding and swallowing abilities.

☐ Roles in Dysphagia Evaluation and Management

In medical settings, the SLP is often a crucial member of a team of individuals involved in assisting patients with dysphagia. Even though the SLP will likely administer the actual therapy, other individuals are needed to oversee additional aspects of patient care, such as overall health and family status. Which professionals are involved depends on the needs of the individual patient.

- A *radiologist* would be required for videofluoroscopy studies, running the X-ray equipment and working with the SLP to determine any difficulties with the patient's swallowing.
- If the patient has difficulty at the esophageal stage, a full barium swallow study may be ordered by a *gastroenterologist,* who would likely manage impediments at this stage.
- The FEES is conducted by an SLP, but an *otolaryngologist* would usually be the person to place the scope through the patient's nasal cavity to view the pharynx during the swallow. An otolaryngologist would also work with patients who have cancer of the head or neck.
- Patients who experience swallowing difficulties due to neurological damage (e.g., car accident or stroke) or disease (e.g., Parkinson's disease or myasthenia gravis) would confer with a *neurologist,* who would, in turn, consult the SLP regarding the patient's swallowing and speech.
- If the patient is experiencing difficulties with swallowing due to dentition (teeth or dentures), a *dentist* may be contacted to assist.
- Patients with cleft palate/lip may require surgery to assist with feeding and swallowing issues, and thus an *orofacial surgeon* could be involved.

In addition to physicians, SLPs work with other professionals to provide care for people with dysphagia. Nurses are important sources of early information, primarily because of their involvement in the patient's feeding. In many cases, the need for evaluation is identified by an observant nursing staff member who notices patients under his or her care experiencing difficulty with swallowing. In a similar manner, certified nursing assistants (CNAs) report problems they see when helping patients eat their meals.

The training that the SLP provides through **in-services** and on-the-job experiences are especially important to those who do much of the hands-on work. The nursing staff involved in feeding must be alert to recommendations for each patient and be knowledgeable about potential dangers, such as coughing and choking. The patient's diet, weight, and nutritional needs will be monitored by the dietician, and it is important that the SLP communicates with this professional regarding recommendations for diet.

Other professionals are also important to patients with dysphagia. Those with respiratory difficulties or who are on ventilators will be monitored by *respiratory therapists*. *Occupational therapists* can assist with patients who have difficulty with hand or arm movements and can also provide specialized plates, spoons, cups, and other devices designed to help the patient eat independently. *Physical therapists* may help patients position themselves properly during meals.

Although many professionals are involved in the evaluation and management of dysphagia, it is often the SLP who provides the actual swallowing therapy. Thus, he or she regularly communicates with all of the other team members.

☐ Synopsis

Swallowing is a complex daily process that involves four stages. Swallowing can be impaired at any of these stages, often due to injury, accident, or illness. SLPs evaluate swallowing disorders and determine the best course of treatment, which may include changing a patient's diet or instructing the patient in safe swallowing techniques. SLPs are often the leaders of teams of individuals who address these issues.

☐ Vocabulary

aspiration—the action of material penetrating the larynx and entering the airway below the true vocal folds (Nicolosi et al., 1989)

aspiration pneumonia—pneumonia infection that develops as a result of foreign material (usually food or saliva) entering the airway

bolus—a ball or lump of masticated (chewed) food ready to swallow (Seikel, King, & Drumright, 2005)

dysphagia—difficulty in swallowing; may include inflammation, compression, paralysis, weakness, or hypertonicity of the esophagus (Nicolosi et al., 1989)

food agnosia—loss of the ability to recognize food as something to eat

gastroesophageal reflux disease (GERD)—backflow of food and stomach acid from the stomach to the esophagus because of failure of the lower esophageal sphincter to keep food in the stomach (Logemann, 1998)

in-service—a presentation given to an audience on a topic related to their profession

peristaltic contractions—rhythmic contractions of the esophageal muscles to propel food through the esophagus to the stomach

silent aspiration—foreign material entering the trachea or lungs (airway) without an outward sign of coughing or throat clearing by the patient

☐ Discussion Questions

1. Why do SLPs work with patients with swallowing disorders?
2. What actually happens in your body when something you are eating or drinking goes "down the wrong way"?
3. What does your body do under normal circumstances when this happens to protect itself?
4. Why does an SLP use an X-ray to study a person's ability to swallow?
5. Name some other professionals who might work with patients with swallowing disorders and tell what they would do for the patient.
6. Why would it be important for an SLP to test different consistencies of both food and liquid?

☐ Recommended Reading

Clark, H. M. (2004). Neuromuscular treatment for speech and swallowing: A tutorial. *American Journal of Speech-Language Pathology, 12,* 400–415.
   This article discusses research support for treatment strategies commonly used in dysphagia treatment.

Kendall, K. A., Leonard, R. J., & McKenzie, S. (2004). Airway protection: Evaluation with videofluoroscopy. *Dysphagia, 19,* 65–70.
   This study examines the timing of the swallowing process. A case study is presented to illustrate the application to real-life situations.

☐ Online Resources

Aaron's Tracheostomy Page. Excellent resource on tracheostomy, including swallowing information.

Compiled by the mother of a young child who had a tracheostomy for the first 4 years of his life. This is a good user-friendly resource. http://www.tracheostomy.com

Dysphagia Resource Center. Provides many links and information on anatomy and physiology, research, and case studies. http://www.dysphagia.com

Resources and frequently asked questions on swallowing problems. http://www.nidcd.nih.gov/health/voice/dysph.asp

Work Settings

The majority of communication sciences and disorders (CSD) professionals work in schools and medical settings (American Speech-Language-Hearing Association [ASHA], 2005; Bureau of Labor Statistics, 2010). In addition, almost a fifth of speech-language pathologists (SLPs) and a smaller number of audiologists do some private practice work.

There are other settings for CSD personnel as well—universities and home health agencies, to name a couple. Although all have their drawbacks, any of these settings will contain benefits conducive to effective assessment and treatment, not to mention potentially rewarding careers.

☐ Private Practice

Starting a private practice is not necessarily limited to those who think big. Some private practitioners operate what is known as a **sole proprietorship**, which means that one owner/clinician is the whole show (Guilford, Graham, & Scheuerle, 2007). Thus, an SLP who keeps his or her therapy materials in the trunk of the car is as much a private practitioner as the audiologist with a three-story office building.

Of course, when people think about private practice, they do not imagine all-day car travel and supplies situated between a spare tire and jumper cables. They think of pristine offices with comfortable waiting rooms, prim receptionists, and treatment rooms chock full of just the right materials for any given client. And indeed, such practices do exist, in the forms of **group practices, partnerships,** and for those thinking big, **corporations** (Guilford et al., 2007).

"Thinking big," of course, requires time, money, and business acumen. Some CSD specialists are in positions to devote the necessary time to such an endeavor. Unfortunately, few of us have any money and fewer still know an S corporation from an IHOP.

But, let us assume that (1) you remember at least the basic idea from that business class you took a decade earlier (make more than you spend), and (2) you have a reliable funding source. Your first step will be to present your potential source of money with a business plan, outlining expenses, sources of income, timelines, and other fiction. I say *fiction* because, similar to the treatment plan described in Chapter 5, a business plan is best thought of as a representation of what is *not* going to happen. Contracts will be lost unexpectedly. New ones will arise. Employees will want to change their work schedules. Others will leave. Testing materials will cost more or less than you anticipated. None of this means that the business plan is an empty exercise in basic math, however. It is essentially a guide regarding what generally needs to occur for the practice to make money. That is important not only because it will allow you to one day eat, but also because it might convince the money person that you will be able to pay back your loan.

Say you get the money and open your office. Well, this is after finding a place, paying for construction, and hiring therapists and office staff, that is. Oh, you need to get furniture, supplies, and diagnostic and therapy materials, then hit up your friend with a truck to help you move it all into one place. At this point, the game on which your business plan was based—bring in more money than you spend—begins. Of course, the therapists have to be paid. And, overhead costs such as those for rent, electricity, equipment, marketing expenses, updating therapy supplies, and the aforementioned receptionist add up (this is the primary reason why private practice owners get so annoyed when clinicians say, "I'm the one who did all the work. Why do I only get $40 for a $60 session?"). Also, you, the private practitioner, are responsible for any benefits you desire, such as life insurance, retirement, dental insurance, and membership in some snooty country club where you are required to wear a suit coat on the tennis court. Clearly, a $40,000 salary as a private practitioner is not the same as a $40,000 salary as someone else's employee.

Along with the money needed to run a practice, there is also the factor of time. Among other tasks, time is needed to:

- Bill the clients and **third-party payers.**
- Take phone calls from people who (1) ask questions, (2) request money, or (3) tell you why they are not going to give you money.

- Market the business, whether this entails putting together pamphlets and flyers or schmoozing school administrators and doctors.
- Hire people.

If you think about it, the last two items—marketing and hiring—overlap in that employees represent the practice to clients and any professionals with whom they come into contact. It follows then that, if you hire someone who presents himself or herself poorly, it reflects badly on your practice and, in the long run, costs you business. Ideally, of course, the clinicians that you hire are professional and competent. Given the high turnover among CSD professionals (in all settings), however, along with the fact that many see private practice work as unstable employment without health or other benefits, the reality is that sometimes the ideal employee is not available when you need someone. Thus, even being your own boss means you might end up working with a dolt or two.

So, given the challenges involved, why would someone start a private practice? The answer is that this type of setting has many rewards—and they are substantial. For one, there is the opportunity to make more money than is probable in other employment settings. Another is flexibility of scheduling. This is true when considering type of therapy (one on one vs. group) or preferred days and times. This flexibility benefits not only clients, of course, but also private practitioners. They catch that afternoon game (or recital, field trip, etc.) and make up the work at night.

It is also worth noting that private practitioners make and receive numerous referrals to and from other professionals. Thus, if additional services are needed, a network for finding them is likely to be available. In addition, private practices can involve the entire family, an important consideration when transferring newly learned skills.

A potential advantage for SLP private practitioners is that they can schedule the types of clients they wish to treat. Of course, economic realities can make it difficult to turn away impending business, but there are opportunities for professionals to do the kind of work they most want to do. Some practices specialize in one disorder area. More common are private clinics with a variety of specialists, all of whom see clients in their area of interest/expertise.

SLPs in private practice also have the opportunity to work in a variety of settings. This is because practitioners often have to go to the clients, not the other way around. For example, school or nursing home contracts might, for obvious reasons, require the professional to see clients on site.

Despite the amount of equipment needed, some audiologists in private practice also work outside their offices. This is made possible by commercial **mobile units** for hearing tests and hearing aid services. In fact, with the advances in telemedicine, audiologists may soon provide services via the Internet or remote clinics.

And, it is the service provided—speech, language, swallowing, hearing, or all—that is most important to any practice, more so than the business plans, cash flow, personnel decisions, or anything else. Not only is this the part of the job that CSD professionals are actually trained to do, but also it is the one that is most crucial to the success of the business. The best word of mouth possible is people talking about the successful therapy experienced in your practice.

☐ Schools

Working in the schools has surface appeals to many, in the forms of midafternoon quitting times, summers off, and the opportunity to wear tennis shoes to work. In talking to school-based therapists, however, additional, less-expected, advantages were also noted. For one, school settings allow them, as one put it, "to gain a broad educational perspective of their clients." What this means is that, by working with classroom teachers, CSD professionals acquire different viewpoints of their clients. They find out what the children are learning in school and how difficulty with communication affects that process. This brings up another benefit. Those in school settings are not lone wolves, but rather part of a community of educators working together.

In addition to workplace advantages, there are benefits related to the treatment itself. If a child needs it, it is possible to increase the frequency of visits. Issues that are pains in the neck in other settings (e.g., insurance denials, loss of funding for treatment, and others) are not part of the work landscape in schools. The abundance of rooms and people can make a school a great place for transfer and generalization (Williams & Dugan, 2002), although as Alvares and Williams (1995) pointed out, this advantage can be counteracted by limited parental involvement.

School personnel encounter a diversity of experiences, not only with respect to the disorders they treat but also in other ways. They learn about the schools in their community, which includes such items as educational budgets, performance evaluations, unions, and more paperwork forms than they ever knew existed. As you might expect, there is not total agreement regarding whether all of these should be considered benefits. Line item budget reviews are not, after all, the most exciting use of time imaginable.

Other listed advantages have their flip sides as well. Being part of a community requires shared responsibilities. However, time spent with pickup and drop-off duties, policing cafeteria food fights, and the like is time away from planning therapy. It is also true that the community of professionals may be lacking a real peer—someone who does the same job and can be useful for consultation and aid. I was told by one school SLP that the only person who reviews her plans is the principal, who is not trained in the field.

The sequence of events taking the SLP through the school year varies from district to district, but in general works as follows: Fall term begins with the screening of either all the students in the school or just those referred by classroom teachers. Those who fail the screening are evaluated, assuming their parents have given permission. If needed, treatment is administered within the school.

At some point during this process, the school SLP may need to observe one or more children in their classrooms. This is because each child's **individualized education plan** (IEP) is designed to be academically relevant. This is good in that the child can learn and progress through his or her schoolwork despite having a communicative difference. It is not so good when disorders that are less overt (e.g., mild stuttering) are left untreated on the basis that they do not interfere with learning.

How the actual therapy is administered varies across school districts. Although the manner in which treatment is provided would ideally depend on the needs of the individual child, legal requirements, administrative policy, and available professional, and financial and physical resources also influence delivery of services (Alvares & Williams, 1995). Two common delivery options are **pull-out therapy** and specialized classrooms.

During pull-out sessions, the SLP may work with a child individually, but a more likely scenario is group therapy. In fact, the schedule of a school SLP is often one group following another. And given the potentially large caseloads, some groups may span different disorders.

Potential disadvantages to the pull-out model are (1) the child misses classroom instruction time, and (2) he or she is singled out as different and may therefore feel socially stigmatized. As someone who was pulled out of class for therapy, I can tell you that I cared not a whit about the former but was deeply concerned about the latter. Particularly in middle school, I hated having to walk out of the classroom while peers asked me where I was going (a question I never answered truthfully). Whenever it was left up to me to leave class voluntarily, I "forgot" to do so.

Although the pull-out model is still used, many early childhood and elementary programs utilize self-contained classroom programs for children with speech and language disorders. The class may be taught by the SLP, a classroom teacher, or both. The rationale for this approach is that language is not a skill that can be isolated from other areas of academics, but rather, it is the foundation on which all learning occurs. Furthermore, if one considers interacting with other people to be a primary function of language, it can be argued that it is best learned within interactive, naturalistic contexts, such as the classroom (Alvares & Williams, 1995).

Although a possible disadvantage to this approach is that the teachers have to accommodate a classroom full of different disorders and learning styles, there are advantages to this sort of a consultative/collaborative approach:

- The children remain in the classroom. They do not miss valuable class time or are identified as being "different" by pulling them away from their peers.
- The SLP and classroom teacher may benefit from each other's expertise and unique perspective about the child. For example, the SLP may provide insight on the relationship between oral language skills and reading, and the teacher can provide information regarding a particular child's learning strengths and weaknesses.
- This approach employs materials the child is already using, thereby enhancing learning and increasing generalization.

Pull-out and classroom-based intervention models can be merged in some instances. For example, the SLP could begin intervention with individual sessions to develop specific skills and then work in collaboration with the teacher to facilitate classroom generalization of the newly learned competencies.

Audiologists working in a public or private school setting may do any or all of the following: hearing screening and testing, in-service training, evaluation of classroom noise and distractions that could impact learning for a child with a hearing loss, fit and recommend amplification, serve on IEP committees, provide programs on hearing loss prevention, and work with children, parents, school personnel, and community agencies to ensure that the child with a hearing loss is receiving the best services possible.

In addition to the public and private schools, audiologists are employed by special schools providing developmental learning services (state or federally funded) to infants and preschool children with disabilities, day care centers, and state schools, as well as group homes, for children with mental retardation.

☐ Medical Settings

Medical settings include hospitals, skilled nursing facilities, and rehabilitation clinics, all of which employ CSD professionals. In these settings, the sequence of treatment is different than it is for public school or private practice therapists. To start, SLPs or audiologists must first get a physician's order to see a client. While this seems somewhat odd on the surface—how could a doctor determine whether someone needs the services of a communication specialist?—there is a stated rationale for it. The attending physician is the person responsible for all aspects of the client's care. Thus, everything goes through him or her.

Once the order is secured, an evaluation is done. In some cases, the subsequent therapy will require a second order (although more often, the original order will be for both evaluation and therapy). The treatment itself might be short term, given that patients can be discharged or transferred (or worse) at any time.

The types of clients vary from place to place, but are likely to be adults, often those who have suffered strokes, head injuries, and other neurological damage. Thus, professionals are apt to treat deficits of hearing, language, speech, cognition, and swallowing.

Although all settings demand paperwork, that required in medical settings probably tops all others. During my time in these places, there were evaluation reports, plans of care, daily progress notes, 14- and 30-day recertification summaries (then every 30 days after that), end-of-month reports, and discharge summaries. In preparing this chapter, I asked a hospital SLP how the paperwork has been streamlined since my time. She told me that they no longer do 14-day summaries.

Medical settings also feature a lot of interaction with other professionals, both informal and during regularly scheduled **staffings**. The latter consist of collaborations between all of the professionals involved with an individual's care. By meeting together, they can relate their goals, the progress they have observed, and any suggestions they have for the others. They also offer the opportunity to ask questions. In these ways, services can be coordinated to the benefit the client. For example, the audiologist can explain the nature of a client's hearing loss and offer suggestions to the SLP regarding how best to present language tasks.

A major upside to staffings is access to additional services a client might need. Because staffings are made up of humans, however, there is always the potential for disagreement. Often, this is no big deal, but sometimes it has an impact on the welfare of the client. For example, say a physician does not wish to write an order for continued speech therapy, despite the SLP's report that the client has not met all goals. In such an instance, the SLP will likely deliberate the balance between maintaining a good working relationship with another professional and advocating for the client. It is hoped that it is possible to do both.

Finally, medical settings may have access to more resources than other settings and might thus be able to offer more intense and thorough evaluations. Treatment is also likely to benefit from the available assets.

CLINICAL AWARDS I HAVE GIVEN MYSELF

DUMBEST MOMENT, MEDICAL SETTING

It was the first day of my first SLP job. A colleague brought me into a client's room in a skilled nursing facility. I looked in the client's mouth and listened to his language. We left the room and the attending SLP asked me what I thought.

"He has trouble with his labiodental sounds," I said confidently, referring to speech sounds made with the teeth and lips.

"He doesn't have any teeth," replied the SLP.

I had to think fast. How could I have missed that? Sensing I should speak, I said the first thing that popped into my mind.

"So I was right!"

MOST UNCOMFORTABLE MOMENT, UNIVERSITY SETTING

Through a two-way mirror, I was observing a female graduate student administering accent reduction therapy tasks to a male undergraduate student. With about 5 minutes left in the session, the client stopped the task, saying that he wanted to thank the clinician for everything she had done for him. She smiled. He was not satisfied.

"I need to do more to thank you," he continued.

"That's really not necessary."

He pretended to think. "I know!" he finally said, as if any of what he was about to say was unrehearsed. "There's a new restaurant downtown. Why don't I buy you dinner?"

The student was clearly blindsided by the offer. "Well, that's very nice of you, but ... "

"I've been meaning to try the new place out anyway," the client interrupted. "This will be fun. How about Friday?"

"I don't know. On Friday, I have to ... um." Clearly, no excuse popped to mind. "I guess Friday would be okay."

"Great."

I was torn watching this. On the one hand, I knew that going out with a client was inappropriate, and I was going to have to tell the student to cancel. On the other hand, I really had to admire the guy's technique in securing a date despite the obvious obstacles involved.

BEST MOMENT, PRIVATE PRACTICE SETTING

Although I am usually the type of guy who tries to order a Whopper at Arby's, every so often I do say the right thing. Maybe I will demonstrate a kind and empathetic understanding of a disorder, a client's circumstances, or more likely, I will get lucky and my brain will squirt out the needed word before I have a chance to think about it. The last time this happened I was treating an adolescent who was trying to remember who the most valuable player of the 2003 World Series was.

"Josh Beckett," I said quickly.

I know I achieved instant respect because I got the *look*, the one that says "Hey, maybe this guy isn't as big an idiot as I thought!"

FEEL GOOD AWARD, GROUP THERAPY SETTING

This one also involves baseball. A 12-year-old boy was upset. It had nothing to do with his communication, but rather, was based on something he considered important: The day before he had made a base running error, resulting in an unnecessary out during a Little League game.

I told the group of a game long ago in which I not only dropped an easy fly ball, but also kicked it a good 20 feet when I attempted to pick it up.

"Nothing you do on a baseball field will ever look as dumb as that," I assured the boy.

Another client who, incidentally, was the most accomplished baseball player in the group, excitedly told me he could top that. He then related an instance in which he had made two errors on one play, including throwing a ball so far over the third baseman's head that it (the ball) landed in a neighboring field. Soon others joined in, telling of bonehead mistakes made on ball fields and elsewhere. It wasn't long before even the base running-impaired kid was laughing.

That day, I learned that sometimes the "emotional support and mutual aid" benefit of group therapy refers to more than just how we communicate.

BEST STORY, SCHOOL SETTING

Technically, I cannot give this award to myself because the story is not mine. I did hear it in enough detail, however, that I can steal it for this book. An SLP told me that he used to take his group of stuttering children around the school to talk to people. They tried various techniques with new listeners, then discussed (and often made fun of) the reactions they got. The clients had so much fun together that, short of severe sickness, none of them ever missed a session. Children who did not stutter asked if they could join the group. For the first time in the lives of the clients, it was cool to stutter.

continued

COOLEST MOMENT, HOME HEALTH THERAPY

The address was Ocean Avenue, so I guessed the building would be close to water. What I did not anticipate was a luxury condo with a balcony overlooking a tropical beach.

The family of my new client could not have been nicer as they provided me with history information. Unfortunately, the client had experienced a series of strokes. Two happened at home, one while sailing the Mediterranean, and the final one when she was overseas, meeting a diplomat of some sort in a castle, embassy, or mansion—I really do not remember as by that time, I was wondering whether the Monet hanging on the wall was an original.

The client herself was more interested in me. Did I have children? Did I bring pictures? Good, let's see them. Oh, they're so cute! She was high functioning and a skilled conversationalist, but she did present some cognitive difficulties. She suggested that we finish the evaluation on the balcony, as it was a beautiful 70-degree day with a slight ocean breeze. As soon as we were seated there, her husband brought a pitcher of tea.

Picture the scenario: I was seated in a deck chair, overlooking the Atlantic Ocean, sipping iced tea while listening to a world traveler describe her life's adventures. And I was on the clock!

As it turned out, the client needed therapy. Thus, I got to travel to the luxury condo twice a week for the next few months.

It never got old.

☐ Other Settings

Universities

As noted, not all CSD professionals work in medical, school, or private practice settings. One example of an additional employment site, one that is likely well known to many of you reading this book, is the college or university setting. Here, those with CSD graduate degrees are employed in both faculty and clinical positions.

You are probably familiar with what professors do—the teaching and research, anyway—but not so much with clinical faculty. These individuals also teach, but do so primarily via one-on-one supervision of graduate students. You see, students of speech-language pathology or audiology have to accumulate client contact hours to graduate. Because of this, universities that offer CSD degrees have their own clinics. Students who treat clients in these clinics must have all their treatment plans approved by certified and licensed professionals. These professionals are also required to observe and grade said students. Thus, university training clinics have a continuous need for clinical supervisors.

A quick glance at the clinical supervisor feedback forms distributed at my university (along with my own familiarity with the job) shows that supervisors spend a great deal of their time observing diagnostic or therapy sessions, meeting with student clinicians, and reading and correcting paperwork. Additional responsibilities include conferencing with clients and their families, facilitating support groups, and collaborating with peers and other professionals.

As components of universities, these clinics are not solely dependent on the fees paid by clients. That, along with the fact that they are training facilities, means that the cost for services is usually lower than clients receive elsewhere. One result of this savings is that there is rarely a shortage of clients, which in turn means that there is likely to be less emphasis on client recruitment than there is in, say, private practices. Also, although students might disagree with this next part, there is often a nurturing atmosphere that comes with training novices. All of these factors combine to produce a working environment that seems relaxed when compared to other settings.

There are advantages from the client's point of view as well. In addition to the lower cost, the presence of researchers should keep the treatment cutting edge. That is, these clinics include individuals whose job is to stay abreast of the most current research in the field.

The primary disadvantage cited by clients is that treatment at training facilities is administered by trainees. Specifically, students may be unable to make the same within-session adjustments that come naturally to the experienced clinician. Also, student clinicians are likely to change each semester. This means that rapport must be reestablished every few months. The upside of this situation is that changing clinicians every few months can be helpful toward generalizing skills to new listeners.

Home Health

Many people who are unable to leave their residences nevertheless require the services of CSD professionals. For this reason, **home health agencies** employ both audiologists and SLPs.

Home health therapy is based on the medical model described previously. That is, a physician's order is secured before the client is seen for an evaluation or therapy. However, unlike other medical professionals, those in home health travel to the client's residence to conduct the session.

This setup obviously necessitates transporting all necessary materials. For this reason, home health therapists' cars are also their offices. Along with this possible inconvenience is another: scheduling. Because their clients often receive multiple services, conflicts occur (for example, you showing up at the same time as the nurse taking vitals).

Once the other professionals are accounted for, however, scheduling can be an advantage in that it is pretty flexible. There are generally a number of available times during a given week that a client can be seen. In addition, home health therapists enjoy the variety of locations that make up their workdays.

Corporate

Corporate speech-language pathology is essentially consulting work. What I mean is that the SLP offers assessment and treatment of speech and language skills needed in the business world. Examples are presentation skills, professional diction and grammar, interviewing skills, business writing, and even foreign and regional accent modification (Corporate Speech Pathology Network, 2006).

☐ Synopsis

The field of CSD offers a variety of employment settings to suit almost any set of preferences. Private practice can be risky, but there are rewards in terms of salary, scheduling flexibility, and opportunities to specialize. Schools offer professionals the chance to be part of an educational team, although heavy client caseloads can lead to difficulties with providing services. Medical settings also offer a team approach and may well be the choice of setting for those who wish to work with adults (and can stand lots of paperwork). Other settings—most notably universities, home health agencies, and corporations—also have their advantages and disadvantages.

☐ Vocabulary

corporations—practice in which a legal entity serves as a management umbrella (Guilford et al., 2007)
group practices—practice in which a clinician owner/manager employs one or more clinicians (Guilford et al., 2007)
home health agencies—entities providing services to home-based clients

individualized education plan—management tool to identify and organize needed services (Smith, 2006)

mobile unit—vehicle that contains a sound-treated room for testing and other tools for hearing services

partnership—practice in which all parties participate in managing the business as well as providing professional services (Guilford et al., 2007)

pull-out therapy—removing a child from a classroom in order that she or he can attend therapy

sole proprietorship—practice in which one person is both owner/manager and clinician (Guilford et al., 2007)

staffings—exchange of information among professionals

third-party payers—entity that pays for services in exchange for premiums collected from an individual or employer

☐ Discussion Questions

1. Pretend you are an SLP or audiologist (your choice). In terms of both work atmosphere and types of clients, what would your ideal job setting look like?
2. If you could, how would you change school settings to improve CSD services? What about medical settings?
3. List what you think are characteristics of a good private practitioner. Do the same for school, medical, university, home health, and corporate CSD professionals.
4. Some traits mesh better with certain work settings than with others. For example, someone who is not a natural risk taker might be uncomfortable starting a private practice. How do your strengths and weaknesses match up with each of the work settings discussed in this chapter?

☐ Recommended Reading

American Speech-Language and Hearing Association. (2007). Frequently asked questions: Speech and language disorders in the school setting. Retrieved from http://www.asha.org/public/speech/development/schoolsFAQ.htm. This page provides a quick overview of what school-based professionals deal with on a daily basis.

Guilford, A. M., Graham, S. V., & Scheuerle, J. (2007). *The speech-language pathologist from novice to expert*. Upper Saddle River, NJ: Pearson Merrill Prentice Hall. Because of the competency of the writing and the ease of reading, this book provides an excellent source for interested students to begin their research of CSD careers.

Multicultural Issues in CSD

Li-Rong Lilly Cheng and Dale F. Williams

Dr. Cheng, professor, School of Speech, Language, and Hearing Sciences, San Diego State University, is also the executive director of the Chinese Study Institute. She is the managing director of the Confucius Institute. She was the former chair of the Multicultural Issues Board for the American Speech-Language-Hearing Association (ASHA) and is the current chair of the Education Committee of the International Association of Logopedics and Phoniatrics. She is a past president of the International Affairs Association, a related professional organization of ASHA. She is also a Fellow of ASHA. Dr. Cheng is the recipient of the 1997 ASHA Award for special contributions to multicultural affairs and the recipient of the 2002 Diversity Award from the California Speech and Hearing Association. Dr. Cheng is on the editorial board of many professional journals, has contributed numerous publications, and has lectured all over the world on topics related to China and the Chinese language and culture. She is a recipient of the Woman's Hall of Fame of San Diego and the Asian Heritage Award. Professor Cheng has provided volunteer clinical services all over the world.

All cultures have their own identity, language, systems of nonverbal communication, material culture, history, and ways of doing things.

Hall, 1972, p. 2

☐ Background

Multiculturalism as it pertains to communication sciences and disorders (CSD) has been investigated by numerous scholars (Banks, 1990; Gay, 1993; Pang & Cheng, 1998; Sleeter, 1995). As the U.S. population grows increasingly diverse in terms of the cultural and linguistic backgrounds of families, there is a corresponding growth in the need for speech-language pathologists (SLPs) to be trained in assessment and treatment of culturally and linguistically diverse (CLD) populations. If current trends continue, the following will hold:

- Hispanics will surpass African Americans as the largest U.S. minority group by the year 2015.
- Immigrants will make up half of all population growth by the year 2015.
- By the year 2030, 20% of the nation's population will be Hispanic.
- Hispanics will account for almost 50% of California's population in 2040 (a population expected to be twice what it is now).
- Asians will triple their share of population in just two generations.
- By 2088, minority populations will become the U.S. majority (Cheng, 1998).

There is a need for SLPs to understand how to work with families from diverse sociocultural and linguistic backgrounds. For one thing, there are challenges presented by children who speak one language at home and who learn English during the preschool and school-age years. These children are often called **English language learners (ELLs)**. In most states, there are growing numbers of ELLs in the public schools. Since the 1990–1991 school year, the ELL population has grown 105%, whereas the general school population has grown only 12% (Kindler, 2002).

These young learners of English perform differently on measures of language proficiency tests than do their monolingual English-speaking peers. They are in the process of acquiring English, and they may produce speech or language errors that sound similar to those produced by children with communicative disorders. These errors occur when they are learning English, and their learning may be influenced by their home languages, from **tonal** to **intonational**, and from alphabetical (English) to **logographic** (Chinese). The logographic writing system is unlike the alphabetical system, and it is complicated with many ways of combining particles together into new words. Those who are familiar with the alphabetical system may need to rethink when dealing with such an entirely different system.

Because some ELLs may have more production errors on verb tense than monolingual age-matched children, they can be easily misdiagnosed as having a language impairment. On the other hand, there is some evidence that children who are learning English as a second language (ESL)[1] and children who are bilingual are underdiagnosed as impaired, and that children who should be identified and diagnosed with language impairments are not receiving services. Both of these situations—overdiagnosis and underdiagnosis—are problematic for children, families, and schools. Children who are mistakenly referred for services may be labeled as language impaired and may feel stigmatized by the label. Parents may have difficulty accepting the labels and may feel mistreated as well. Children who are not diagnosed may fall behind their peers academically and miss valuable intervention time and learning opportunities.

SLPs face similar challenges in differentiating language differences from language disorders in children who speak nonstandard dialects of English, such as **African American English (AAE)**, frequently referred to as **Ebonics (Ebony Phonics)** or **African American Vernacular (AAV)** and **Appalachian English**. Children who are adopted internationally as infants, toddlers, and young children also present special challenges for SLPs. In sum, the responsibilities of SLPs are to assist with prevention of language impairment, identify children at risk for impairment, make accurate diagnoses, and provide appropriate intervention services.

In the United States, about 19% of the population speaks a language other than English at home. In 13 states, more than 20% of the population use different languages, and in California, New Mexico, and Texas, more than 30% of the people do (U.S. Bureau of the Census, 2005). Of the many languages spoken, Spanish has the largest number of speakers. In 10 states, more than 12% of the state population speaks Spanish at home.

Even in parts of the country that are presumed to be predominantly Spanish speaking, many languages are represented. For example, in Palm Beach County and Miami-Dade County in South Florida, school district officials reported more than 140 different languages spoken by families of children enrolled in the schools (Perrie & Core, 2006). In Los Angeles County, more than 150 languages are spoken by families of children enrolled in the schools. In many parts of the United States, pockets of ELLs reside in small towns and rural areas such as Liberty, Kansas, with its large Vietnamese population. Access to appropriate speech and language services presents a challenge for many students and families.

☐ African American English

The African Americans are diverse with different history, culture, social class, and family roles and relationships. Many are traditional African Americans or the descendants of the American slave industry. But, many are not. According to the 2000 census, 34.7 million persons or 12.3% of the population of the United States identified their race as Black, while 1.7 million classified themselves as Black and at least one other race (U.S. Bureau of the Census, 2000). In addition, approximately 600,000 Blacks are descendants of the Caribbean region, including Haiti, Barbados, Jamaica, and other areas of the non-Hispanic Caribbean and Central America. Many Black persons who reside in the United States came from African countries such as Kenya, Ethiopia, Sudan, and Somalia; they do not consider themselves to be African Americans. In general, they maintain their cultural identity based on their country of origin (Battle, 2007). There are 53 countries in Africa, and immigrants/refugees from Africa speak a variety of languages and dialects. For example, there are 13 official languages in South Africa, and many **dialects** are spoken in that country. Immigrants from South Africa are generally multilingual. According to the Mumford Center at the State University of New York (SUNY) at Albany, 25% of the growth of the Black population in the United States between 1990 and 2000 was due to immigrants from Africa and the Caribbean (U.S. Bureau of the Census, 2005). By 2000, there were more than 2.2 million persons from African countries living in the United States, including immigrants from Nigeria, Ghana, Ethiopia, Eritrea, Egypt, Sierra Leone, Somalia, South Africa, Angola, Cape Verde, Mozambique, Kenya, and Cameroon. The largest percentage of immigrants from Africa was from Angola, Somalia, and Mauritania (Battle, 2007; U.S. Census Bureau, 2005). Children who use AAE or AAV in their home community are exposed to **Standard American English (SAE)** at home as well as through the media contact. Others from Africa may speak English with the influence of their mother tongues. SLPs need to understand the diversity that exists among the Black populations.

☐ Spanish

Spanish is the second most common language spoken in the United States. According to the 2007 American Community Survey conducted by the U.S. Census Bureau, Spanish is the primary language spoken at home by over 34 million people aged 5 or older. The United States is home to more than 45 million Hispanics, making it the world's second-largest Spanish-speaking community, only after Mexico (Langdon, 2007). More than 50% of all U.S. Spanish speakers also speak English "very well," based on the self-assessment census questioning respondents. Research in bilingual child language indicated that Hispanic ESL children frequently lag behind their non-Hispanic peers in academic skills in preschool, elementary, and middle school years (Gutierrez-Clellen,

1999). These students reportedly have lower reading skills than native English or Asian language-speaking children (Klinger, Artiles, & Mendez Barletta, 2006). Approximately 22% of Spanish-speaking children in later grades with reading difficulties were found not to have been identified with reading problems in earlier grades (Torgesen, 1998).

☐ Number of Bilingual SLPs/Need for SLPs

The field of speech-language pathology has a critical shortage of bilingual service providers (ASHA, 2005). The American Speech-Language-Hearing Association (ASHA) developed a focused initiative in the area of culturally/linguistically diverse populations and continues its efforts to recruit bilingual, bicultural SLPs to serve ELL students and their families. The continuing education series of ASHA also focused on meeting the needs of ELL students with communication disorders (e.g., Roseberry-McKibbin, 2001). The solution to the shortage of bilingual SLPs cannot be easily met since there are hundreds of languages spoken in our schools. It would be impossible to have SLPs for each language represented in a community. For example, in the school district of Palm Beach County, there are children with more than 140 different home languages. It would not be feasible to think that the SLPs could be proficient in all 140 home languages spoken by the children and their families.

In 1990, a survey was sent out to public school SLPs all over the United States to determine current conditions regarding service delivery to ELLs as well as respondents' needs and interests for more information in this area (Roseberry-McKibbin & Eicholtz, 1994). In 2001, another survey was sent to public school SLPs, and a total of 1,736 surveys were returned. A comparison of the two was made (Roseberry-McKibbin, Brice, & O'Hanlon, 2005). Here are some highlights:

- In both surveys, the most commonly represented racial/ethnic group on respondents' caseload was "Hispanic," followed by "Asian."
- In 1990, 49% of ELL students on respondents' caseloads received treatment for language disorders; in 2001, the number was 91%.
- In both surveys, the majority of ELL students received intervention for language disorders; the number had almost doubled in 11 years.
- The number one problem indicated was "don't speak the language of the student."
- Another problem indicated in both surveys was "lack of less-biased assessment instruments."
- An additional problem was "lack of other professionals who speak students' languages."

- In 1990, 76% of respondents indicated that they had no course work addressing service delivery to ELL students, but in 2001, 77% of respondents did. Thus, it appeared that the topic area of greatest interest for respondents in both surveys was assessment of ELL students with communication disorders.
- "Effects of bilingualism on language learning" was the next topic area of greatest interest for respondents.

Bilingual individuals are those who are proficient in two languages. They are fluent in using the two languages orally, but they may not be **biliterate**. Some bilingual children are **simultaneous** learners, and some are **sequential** learners. Children who are simultaneous bilinguals are those who acquire two languages from birth. This type of simultaneous bilingualism from a very young age can be called *bilingual first language acquisition*. Sequential bilinguals are bilinguals who first acquired one language, then acquired a second language. ELLs make up a large percentage of many school districts. They are children who acquired one language at home, then began acquiring English at school entry. Many children speak English with siblings, peers, and friends, using English as a social language, and they speak their home language with parents and elders, using the home language as a maintenance language. So, many go through *language attrition*, which means losing home language and *language shift*, which means gaining competence in the school language.

Bilingualism encompasses a wide variety of proficiencies in receptive and productive language abilities. Some children who are raised in bilingual homes become proficient only in their language comprehension abilities but never develop oral language proficiency. The two concepts proposed by Cumminis (1981) are applicable here. Cumminis proposed the concept of **basic interpersonal communication proficiency (BICS)** and the concept of **cognitive academic linguistic proficiency (CALP)** (Cumminis, 1984).

Many ELLs present sufficient BICS but are insufficient in CALP. This presents a challenge to the schools since higher education requires competency in CALP. SLPs work on BICS, and many assessment instruments also focus on BICS. Assessment aimed at CALP is suggested to get at the deeper issue of the acquisition of literacy. Children have been found to be at risk for grade-age appropriate word recognition if they have poor proficiency in learning the English language (MacDonald & Cornwall, 1955; Roth, Speece, & Cooper, 2002). They may also have difficulty with complex reading tasks (Silliman & Diehl, 2002). In addition, it may be very important to assess **phonological awareness** in younger children to prevent later reading difficulties (Levey, 2009). Findings from second language learners' academic difficulties point to the need for early screening

CASE 15.1   DAVID

David is 5-year-old boy who was born in Fujian, China. He moved to New York with his parents, Li and Hua, and grandparents when he was a baby. Both parents work two jobs in Chinatown and speak no English. His grandparents take care of him and speak Fujianese to him at home. The home language is Fujianese. He has very few play-mates and is quite pampered and sheltered. He started kindergarten and could not communicate with the students and the teachers. He played by himself for the most part and did not socialize in school.

His teacher was concerned that he might have a speech or lan-guage disorder. A referral was made to a Chinese-speaking bilin-gual SLP.

Unfortunately, the SLP did not speak Fujianese. The parents were asked to come to school, and they could speak Mandarin. By asking the parents questions in Mandarin, the SLP learned that they were not at all concerned about David and thought that David was developing normally in Fujianese. They believed that David would learn English in time.

to prevent these difficulties (Limbos & Geva, 2001). Some of the other factors that have been found to play a role in good literacy skills are socio-economic level (Silliman, Wilkinson, & Brea-Spahn, 2004) and word read-ing skills (Bialystok, 2002; Snowling, 1991).

For most bilingual people, being bilingual is not a choice. People are bilingual because they are exposed to two languages and because they want or need to speak those languages to communicate with family members or with people in their community. Because bilingual speakers often communicate with speakers from each of their languages within the same conversation, they can use words or phrases from one language while holding a conversation in the other language. Different terms are used to describe the different varieties of such phenomena. A frequently used term is **code switching**, which means the speaker switches from one language to another. Another term that is frequently used is **code mixing**. Code mixing is not a matter of confusion or lack of linguistic knowledge. Many speakers code mix when there is a lexical gap in their language, or if they have difficulty recalling a lexical item, they will substitute an item from their other language. When speaking with other bilinguals, code switching and code mixing take on a sociolinguistic function to identify the speaker as a member of both language communities (Butler, 1996). Bilingual speakers not only switch codes but also switch phonol-ogy depending on with whom they are speaking. For example, Jesus is a common Spanish surname, and it may be pronounced in the English way or the Spanish way depending on the situation.

☐ Information About Bilingual and ELL Development

Language is not a machine you can break and fix with the right technique, it is a function of the whole person, an expression of culture, desire, need. … Inside our language is our history, personal and political.

Yaeger Kaplan, 1994, p. 66

In general, there is no good evidence to suggest that children exposed to two languages from birth (bilingual first language acquisition) learn language any differently from monolinguals of each of their languages. Children who receive input in both languages from birth can be expected to learn sounds, words, and the grammar of each of their languages at about the same ages as monolingual children from each of their languages. That is, there is no reason to think that being exposed to two languages causes a delay in language acquisition.

However, it is not typically the case that children receive equal input in each of their languages, and if a child receives very little input in one of the languages (less than 40% or so), then it is not likely that the child will acquire the two languages at the same rate. In the case of children who are exposed to three languages, very little is known about their developmental patterns, but it seems that a child must receive at least 10% of his or her total language input in a language to acquire it.

☐ What We Know About Bilingual Language Disorders

Bilingual children who have speech and language disorders in one of their languages also have evidence of impairment in their other language. Still, children who are exposed to two languages do not get confused by them. SLPs should not encourage families to restrict children with language impairment to only one of their languages. It is important for families to continue to use the parents' most proficient language to provide well-formed, grammatical input. Children may use input in their home language to acquire the features of their second language. It is worth

CASE 15.2   JESUS

Jesus, a 4-and-a-half-year-old boy, grew up in San Ysidro, California. He is the youngest of three children of Juan and Maria. Juan is a gardener, and Maria cleans houses. Maria takes Jesus with her to work. The two older siblings are in school and speak Spanish and English very well. Juan and Maria have minimal English and speak to each other and to their children in Spanish. Jesus seems to understand some Spanish but speaks very little. He is quiet and likes to watch the same cartoon over and over again and loves his train set. He is a very picky eater and only eats rice and beans. Maria thinks Jesus is different from her two other children and takes him to the doctor for a checkup; the doctor thinks that Jesus is fine.

noting also that children with language and cognitive impairments can become bilingual. Thus, it is important to encourage families to use the language of their choice with their child.

☐ Assessment of African American English

African American English (AAE) is a rule-governed linguistic system and discourse variety used primarily in informal situations by many working-class African Americans. AAE is influenced by contextual and status variables (Battle, 1998).

Fasold and Wolfram (1978) identified the contrastive features between AAE and SAE. The phonological features of AAE are usually identified as final consonant deletion, final consonant cluster reduction, unstressed syllable deletion, and interdental fricative substitution (for example, *wif* for "with"). These features are part of the normal development of AAE speakers, and they should not be considered disordered. To distinguish phonological disorders from normal development, SLPs need to focus on the noncontrastive features between AAE and SAE. Phoneme inventory differences are not evident until after 5 years of age. Awareness of the features that do not contrast between AAE and SAE is necessary to distinguish normal from disordered speech among African American children.

The morphosyntactic development of African American children is similar to that of White children up to the age of 3 years, including the development of **mean length of utterance (MLU)**. Children learning AAE acquire morphology that includes the use of plural, possessive, past tense, and third-person singular in the same pattern as children learning

SAE (Cole, 1980; Stockman, 1986). To distinguish true disorders from normal use, SLPs need to look at noncontrastive features of AAE morphology. Copula usage or absence can be highly variable depending on the linguistic context (Battle, 1998). In recent decades, the use of AAE in the entertainment industry (e.g., hip-hop music) and on YouTube makes it easier for professionals who are not familiar with AAE to have samples.

☐ Differential Diagnosis of Difference Versus Disorder

How can SLPs differentiate language differences from disorders? Superficially, a child who does not speak clearly may have a speech disorder or he or she may be in the process of learning English. The following is a list of some of the common features of learning English as a second language or new language:

1. Insufficient vocabulary (a vocabulary test may show a delay)
2. Inappropriate usage of common colloquialism (the user is not familiar with the proper usage)
3. Phonological variations (substituting /f/ for /th/, for example)
4. Syntactic errors (lack of plurality, lack of tense markers)
5. Inappropriate pragmatics (turn taking, delay in response, yes/no confusion)
6. Lack of culturally important content (not knowing Abraham Lincoln; Washington, D.C.; the Gettysburg Address)

Using Standardized Tests

As noted in Chapter 4, standardized tests are based on data from large samples. In general, national norms are established based on populations that use English as their home language/first language. The need to have local norms is a necessary step when the populations have varied backgrounds. For example, the U.S. Southwest has a large Hispanic population; the speech and language norms should reflect that factor (Langdon, 2009).

Linguistic and Cultural Influences on Standardized Testing

Research on language tests has revealed the impact of culture on the testing-taking process. Tests can be biased against certain cultures. People living on a Pacific island might not know what a polar bear is. By the

CASE 15.3   TATIANA

Tatiana was born in Russia. Her parents were divorced when she was 2 years old. Her mother, Svetlana, brought Tatiana with her to Baltimore when Tatiana was 3 years old. Tatiana is now 4 years old and only points and seems very alert. She likes to draw and plays with puzzles. Svetlana works as a nurse assistant, and Tatiana has a Russian-speaking babysitter. Tatiana is happy and content, but Svetlana is a little worried. What do you think?

same token, people who live in Alaska might not know what sugarcane looks like. Battle (2009), Cheng (1991, 1993), Iglesias (1985), and others have argued that there are biases in the following areas:

1. The client/student is not familiar with the items being presented (e.g., polar bear).
2. The client/student has a different cultural experience (the pyramid in Egypt looks different from the pyramid in Teotihuacán; putting sugar in tea versus drinking tea in a cup with tea leaves).
3. The client/student has a different word/term for the same object (dish for plate, cup for mug).
4. The client/student has a different cultural interpretation of the same word (*dragon* in Chinese means "auspicious," but *dragon* in Western cultures may mean something to fear; in the Chamorro culture, *ambulance* means a "car" that takes people to the hospital to die).
5. The test item may be translated into something that gives a clue to the answer (the Chinese word for "bicycle" is *foot-pedal-wheels*).
6. The test item may be confusing (the Spanish word *embarrasado* means "being pregnant," not embarrassed).

Why We Should Not Just Translate Standardized Tests

In the 1980s and 1990s, many standardized tests, such as the **Peabody Picture Vocabulary Test (PPVT)**, were translated into other languages for the test of vocabulary. The PPVT aims at testing receptive vocabulary by showing the students four pictures and asking the student to point or identify the correct picture by saying a stimulus word. Practitioners found the test results using the translated version unreliable. The difficulty in translating tests lies in the differences in culture. Words in English may not be easily translated into another language. In addition, norms were not established. Alternative strategies were suggested, including collecting local norms, modifying test items, using alternative scoring, and making notes of the explanations regarding why certain items are incorrect.

Over-/Underdiagnosis

Overdiagnosis of language disorders can occur when children are simply performing below their peers due to their language difference. By the same token, underdiagnosis can happen when clinicians think that more time should be given to the students while they are learning the school language. How to strike a balance and provide equitable care is the question at hand. SLPs need to know that when students are learning English, they will go through a learning curve, and it takes time for them to develop the language. An important piece of information for the practitioner is how the clients' home language is developing. Did they have difficulties with the acquisition of the home language? Did family members have difficulty understanding them? Did their siblings have difficulty understanding them? Did they develop more slowly than their younger siblings? Many children develop their home language but have difficulty with English due to a limited exposure to the English language. That is, they learn English in the classroom in limited settings, and they go home to an entirely different linguistic and cultural environment. This limited exposure to English may cause a delay in their English language development. This, however, does not mean that the delay is a disorder. Finding out the home language environment is a crucial step in the decision-making process. In the case of the limited exposure, an intensive English program may need to be implemented. On the other hand, if a student continues to exhibit difficulty in learning English and is also having difficulty with his or her home language, then the risk factor is much higher, and a thorough assessment of language development is indicated. Another clue is to compare the student with peers from the same linguistic, social, and cultural background. In addition, an examination of the English language proficiency of his or her older and younger siblings will provide needed data to make a determination regarding whether the condition is normal second language acquisition or there are some red flags. The following list provides SLPs with some indicators of possible speech and language disorders in the ELL populations:

1. Overall delay in home language development
2. Past medical records indicate problems with language learning
3. Abnormal behaviors (supersensitivity, hyperactive, lacking attention)
4. Family members with difficulty understanding the students
5. Siblings translate for the students
6. Parents show some concerns about the students
7. Lack of interactions with peers
8. Oral speech mechanism weaknesses
9. Other disabling conditions
10. Low MLU
11. Low working vocabulary

Alternative Assessments

One recommended alternative assessment strategy is the use of **dynamic assessment**. Lidz and Peña (1996) and Gutierrez-Clellen (1999) have advocated for the use of dynamic assessment. Dynamic assessment is based on the fundamental belief that most children will be able to learn languages as long they are given the right instructions and the right environment. The methodology includes test-teach-test. Students are given the opportunity to learn and to be tested again over time to track their learning. This methodology has been widely adopted as a preferred method of assessing ELL children.

Use of Interpreters

When clinicians do not speak the language of their clients/students, it is imperative that interpreters be used to facilitate communication. Langdon and Cheng (2002) presented a guide to clinicians in working with interpreters. In general, there are three steps that must be followed to ensure quality of service.

1. Briefing
2. Interaction
3. Debriefing

In short, interpreters must be briefed before a student is seen, and the interpreter needs to debrief the clinician after the session. Interpreters must be trained to understand the diagnostic process and be knowledgeable and ethical.

World Englishes

Many people in the United States grew up with many forms of English. In an article, "Mother Tongue," Amy Tan, a Chinese American author, described many forms of English (2003):

> I began to write stories using all the Englishes I grew up with: the English I spoke to my mother, which for lack of a better term might be described as simple; the English she used with me, which for lack of a better term might be described as broken; my translation of her Chinese, which could certainly be described as watered-down; and what I imagine to be her translation of her Chinese if she could speak in perfect English, her internal language, and for that sought to

preserve the essence, but neither an English nor a Chinese structure. I wanted to capture what language ability tests can never reveal: her intent, her passion, her imagery, the rhythms of her speech and the nature of her thoughts. (pp. 256–257)

Learning from her experience, SLPs need to be aware of the many forms of English our students bring into the school and to consider the interpretations of these many forms of English. Furthermore, attention to nonverbal communication is also an essential part of our interaction with CLD populations.

Nonverbal Communication

Nonverbal communication includes facial expressions, gazing, postures, proximity, and gestures. Different cultures have different interpretations of these nonverbal codes. The lack of familiarity with other languages may lead SLPs to misinterpret not only the verbal communication but also the nonverbal communication of their clients, patients, or families. Some Americans feel that when they hear two Vietnamese speakers talk, they think they are arguing. This is due to their unfamiliarity with the tonal language and the mannerism in which discourse is conducted.

The RIOT Approach

To process the assessment of a bilingual/multicultural child or adult with possible communicative disorder, the **RIOT** procedure is recommended (Cheng, 2007).

R stands for **review**.
I stands for **interviews**.
O stands for **observations**.
T stands for **test**.

Review precedes all other procedures and may include the following, which can be accomplished by reviewing reports or by obtaining answers from a questionnaire regarding:

- previous medical records
- previous school records
- previous test results
- birth history

- development history
- relevant information regarding refugee/immigrant history
- language learning history
- caretaker history

The second component of the assessment and intervention process is the interviews. Interviews may be conducted using an interpreter or an informant. The following persons need to be interviewed through informal or formal process:

- parents
- teachers/teacher's aid
- classmates/schoolmates
- friends
- other family members/siblings/grandparents
- professionals: SLPs, psychologist, counselors
- community members and others who have some knowledge about the family and the child
- caretakers

Observation is the third part of this recommended procedure. Guided observations are keys to obtaining useful information about the child. Observation may take place in the following locations:

- home
- school
- community centers (church, activity center, etc.)
- play environment (school yard, neighborhood)
- any setting where there are interactions

The following are key areas of observation:

- communication in general
- who the partners in communication are
- what language is used
- the quality of the language
- whether the interactants understand the output
- comprehension
- samples of language
- areas of frustration or avoidance
- other behaviors that warrant attention
- general affect

Testing is the final step in this recommended procedure. The choice of appropriate test is important. For assessment of the Hispanic populations, a number of tests have been field tested, and normative data are available. These tests can be used for assessment. The language sample approach is considered one of the most appropriate ways to find out the language development of the child. Language samples need to be collected in the home language and in English.

Although there are some existing tests that can be used for the assessment, on many occasions, tests are not available, and alternative procedures may need to be adopted. For more information about the language-sampling techniques, read Miller and Iglesias (2006).

☐ Bilingual Aphasia

As noted in Chapter 7, bilingual/multilingual individuals who suffer from aphasia present a variety of recovery patterns. Unfortunately, there is little information available for SLPs about bilingual adults and how aphasia affects their linguistic abilities in each of their languages.

☐ Intervention: Creating a Multicultural Landscape

Bloom and Lahey (1978) maintained that language is the interaction of form (phonology, morphology syntax), function (pragmatics), and content (semantics). Complete mastery of any language/dialect requires social/cultural knowledge and understanding, and this was not an area of focus for Bloom and Lahey. Bilingualism poses some particular challenges for selecting a language for language intervention services. First, in most cases it will not be possible to find a bilingual SLP with native-like language proficiency in both (or all) of a child's languages. In addition, simply having a large working vocabulary and substantial lexicon is not enough to comprehend all the different meanings and connotations of words and expressions. For example, a person may know the meaning of the word *shower* as in to take a shower (noun) or as in the rain shower (noun) is unexpected. Further, the person might know that shower can also be a verb—to shower his girlfriend with love. However, shower can also mean going to a baby shower or going to a bridal shower. If the person has never been to a shower, the person might not know what to bring or what to buy.

Reasons to Support Home Language Development and Use

There is reason to believe that, once bilingual children enter school and begin acquiring the majority language through academic instruction and peer interactions, their native or home language skills will diminish. While this belief has not been clearly established, it does seem that the home language does not continue to develop or be acquired in the same way that the majority language is acquired. There are several reasons this might be the case. First, for many home languages, which are also community minority languages, children receive no formal instruction in reading and writing. Second, language learning, particularly lexical learning, is domain and context specific. The formal academic domains of science, for example, do not usually arise at home, so children do not acquire the vocabulary of that domain. Third, children spend a lot of time in school and less time at home as they grow. There is also a strong peer language influence for children as they approach adolescence and go into young adulthood.

Children Adopted Internationally

Each year, more than 5,000 children are adopted into the United States from foreign countries. Most of these children receive no exposure to English prior to their arrival in the U.S. Most children adopted internationally are over 1 year of age at the time they arrive in the United States. These children present a unique challenge for SLPs. First, they represent a heterogeneous population of children from many different kinds of cultures and language backgrounds. These children are considered to be at risk for developmental disabilities. They may have received inadequate nutrition, medical care, or attention prior to their U.S. arrival. Many of the children adopted internationally are identified as having special needs prior to their adoption, so they enter the country with known medical needs; yet, their medical history, family history, or birth history is unknown.

Cultural Intelligence and Cultural Competence

It is crucial for SLPs and audiologists to develop **cultural competence** to work effectively with families from diverse backgrounds. Developing one's diversity consciousness and implications for understanding culturally diverse families is a necessary step toward the acquisition of cultural competence. SLPs have an important responsibility to develop their own cultural competence to meet the increasing and ever-changing demands of today's global and diverse workplace. This is accomplished through the development of one's multiperspective identity (MI). **Cultural intelligence** (**CQ**), one component of cultural competence, is defined as "a person's capability to adapt effectively to new cultural contexts" (Earley & Ang, 2003, p. 59). Earley and Ang (2003) in their book, *Cultural Intelligence,* described the importance of cultural intelligence. Van Dyne (2005–2006) has developed a Web site on the concept as well. Earley and Mosakowski (2004) presented a screening test for cultural competence. Culture is language, and language is embedded in culture. As a result, culture does influence thought patterns and ways with words (Heath, 1983).

Van Dyne (2005–2006) discussed four aspects of cultural intelligence, which include CQ-strategy, CQ-knowledge, CQ-motivation, and CQ-behavior. The development of cultural intelligence begins with a study of self and the awareness that everyone has a **multiperspective identity (MI)**. MI is defined as characteristics of our identity that enable each individual to view reality through a specific perspective based on ability, age, ethnicity, gender, race, religion, sexual orientation, and socioeconomic class (Perlis, 2001, p. 11). MI theory is the study of how groups perceive the cultural differences between individual members of the group and how groups perceive the cultural differences between individual members of the group and how those differences may or may not become interconnected to each other. Concepts of difference and the **interconnectedness** of difference "shape the culture of a group or subgroup of people" (Perlis, 2001, p. 40). As SLPs begin to see themselves as multiperspective individuals and understand the interrelationships between these forms of their identity, they will develop cultural intelligence. One way to develop MI is to encourage dialogue regarding forms of difference. Through staff development activities, SLPs are provided with opportunities to recognize their MI as well as the identities of others. McIntosh (1980) encouraged us to unpack our invisible knapsacks and look at those characteristics of our identity that enable us to be privileged or oppressed. McIntosh's now-classic work on understanding privilege and oppression related to forms of identity difference asks each of us to accept our privilege or oppression and to acknowledge that when they serve others. Hicks (1998) stated that to deny any form of difference, is to deny the basic identity of an individual. Others have indicated that we should spend time exploring the interconnected nature of difference to fully understand the worldview of others (DuCette, Shapiro, & Sewell, 1993). Regardless of the MI of their clients and families, SLPs must affirm the identity of those they serve.

The Role of Family

Different cultures define *family* differently. Some cultures look at all members of a clan or village as family. Others may consider individuals with the same last name as family. The views vary from culture to culture and are not static. When societies make contact with other societies, adaptations and modifications take place, and changes about family-related attitudes occur.

Two broad perspectives exist when thinking about family systems and structures: **collectivism** and **individualism**. The collectivism perspective views the family as an extremely large unit and can include the family nucleus, extended family members, and other members of the community/society that share the culture. Events affecting the well-being of an individual affect the entire family unit. The Eastern cultures have the collectivist view of family, and a member of the family can be a distant relative, an adopted child, a neighbor, a member of a clan, or a good friend. Children learn from their family, school, and community. Matsuo (2005) investigated the Bosnian refugee settlement in St. Louis and learned that the Bosnian's notion of family extends to relatives. In addition, she found that the Bosnian community understood the meaning of postponing immediate fulfillment to achieve a better outcome in the future for the entire family. Understanding the family systems and various family structures of our diverse populations is one of the most important tasks of professionals in education (Cheng, 2009).

In contrast, individualism, which is commonly found in many Western cultures, "values the importance of individuals and one is responsible for one's own actions" (Cheng, 2009, p. 70). Family is generally the immediate family, parents and children and sometimes grandparents. Relatives who are considered extended family include cousins and others. In the individualist view, family is considered as a "nucleus." This implies those members of the family are only members of the immediate family and not part of the clan. This also means that an individual is independent and unique, is responsible for his or her own behaviors, and takes responsibility for the consequences of his or her doings (including those related to treatment). On the contrary, in the collectivist view, if a member of the family is ashamed, the whole extended family feels ashamed, and therefore the whole clan feels ashamed. This means treating a child's disability is treating the whole extended family and even the whole clan, village, or tribe. Members of the extended family or the clan leader are often consulted about such cases.

Indeed, the role of culture is very important in understanding the development of family relationships (Cheng, 2009). Only by rooting ourselves in the concepts of cultural proficiency and competency can SLPs begin to work effectively with families from diverse backgrounds. To create optimal language learning environments (OLLEs), SLPs must recognize, appreciate, and respect the vital role parents and family members have in educating their children (Cheng, 2009). Children typically spend more time with their parents and family members. They eat together, they

CULTURE AND FAMILY

In the Christian religion, the Ten Commandments include honoring your parents (Grady, 2007). Similarly, **Buddhism** accepts and promotes the family and filial love within the lay community. Piety is fundamental to the social and cosmological order. Children support parents in five ways: returning the care and nurturing the parents gave to the child; carrying out their duties; maintaining the family tradition; becoming worthy of one's inheritance; and respecting one's ancestors (Schmid, 2007).

According to **Confucianism**, no love is greater than that between parent and child. Even romantic love pales before one's feelings for your parents. The Confucian philosopher Mencius said that:

> Great filial piety consists of yearning for your parents all your life. ... Because of children's devotion to their parents, they will marry whomever their parents choose. Children express filial love by making sure that their parents' desires are always satisfied. Further, filial piety does not end with one's parents. By extension, the same sense of debt is owed to one's ancestors. (Knapp, 2007)

In **Hinduism**, the love reaches beyond the realms of the nuclear family to incorporate the large extension of family members. It says each person has three debts: to the sage, to the gods, and to the ancestors. The relationship between parents and children is more than just a fulfillment of a debt; it is a lifetime commitment (Simmons, 2007). Many cultures teach family traditions in the homes. Cultures with a strong oral tradition will teach family values through orality and aurality.

play together, they go on vacations together, and they are surrounded by family for the most part. This involves understanding that families are defined differently depending on the norms, beliefs, values, and rules of their culture.

In the Native American tradition, storytelling is a very important part of the culture; stories about the history of the people, how tribesmen work together, how people help each other, how family is defined are all part and parcel of the oral tradition, and many of the stories are memorized and passed down from generation to generation. Many families use memorization to remember the credo—creating opportunities for learning together and using questions to guide children's behaviors.

Optimal Language Learning Environment

All families in different societies engage in meaningful teaching. Parents teach their children how to behave, and what is expected of them. Creating an optimal learning environment (OLE) is critical. Since so much of the teaching is done orally through the use of language, it creates an optimal *language* learning environment (OLLE). Further, not only is the environment necessary but also the exposure to diverse experience is crucial. Thus, the concept of optimal language learning environment *and experience* (OLLEE) is an important ingredient in a child's learning and family's teaching. The following example illustrates a child who decoded the Pledge of Allegiance using somewhat limited language resources: "I pledge a lesson to the frog of the United States of America and to the wee puppet for witches' hands. One Asian, in the vestibule, with little tea and just rice for all" (Lord, 1985, p. 86).

So, how can OLLEE be achieved? How can a rich environment and experience be accomplished? The following suggestions might be helpful: As mentioned, simply having a large working vocabulary and substantial lexicon in one's repertoire is not enough to permit one to comprehend all the different meanings, including the connotations, of words or expressions. However, metalinguistic skills are not sufficient in cross-cultural encounters since culture plays a significant role in the actual interpretation of social interactions. Multicultural ability is needed to discover the true meaning of words, stories, and contexts.

1. Engage children in meaningful discourse, such as reading stories to children and reading the same stories repeatedly. Then, ask critical questions about the stories.
2. Ask hypothetical questions, such as, What if Snow White did not take a bite of the poisoned apple?
3. Provide a variety of reading materials: brochures, maps, magazines, newsletters, newspapers, books, journals, and so on.
4. Use memorization exercises and rhymes (metalinguistic tasks).
5. Create collective stories based on real experiences and customize stories based on the individual child's interest.
6. Compare and contrast, for example, the difference between chopsticks and forks.
7. Use wordplay: crossword puzzles, riddles, and so on.

Beyond BICS and CALP

Many individuals can learn English with native or near-native fluency and communicate freely. Others may use limited English in school and have difficulty acquiring BICS and CALP (Cumminis, 1981). They find school activities—including communication with teachers, administrators, peers, and staff—incomprehensible, threatening, and foreign. They go home to non-English-speaking environments, likely with only home language television programs, newspapers, books, and magazines available. Lack of practice in English can lead to disenfranchisement and school failure; thus, intensive English language training is crucial for students at risk. On the other hand, many exhibit high BICS and CALP and yet are still confronted with communication difficulties. The following discussion offers some suggestions for improving language proficiency.

Cross-Cultural Communicative Competence

SLPs are constantly challenged by the diverse cultural mandates from the families with which they work. The development of cultural competence is a continuous and dynamic process. We learn by interviewing people, reading up on background information, observing various contexts, and keeping in mind the central question: How does this culture look at family and the importance of family? Cultural competence is the integration of one's knowledge and skills, passion for engagement in further research, and exposure to various learning contexts in environments. The concept of OLLEE also works well for clinicians. We need to find ways to provide training and education for professionals in their ongoing quest for understanding in dealing with diverse families and values. The process of acquiring cross-cultural communicative competence is extremely complex and requires not only competence in language, but also social cultural competence beyond language.

Communication Breakdown

Breakdown in communication happens when people make false assumptions about each other's knowledge, culture, and experience. Mastering a language and culture means being able to say the right thing at the right time in the right manner. Language is so embedded in culture that without understanding and experiencing cultures and socialization, cross-cultural communicative competence cannot be achieved. True competence requires the individual's ability to integrate language, culture, social knowledge, and cognition. As Hall put it so aptly, "All [cultures] have their own identity, language, systems of nonverbal communication, material culture, history, and *ways of doing things*" (Hall, 1977, p. 2). By developing their MI, SLPs develop cultural intelligence and evolve into culturally competent professionals and thus are better equipped to work with families from diverse backgrounds.

☐ Synopsis

As professionals in CSD will assess and treat clients from various backgrounds and cultures, they need to understand such topics as bilingualism, cultural intelligence, and the difference between dialects and disorders. A multicultural perspective not only will allow professionals better interpersonal interaction with their clients but also will improve the validity of evaluations and treatment outcomes.

☐ Vocabulary

African American English (AAE), African American Vernacular English (AAV)—African American varieties of American English. AAVE is the variety formerly known as Black English Vernacular or Vernacular Black English among sociolinguists.

Appalachian English—also known as Southern Midland dialect of American English. It is spoken primarily in the central and southern Appalachian Mountain region of the eastern United States.

Basic Interpersonal Communication Skills (BICS)—refers to the ability of conversational fluency. The distinction between CALP was drawn because of the time difference it takes for immigrant children to acquire the two. Conversational fluency is often acquired to a functional level within about 2 years.

bilingualism—the ability to speak two languages or the frequent use of two languages

biliterate—the ability to read in two languages

Buddhism—a religion of eastern and central Asia growing out of the teaching of Gautama Buddha that suffering is inherent in life and that one can be liberated from it by mental and moral self-purification

code mixing—refers to any admixture of linguistic elements of two or more languages. The term *code mixing* emphasizes the hybridization of the two languages.

code switching—process of varying between two or more languages. The term *code switching* emphasizes the movement from one language to another.

Cognitive Academic Linguistic Proficiency (CALP)—grade-appropriate academic proficiency. The distinction between BICS was drawn because of the time difference it takes for immigrant children to acquire the two. Academic proficiency can take at least 5 years.

collectivism—emphasis on collective rather than individual action or identity

Confucianism—philosophies that are of or relating to the Chinese philosopher Confucius or his teachings or followers

cultural competence—an ability to interact effectively with people of different cultures

cultural intelligence (CQ)—one component of cultural competence. Refers to a person's capability to adapt effectively to new cultural contexts.

dialect—a regional variety of language distinguished by features of vocabulary, grammar, and pronunciation from other regional varieties and constituting together with them a single language

dynamic assessment—an interactive approach to conducting assessments. It is based on the fundamental belief that most children will be able to learn languages as long they are given the right instructions and the right environment. The methodology includes test-teach-test. Students are given the opportunity to learn and to be tested again over time to track their learning.

Ebonics—African American varieties of American English, term for Ebony Phonics. Commonly called Ebonics outside the academic community.

English language learner (ELL), English as a second language (ESL)—generally refers to children who speak one language at home and who learn English during the preschool and school-age years

English as a new language (ENL)—a new term proposed to refer to children who speak one language at home and who learn English during the preschool and school-age years

Hinduism—the dominant religion of India that emphasizes dharma with its resulting ritual and social observances and often mystical contemplation and ascetic practices

individualism—the conception that all values, rights, and duties originate in individuals

interconnectedness—mutually joined or related; refers to how groups perceive the cultural differences between individual members of the group and how those differences may or may not become interconnected to each other.

intonational—intonational languages refer to languages for which the variation of pitch while speaking is not used to distinguish words (e.g., English)

limited English proficient (LEP)—refers to individuals who have a limited ability to read, write, speak, or understand English

logographic—in a logographic language or logographic writing system, a single written symbol represents an entire word or phrase without indicating its pronunciation

mean length of utterance (MLU)—a measure of complexity in children's speech taken by calculating the average number of morphemes per utterance, using standardized rules; its purpose is to compare children at the same level of language knowledge, thus establishing stages of acquisition independent of chronological age

multiperspective identity (MI)—characteristics of our identity that enable each individual to view reality through specific perspective based on ability, age, ethnicity, gender, race, religion, sexual orientation, and socioeconomic class

Peabody Picture Vocabulary Test (PPVT)—a test to measure an individual's receptive vocabulary for Standard American English. It can be used for assessing the English vocabulary of non-English-speaking individuals and assessing adult verbal ability.

phonological awareness—refers to one's awareness of the sound structure or phonological structure of a spoken word; the ability to segment and blend phonemes

review, interview, observation, test (RIOT)—a procedure to process the assessment of a bilingual/multicultural child or adult with possible communicative disorder

sequential bilingual—children exposed to more than one language before the age of 3

simultaneous bilingual—children acquiring a second language after 3 or soon after birth

Standard American English (SAE)—the language used in most public communication in the United States; the formalized, standardized language in which people are educated, informed, entertained, and governed

tonal—tonal languages refer to languages in which a combination of high-low pitch has a phonemic distinction (e.g., Chinese)

☐ Discussion Questions

1. What is your personal definition of CLD?
2. What are some of the distinctive phonological features of AAE?
3. What is ASHA's position on the teaching of ESL for SLPs?
4. What is the definition of BICS?
5. What is the definition of CALP?
6. How do you differentiate language disorder from language difference?
7. In your opinion, can standardized procedures be translated for usage for bilingual populations?
8. What are some alternative strategies that can be used when there are no standardized tests?
9. What is the definition of cultural competence?
10. Why is cultural competence important?

☐ Note

1. Many terms have been used in the past to refer to these children, including **limited English proficient (LEP)**, **English as a second language (ESL)**, and so on. Currently, the favored term is **English as a new language (ENL)**.

☐ Recommended Reading

Ajax, B., Bernstein, J. A., Deng. B. A., & Deng A. (2005). *They poured fire on us from the sky*. Cambridge, MA: Public Affairs.
   This book gives a vivid description of the lost boys from Sudan. It details the stories of several boys from the same village traveling for 10 years during the civil war in Sudan. This book helps us understand the refugees from Africa.

Cisneros, S. (1991). *The house on Mango Street*. New York: Vintage Contemporaries.
   This book gives us the lifestyles of Hispanic Americans.
   It helps us understand the ways of life in the Hispanic bilingual, bicultural community.

Fadiman, A. (1998). *The spirit catches you and you fall down*. New York: Farrar, Straus & Giroux.
   This book tells us about a Hmong girl who suffers epilepsy, and due to cultural conflicts and mismanagement, her condition got worse, and a tragedy took place. This true story reveals the importance of cross-cultural competence in case management.

Li, Y. (2007). *A thousand years of good prayers*. New York: Random House.
   This book provides a background of Chinese thoughts and philosophy and provides interesting reading for understanding the Chinese way of life.

Morrison, T. (1987). *Beloved*. New York: Alfred Knopf.
   This is a book about the African American family and community. It talks about identity and identity crisis. This is a great example of African American cultural discourse.

Mortenson, G. (2007). *Three cups of tea*. New York: Penguin.
   This book details a true personal journey of an American traveling to the remote mountains of Pakistan to help build schools for girls. He outlines the lessons learned from his journey, which helps us understand the Muslim tribal culture.

Seierstad, A. (2003). *Bookseller from Kabul*. New York: Little, Brown.
   This true story is about a European writer in Afghanistan. She wrote about the lives of a family, a bookseller. She lived with them and wrote her story based on what she observed; this is a book about diverse views of looking at the same situation—cultural conflicts and misinterpretations.

Tan, A. (1989). *The joy luck club*. New York: Putnam.
   This book tells the stories of four pairs of mothers and daughters. The mothers are from China, and the daughters were born in the United States. It talks about the conflicts between them due to cultural differences and linguistic differences. It provides excellent information for understanding generational conflicts in bicultural families.

16
CHAPTER

Professional Issues

Preparation and Practice

Deena Louise Wener and Dale F. Williams

We are going to assume that, because you have read this far, you are still interested in a career in communication sciences and disorders (CSD). If so, you might have had new questions emerge: How do I qualify to practice? How long will it take? What are the steps? To whom do I report? What issues will I face? When will I actually feel competent? Do I need a license? How do I get it? Do I take a test? Pull a sword from a stone?

Fear not: in this chapter all shall be revealed.

☐ Becoming a Speech-Language Pathologist: What Do I Have To Do and How Long Will It Take?

To meet requirements for clinical certification as a speech-language pathologist (SLP), students must graduate from an accredited graduate program (discussed further in this chapter). That means the student must meet national academic and clinical requirements, complete a supervised *clinical fellowship*, and earn a passing score (currently 600) on the *National Examination in Speech-Language Pathology and Audiology* (NESPA). Most graduate programs take 2 years (give or take a semester) to complete if

347

attended full time. The clinical fellowship is a supervised term of 9 months completed in the first employment setting.

Some individuals come to CSD master's degree programs with out-of-field baccalaureate degrees. In these instances, prerequisite course work must be completed. Graduate programs vary in their policies on accepting students who have not completed the prerequisites as undergraduates. Some will require completion of the prerequisites prior to acceptance, while others will accept students and require them to complete prerequisite course work as a graduate student. All programs, however, will require students to have the prerequisites completed before beginning their graduate curriculum.

☐ Educational Requirements for the Aspiring Speech-Language Pathologist

Undergraduate

The intent of the American Speech-Language-Hearing Association (ASHA) standards with regard to undergraduate preparation is to require students to have a broad liberal arts and science background. With that in mind, students are required to have foundations in the biological and physical sciences, mathematics, and the social and behavioral sciences at the college level. Generally, these courses are a part of a student's "general requirements" during the first 2 years of college; therefore, just about anyone with a bachelor's degree has completed these prerequisites.

In addition to basic science course work, there are prerequisites specific to CSD. A student majoring in speech-language pathology will likely complete these courses during the junior and senior years, although some programs will require additional or other undergraduate classes. It is important to check the prerequisite requirements for the graduate schools to which you hope to apply. This information is easily accessible on the Web sites of the graduate programs.

Students who do not attend a college/university with an undergraduate preparation program, or who decide on a career in speech-language pathology after majoring in another area, will have to complete the prerequisites for graduate study. Some students may be able to take some of these prerequisite courses as electives; others will have to take the prerequisite courses in addition to the requirements for their majors; still others will have to take the prerequisite requirements after the bachelor's degree is awarded. We are often asked what the "best" undergraduate major is if a CSD major is not offered. The truth is that there is no one best major for this purpose. Assuming the required prerequisites are available, a major that allows flexibility in electives could be viewed as preferable to one that does not. Some universities and colleges have a sort of "design your own major" under headings such as liberal, general, interdisciplinary, or basic studies, while other schools enable you to declare a "minor" (usually 15–18 credits) that allows you to take speech-language courses. Majors that provide information that may be related to speech-language pathology are also a good choice. Still, while many students we know have earned majors of this type (e.g., special education, psychology, or linguistics), just as many have had majors in business, the sciences, and the arts. Moreover, there have been students from all of these fields who were successful in CSD.

The prerequisite classes related to basic and disordered human communication processes that are required for graduate study include, at a minimum:

- 3 credit hours of an introductory course in communication disorders
- 3 credit hours in anatomy and physiology of the speech, hearing, and swallowing mechanisms
- 3 credit hours in the neuroanatomical bases of speech, language, hearing, and swallowing
- 3 credit hours in speech and hearing science (courses that focus on the physics of sound, hearing science, speech science, etc.)
- 3 credit hours in the normal development of speech, language, and hearing
- 3 credit hours in phonetics
- 3 credit hours in audiology (hearing and hearing problems)

Early on, students in SLP programs will be required to observe clinical sessions. Observations can be done on or off campus. ASHA requires the accrual of 25 clock hours of observation. These hours can be completed at the undergraduate or graduate level. Most master's programs will require students to complete them prior to beginning any practicum. Others will allow students to begin a clinical practicum and complete their observation hours concurrently.

Clinical practicum is a supervised clinical experience in which the student meets with a client or clients (groups, pairs, etc.) and is responsible for the planning, implementation, and documentation of treatment for those clients. Although some undergraduate programs do provide a clinical practicum during the senior year, most students will not engage in such experiences until graduate school. ASHA will accept only 50 hours not completed at the graduate level toward the overall 400 required (25 observation + 375 clinical) hours. Table 16.1 charts additional steps in the journey from student to certified SLP.

TABLE 16.1 ASHA Standards for Education and Certification

ASHA Requirements

Step 1: The Baccalaureate Degree

Undergraduate   The student must have prerequisite knowledge of the biological sciences, physical sciences, mathematics, and the social/behavioral sciences.

(Standard III-A)

⇒ The student must demonstrate through transcript credit (e.g., course work, advanced placement, CLEP, or examination of equivalency) for each of the following areas:

- biological sciences: course work in biological sciences may include, but is not limited to, biology, general anatomy and physiology, neuroanatomy and neurophysiology, and genetics
- physical sciences: course work in physical sciences may include, but is not limited to, physics and chemistry
- mathematics: course work in math may include, but is not limited to, statistics and nonremedial mathematics
- social/behavioral sciences: course work in social/behavioral sciences may include, but is not limited to, psychology, sociology, and cultural anthropology.

Courses in biological and physical sciences specifically related to communication sciences and disorders (CSDs) cannot be applied for certification purposes in this category. Methodology courses, such as methods of teaching mathematics, may not be used to satisfy the mathematics requirement.

(Standard III-B)

The student must demonstrate the ability to integrate information pertaining to normal and abnormal human development across the life span, including basic communication processes and the impact of cultural and linguistic diversity on communication. Similar knowledge must also be obtained in swallowing processes and new emerging areas of practice.

Course work meeting this standard may include, but is not limited to,

⇒ Anatomy and Physiology of the Speech, Hearing, and Swallowing Mechanisms
⇒ Speech and Hearing Science
⇒ Phonetics
⇒ Neurological Bases of Communication and Hearing
⇒ Normal Development of Speech, Language, and Hearing
⇒ Normal Swallowing Function
⇒ Introduction to Communication Disorders
⇒ Introduction to Audiology (includes hearing, hearing problems, hearing testing)

Note: Graduate programs may stipulate specific courses or additional courses to meet program requirements.

TABLE 16.1 (continued) ASHA Standards for Education and Certification

Step 2: Master's Degree

Graduate
All graduate course work and graduate clinical practicum required in the professional area must have been initiated and completed at an institution whose program was accredited by the Council on Academic Accreditation (CAA) in Audiology and Speech-Language Pathology of the American Speech-Language-Hearing Association.

ASHA has identified 9 content areas in which a student must demonstrate both knowledge and skill. These areas are:

⇒ articulation

⇒ fluency

⇒ voice and resonance, including respiration and phonation

⇒ receptive and expressive language (phonology, morphology, syntax, semantics, and pragmatics) in speaking, listening, reading, writing, and manual modalities

⇒ hearing, including the impact on speech and language

⇒ swallowing (oral, pharyngeal, esophageal, and related functions, including oral function for feeding; orofacial myofunction)

⇒ cognitive aspects of communication (attention, memory, sequencing, problem solving, executive functioning)

⇒ social aspects of communication (including challenging behavior, ineffective social skills, lack of communication opportunities)

⇒ communication modalities (including oral, manual, augmentative, and alternative communication techniques and assistive technologies)

Knowledge

The student must demonstrate knowledge of principles and methods of prevention, assessment, and intervention for people with communication and swallowing disorders. This includes the anatomical and physiological, psychological, developmental, and linguistic and cultural correlates of the disorders.

Other areas in which the student must demonstrate knowledge are

⇒ standards of ethical conduct

⇒ processes used in research

⇒ the integration of research principles into evidence-based clinical practice

⇒ contemporary professional issues

⇒ certification, specialty recognition, licensure, and other relevant professional credentials

Skill

The student must demonstrate skill in oral, written, or other forms of communication sufficient for entry into professional practice.

The student must complete a minimum of 400 clock hours of supervised clinical experience in the practice of speech-language pathology.

continued

TABLE 16.1 (continued) ASHA Standards for Education and Certification

⇒ 25 hours must be in clinical observation

⇒ 375 hours must be spent in direct client contact

    ⇒ 325 hours of the clinical practicum must be completed at the graduate level

    ⇒ Experiences must include diagnosis and treatment, across the life span from the range of disorders and differences covered by the nine content areas

    ⇒ Experiences must provide opportunities for students to demonstrate that they communicate effectively, recognizing the needs, values, preferred mode of communication, and cultural/linguistic background of the client, family, caregivers, and relevant others

    ⇒ Experiences must provide opportunities for collaboration with others

    ⇒ Experiences must provide opportunities for counseling regarding communication and swallowing disorders

    ⇒ Students must adhere to the ASHA Code of Ethics and behave professionally

Step 3: The National Exam

NESPA[a]   Evidence of a passing score (currently 600) must be submitted to the ASHA by the testing agency administering the examination.

⇒ Some graduate programs require a passing score prior to graduation.

⇒ If not required by your graduate program, it is recommended that students take the NESPA after completing academic course work or shortly after graduation.

Step 4: The Clinical Fellowship

SLPCF[b]   After completion of all academic course work and clinical practicum, a Speech-Language Pathology Clinical Fellowship (SLPCF) must be completed.

⇒ The clinical fellow's major responsibilities must be in direct client/patient contact, consultations, record keeping, and administrative duties.

⇒ The SLPCF may not be initiated until completion of the graduate course work and graduate clinical practicum.

⇒ It is the responsibility of the clinical fellow to secure an ASHA-certified speech-language pathologist (CCC-SLP) to serve as his or her mentor.

⇒ The clinical fellow must develop, with the mentoring SLP, outcome and performance levels for the fellowship period within 4 weeks of initiating the SLPCF.

⇒ The clinical fellow will submit the SLPCF Report and Rating Form to the Council for Clinical Certification at the conclusion of the SLPCF.

TABLE 16.1 (continued) ASHA Standards for Education and Certification

⇒ The SLPCF consists of the equivalent of 36 weeks of full-time clinical practice.

⇒ Full-time clinical practice is defined as a minimum of 35 hours per week in direct patient/client contact, consultations, record keeping, and administrative duties.

⇒ The length of the SLPCF is modified if the clinical fellow is engaged in less than full-time employment.

⇒ Professional experience of less than 15 hours per week does not meet the requirement and may not be counted toward the SLPCF.

Step 5: Certification

CCC-SLP[c]   *Obtaining the Certificates of Clinical Competence*

⇒ Submit to the ASHA certification office one complete packet including the following:

⇒ a properly completed and signed application

⇒ verification of receipt of graduate degree

⇒ course descriptions or transcripts

⇒ appropriate payment

⇒ Complete the clinical fellowship (SLPCF) experience.

⇒ Submit the clinical fellowship evaluations and observations.

⇒ Submit the signed clinical fellowship report and rating form.

⇒ Submit a passing score on the national examination (NESPA).

⇒ Exam results must be sent directly from the Educational Testing Service (ETS) to be applicable toward certification.

⇒ Once certification has been awarded, you have the option of ordering the certificate.

⇒ To maintain certification, you must pay annual dues and fees when the annual invoice is received as the maintenance of certification is contingent on the timely payment of annual dues and fees.

⇒ Individuals who hold the Certificate of Clinical Competence (CCC) in Speech-Language Pathology must accumulate 30 contact hours of professional development over a 3-year period.

Source: Adapted from American Speech-Language-Hearing Association. (2009). Membership and certification manual. Retrieved January 16, 2010, from http://www.asha.org/members/international/caslpa/certification.htm.

[a] National Examination in Speech-Language Pathology and Audiology (Praxis examination).
[b] Speech-Language Pathology Clinical Fellowship.
[c] Certificate of Clinical Competence-Speech-Language Pathology.

Graduate Study and KASA

The entry-level degree for professional practice in the field of speech-language pathology is the master's degree. Admission to graduate programs is highly competitive, and as noted, the programs of study are rigorous. Although specific courses and credit requirements will vary, students must meet the knowledge and skill requirements set out by ASHA.

KASA stands for knowledge and skill assessment. The Council on Academic Accreditation (CAA) requires all accredited graduate programs to provide evidence that students have met the circumscribed knowledge and skill competencies set out in the *Standards for Accreditation of Graduate Education Programs in Audiology and Speech-Language Pathology* (ASHA, 2008b). New standards went into effect on January 1, 2008, and provide programs with greater flexibility in regard to curriculum design. However, all graduate programs are required to supply:

The opportunities for students to acquire and demonstrate knowledge of the nature of speech, language, hearing, and communication disorders and differences, as well as swallowing disorders, including etiologies, characteristics, and anatomical/physiological, acoustic, psychological, developmental, linguistic, and cultural correlates. These opportunities must be provided in the following areas:

- articulation
- fluency
- voice and resonance, including respiration and phonation
- receptive and expressive language (phonology, morphology, syntax, semantics, and pragmatics) in speaking, listening, reading, writing, and manual modalities
- hearing, including the impact on speech and language
- swallowing (oral, pharyngeal, esophageal, and related functions, including oral function for feeding; orofacial myofunction)
- cognitive aspects of communication (e.g., attention, memory, sequencing, problem solving, executive functioning)
- social aspects of communication (e.g., behavioral and social skills affecting communication)
- communication modalities (e.g., oral, manual, and augmentative and alternative communication techniques and assistive technologies)... (ASHA, 2008b).

Many in the field refer to the above-mentioned areas as "KASA-9," others as "the big nine." We prefer the "K-9." Regardless of the moniker, however, graduate programs must provide evidence that students have acquired and demonstrated knowledge and skills in these content areas, including course work and practicum experiences across the life span and in linguistic and cultural differences correlated with the disorders. Students must be informed of and follow the standards of ethical conduct in the ASHA Code of Ethics. In addition, students must have knowledge of research processes, evidence-based practice, and contemporary professional issues, as well as information pertaining to professional credentialing at the state and national levels. Graduate programs must provide students with academic and clinical practicum experiences across the nine content areas that will allow students to acquire and demonstrate skills in oral and written communication; the prevention, evaluation, and treatment of communication and swallowing disorders; the application of evidence-based practice; interactions with patients, families or significant others, and professionals; and self-evaluation of the effectiveness of their clinical practice. Students are required to have a graduate education that reflects the ASHA's current scope of practice and access to current technology. It should also be mentioned (as previously indicated in this chapter in reference to the attributes of a successful graduate student) that students must exhibit the interpersonal and personal qualities that will allow them to be successful clinicians. This includes the ability to provide effective counseling to clients and others regarding communication disorders and professional behaviors such as punctuality, dependability, patience, tolerance, and sensitivity, to mention only a few.

☐ Council on Academic Accreditation

ASHA affects the academic and professional lives of CSD professionals in a number of ways. For one thing, they stipulate the academic and clinical skills required to earn the monikers of speech-language pathologist and/or audiologist. Graduate programs training aspiring speech-language pathologists must be accredited by ASHA's Council on Academic Accreditation (CAA).

There are several responsibilities assigned to the CAA. The first is to formulate standards for the accreditation of graduate education programs that provide entry-level professional preparation in either or both audiology and speech-language pathology. In addition to formulating, revising, and updating these standards, the CAA evaluates programs for accreditation and accredits programs that have met the requirements set out in the standards. Last, a registry of accredited programs is maintained, and programs are monitored through yearly accreditation reports. As stated in the ASHA "Membership and Certification Manual" (2009d):

All graduate course work and graduate clinical practicum required in the professional area for which the Certificate is sought must have been initiated and completed at an institution whose program was accredited by the Council on Academic Accreditation in Audiology and Speech-Language Pathology (CAA) of the American Speech-Language-Hearing Association in the area for which the Certificate is sought.

Quite simply, a program *must* be accredited by the ASHA-CAA if its graduates desire to be certified practitioners.

The most current revision of the CAA standards went into effect on January 1, 2011. These standards establish six areas deemed "essential to quality education in the professions" (ASHA, 2011a). These areas are:

- administrative structure and governance
- faculty
- curriculum (academic and clinical education)
- students
- assessment
- program resources

☐ Certification

The ASHA Council for Clinical Certification (CFCC) is the granting body for the Certificates of Clinical Competence (CCC) in both speech-language pathology and audiology. An individual with the CCC may provide clinical services independently, as well as supervise student clinicians, clinicians who do not hold certification, and support personnel.

To meet the requirements for the CCC in speech-language pathology (CCC-SLP), an individual must, after earning the baccalaureate degree,

- complete a graduate degree program that meets the established academic course work and clinical practicum requirements,
- complete a supervised clinical fellowship equal to 9 months of full-time employment, and
- earn a passing score (currently 600) on the National Examination in Speech-Language Pathology and Audiology (NESPA-Praxis examination).

Any ASHA member providing services in speech-language pathology and audiology must hold the appropriate CCC. A member in the process of obtaining that certificate must be supervised by an individual who holds the appropriate CCC. Failure to meet this condition is a violation of ASHA's Code of Ethics.

Maintenance of the CCC requires on-time payment of annual dues and fees and the completion of 30 certification maintenance hours of **professional development** every 3 years. The 3-year maintenance cycle is determined by the initial certification date.

☐ Licensure

In most states, SLPs must comply with state regulatory (licensure) standards to practice or have state education certification. At present, 47 states regulate SLPs. Colorado, Michigan, and South Dakota do not (neither does the District of Columbia). Of the states regulating the practice of speech-language pathology, 41 require continuing education for license renewal. These requirements are in addition to what ASHA requires. However, continuing education activities completed for state licensure may be used for ASHA continuing education requirements during overlapping renewal periods. In other words, a continuing education course can count for both the ASHA and state requirements.

To work in the public schools, some states will require a state teaching credential. Others allow individuals who hold a state license in speech-language pathology to work in any setting. There are, currently, eight states that have a comprehensive licensure law that requires the individual to hold a state license regardless of the setting in which he or she is employed. These states are: Delaware, Hawaii, Kansas, Maryland, Michigan, Montana, New Mexico, and Texas. Six states require licensure plus additional requirements, for example, an educator certificate requiring coursework in educational foundations, classroom instruction and management, bilingual/bicultural education, and behavior management.

Twenty-nine states and the District of Columbia require a master's degree for initial employment in the public schools. In Florida, Maine, and New York, an individual may obtain a provisional teaching license with a bachelor's degree. However, a Master's degree must be obtained within three to five years. Arizona, Oregon, and Nevada will grant a full teaching license with only a bachelor's degree.

A number of states will accept the CCC-SLP from ASHA in lieu of a teaching certificate, so it is important to check state requirements before applying for employment. ASHA provides a state-by-state listing of credentialing requirements on its website.

☐ Becoming an Audiologist: Big Changes to Standards and Education Requirements

New audiology standards went into effect on January 1, 2007. One notable feature of these standards is that starting January 1, 2012, a master's in audiology will no longer serve as the terminal degree for clinical practice in the field. Any master's-level audiologist who failed to apply for certification by December 31, 2007, now is required to meet the 2007 standards for the CCC in audiology (CCC-A).

The implementation of the new standards is to occur in two steps. The first step went into effect on January 1, 2007. At that time, requirements for the postbaccalaureate degree were increased. Also required was a reconfiguration of practicum and evidence of the formative (i.e., ongoing) assessment of all knowledge and skills. The second step will go into effect on January 1, 2012. As of that date, a doctoral degree will be required of all applicants for certification in audiology. The AuD is the designator for the professional doctorate in audiology. However, the requirement for an earned doctoral degree will not exclude other doctoral degrees, such as PhD (doctor of philosophy), EdD (doctor of education), or ScD (doctor of science), to meet the standard. In other words, all of them meet the certification requirement.

Just as in speech-language pathology, applicants for certification in audiology must have initiated and completed all graduate-level academic course work and a clinical practicum in a program that is accredited by the CAA in audiology and speech-language pathology. While the graduate degree does not have to be a degree in audiology, an applicant will be required to have "75 semester credit hours of post-baccalaureate study addressing the knowledge and skills pertinent to the field of audiology" (ASHA, 2009c).

If an individual already holds the CCC-A, he or she will not be required to earn a doctoral degree. This holds true only for individuals applying for initial certification on or after January 1, 2012 (ASHA, 2009c). It is extremely important to note that payment of annual dues and fees must remain current. In addition, continuing education requirements for the maintenance of certification must be met every 3 years. If an individual holding a master's degree allows the current certification to lapse and then applies for the reinstatement of certification after January 1, 2012, he or she will be required to earn a doctoral degree.

The major changes to the audiology standards are highlighted in the introduction to the 2007 standards, discussed next.

Overview of Standards

Salient features of the new standards for entry-level practice include the following:

A. A minimum of 75 semester credit hours of post-baccalaureate study that culminates in a master's, doctoral, or other recognized academic degree from a program accredited by the CAA of the ASHA.
B. The requirement for a doctoral degree is mandatory for persons who apply for certification after December 31, 2011.
C. Practicum experience that is equivalent to a minimum of 12 months of full-time, supervised experience.
D. Skills in oral and written communication and demonstrated knowledge of ethical standards, research principles, and current professional and regulatory issues.

Educational Requirements for the Aspiring Audiologist

Because of the change in audiology certification standards, the CAA removed accreditation from all existing master's programs in audiology on December 31, 2006. The council also changed its eligibility standards for the accreditation of audiology programs to support the new degree requirements. Earning the AuD requires, typically, 4 years of postbaccalaureate study. In general, there is no specific undergraduate degree in audiology such as exists in speech-language pathology. ASHA recommends that:

> During high school, prospective audiologists should consider a program with courses in biology, physics, mathematics, and psychology. On the undergraduate level, a strong liberal arts focus is recommended, with course work in linguistics, phonetics, psychology, speech and hearing, mathematics, biological sciences, physical sciences and social sciences. A program of study in audiology is not available at the undergraduate level. Typically, students obtain an undergraduate degree in communication sciences which provides introductory course work in audiology. (ASHA, 2009b)

Undergraduate

The *Audiology Foundation of America* (AFA) (2007) recommends a pre-AuD curriculum at the undergraduate level that includes the following:

Biology/zoology	6 credits
Chemistry	4–8 credits
Mathematics	6 credits
Physics	4–8 credits
Communication	3 credits
Statistics	3 credits
English	6 credits
Psychology	3 credits
Humanities	9 credits
Social sciences	9 credits
Foreign language	6 credits
Business management	3 credits

However, students are strongly advised by both the AFA and the American Academy of Audiology (AAA) to check with the graduate program of their choice for the prerequisite course work required at the bachelor's level.

The 2007 standards (Standards IV-A: A1 and A2) provide general guidance with regard to the required prerequisite knowledge and skills required for clinical certification in audiology.

A1. The applicant must have prerequisite skills in oral and written or other forms of communication.

Implementation: The applicant must demonstrate communication skills sufficient to achieve effective clinical and professional interaction with clients/patients and relevant others. For oral communication, the applicant should demonstrate speech and language skills in English, which, at a minimum, are consistent with ASHA's most current position statement on students and professionals who speak English with accents and nonstandard dialects. For written communication, the applicant must be able to write and comprehend technical reports, diagnostic and treatment reports, treatment plans, and professional correspondence.

Individuals educated in foreign countries must meet the criteria required by the International Commission of Healthcare Professions (ICHP) to meet this standard.

A2. The applicant must have prerequisite skills and knowledge of life sciences, physical sciences, behavioral sciences, and mathematics.

Implementation: The applicant must demonstrate through transcript credit (which could include course work, advanced placement,

College Level Examination Program (CLEP), or examination of equivalency) knowledge and skills in the areas delineated in this standard. Appropriate course work could include human anatomy and physiology, neuroanatomy and neurophysiology, genetics, physics, inorganic and organic chemistry, psychology, sociology, anthropology, and nonremedial mathematics. The intent of this standard is to require students to have a broad liberal arts and science background in addition to knowledge of life sciences and physical sciences specifically related to CSD. Therefore, science courses in speech-language pathology may *not* be counted for certification purposes in both this category and the professional areas. In addition to transcript credit, applicants may be required by their graduate program to provide further evidence of meeting this requirement.

As mentioned, because there is no baccalaureate degree in audiology, students who decide on a career in audiology may have to take additional courses, postbaccalaureate, to meet the prerequisite requirements of an AuD program. Each AuD program has flexibility in determining which prerequisites best prepare a student for a career as an audiologist. Because there is no standardized curriculum in audiology, students must show transcript credit that courses were completed in life sciences, physical sciences, behavioral sciences, and mathematics.

Introducing the AuD

Applicants for certification in audiology must meet the degree requirements in Standard 1 of the 2007 audiology standards.

Standard I: Degree

Applicants for certification must have a minimum of 75 semester credit hours of postbaccalaureate education culminating in a doctoral or other recognized graduate degree. This is a transitional standard that will be in effect until January 1, 2012, at which time applicants for certification must have a doctoral degree. Seventy-five semester credit hours are equal to 112.5 quarter hours.

Students must demonstrate, also, that they have acquired the knowledge and developed the skills listed in the 2007 audiology standards in the following four areas:

- foundations of practice
- prevention and identification

- evaluation
- treatment

Which Professional Courses Are Required?

Unlike the 1993 audiology standards, for which the focus was on completion of specific courses, the 2007 standards focus on the acquisition of knowledge and skills in the foundations of practice, prevention and identification, evaluation, and treatment (Standards IV-B through IV-E). Each graduate training program is charged with the responsibility of determining learning outcomes and how those outcomes will be assessed to ensure that students have the knowledge and skills set down in the standards. Assessments must be ongoing and the results used for continuous program improvement.

One of the major differences between the 1993 and 2007 standards is that earning a passing grade in a course is no longer sufficient to show mastery of knowledge and skills. The CFCC expects the academic and clinical instructors of the program to identify where (e.g., courses, practicum) specific knowledge and skills are met and how they have been assessed. In essence, no specific audiology courses are identified as required for certification. Rather, certification requirements specify the minimum number of academic credits and clinical hours needed to receive the CCC-A.

While the 2007 standards in audiology do speak to the attainment of knowledge related to areas in speech and language, there is no requirement, as in the 1993 standards (6 semester hours/20 clinical hours), for specific courses or practicum hours in speech-language pathology. The rationale given for this change is that speech-language pathology is not within the scope of practice for audiology.

Clinical Practicum

In the area of clinical practicum, another major difference may be identified between the 1993 and 2007 certification standards. The new standards require that applicants for certification:

> complete a minimum of 12 months' full-time equivalent of supervised clinical practicum. ... Clinical experience under new standards must equal 52 weeks of experience, with a week of clinical practicum defined as 35 hours per week in direct patient/client contact, consultation, record keeping, and administrative duties relevant to

audiology service delivery. The aggregate total is 1,820 clock hours of clinical practicum. (ASHA, 2009a)

A Colossal Number of Hours

The 1993 audiology standards required 350 hours of supervised clinical practicum hours. The difference in practicum hour requirements reflects the elimination of the clinical fellowship year for individuals pursuing an AuD degree. During the development of the new standards, the Standards Council solicited and received input from a number of sources. Practicing professionals as well as graduate training programs chimed in. In addition, a "Skills Validation Study" was carried out. The validation study identified the skills that needed to be mastered while an individual was in his or her graduate program. Those required for the AuD were of greater scope and complexity than those needed for the master's degree.

The rationale for eliminating the clinical fellowship component of the certification process in audiology appears on ASHA's *Frequently Asked Questions About the 2007/2012 Standards in Audiology* Web page.

> An increase in the amount of practicum was the logical answer to increase the depth of skills acquired during the program and thereby eliminate the need for the clinical fellowship experience after the degree was awarded.

The 2005 standards for speech-language pathology identified nine content/clinical areas that must be covered by graduate training programs. The 2007 audiology standards do not address how many hours of clinical practicum must be earned in different categories. However, state licensure requirements may be different. Students should be mindful of what their states require for licensure in audiology to be certain that they meet those requirements clinically and academically.

Certification

Graduate programs in audiology must assess and document the attainment of knowledge and skills for all students in their programs. The programs must develop, as needed, remediation plans for students who require further assistance in meeting the knowledge and skills requirements. As in speech-language pathology, most programs will use the KASA form to document progress through the program.

ASHA has a new application for certification in audiology that reflects the changes that have occurred in the audiology requirements.

Applicants for initial certification in audiology must submit the following (Table 16.2):

1. Sections I, II, and the "Verification by Program Director" page of the application for certification, if submitted no more than 3 years after the awarding of the graduate degree. The entire application must be submitted, with a completed KASA form, if application for certification is made after the 3-year period.
2. Official graduate transcripts with the date on which the degree was rewarded.
3. Submission of payment of all dues and fees with the application.
4. A passing score (currently 600) on the Praxis series examination in audiology administered by the Educational Testing Service (ETS). Results must be sent to the ASHA National Office directly from the ETS. Score reports sent by applicants are not acceptable. All scores must not be more than 5 years old when the initial application for certification is submitted.

A Final Word on Graduate Study in Audiology

The National Association of Future Doctors of Audiology (NAFDA) provides information on both residential and distance learning AuD programs. Information is also available on the AFA and AAA Web sites. About 120 colleges and universities offer CAA-accredited graduate programs in audiology in the United States. The AuD is available in both residential and distance learning formats. Course work includes anatomy and physiology, basic science, math, auditory, balance, and normal and abnormal communication development. NAFDA (2007) stated:

> The Au.D. is a, postbaccalaureate clinical degree that includes an in-depth, broad-scope educational element. The clinical training is patient-based and includes audiometric evaluations, electrophysiologic testing, pediatrics, geriatrics, special needs audiology, advanced hearing amplification, aural habilitation and rehabilitation, cerumen management, tinnitus training, vestibular balance care, Electronystagmography (ENG), as well as other scope of practice training. The scientific basis of audiology includes acoustics and instrumentation, anatomy and physiology of the auditory and nervous systems, and auditory and speech perception. ... Direct client contact hours are required for certification in audiology. It is expected that students will accrue more than 2000 hours of clinical practicum during their four years of graduate school. Students also complete a research project during their second and third years of most programs. There are 60+ Au.D. programs in the United States today.

TABLE 16.2 ASHA Requirements for Initial Certification in Audiology

Step 1: The Baccalaureate Degree

Undergraduate   There is no specific undergraduate degree or uniform curriculum in audiology.

Students must demonstrate, through transcript credit, evidence of courses completed in the life sciences, physical sciences, behavioral sciences, and mathematics.

Course work meeting this standard may include: human anatomy and physiology, neuroanatomy and neurophysiology, genetics, physics, inorganic and organic chemistry, psychology, sociology, anthropology, nonremedial mathematics.

Students must have prerequisite skills in oral and written or other forms of communication. These skills must be sufficient to achieve "effective" clinical and professional interactions.

Students should demonstrate speech and language skills in English.

Students' written communication skills must be sufficient for professional demands.

Individuals educated in foreign countries must meet the criteria required by the International Commission of Healthcare Professions (ICHP) in order to meet this standard.

Note: Graduate programs may stipulate specific courses or additional courses to meet program prerequisite requirements.

Step 2: AuD (Doctor of Audiology)

Graduate   *All graduate course work and graduate clinical practicum required in the professional area must have been initiated and completed at an institution whose program has been accredited by the Council on Academic Accreditation (CAA) in Audiology and Speech-Language Pathology of the American Speech-Language-Hearing Association.*

Students must complete a program of graduate study (a minimum of 75 semester credit hours) that includes academic course work and a minimum of 12 months of full-time equivalent supervised clinical practicum (aggregate total is 1,820 clock hours) sufficient in depth and breadth to achieve the knowledge and skills outcomes stipulated in the standards.

Students must show achievement of knowledge and skills in the following areas:

Standard IV-B: Foundations of Practice

⇒ Professional codes of ethics and credentialing

⇒ Patient characteristics (e.g., age, demographics, cultural and linguistic diversity, medical history and status, cognitive status, and physical and sensory abilities) and how they relate to clinical services

⇒ Educational, vocational, and social and psychological effects of hearing impairment and their impact on the development of a treatment program

continued

TABLE 16.2 (continued) ASHA Requirements for Initial Certification in Audiology

⇒ Anatomy and physiology, pathophysiology and embryology, and development of the auditory and vestibular systems

⇒ Normal development of speech and language

⇒ Phonologic, morphologic, syntactic, and pragmatic aspects of human communication associated with hearing impairment

⇒ Normal processes of speech and language production and perception over the life span

⇒ Normal aspects of auditory physiology and behavior over the life span

⇒ Principles, methods, and applications of psychoacoustics

⇒ Effects of chemical agents on the auditory and vestibular systems

⇒ Instrumentation and bioelectrical hazards

⇒ Infectious/contagious diseases and universal precautions

⇒ Physical characteristics and measurement of acoustic stimuli

⇒ Physical characteristics and measurement of electric and other nonacoustic stimuli

⇒ Principles and practices of research, including experimental design, statistical methods, and application to clinical populations

⇒ Medical/surgical procedures for treatment of disorders affecting auditory and vestibular systems

⇒ Health care and educational delivery systems

⇒ Ramifications of cultural diversity on professional practice

⇒ Supervisory processes and procedures

⇒ Laws, regulations, policies, and management practices relevant to the profession of audiology

⇒ Manual communication, use of interpreters, and assistive technology

Standard IV-C: Prevention and Identification

⇒ Interact effectively with patients, families, other appropriate individuals, and professionals

⇒ Prevent the onset and minimize the development of communication disorders

⇒ Identify individuals at risk for hearing impairment

⇒ Screen individuals for hearing impairment and disability/handicap using clinically appropriate and culturally sensitive screening measures

⇒ Screen individuals for speech and language impairments and other factors affecting communication function using clinically appropriate and culturally sensitive screening measures

⇒ Administer conservation programs designed to reduce the effects of noise exposure and of agents that are toxic to the auditory and vestibular systems

TABLE 16.2 (continued) ASHA Requirements for Initial Certification in Audiology

Standard IV-D: Evaluation

⇒ Interact effectively with patients, families, other appropriate individuals and professionals

⇒ Evaluate information from appropriate sources to facilitate assessment planning

⇒ Obtain a case history

⇒ Perform an otoscopic examination

⇒ Determine the need for cerumen removal

⇒ Administer clinically appropriate and culturally sensitive assessment measures

⇒ Perform audiologic assessment using physiologic, psychophysical, and self-assessment measures

⇒ Perform electrodiagnostic test procedures

⇒ Perform balance system assessment and determine the need for balance rehabilitation

⇒ Perform aural rehabilitation assessment

⇒ Document evaluation procedures and results

⇒ Interpret results of the evaluation to establish type and severity of disorder

⇒ Generate recommendations and referrals resulting from the evaluation process

⇒ Provide counseling to facilitate understanding of the auditory or balance disorder

⇒ Maintain records in a manner consistent with legal and professional standards

⇒ Communicate results and recommendations orally and in writing to the patient and other appropriate individual(s)

⇒ Use instrumentation according to manufacturer's specifications and recommendations

⇒ Determine whether instrumentation is in calibration according to accepted standards

Standard IV-E: Treatment

⇒ Interact effectively with patients, families, other appropriate individuals, and professionals

⇒ Develop and implement treatment plan using appropriate data

⇒ Discuss prognosis and treatment options with appropriate individuals

⇒ Counsel patients, families, and other appropriate individuals

⇒ Develop culturally sensitive and age-appropriate management strategies

⇒ Collaborate with other service providers in case coordination

⇒ Perform hearing aid, assistive listening device, and sensory aid assessment

continued

TABLE 16.2 (continued) ASHA Requirements for Initial Certification in Audiology

⇒ Recommend, dispense, and service prosthetic and assistive devices

⇒ Provide hearing aid, assistive listening device, and sensory aid orientation

⇒ Conduct aural rehabilitation

⇒ Monitor and summarize treatment progress and outcomes

⇒ Assess efficacy of interventions for auditory and balance disorders

⇒ Establish treatment admission and discharge criteria

⇒ Serve as an advocate for patients, families, and other appropriate individuals

⇒ Document treatment procedures and results

⇒ Maintain records in a manner consistent with legal and professional standards

⇒ Communicate results, recommendations, and progress to appropriate individual(s)

⇒ Use instrumentation according to manufacturer's specifications and recommendations

⇒ Determine whether instrumentation is in calibration according to accepted standards

Step 3: The National Exam

NESPA[a]

Evidence of a passing score (currently 600) must be submitted to the ASHA by the ETS (Educational Testing Service). The score may not be more than 5 years old at the time of submission of the initial certification application.

Step 4: Certification

CCC-A[b]

Students must submit the following:

⇒ 2007 Standards for Certification in Audiology application form completed in black ink.

⇒ Applications must have *the original* signature of both the applicant and the director of the educational program.

⇒ Payment in the form of a check or charge authorization. Applications submitted without the full, appropriate payment will be returned.

⇒ All applicants for certification must submit official graduate transcripts verifying receipt of the graduate degree.

Individuals educated under 2007 Standards for Certification in Audiology who apply within 3 years of graduation, need to complete only the first two pages of the application and the *Verification by Program Director* page.

Individuals who are applying more than 3 years after receipt of the graduate degree must complete the application in its entirety.

⇒ To maintain certification, you must pay annual dues and fees when the annual invoice is received, as the maintenance of certification is contingent on the timely payment of annual dues and fees.

TABLE 16.2 (continued) ASHA Requirements for Initial Certification in
Audiology

> ⇒ Individuals who hold the Certificate of Clinical Competence (CCC)
> in Audiology must accumulate 30 contact hours of professional
> development over a 3-year period.

Source: Adapted from 2007 audiology standards and information from the AFA, AAA, and
NAFDA (National Association of Future Doctors of Audiology, 2007).
[a] National Examination in Speech-Language Pathology and Audiology (Praxis examination).
[b] Certificate of Clinical Competence-Audiology.

☐ American Speech-Language-Hearing Association (ASHA)

Audiologists and SLPs make up ASHA. This organization has a 79-year
history, beginning as the American Academy of Speech Correction in
1925. The current name was adopted in 1978.

In 1958, ASHA's first "official" national office was established. It was
relatively small compared to today's facility, which is staffed by approximately 225 individuals. This staff includes about 30 professionals in audiology and speech-language pathology. Other professionals come from
backgrounds in accounting, adult learning, association management,
human resources, lobbying, marketing, meetings and conference management, publications, and research, among others.

Currently, more than 127,000 speech-language-hearing professionals
belong to ASHA. These individuals include audiologists, SLPs, and
speech-language-hearing scientists. ASHA membership is required to
maintain the CCC. However, individuals who are not engaged in clinical
practice can still be members of the ASHA.

ASHA publishes four peer-reviewed, scholarly journals:

- *American Journal of Audiology*
- *American Journal of Speech-Language Pathology*
- *Journal of Speech, Language, and Hearing Research*
- *Language, Speech, and Hearing Services in Schools*

The organization also circulates *Contemporary Issues in Communication
Science and Disorders (CICSD)*, the journal of the National Student Speech-
Language-Hearing Association (NSSLHA). All ASHA members are entitled
to free online access to the full text of the four ASHA journals from 1980
to the present.

Sixteen times a year, *The ASHA Leader* is published. This professional newspaper provides member and association news, employment recruitment ads, and in-depth coverage of issues and stories that impact the professions now and will do so in the future. Major stories are posted on the *Leader* online. This easy-to-read publication is a good way for students (at any level) to keep up on what is happening in CSD professions. Finally, ASHA also provides *Access E-newsletters*, bimonthly electronic publications targeted to different audiences and focusing on different professional interests.

There are 18 special interest divisions of ASHA focusing on various areas of professional concentration. Membership in any division is open to ASHA members, ASHA international affiliates, consumers, and students who are members of the NSSLHA or are full-time doctoral students. A yearly fee is charged for membership. Members of special interest divisions receive access to the division listserv and member-only online content. In addition, special interest division members may participate in Web forums and receive discounts at the ASHA national conventions.

The special interest divisions gave rise to the *Clinical Specialty Recognition* Program. This recognition program is for ASHA-certified members who wish to become board-recognized specialists in a specialty area. Members of a special interest division may petition to establish recognition in a specialty area. The specialty areas of child language, fluency, and swallowing and swallowing disorders have established specialty boards and have application requirements and procedures for specialty recognition.

☐ American Academy of Audiology

The American Academy of Audiology (AAA) is, like ASHA, a professional organization devoted to education, research, and advocacy. The difference is that AAA is, as the name implies, strictly devoted to the profession of audiology. In fact, it is the largest audiology organization in the world. Only two decades old, AAA already boasts a membership of 10,000 (AAA, 2011). AAA publications include the *Journal of the American Academy of Audiology*, a research journal; *Audiology Today*, with membership information and updates on the association; and *AT Extra*, a monthly newsletter.

☐ Ethics

All CSD practitioners are expected to adhere to codes of ethics. Both ASHA and AAA have codes covering such areas as service delivery, research, and client confidentiality.

TABLE 16.3 Titles and Descriptions of ASHA Special Interest Divisions

Specialty Division	Description
Division 1: Language Learning and Education	Activities related to (1) linguistic knowledge and communicative interaction of infants, children, and youth from diverse cultures; (2) how knowledge, interactions, and culture affect language learning and literacy; (3) ways in which contexts influence children's communication; and (4) assessment and intervention approaches for people with developmental disabilities or speech-language-hearing disorders.
Division 2: Neurophysiology and Neurogenic Speech and Language Disorders	Promote, interpret, and disseminate information that is relevant to neurogenic communication disorders and to serve as a conduit for the exchange of information and ideas among division affiliates.
Division 3: Voice and Voice Disorders	Interests related to voice production and voice disorders through continuing education, networking, demonstrations, and study sessions.
Division 4: Fluency and Fluency Disorders	Focuses on the study of characteristics and processes related to normal fluency of speech; prevention, assessment, and treatment of fluency disorders, including neurophysiologic, cognitive, psychological, social, and cultural factors.
Division 5: Speech Science and Orofacial Disorders	Interaction among colleagues concerning specific areas of mutual interest. Affiliate members have a direct voice in addressing issues that impact their scholarly pursuits and delivery of service.
Division 6: Hearing and Hearing Disorders: Research and Diagnostics	Opportunity for basic and applied hearing researchers to pursue topics of mutual interest within the larger framework of the Association. Encourages membership of clinical practitioners with an interest in hearing research. Provides forum in which the clinician can suggest areas in need of further research to develop productive collaborations with the researchers.
Division 7: Aural Rehabilitation and Its Instrumentation	Dedicated to creating and maintaining a forum allowing clinicians and researchers to affiliate formally to focus on (a) the study, development, and application of amplification systems and communication devices; (b) techniques for amelioration of expressive and receptive communication problems in children and adults with hearing impairments; and (c) technology for habilitation of deafened children and adults. Underlying purposes are to foster an exchange of information among affiliates sharing the common interest of aural rehabilitative methodologies and to disseminate information to other professionals as well as consumers of audiological services.
Division 8: Hearing Conservation and Occupational Audiology	The mission of the division is to prevent hearing impairment from exposure to noise and other toxic agents by (a) increasing understanding of the problem and knowledge of effective intervention strategies; (b) monitoring and promoting appropriate regulatory activity and legislation; (c) educating the public and related professionals; (d) facilitating communication within ASHA and among related professional organizations; (e) promoting excellence in hearing conservation; and (f) promoting needed research.

continued

TABLE 16.3 (continued) Titles and Descriptions of ASHA Special Interest Divisions

Specialty Division	Description
Division 9: Hearing and Hearing Disorders in Childhood	The main focus is on all areas related to childhood hearing. The mission is to provide a unified voice and advocacy for childhood hearing issues within ASHA. Other functions: to permit interaction between members who share the same concerns; to provide for study sections within the division, with members of other divisions, and with members of allied health groups; to provide a forum for demonstration and sharing of new technologies, research, clinical developments, and treatment outcomes; and to provide a vehicle for input into education and training issues related to hearing in childhood.
Division 10: Issues in Higher Education	The mission is to foster development of ever-expanding knowledge of instruction, learning strategies, and curriculum to provide the underpinnings of education and skills for practice of the profession. To foster collaboration among programs, faculty, research laboratories, and administration so that common concerns are addressed and resolved in the best interests of our academic members.
Division 11: Administration and Supervision	The mission is to promote best practices in administration and supervision by serving as the primary resource for leaders, administrators, and supervisors at all levels of professional development, working in a variety of settings.
Division 12: Augmentative and Alternative Communication	The goal is to promote continuing education for ASHA members at introductory, intermediate, and advanced levels; advocate for ASHA membership regarding clinical service needs; and advocate for preservice and in-service personnel preparation in the area of augmentative and alternative communication.
Division 13: Swallowing and Swallowing Disorders (Dysphagia)	The mission is to provide leadership and advocacy for issues in swallowing and swallowing disorders and to serve affiliates who evaluate and manage individuals with swallowing and feeding disorders across the life span by supporting professional development, research, education, and communication necessary for delivery of the highest-quality services.
Division 14: Communication Disorders and Sciences in Culturally and Linguistically Diverse (CLD) Populations	The mission is to provide leadership and advocacy for best practices relating to speech-language pathology and audiology services to members of CLD populations and research, networking, and mentoring opportunities for its members.
Division 15: Gerontology	Concerned with the interdisciplinary study and communication behaviors and disorders in older individuals. The mission is to provide an opportunity for members concerned with the communication problems associated with the aging process to (a) affiliate with one another to promote specific professional and scientific interests, (b) develop communication and networking in diverse professional and scientific settings, (c) advocate for positive outcomes on issues concerning older individuals.

TABLE 16.3 (continued) Titles and Descriptions of ASHA Special Interest Divisions

Specialty Division	Description
Division 16: School-Based Issues	The mission is to provide leadership and advocacy for all speech-language pathologists and audiologists with interests in school-based issues. Additionally, the group strives to promote quality services within both early childhood and school programs at local, state, and federal levels.
Division 17: Global Issues in Communication Sciences and Related Disorders	The group's main mission is to provide international leadership related to services provided by the professions, audiology, and speech-language pathology, by promoting research, networking, collaboration, education, and mentoring in the global marketplace.
Division 18: Telepractice	The mission of this group is to provide education, leadership, and leadership for issues in telepractice in both speech and audiology.

Source: American Speech-Language-Hearing Association (2011b). Special Interest Divisions. Retrieved June 13, 2011 from http://www.asha.org/members/divs/.

The most recent version of the ASHA Code of Ethics was completed in 2003. Revisions to the code were necessary over the years because of the expanding scope of practice for CSD professionals and to reflect changing attitudes, information, and research on areas of practice and professional behavior. A good example of changing attitudes is the code of ethics statement on advertising. Early codes of ethics allowed professionals to "tastefully" announce their services in community publications or mailings, but not to advertise directly. The current code of ethics, on the other hand, provides a much broader and competition-friendly stance toward the advertising of our professional services.

The admonition on ethical treatment of research participants is another example of a recent modification to the code of ethics. This principle emphasizes the importance of protecting and honoring the clients we serve.

It is expected that every individual who is a member of the ASHA, whether or not he or she is certified, will abide by the code of ethics. In addition, applicants for membership or certification and clinical fellows are also expected to follow the code. In fact, a board of ethics exists for the purpose of making sure members do exactly that. This board has adopted practices and procedures to be followed in both the administration and enforcement of the code of ethics. Each case brought before the board of ethics is judged individually on its merits and shortcomings. If appropriate, the board may apply one or more of the following sanctions: reprimand; censure; withhold, suspend, or revoke membership or the CCC(s).

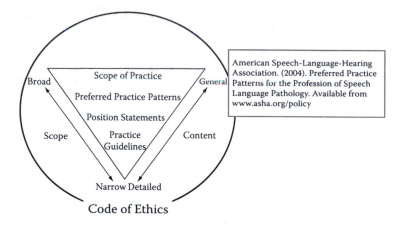

FIGURE 16.1 A conceptual framework of ASHA policy statements.

Encompassed within the ASHA Code of Ethics are various types of policy statements (see Figure 16.1). These are explained individually.

- Scope of practice statement: a list of professional activities that define the range of services offered within the profession of speech-language pathology.
- Preferred practice patterns: statements that define generally applicable characteristics of practice.
- Position statements: statements that specify ASHA's policy and stance on a matter that is important not only to the membership but also to other outside agencies or groups.
- Practice guidelines: a recommended set of procedures for a specific area of practice, based on research findings and current practice; detail the knowledge, skills, or competencies needed to perform the procedures effectively.

Scope of Practice

There are scopes of practice for both speech-language pathology and audiology. The purpose of both documents is to provide "the breadth of professional practice" within the professions. Because CSD fields are dynamic and ever changing, these documents may not include new or emerging areas of practice. However, this does not restrict professionals from helping those in need. For example, the *Scope of Practice in Speech-Language Pathology* (2007) allows engagement in areas of practice that serve the needs of clients even if these areas are not addressed in *Scope of Practice* (assuming individuals have the requisite knowledge and skills to do so).

Practice scopes include, among other topics, a framework for research and clinical practice, specialized qualifications, professional roles and activities, and practice settings. Further, ASHA requires that individuals engaging in clinical practice consider the impact of cultural and linguistic exposure/acquisition and use the best-available evidence to select clinical procedures and ensure optimal outcomes for clients.

Preferred Practice Patterns

Current preferred practice statements are intended as a guide for practitioners and as an educational tool for those outside the professions (e.g., consumers, administrators, third-party payers). They are intentionally broad enough to apply across all practice settings, with the practitioner paying attention to cultural and linguistic differences and the needs of clients/patients and their families.

Position Statements

Position statements present the association's stands on numerous professional and practice issues. There are statements related to the treatment of different disorders, as well as positions on new forms of practice such as **telepractice**. ASHA has position statements on the use of support personnel, clinical supervision, areas of practice, and evidence-based practice, to highlight only a very few.

Practice Guidelines

ASHA provides practitioners with a variety of guidelines designed to assist in clinical practice and educational training. The guidelines are the official statements of the association and define the roles and responsibilities of the professional with regard to disorders, documentation, best practices, and training or educational requirements.

Other Efforts

Along with the setting of ethical and practice codes, ASHA provides additional functions. Two noteworthy programs are the American Speech-Language-Hearing Foundation (ASHF) and the American Speech-Language-Hearing Association Political Action Committee (ASHA-PAC).

The ASHF was created in 1946 and is a charitable foundation. Its general purpose is

> to generate and allocate funds to support the advancement of knowledge and improvement of practice in serving children and adults with speech, language, or hearing disorders by (a) furthering education and supporting research and similar endeavors and (b) identifying and facilitating new directions in the field of communication sciences and disorders through support of such vehicles as conferences, publications, and other media. (ASHA, 1994)

The foundation provides merit-based graduate scholarships, funds research, recognizes distinguished professionals for their clinical achievements, and supports projects to advance innovative practice and technology.

The ASHA-PAC is a voluntary, nonprofit, and unincorporated committee. Comprised solely of SLPs and audiologists, the ASHA-PAC is not affiliated with any political party, other political action committees, or any national, state, or local speech-language-hearing associations. Its central purposes are

1. To influence or attempt to influence the nomination or election of individuals to national office to promote the interests and needs of the speech-language pathology and audiology professions and of persons with disabilities.
2. To raise funds to influence the nomination or election of such individuals.
3. To encourage SLPs and audiologists to understand the institutions and procedures of government and the public issues acted on by governmental officials that affect the professions and those they serve.
4. To promote the interests of the professions and of those they serve by facilitating the participation of SLPs and audiologists in the political process.
5. To do all of the above to promote public policies that result in accessible and appropriate services in the areas of education and health care, in the training of qualified personnel to deliver these services, and in research that leads to more effective and quality services and benefits.

☐ Synopsis

The fields of speech-language pathology and audiology are in constant motion. Educational, certification, practice, and even ethical standards all change with the times, affected by educational policy and funding, health care guidelines, the economy, and numerous other factors. Within this changing environment, procedures are in place for becoming a CSD professional and, once this is accomplished, for effective delivery of services to the communicatively impaired.

☐ Vocabulary

professional development—the advancement of skills or expertise through continued education

telepractice—the application of telecommunications technology to delivery of professional services at a distance by linking clinician to client, or clinician to clinician, for assessment, intervention, or consultation (ASHA, 2010)

☐ Discussion Questions

1. Should support personnel be permitted to diagnose, prescribe, treat, and discharge patients independently?
2. Should services to bilingual/bidialectal clients be provided only by a bilingual/bidialectal SLP fluent in that client's language or dialect?
3. Should private practitioners be required to provide a small percentage of their services "pro bono"?
4. Should there be minimum intelligibility or language competency requirements for students studying to be SLPs and whose primary language is not English?

☐ Recommended Reading

Detailed information on the KASA and the CAA standards may be found on the ASHA Web site as follows:

KASA Summary Form-SLP: http://www.asha.org/NR/rdonlyres/3B9B6A8F-4AA7–4203–8447-BCFD754D64F9/0/KASA_SummaryFormSLP.pdf

Preferred practice patterns: http://www.asha.org/docs/html/PP2004–00191.html#top

Scope of practice: http://www.asha.org/docs/html/SP2007–00283.html

2008 Standards for accreditation of graduate education programs in audiology and speech-language pathology: http://www.asha.org/NR/rdonlyres/686AF94D-5DA9–4D2C-96FB 2CA5E047527F/0/AccreditationStds0307.pdf

CHAPTER

A Few Final Thoughts

Having read, to this point, the bulk of this text, I hope you have learned a few things about communication sciences and disorders (CSD). Aside from the most evident points (e.g., speech is different from swallowing, which is different from hearing), there were items covered that were perhaps not as apparent at the outset:

- There is a connection (perhaps working memory) between literacy and language.
- Cleft palates are associated not only with speech difficulties but also with language disorders.
- Hearing impairments often lead to delayed language development and differences in speech.
- Children who stutter are more likely to present concomitant communication disorders than are their nonstuttering peers.
- Those with neurological trauma (e.g., subcortical aphasia) quite often present disorders of language, both receptive and expressive, as well as impairments that make speech production difficult.

In addition to such new material, there were likely points you thought you knew that are now perhaps less clear. For example, language is different from speech—but doesn't language expression include speech? Wouldn't a disorder of one necessarily result in a disorder of the other?

If a child has articulation and stuttering disorders, the speech-language pathologist (SLP) would obviously treat both, right? But how? How do you teach the kid easy speech simultaneous with precise instruction on where to place his or her articulators? How do you tell the parents that stuttering necessitates a focus on the content of speech and articulation on the production?

SHOULD SLPS TREAT SWALLOWING DISORDERS?

"First of all, that's a lousy title for a debate."

"Why?"

"It presents the question as if it's legitimate, worthy of response. Why not ask 'Why do football players play football?' Because they're qualified, that's why!"

"Actually, a better analogy would be 'Why do greeting card stores also sell those cutesy little knick-knacks?'"

"You lost me on that one."

"What I'm trying to say is that just because one person can do—and get paid for doing—two things, that alone doesn't make it a great idea."

"So there should be separate cutesy little knick-knack stores?"

"I'm saying that when I'm looking for a Mother's Day card, I don't want to first have to make my way past four bookshelves of ceramic puppies and singing bottle openers. More to the point, I think swallowing should be a separate field from speech-language pathology."

"Why?"

"Let's start with the basics. We're communication professionals. By whose definition does that include speech, language, hearing, and *swallowing*? What's that Sesame Street song? 'One of these things is not like the other. One of these things just doesn't belong… .'"

"Please stop singing. It's not as different as you think. Swallowing is performed by the same structures used for communication. And SLPs know those structures better than anyone."

"SLPs know all about respiration, too. Why don't they just take over respiratory therapy?"

"Interesting that you should mention respiration. The anatomy we're talking about exists for the purposes of respiration and swallowing. Communication is a secondary function."

"So?"

"So SLPs need to understand the relationship between these functions. Would you want an SLP to treat your voice problem in a way that interferes with your ability to swallow?"

"You're saying SLPs need to be experts in all three areas? Then, I'll ask again: Why are SLPs doing swallowing and communication therapy, but not respiratory therapy?"

"Some do limited amounts of respiratory therapy, when communication is impacted."

"Aha!"

"Aha what?"

"When communication is impacted. That's the difference right there. With swallowing therapy, they treat whether or not there's an impact on communication."

"They have to."

"Why?"

"Well, as I already said, they're the most qualified. Added to that is the fact that nobody else treats swallowing disorders. Your assertion that it's not technically communication is a nice ivory tower argument. Now, it's time to join the real world and admit that someone needs to help the client who is lying in a hospital bed unable to swallow. SLPs should be admired for stepping up to the plate."

"But do they need to be batting at all? Who worked on swallowing before SLPs entered the game? And why did SLPs take it away? Look, no one is saying that swallowing therapy is unimportant. I'm just saying there was no good reason for SLPs to get involved."

"And just where did you observe people doing swallowing therapy before SLPs got involved? The Mayo Clinic? Boston General? News flash: Some people had to go to their local hospitals. And nobody was there to help them. Those people are certainly thankful that SLPs stepped up."

"Even if I admit, for the sake of argument, that that may have been true last century, let's talk about now. Hospitals need SLPs, and they need swallowing therapists. But the two shouldn't overlap."

"Why not?"

"Well, to start with, swallowing therapy takes up a huge amount of a hospital SLP's workday. Add to that that it's reimbursable, and the equation becomes clear: a limited number of SLPs plus dysphagia therapy equals patients with real communication disorders not getting therapy."

"Even if it was happening someplace, the concern shouldn't be that SLPs know how to do swallowing therapy. The problem was that the hospital wasn't taking care of their patients. They needed to hire more SLPs."

"Now you're the one living in dreamland. What actually happens is that hospital administrators say they have an SLP on staff. And since the profession covers speech and swallowing, they don't have to fork out the money to hire anyone else."

continued

"Do you have one single ounce of data to back up that claim? And even if you did, I'll tell you again: What you're describing is a problem with a hospital, not the field of speech-language pathology."

"It's all related. Let's look at how SLPs are trained. Learning about swallowing takes up hours of students' time that could be devoted to communication problems. And even after they've graduated, how are they supposed to keep up on the ever-changing areas of communication when this new area is piled on?"

"It's not unheard of for health-related professions to require a lot of knowledge. People learn it if they want to do the job."

"And people work jobs to make money, which, ultimately, is what this is all about. There's gold in them thar' swallows. And because there is, SLPs want it, even if it means sacrificing people's communication treatment."

"Leaving aside my opinion that there's nothing wrong with SLPs making money, let me again point out that you're not addressing the central question. Yes, insurances and other agencies do reimburse well for swallowing therapy. Here's something else you should know about these payers: Recent changes, like reducing the maximum payments and number of visits allowed, have seriously hindered what SLPs can do for communication problems. It's not the SLPs who are sacrificing anyone's treatment. Again, the problem lies outside the profession."

"Perhaps if the profession were as concerned with communication problems as they are with swallowing, they could fight these changes."

"They've tried."

"Then they can try again. They need to do what's best for the patients."

"I know. I also know that dysphagia, as an area of speech-language pathology, is here to stay. Regardless of what people say, students have to learn it and know how to do it."

What do *you* think?

What about hearing information versus processing it? Yes, those are different, but perhaps not as much as you thought going into this book. They are basically parts of the same system, an idea that is key to this chapter.

As the list at the start of this chapter indicates, it is not uncommon for clients to present multiple speech and language disorders. I remember one child who was referred to me with vocal nodules, a language delay, stuttering, and a phonological disorder. What was interesting was how

CSD IN EAST AFRICA

The flight from Washington, D.C., to Kigali was absolutely brutal. It was 10 hours to Rome, an hour on ground refueling (during which passengers were not allowed out of the plane), then 6 hours to Addis Ababa, a 2-hour layover (but out of the plane this time), and finally about 2 more hours to our destination. I wish I could sleep on airplanes. As it was, I was awake for over 30 hours before finally passing out in a strange bed an ocean away from home.

Sleep, unfortunately, was fitful, yet I still had to awaken the following morning and attend a meeting. Along the way, I got my first taste of Rwanda. The countryside is absolutely layered with mountains. Every route is uphill or down; there seemed to be no flat space anywhere. Although it sits close to the equator, the elevation keeps the climate cool.

The city of Kigali is disjointed in that one can see modern building next to slum, traditional house next to clay hut. The people were friendly and very respectful (I had not yet met the market sellers). Armed soldiers were present, which probably added to the overall feel of orderliness. Despite the order, however, there was a surprising indifference to rules. The plane landed with seats back and tray tables out. After reaching the hotel, the staff opened the restaurant after it had been closed for hours because someone requested it.

My meeting was with a local Rwandese[1] businessman. The sole agenda item was the very reason I was there: the development of a distance CSD treatment program. Specifically, my goal was to deliver speech and language services to residents of Rwanda who do not have access to such opportunities. This would be done by Florida Atlantic University (FAU) student clinicians via webcam videoconferencing.

Even more specifically, I was invited by the Koinonia Foundation to travel to Rwanda during the summer of 2009. Koinonia primarily provides this nation with solar power and other forms of clean energy. To accomplish their mission, they must utilize local businesses. Thus, communication between the foundation and Rwandese individuals is paramount. Unfortunately, it is often difficult as well.

Such difficulty led to Rwandese businessmen's interest in improving their communication with Koinonia and other American companies. Koinonia wished to help them do so and asked me to set up an accent reduction program. What the businessmen needed, however, was a speech and language program. That is, accent reduction was

continued

only part of the communication gap. To make them understandable to listeners unfamiliar with the local English dialect, linguistically based features such as phonology, rate, and intonation would all need to be addressed.

With that in mind, I began administering evaluations. Time was always limited, so they had to be efficient. Had we been in a hospital, I would have called them bedside evals. Among other undertakings, I transcribed words, sentences, and conversational speech; asked them to explain idioms and idiomatic verbs (e.g., *fall behind*, *shut up*) common to Standard American English (SAE), and define homonyms ("Give me two definitions for the word *park*."). I also asked them what Americans say that is difficult to understand and, conversely, what they say that is misunderstood.

All told, there was some consistency across subjects. This was not entirely surprising, given their similar communication histories: The first language for all of the subjects was Kinyarwanda, and all used French in school. Both languages influenced their third, English. As expected, the production of many vowels was different. There were also consonant variations from SAE. Plosives, particularly /t/ and /d/, were produced with far more aspiration than what I was accustomed to hearing. Continuant sounds were sometimes prolonged in comparison to SAE. The /r/ sound was either more extreme (what is often referred to as "rolled") or omitted (e.g., "hard" rhymed with "cod").

More troubling to the American ear than articulation differences, however, were unfamiliar stress and intonation patterns. There was not always a pitch rise at the end of questions. Different words were stressed within sentences and different syllables in words (e.g., *en-GIN-eer*). As one subject put it, "The music of the language is not like in America." This was particularly true in longer utterances or when speech rate was accelerated.

Defining words was tough for some, simple for others. One subject had an easy time explaining idiomatic verbs; the rest struggled with this task. When asked about speaking to Americans, two reported more difficulty on the telephone because they could not communicate with gestures or use facial expressions. Another noted that he sometimes uses a literal English interpretation of a Kinyarwanda expression (e.g., "working on your own tree") before realizing that American listeners will not understand it.

When they were not understood, subjects reported implementing a variety of strategies: talking slower, using simpler language, and repeating the misconstrued utterance. All stated that they would request a repeat of phrases they did not understand, yet when I asked them to do so during conversation with me, only one signaled me when he was not following my words. On the same topic, three subjects reported that Americans do not pronounce /t/, which they found confusing. Indeed, after one subject told me about the Rwandan Information and Technology Agency (RITA), I asked him if there were RITA centers in Kigali. Because I had used an American pronunciation, however ("ree-da"), he told me that he sincerely did not know what I was asking.

The recommendations from these evaluations were to address:

1. SAE prosody. This would likely have the greatest impact on intelligibility.
2. Vocabulary common to American speakers.
3. Production of vowels and, to a lesser extent, selected consonants.
4. Use of figurative language in conversation.

These goals served as the basis for the treatment plans when, beginning in 2010, students in the CSD program at FAU began conducting therapy across six time zones.

Additional highlights of the trip included the scenes shown in Figures 17.1–17.3.

FIGURE 17.1   The Rwandan countryside.

continued

FIGURE 17.2   Helping to install solar power in a school (under the watchful eyes of every child there).

FIGURE 17.3   Finally, watching my son make some new friends.

improvement in one area enhanced additional skills. I remember in particular how direct voice therapy (designed to eliminate abusive behaviors such as yelling) yielded a corresponding decrease in the rate and tension of his speech. In other words, voice therapy instruction facilitated the easy speech conducive to fluency. It was a valuable reminder that, as a CSD professional, I do not really deal with language, articulation, voice, resonance, and fluency. Rather, these are parts of one big system; a change in one is likely to affect the others.

Thus, I leave the reader with this: Do not think of communicative disorders as a list of topics discussed in the previous 16 chapters. Instead, understand that these topics overlap in terms of definitions, manifestations, assessment, and treatment. It is difficult to learn about one without gaining knowledge of the others.

And, it is impossible to treat any of them without understanding the rest of the system.

☐ Discussion Questions

1. Think of any of the communication disorders covered in this text. What is its connection to language, phonology, hearing, fluency, voice, and hearing?
2. How would treating your selected disorder change without any knowledge of the other systems (for example, how would the treatment of stuttering change without knowing anything about language, voicing, etc.)?
3. Should clinicians providing dysphagia services earn a specialized degree?

☐ Note

1. According to Gilbert Kayumba, a Kigali businessman who was instrumental in scheduling and transporting me to meetings and evaluations, "Only Americans say 'Rwandan,'" and everyone else—including those in Rwanda—use "Rwandese."

☐ Online Resource

Koinonia Foundation Web site: http://www.kfaid.com/

REFERENCES

About.com:Stroke. (2009). What is muscle rigidity? Retrieved November 12, 2009, from http://stroke.about.com/od/glossary/g/rigidity.htm

Adler, R. K., Hirsch, S., & Mordaunt, M. (2006). *Voice and communication therapy for the transgender/transsexual client: A comprehensive clinical guide.* San Diego, CA: Plural.

Ajzen, I. (1988). *Attitudes, personality, and behavior.* Chicago: Dorsey Press.

Akshoomoff, N. (2000). Neurological underpinnings of autism. In A. Wetherby & B. Prizant (Eds.), *Autism spectrum disorders: A transactional developmental perspective* (pp. 167–190). Baltimore: Brookes.

Allyn & Bacon Communication Disorders Supersite. (2008). "Glossary of Terms: E–G" 1995–2010, Pearson Education, Inc. Retrieved from http://wps.ablongman.com/ab_disorders_supersite/234/59906.cw/index.html

Alvares, R. L., & Williams, D. F. (1995). Students with speech and/or language impairments. In R. L. Taylor, L. Sternberg, & S. B. Richards (Eds.), *Exceptional children: Integrating research and teaching* (pp. 191–216). San Diego, CA: Singular.

American Academy of Audiology (2011). Academy information. Retrieved June 11, 2011 from http://www.audiology.org/about/Pages/default.aspx

American Academy of Otolaryngotomy. (2008). Fact sheet: Laryngeal (voice box) cancer. Retrieved June 6, 2008, from http://entlink.org/healthinfo/throat/Throat_Cancer.cfm

American Cancer Society. (2007, May). Detailed guide: Laryngeal and hypopharyngeal cancer. Retrieved June 6, 2008, from http://www.cancer.org

The American Heritage Medical Dictionary. (2008). Boston: Houghton Mifflin Company.

American Psychological Association (2011). Practitioners working with older adults. Retrieved June 11, 2011 from http://www.apa.org/pi/aging/resources/guides/practitioners-should-know.aspx.

American Speech-Language-Hearing Association. (1990). Knowledge and skills needed by speech-language pathologists providing services to dysphagic patients/clients. *Asha, 32*(Suppl. 2), 7–12.

American Speech-Language-Hearing Association. (1993). *Definitions of communication disorders and variations.* Retrieved from http://www.asha.org/policy

American Speech-Language-Hearing Association. (1994). Bylaws of the American Speech-Language-Hearing Foundation [Bylaws]. Retrieved from http://www.asha.org/policy

American Speech-Language-Hearing Association. (1997). Position Statement: Multiskilled Personnel. ASHA, (Supplement 17), 13.

American Speech-Language-Hearing Association. (1998). Provision of instruction in English as a second language by speech-language pathologists in school settings [position statement]. Retrieved from http://www.asha.org/policy

American Speech-Language-Hearing Association. (2003). Code of ethics. Retrieved January 16, 2010, from http://www.asha.org/docs/html/ET2003–00166.html

American Speech-Language-Hearing Association. (2005). Cultural competence. *ASHA Supplement 25.*

American Speech-Language-Hearing Association. (2007). Scope of practice in speech-language pathology. Retrieved from http://www.asha.org/policy

American Speech-Language-Hearing Association. (2008a). Retrieved June 17, 2008, from http://www.asha.org/public/hearing/testing/

American Speech-Language-Hearing Association. (2008b). Council on academic accreditation standards. Retrieved January 16, 2010, from http://www.asha.org/academic/accreditation/CAA_roster.htm

American Speech-Language-Hearing Association. (2009a). Certification. Retrieved January 16, 2010, from http://www.asha.org/certification/

American Speech-Language-Hearing Association. (2009b). Fact sheet: Audiology—nature of work. Retrieved January 16, 2010, from http://www.asha.org/careers/professions/audiology.htm

American Speech-Language-Hearing Association. (2009c). Frequently asked questions about the 2007/2012 standards in audiology. Retrieved January 16, 2010, from http://www.asha.org/certification/2007AudFAQ.htm

American Speech-Language-Hearing Association. (2009d). Membership and certification manual. Retrieved January 16, 2010, from http://www.asha.org/members/international/caslpa/certification.htm

American Speech-Language-Hearing Association. (2009e). 2007 standards and implementation procedures for the certificate of clinical competence in audiology. Retrieved January 16, 2010, from http://www.asha.org/certification/aud_standards_new.htm

American Speech-Language-Hearing Association. (2010). Telepractice for SLPs and Audiologists. Retrieved July 31, 2010, from http://www.asha.org/practice/telepractice//.

American Speech-Language-Hearing Association (2011a). Standards for accreditation of graduate education programs in audiology and speech-language pathology. Retrieved June 11, 2011 from http://www.asha.org/academic/accreditation/accredmanual/section3.htm#standards1.

Anderson, N. B., & Shames, G. H. (2006). *Human communication disorders: An introduction*. Needham Heights, MA: Allyn & Bacon.

Anderson, N. B., Shames, G. H., & Chabon, S. (2006). Introduction. In N. B. Anderson & G. H. Shames (Eds.), *Human communication disorders: A philosophy and practice of service. Human communication disorders: An introduction*. Needham Heights, MA: Allyn & Bacon, 1–15.

Andrews, G., Guitar, B., & Howie, P. (1980). Meta-analysis of stuttering treatment. *Journal of Speech and Hearing Disorders, 45*, 287–307.

Andrews, M. (2007). *Manual of voice treatment* (3rd ed.). Clifton Park, NY: Delmar Cengage.

Apel, K., & Masterson, J. J. (2001). Theory-guided spelling assessment and intervention: A case study. *Language, Speech, and Hearing Services in Schools, 32*, 182–195.

Apel, K., & Swank, L. K. (1999). Second chances: Improving decoding skills in the older student. *Language, Speech, and Hearing Services in Schools, 30*, 231–242.

Archibald, L., & Gathercole, S. (2007). The complexities of complex memory span: Storage and processing deficits in specific language impairment. *Journal of Memory and Language, 57*, 177–194.

Archibald, L. M., & Gathercole, S. E. (2006). Short-term and working memory in specific language impairment. *International Journal of Language and Communication Disorders, 41*(6), 675–693.

Aram, D. M., & Hall, N. E. (1989). Longitudinal follow-up of children with pre-school communication disorders: Treatment implications. *School Psychology Review*, *18*(4), 487–501.

Armstrong, D., & Wilcox, S. (2005). Origins of sign languages. In M. Marshark & P. E. Spencer (Eds.), *Oxford handbook of deaf studies, language, and education* (pp. 305–318). New York: Oxford University Press.

Aronson, A. E. (1990). *Clinical voice disorders* (3rd ed.). New York: Thieme.

Arvedson, J. C., & Brodsky, L. (1993). *Pediatric swallowing and feeding: Assessment and management*. San Diego, CA: Singular.

Association for Families of Children With a Communication Disorder. (2008). Retrieved May 22, 2008, from http://www.beyond-words.org/definitions.htm

Audiology Foundation of America. (2007). Audiology: A doctoring profession. Retrieved January 16, 2010, from http://www.audfound.org/files/AuDProfession.pdf

Audiology Online. (2008). Retrieved May 22, 2008, from http://www.audiology-online.com/articles/pf_article_detail.asp?article_id=286

Baddeley, A. D. (1986). *Working memory*. Oxford, UK: Clarendon Press.

Baddeley, A. (2003). Working memory and language: An overview. *Journal of Communication Disorders, 36*, 189–208.

Bailey, B. J., Johnson, J. T., & Newlands, S. D. (2006). *Head and neck surgery—Otolaryngology* (4th ed.). Philadelphia: Lippincott Williams & Wilkins.

Baker, G. P., & Hacker P. M. S. (2005). *Wittgenstein: Understanding and meaning*. Chicago: University of Chicago Press.

Banks, J. A. (1990). Transforming the curriculum. Conference on diversity. Oakland, CA: Teacher Credentialing Commission. February.

Barker, R. L. (1999). *The social work dictionary* (4th ed.). Washington DC: NASW Press.

Bartley, W. W. (1984). The retreat to commitment. New York: Albert A. Knopf.

Battle, D. E. (1998). *Communication Disorders in Multicultural Populations* (2nd ed.). Newton, MA: Butterworth-Heinemann.

Battle, D. E. (2007). Children, education, and living in poverty. Retrieved from http://div16perspectives.asha.org/cgi/reprint/8/3/14.

Bauman-Waengler, J. (2004). *Articulatory and phonological impairments: A clinical focus*. Boston: Pearson.

Bauman-Waengler, J. (2008). *Articulatory and phonological impairments: A clinical focus* (3rd ed.). Boston: Pearson Education.

Bender, P. E., & Small, L. L. (1994, May). A top pediatrician explains stuttering. *Parents*, 88–89.

Bialystok, E. (2002). Acquisition of literacy in bilingual children: A framework for research. *Language Learning, 52*(1), 159–199.

Bishop, D. V., & Adams, C. (1990). A prospective study of the relationship between specific language impairment, phonological disorders and reading retardation. *Journal of Child Psychology and Psychiatry, and Allied Disciplines, 31*(7), 1027–1050.

Black's medical dictionary (41st ed.). (2006a). London: Scarecrow Press. Marcovitch, H. (Ed.).

Blackstone, S., & Hunt Berg, M. (2003). *Social networks: A communication inventory for individuals with severe communication challenges and their communication partners*. Monterey, CA: Augmentative Communication.

Bleile, K. M. (2004). *Manual of articulation and phonological disorders: Infancy through adulthood* (2nd ed.). New York: Thomas Delmar Learning.

Blitzer, A., & Sulica, L. (2001). Botulinum toxin: Basic science and clinical uses in otolaryngology. *The Laryngoscope, 111*:2, 218–226.

Blood, G. W., Ridenour, V. J., Qualls, C. D., & Hammer, C. S. (2003). Co-occurring disorders in children who stutter. *Journal of Communication Disorders, 36*(6), 427–448.

Bloodstein, O. (1981). *A handbook on stuttering.* Chicago: National Easter Seal Society.

Bloodstein, O. (1993). *Stuttering: The search for a cause and cure.* Boston: Allyn and Bacon.

Bloom, L., & Lahey, M. (1978). *Language development and language disorders.* New York: Wiley.

Boone, D. R., & McFarlane, S. C. (1994). *The voice and voice therapy* (5th ed.). Englewood Cliffs, NJ: Prentice Hall.

Botting, N., & Conti-Ramsden, G. (2004). Social difficulties and victimization in children with SLI at 11 years of age. *International Journal of Language and Communication Disorders, 39*, 215–227.

Bowen, C. (1998). *Developmental phonological disorders: A practical guide for families and teachers.* Melbourne: Australian Council for Educational Research.

Boysson-Bardies, B., de Sagart, L., & Durand, C. (1984). Discernible differences in the babbling of infants according to target language. *Journal of Child Language, 11*, 1–15.

Brady, J. P. (1991). The pharmacology of stuttering: A critical review. *American Journal of Psychiatry, 148*, 1309–1316.

Brain Injury Association of America. (2009). Retrieved September 18, 2009, from http://biausa.org/

Brain Injury Association of Queensland, Inc. (2008). Retrieved from http://braininjury.org.au/portal/fact-sheets/emotional-lability-fact-sheet.html

Brown, R. (1973). *A first language: The early stages.* Cambridge, MA: Harvard University Press.

Brunner, B. (2009). Urdu spoken here: The U. S. is more multilingual than you might think. Retrieved July 27, 2010, from http://www.infoplease.com/spot/multilingual1.html

Bunge, M. (1967). *Scientific research.* London: Springer Verlag

Bureau of Labor Statistics (2011). *Occupational outlook handbook, 2010–11 edition.* Retrieved May 31, 2011 from http://www.bls.gov/oco/ocos099.htm.

Business2000. (2009). A–Z glossary. Retrieved January 16, 2010, from http://www.business2000.ie/resources/Glossary_P.html

Butler, K. (1996). From the editor. *Topics in Language Disorders, 16*(4), 3–5.

Campbell, T. F., Dollaghan, C., Needleman, H., & Janosky, J. (1997). Reducing bias in language assessment: Processing dependent measures. *Journal of Speech, Language, and Hearing Research, 40*, 519–525.

Campbell, T. F., Dollaghan, C. A., Rockette, H. E., Paradise, J. L., Feldman, H. M., Shriberg, L. D., Kurs-Lasky, M. (2003). Risk factors for speech delay of unknown origin in 3-year-old children. *Child Development, 74*(2), 346–357.

Campbell psychiatric dictionary (7th ed.). (1996). Campbell, R. J. (Ed.), New York: Oxford University Press.

Case, J. (2002). *Clinical management of voice disorders* (4th ed.). San Antonio, TX: Pro Ed.

Cheng, L. L. (1991). *Assessing Asian language performance: Guidelines for evaluating LEP students* (2nd ed.). Oceanside, CA: Academic Communication Associates.

Cheng, L. L. (1993). *Assessing Asian language performance*. Oceanside, CA: Academic Communication Associates.

Cheng, L. L. (1998). *Beyond multiculturalism*. In V. O. Pang and L. L. Cheng, Struggling to heard (pp. 105–124). Albany NY: SUNY Press.

Cheng, L. L. (2007). Cultural intelligence (CQ): A quest for cultural competence. *Communication Disorders Quarterly, 29*(1), 36–42.

Cheng, L. L. (2009). Creating an optimal language learning environment: A focus on family and culture. *Communication Disorders Quarterly, 30*(2), 69–76.

Childress, D. (2002). Myths and realities of aging: American perspectives of aging in the 21st century. *Innovations, 1*, 16, 25–26. Retrieved September 18, 2009, from http://www.healthyagingprograms.org/content.asp?sectionid=75& ElementID=216

Cole, L. (1980). *Developmental analysis of social dialect features in the spontaneous language of preschool Black children*. Unpublished doctoral dissertation, Northwestern University, Evanston, il.

Colman, A. M. (2001). *Dictionary of psychology*. Oxford, UK: University Press.

Colton, R. H., & Casper, J. K. (1996). *Understanding voice problems. A physiological perspective for diagnosis and treatment* (2nd ed.). Baltimore: Williams & Wilkins.

Colton, R. H., Casper, J. K., & Leonard, R. (2006). *Understanding voice problems: A physiological perspective for diagnosis and treatment* (3rd ed.). Philadelphia: Lippincott, Williams, & Wilkins.

Conti-Ramsden GM, Botting, NF. (2004). Social Difficulties and victimization in children with SLI at 11 years of age. *Journal of Speech, Language, and Hearing Research, 47*(1), 145–161.

Conture, E. G. (1996). Treatment efficacy: Stuttering. *Journal of Speech and Hearing Research, 39*, S18–S26.

Conture, E. G. (2001). *Stuttering: Its nature, diagnosis, and treatment*. Needham Heights, MA: Allyn & Bacon.

Coon, D., & Mitterer, J. O. (2008). *Introduction to psychology: Gateways to mind and behavior*. Belmont, CA: Cengage Learning.

Cooper, E. B. (1987). The chronic preservative stuttering syndrome: Incurable stuttering. *Journal of Fluency Disorders, 12*, 381–388.

Cooper, E. B., & Cooper, C. (1985). Clinician attitudes toward stuttering: A decade of change (1973–1983). *Journal of Fluency Disorders, 10*, 19–33.

Coriat, I. H. (1928). Stammering: A psychoanalytical interpretation. *Nervous and Mental Diseases Monographs, 47*, 1–68.

Corporate Speech Pathology Network. (2006). Retrieved October 14, 2007, from http://www.corspan.org

Crago, M., & Gopnik, M. (1994). From families to phenotypes: Theoretical and clinical implications of research into the genetic basis of specific language impairment. In R. Watkins & M. Rice (Eds.), *Specific language impairments in children*. Baltimore: Brookes, 35–51.

Craig, A., Tran, Y., & Craig, M. (2003). Stereotypes towards stuttering for those who have never had direct contact with people who stutter: A randomized and stratified study. *Perceptual and Motor Skills, 97*, 235–245.

Crary, M. A., Haak, N. J., & Malinsky, A. E. (1989). Preliminary psychometric evaluation of an acute aphasia screening protocol. *Aphasiology, 3*(7), 611–618.

Culatta, R., & Goldberg, S. A. (1995). *Stuttering therapy: An integrated approach to theory and practice*. Boston: Allyn & Bacon.

Cumminis, J. (1984). *Bilingualism and special education: Issues in assessment and pedagogy*. Clevedon, UK: Multilingual Matters.

Cumminis, J. (1981). The role of primary language development in promoting educational success from language minority students. In California State Department of Education, Office of Bilingual Bicultural Education (Ed.), *Schooling and language minority students: A theoretical framework*. Los Angeles: Evaluation Dissemination and Assessment Center, California State University, 29.

Curlee, R. F., & Yairi, E. (1997). Early intervention with early childhood stuttering: A critical examination of the data. *American Journal of Speech-Language Pathology, 6*, 8–18.

Daly, D. A. (1993). Cluttering, another fluency syndrome. In R. Curlee (Ed.), *Stuttering and related disorders of fluency*. New York: Thieme, 179–204.

Davidow, J. H., Crowe, B. T., & Bothe, A. K. (2004). "Gradual Increase in Length and Complexity of Utterance" and "Extended Length of Utterance" treatment programs for stuttering: Assessing the implications of strong but limited evidence. In A. K. Bothe (Ed.), *Evidence-based treatment of stuttering: Empirical bases and clinical implications*. Mahwah, NJ: Erlbaum, 201–230.

Deal, J. L. (1980). Sudden onset of stuttering: A case report. *Journal of Speech and Hearing Disorders, 47*, 301–304.

Delaney, A. L., & Kent, R. D. (2004, November). *Developmental profiles of children diagnosed with apraxia of speech*. Poster session presented at the annual convention of the American-Speech-Language-Hearing Association, Philadelphia.

DeNil, L., & Brutten, G. J. (1987). *Communication attitudes of stuttering, speech disordered and normal speaking children*. Paper presented at the American Speech-Language-Hearing Association Convention, New Orleans.

DeRennzi, E., & Ferrari, C. (1978). The reporter's test: A sensitive test to detect expressive disturbances in aphasics. *Cortex*: Jun;14(2):279–93.

Devices are not a cure, Foundation reports. (2004). *Advance for Speech-Language Pathologists and Audiologists, 14*(19), 14.

Dietrich, S. (2000). Tension control therapy: An integrated approach to the treatment of stuttering. In H.-G. Bosshardt, J. S. Yaruss, & H. F. M. Peters (Eds.), *Fluency disorders: Theory, research, treatment and self-help* (Proceedings of the Third World Congress on Fluency Disorders). Nijmegen, Holland: Nijmegen University Press.

Dirckx, J. H. (Ed.). (1997). *Stedman's concise medical dictionary for the health professions* (3rd ed.). Baltimore: Williams & Wilkins, 274–278.

Dobie, R. (1978). Rehabilitation of swallowing disorders. *American Family Physician. 17*, 84–85.

Dollaghan, C., & Campbell, T. F. (1998). Nonword repetition and child language impairment. *Journal of Speech, Language, and Hearing Research, 41*, 1136–1146.

Donaher, J. (2003). *Intervention strategies for the school-aged child who stutters*. Workshop presented at the National Stuttering Association Convention, Nashville.

Dorsey, M., & Guenther, R. K. (2000). Attitudes of professors and students toward college students who stutter. *Journal of Fluency Disorders, 25*, 77–83.

DuCette, J. P., Shapiro, J. P., & Sewell, T. E. (1993). *Diversity in education: Problems and possibilities.* In *AACTE Handbook, A Knowledge Base for Teacher Education.*

Duffy, J. R. (2005). *Motor speech disorders: Substrates, differential diagnosis, and management* (2nd ed.). St. Louis, MO: Elsevier Mosby.

Dunn, L., Smith, J., Horton, K., & Smith, D. (1981). Peabody language development kits—revised manuals Level P, 1, 2, and 3. Circle Pines, MN: American Guidance Service.

Earley, C., & Mosakowski, E. (2004). Cultural Intelligence. *Harvard Business Review,* 82(10), 139–146.

Earley, P. C., & Ang, S. (2003). *Cultural intelligence: Individual interactions across cultures.* Stanford, CA; Stanford University Press.

Eleweke, C. J., & Rodda, M. (2000). Factors contributing to parents' selection of a communication mode to use with deaf children. *American Annals of the Deaf,* 145(4), 375–383.

Ellis Weismer, S., Evans, J., & Hesketh, L. (1999). An examination of verbal working memory capacity in children with specific language impairment. *Journal of Speech, Language, and Hearing Research, 42,* 1249–1260.

Enderby, P. M., Wood, V., & Wade, D. (2006). Frenchay Aphasia Screening Test, 2nd ed. Indianapolis, IN: Wiley.

Emanuel, F. (1985). About reliability and validity. *Speech Science Notes.* Unpublished paper.

Evans, J., & Mainela-Arnold, E. (2005). Beyond capacity limitations: Determinants of word recall performance on verbal working memory span tasks in children with SLI. *Journal of Speech, Language, and Hearing Research, 48,* 897–909.

Farlex. (2008). The Free Dictionary by Farlex. Retrieved June 17, 2008, from http://medical-dictionary.thefreedictionary.com

Fasold, R. W., & Wolfram, W. (1978). Some linguistic features of Negro dialect. In P. Stroller (Ed.), *Black American English.* New York: Delta, 41–86.

Feeney, P. (2006, May 2). Primer on research: An introduction. *The ASHA Leader,* Referenced June 11, 2011 from http://www.asha.org/Publications/leader/2006/060502/060502c/

Fenichel, O. (1945). *The psychoanalytic theory of neurosis.* New York: Norton.

Ferrand, C. T. (2001). *Speech science: An integrated approach to theory and clinical practice.* Boston: Allyn & Bacon.

Fitch-West, J., & Sands, E. S. (1998). *Bedside evaluation screening test.* Austin, TX: PRO-ED, Inc.

Flax, J. F., Realpe-Bonilla, T., Hirsch, L. S., Brzustowics, L. M., Bartlett, C. W., & Tallal, P. (2003). Specific language impairment in families: Evidence for co-occurrence with reading impairments. *Journal of Speech, Language, and Hearing Research, 46,* 530–543.

Froeschels, E. (1952). Chewing method as therapy. *Archives of Otolaryngology, 56,* 427–434.

Fujiki, M., & Brinton, B. (1996). Social skills of children with specific language impairment. *Language, Speech, and Hearing Services in Schools, 27,* 195–202.

Fujiki, M., Brinton, B., & Isaacson, T. (2001). Social behaviors of children with language impairment on the playground. *Language, Speech, and Hearing Services in Schools, 32,* 101–113.

Fuller, D. R., & Lloyd, L. L. (1991). Toward a common usage of iconicity terminology. *Augmentative and Alternative Communication. 7,* 215–220.

Fuller, D. R., Lloyd, L. L., & Schlosser, R. W. (1992). Further development of an augmentative and alternative communication symbol taxonomy. *AAC: Augmentative and Alternative Communication, 8*(1), 67–74.

Gallena, S. K. (2007). *Voice and laryngeal disorders*. St. Louis, MO: Elsevier Mosby.

Gathercole, S. E., Pickering, S. J., Knight, C., & Stegmann, Z. (2004). Working memory skills and educational attainment: Evidence from National Curriculum assessments at 7 and 14 years of age. *Applied Cognitive Psychology, 40*, 1–16.

Gathercole, S. E., Alloway, T. P., Willis, C., & Adams, A. (2006). Working memory in children with reading disabilities. *Journal of Experimental Child Psychology, 93*(3), 265–281.

Gay, G. (1993). *At the essence of learning: Multicultural education*. West Lafayette IN: Kappa Delta Pi, p. 152.

Geirut, J. A. (1989). Maximal opposition approach to phonological treatment. *Journal of Speech and Hearing Disorders, 54*, 9–19.

Geirut, J. A. (1990). Differential learning of phonological oppositions. *Journal of Speech and Hearing Research, 33*, 540–549.

Geirut, J. A. (1998). Treatment efficacy: Functional phonological disorders in children. *Journal of Speech-Language-Hearing Research, 41*, 85–100.

Geng, L., Jacobson, R., Mikel, G., Mustafa, C., & Morin, T. Speech express. Retrieved August 21, 2007, from http://www.speech-express.com/glossary.html

Gerrig, R. J., & Zimbardo, P. G. (2002). *Psychology and life* (16th ed.). Boston: Allyn & Bacon.

Gillam, R. B., Cowan, N., & Day, L. S. (1995). Sequential memory in children with and without language impairment. *Journal of Speech-Language-Hearing Research, 38*, 393–402.

Gillon, G. T. (2005). Facilitating phoneme awareness development in 3- and 4-year-old children with speech impairment. *Language, Speech, and Hearing Services in Schools, 36*, 308–324.

Goldman-Eisler, F. (1961). Continuity of the speech utterance, its determinants and its significance. *Language and Speech, 4*, 220–231.

Goldstein, B., & Kohnert, K. (2005). Speech, language, and hearing in developing bilinguals: Current findings and future directions (Issue Epilogue). *Language, Speech, and Hearing Services in School, 36*, 264–267.

Golper, L. C. (1998). *Sourcebook for medical speech pathology* (2nd ed.). San Diego, CA: Singular.

Good Talking With You Series: Oh Say What They See An Introduction to Indirect Language Stimulation Techniques. (2007). Wachter, T. (Ed.), Portland, OR: Educational Productions.

Goodglass, H., Kaplan, E., & Barresi, B. (2001). *Boston diagnostic aphasia examination*. San Antonio, TX: Pearson Education, Inc.

Goodglass, H. & Kaplan, B. (2001). *Boston naming test, 2nd ed.* Baltimore, MD: Lippincott Williams & Wilkins.

Goodwin, C. (2003). *Conversation and brain damage*. New York: Oxford University Press.

Goossens, C. (1989). Aided communication intervention before assessment: A case study of a child with cerebral palsy. *Augmentative and Alternative Communication, 5*(1), 14–26.

Gracco, V. L., & Abbs, J. H. (1986). Variant and invariant characteristics of speech movements. *Experimental Brain Research, 65*, 156–166.

Grady, J. A. (2007). Love in Christianity. In Y. K. Greenberg (Ed.,), *Love in world religions* (pp. 217–218). Oxford, UK: ABC-CLIO.

Green, G. (1996). Evaluating claims about treatments for autism. In Maurice, C., Green, G., & Luce, S.C. (Eds.), *Behavioral intervention for young children with autism: A manual for parents and professionals.* Austin, TX: Pro-Ed, 15–28.

Greenwald, C., & Leonard, L. (1979). Communicative and sensorimotor development of Down's syndrome children. *American Journal of Mental Deficiency, 84*, 296–303.

Gregory, H. H. (1991). Therapy for elementary school-age children. In W. H. Perkins (Ed.), *Stuttering: Challenges of therapy—Seminars in speech, language, and hearing* (pp. 323–335). New York: Thieme.

Guilford, A. M., Graham, S. V., & Scheuerle, J. (2007). *The speech-language pathologist from novice to expert.* Upper Saddle River, NJ: Pearson Merrill Prentice Hall.

Guisti Braislin, M. A., & Cascella, P. W. (2005). A preliminary investigation of the efficacy of oral motor exercises for children with mild articulation disorders. *International Journal of Rehabilitation Research, 28*, 263–266.

Guitar, B. (1998). *Stuttering: An integrated approach to its nature and treatment.* Baltimore: Williams & Wilkins.

Guitar, B., & Conture, E. G. (Eds.). (2006). *The child who stutters: To the pediatrician* (4th ed., publication 0023). Memphis, TN: Stuttering Foundation of America.

Gutierrez-Clellen, V. F. (1999). Mediating literacy skills in Spanish-speaking children with special needs. *Language, Speech, and Hearing Services in Schools, 30*, 285–292.

Hadi, U., & Nuwayid, N. S. (1987). An unusual complication following tracheo-esophageal puncture for alaryngeal voice restoration. *Journal of Laryngology & Otology, 101*, 855–860.

Hall, E. T. (1972). *The silent language.* Garden City, NY: Doubleday.

Hall, E. T. (1977). *Beyond culture.* Garden City, NY: Doubleday.

Hammer, C. S., Tomblin, J. B., Zhang, X., & Weiss, A. L. (2001). Relationship between parenting behaviours and specific language impairment in children. *International Journal of Language and Communication Disorders, 36*, 185–205.

Hand, C. R. & Haynes, W. O. (1983). Linguistic processing and reaction time differences in stutterers and nonstutterers. *Journal of Speech and Hearing Research, 26*, 181–185.

Hardin, C., Pindzola, R., & Haynes, W. (1992). A tachistoscopic study of hemispheric processing in stuttering and non-stuttering children. *Journal of Fluency Disorders, 17*, 4. 265–281

Haynes, W. O., Moran, M. J., & Pindzola, R. H. (1999). *Communication disorders in the classroom an introduction for professionals in school settings.* Dubuque, IA: Kendall/Hunt.

Haynes, W. O., & Pindzola, R. H. (2004). *Diagnosis and evaluation in speech pathology* (6th ed.). Boston: Allyn & Bacon.

Heath, S. B. (1983). *Ways with words: Language, life and work in communities and classrooms.* Cambridge, UK: Cambridge University Press.

Hegde, M. N. (1995). *Introduction to communicative disorders* (2nd ed.). Austin, TX: Pro-Ed.

Hegde, M. N. (2005). *A coursebook on aphasia and other neurogenic language disorders* (3rd ed.). Clifton Park, NY: Thomson Delmar Learning.

Hegde, M. N. (2006). *A coursebook on aphasia and other neurologic disorders, 3rd edition.* Clifton Park, NY: Thomson Delmar Learning.

Hegde, M. N., & Davis, D. (1999). *Clinical methods and practicum in speech-language pathology.* San Diego, CA: Singular.

Helm-Estabrooks, N. (1992). *Aphasia diagnostic profiles.* Austin, TX: PRO-ED, Inc.

Herbert, J. D., Lilienfield, S. O., Lohr, J. M., Montgomery, R. W., O'Donhue, W. T., Rosen, G. M., & Tolin, D. F. (2000). Science and past science in the development of eye desensitization and reprocessing: Implications for clinical psychology. *Clinical Psychology Review, 20,* 945–971.

Hicks, M. A. (1998). The stranger at home: Toward a philosophy of a multicultural self. Doctoral dissertation. Teachers College, Columbia University, New York.

Hillman, R. E., Gress, C. D., Hargrave, J., Walsh, M., & Bunting, G. W. (1990). Efficacy of speech-language pathology intervention: Voice disorders. *Seminars in Speech and Language, 11,* 150–161.

Hoag, L., Bedrosian, J., McCoy, K., & Johnson, D. (2004). Trade-offs between informativeness and speed of message delivery in augmentative and alternative communication. *Journal of Speech, Language, and Hearing Research, 47,* 1270–1285.

Hodson, B. W., & Paden, E. P. (1991). *Targeting intelligible speech: A phonological approach to remediation.* Austin, TX: Pro-Ed.

Hoffman, P. R., & Norris, J. A. (2005). Intervention: Manipulating complex input to promote self-organization of a neuro-network. In A. G. Kamhi and K. E. Pollock (Eds.), *Phonological disorders of children: Clinical Decision Making in Assessment and intervention* (pp. 139–146). Baltimore: Paul H. Brookes.

Hogikyan N. D., & Sethuraman G. (1999). Validation of an instrument to measure voice-related quality of life (V-RQOL). *Journal of Voice, 13*(4), 557–569.

Holland, A., Frattali, C. M., & Fromm, D. (1998). *Communicative abilities of daily living, 2nd Ed.* Austin, TX: PRO-ED, Inc.

Hooper, C. R. (2004) Treatment of voice disorders in children. *Language Speech and. Hearing Services in Schools, 35,* 320–326.

Hotz, M. A., Baumann, A., Schaller, P., & Zbären, P. (2002). Success and predictability of provox prosthesis voice rehabilitation. *Archives of Otolaryngology—Head and Neck Surgery, 128,* 687–691.

Huer, M. B., & Parette, H. P. (1999). Examining the perspectives of families: Issues related to conducting cross-cultural research. In F. Loncke, J. Clibbens, H. Arvidson, & L. Lloyd (Eds.), *Augmentative and alternative communication: New directions in research and practice* (pp. 291). London: Whurr.

Huitt, W., & Hummel, J. (1997). An introduction to operant (instrumental) conditioning. *Educational Psychology Interactive.* Valdosta, GA: Valdosta State University. Retrieved June 17, 2008, from http://chiron.valdosta.edu/whuitt/col/behsys/operant.html

Hungerford, S., & Gonyo, K. (2007, November). *Relationships between executive functions and language variables.* Poster session presented at the meeting of the American Speech Language Hearing Association, Boston.

Hurst, M. I., & Cooper, E. B. (1983a). Employer attitudes toward stuttering. *Journal of Fluency Disorders, 8,* 1–12.

Hurst, M. A., & Cooper, E. B. (1983b). Vocational rehabilitation counselors' attitudes toward stuttering. *Journal of Fluency Disorders, 8,* 13–27.

Hwa-Froelich, D. A. (2009). Foreword. *Topics in Language Disorders, 29*(1), 3–5.

Iglesias, A. (1985). Cultural conflict in the classroom: The communicatively different child. In D. N. Ripich & F. M. Spinelli (Ed.), *School discourse problems* (pp.79–96). San Diego, CA: College-Hill Press.

Iverson, J. M., & Goldin-Meadow, S. (2005). Gesture paves the way for language development. *Psychological Science, 16*(5), 367–371.

Jacobson, B., Johnson, A., Grywalski, C., Silbergleit, A., Jacobson, G., Benninger, M., et al. (1997). The Voice Handicap Index (VHI): Development and validation. *American Journal of Speech-Language Pathology, 6,* 66–70.

Jankovic, J. (1994). Botulinum toxin in the treatment of dystonic tics. *Movement Disorders. 9*:3, 347–349.

Jankovic, J. (2004). Botulinum toxin in clinical practice. *Journal of Neurology, Neurosurgery, and Psychiatry, 75*:7, 951–957.

Johnson, A. F., & Jacobson, B. H. (2007). *Medical speech-language pathology: A practitioner's guide* (2nd ed.). New York: Thieme Medical.

Justice, L. M. (2006). *Communication sciences and disorders: An introduction.* Upper Saddle River, NJ: Pearson/Merrill Prentice Hall.

Kaderavek, J. N., & Sulzby, E. (2000). Narrative production by children with and without specific language impairment: Oral narratives and emergent readings. *Journal of Speech, Language, and Hearing Research, 43*(1), 34–49.

Kalinowski, J., Noble, S. Armson, J., & Stuart, A. (1994). Pretreatment and posttreatment speech naturalness ratings of adults with mild and severe stuttering. *American Journal of Speech-Language Pathology, 3,* 61–66.

Kaplan, A,Y. (1994). On language memoir. In A. Bammer (Ed.), *Displacements: Cultural identities in question.* Bloomington, IN: Indiana University Press, 59–70.

Katz, J. (1970). Audiologic diagnosis: cochlea to cortex. *Menorah Medical Journal.*

Katz, J. (1992). Classification of auditory processing disorders. In J. Katz, N. Stecker, D. Henderson (Eds.), *Central auditory processing: A transdisciplinary view.* Chicago: Mosby, 81–92.

Kay, J., Lesser, R., & Coltheart, M. (1992). *Psycholinguistic assessments of language processing in aphasia.* Florence, KY: Psychology Press.

Keenan, J. S., & Brassell, E. G. (1975). *Aphasia language performance scales.* Canton, OH: Pinnacle Press.

Kent, L. R. (1963). The use of tranquilizers in the treatment of stuttering. *Journal of Speech and Hearing Disorders, 28,* 288–294.

Kertesz, A. (1982). *Western aphasia battery-revised.* San Antonio, TX: Pearson Education, Inc.

Keys, W. T., & Ruder, K. F. (1992). A review of commercialized fluency treatment programs (CFTPS). *ECHO, 14,* 14–24.

Kindler, A. (2002). *Survey of the states' limited English proficient students and available educational programs and services: 2000–2001 summary report.* Washington, DC: National Clearinghouse for English Language Acquisition.

Kindred, D. (2006). *Sound and fury: Two powerful lives, one fateful friendship.* New York: Free Press.

Kinsella, K., & Wan, H. (2009). *An aging world: 2008* (U. S. Census Bureau Publication No. P95/09-1). Washington, DC: U.S. Government Printing Office.

Kiser, A. M., Lass, N. J., Lockhart, P., Mussa, A. M., Pannbacker, M., Ruscello, D. M., et al. (1994). School administrators' perceptions of people who stutter. *Language, Speech, and Hearing Services in Schools, 25,* 90–93.

Klima, E. S., & Bellugi, U. (1979). *The signs of language*. Cambridge, MA: Harvard University Press.

Klinger, J. K., Artiles, A. J., & Mendez Barletta, L. (2006). English language learners who struggle with reading: Language acquisition or LD? *Journal of Learning Disabilities, 39*(2), 108–128.

Knapp, K. N. (2007). Love in Confucianism. In Y. K. Greenberg (Ed.), *Love in world religions* (pp. 218–219). Oxford, UK: ABC CLIO.

Kohnert, K., & Goldstein, B. (2005). Speech, language, and hearing in developing bilinguals: From practice to research. *Language, Speech, and Hearing Services in Schools, 36*, 169–171.

Kuster, J. (2004). Electronic devices and stuttering treatment. Retrieved from the Stuttering Home Page at http://www.mnsu.edu/comdis/kuster/TherapyWWW/dafjanus.html

Lahey, M., Liebergott, J., Chesnick, M., & Menyuk, P. (1992). Variability in children's use of grammatical morphemes. *Applied Psycholinguistics, 13*, 373–398.

Langdon, H. W. (2003). *Working with interpreters to serve bilingual children and families*. Rockville, MD: American Speech-Language-Hearing Association.

Langdon, H. W. (2007). *Assessment and intervention for communication disorders in culturally and linguistically diverse populations*. New York: Delmar Learning.

Langdon, H. W. (2009). Providing optimal special education services to Hispanic children and their families. *Communication Disorder Quarterly, 30*(2), 83–96.

Langdon, H. W., & Cheng, L. L. (2002). *Collaborating with interpreters and translators: A guide for communication disorders professionals*. Eau Claire, WI: Thinking Publications.

Langmore, S. (2001). *Endoscopic evaluation and management of swallowing disorders*. New York: Thieme.

Langmore, S. E., Schatz, K., & Olsen, N. (1988). Fiberoptic endoscopic examination of swallowing safety: A new procedure. *Dysphagia, 2*, 216–219.

LaPointe, L., & Horner, J. (1998). *Reading comprehension battery for aphasia, 2nd ed.* Austin, TX: PRO-ED, Inc.

Lass, N. J., Ruscello, D. M., Pannbacker, M., Schmitt, J. F., Kiser, A. M., Mussa, A. M., et al. (1994). School administrators' perceptions of people who stutter. *Language, Speech, and Hearing Services in Schools, 25*, 90–93.

Latulas, M., Tetnowski, J., & Bathel, J. (2003). *Getting ready for therapy: Self-esteem and "coachability."* Paper presented at the National Stuttering Association Convention, Nashville.

Leith, W. R. (1993). *Clinical methods in communication disorders*. Austin, TX: Pro-Ed.

Leonard, L. B., Weismer, S. E., Miller, C. A., Francis, D. J., Tomblin, B. J., & Kail, R. V. (2007). Speed of processing, working memory, and language impairment in children. *Journal of Speech, Language, and Hearing Research, 50*, 408–428.

Levey, S. (2009). *Factors that are associated with bilingual Spanish/English-speaking children's sentence reading comprehension*. Unpublished manuscript.

Lewis, B. A., Freebairn, L. A., Hansen, A. J., Miscimarra, L., Iyengar, S. K., & Taylor, H. G. (2007). Speech and language skills of parents of children with speech sound disorders. *American Journal of Speech-Language Pathology/American Speech-Language-Hearing Association, 16*(2), 108–118. doi:10.1044/1058-0360(2007/015).

Lewin, J., Kohen, D., & Mathew, G. (1993). Handedness in mental handicap: Investigated into populations of Down's syndrome, epilepsy, and autism. *The British Journal of Psychiatry, 163*, 674–676.

Lewis, B. A., Freebairn, L. A., & Taylor, G. H. (2000). Follow-up of children with early expressive phonology disorders. *Journal of Learning Disabilities, 33*(5), 433–444.

Lewis, B. A., Shriberg L. D., Freebairn L. A., Hansen A. J., Stein C. M., Taylor H. G., et al. (2006). The genetic bases of speech sound disorders: Evidence from spoken and written language. *Journal of Speech, Language, and Hearing Research, 49*(6), 1294–1312.

Lidz, C. S., & Peña, E. D. (1996). Dynamic assessment: The model, its relevance as a nonbiased approach, and its application to Latino American preschool children. *Clinical Forum: Cultural/Linguistic Variation*. Language, Speech, and Hearing Services in Schools Oct 01, *27*, 367–372.

Limbos, M. M., & Geva, E. (2001). Accuracy of teacher assessments of second language students at risk for reading disability. *Journal of Learning Disabilities, 28*, 523–527.

Lloyd, L. L., & Fuller, D. R. (1986). Toward an augmentative and alternative communication symbol taxonomy: A proposed superor-dinate classification. *Augmentative and Alternative Communication, 2*, 165–171.

Lof, G. L. (2006). Logic, theory, and evidence against the use of non-speech oral motor exercises to change speech sound productions. Paper presented at the American Speech, Hearing, and Language Convention, Miami.

Logemann, J. A. (1993). *Manual for the videofluorographic study of swallowing.* (2nd ed.). Austin, TX: Pro-Ed.

Logemann, J. A. (1994). Evaluation and treatment of swallowing disorders. *American Journal of Speech-Language Pathology, 3*(3), 41–44.

Logemann, J. A. (1996). Screening, diagnosis, and management of neurogenic dysphagia. *Seminars in Neurology, 16*(4), 319–327.

Logemann, J. A. (1997). Structural and functional aspects of normal and disordered swallowing. In C. T. Ferrand & R. L. Bloom (Eds.), *Introduction to organic and neurogenic disorders of communication: Current scope of practice.* Boston: Allyn and Bacon, 229–246.

Logemann, J. A. (1998). *Evaluation and treatment of swallowing disorders* (2nd ed.). Austin, TX: Pro-Ed.

Lomas, J., Pickard, L., Bester, S., Elbard, H., Finlayson, A., & Zoghaib, C. (1989). Development and psychometric evaluation of a functional communication measure for adult aphasia, *Journal of Speech and Hearing Disorders* Vol. 54 113–124.

Loncke, F., Campbell, J., England, A, & Haley, T. (2006). Multimodality: A basis for augmentative and alternative communication—psycholinguistic, cognitive, and clinical/educational aspects. *Disability and Rehabilitation, 28*(3), 169–174.

Lord, B. B. (1985). *Eighth moon: The true story of a young girl's life in Communist China.* London: Firecrest.

Ludlow, C. L. (1990). Treatment of speech and voice disorders with botulinum toxin. *Journal of the American Medical Association, 264*:20, 2671–2675.

MacDonald, G. W., & Cornwall, A. (1955). The relationship between phonological awareness and spelling achievement eleven years later. *Journal of Learning Disabilities, 28*, 523–527.

Maguire, G., Riley, G., Wu, J. C., Franklin, D., & Potkin, S. (1997). PET scan evidence of parallel cerebral systems related to treatment effects: Effects of risperidone in the treatment of stuttering. In W. Hulstijn, H. Peters, & P. H. H. M. Van Lieshout (Eds.), *Speech production, motor control, brain research, and fluency disorders.* Amsterdam: Elsevier Science, 379–382.

Manning, W. H. (2001). *Clinical decision making in fluency disorders.* Vancouver, BC, Canada: Singular.

Martin, F. N., & Clark, J. G. (2003). *Introduction to audiology* (8th ed.). Boston: Allyn & Bacon.

Martin, F. N., & Clark, J. G. (2006). *Introduction to audiology.* Boston: Pearson/Allyn & Bacon.

Marton, K., & Schwartz, R. (2003). Working memory capacity and language processes in children with specific language impairment. *Journal of Speech, Language, and Hearing Research, 46,* 1138–1153.

Masterson, J. J., & Crede, L. A. (1999). Learning to spell: Implications for assessment and intervention. *Language, Speech, and Hearing Services in Schools, 30,* 243–254.

Matsuo, H. (2005). Bosnian refugee resettlement in St. Louis, Missouri. In P. Waxman & V. Colie-Peisker (Eds.), *Homeland wanted* (pp. 109–125). New York: Nova Science.

McCaffrey, P. (2008). *Neuropathologies of swallowing and speech.* Retrieved from the Neuroscience on the Web Series online Web site at http://www.csuchico.edu/~pmccaffrey/syllabi/SPPA342/342unit14.html

McCauley, R. J. (2001). *Assessment of language disorders in children.* Mahwah, NJ: Erlbaum.

McClure, J. A., & Yaruss, S. (2003). Stuttering survey suggests success of attitude-changing treatment. *ASHA Leader, 8*(9), 3, 19.

McIntosh, P. (1980, July/August). *White privilege: Unpacking the invisible knapsack.* Peace and Freedom, p.10–12.

McKeehan, A. B., & Child, D. R. (1990). *Parents as partners: Direct treatment of childhood stuttering* (Professional Guide).

McKenna, M. C., & Stahl, S. A. (2003). *Assessment for reading instruction.* New York: Guilford Press.

McManus, C. (2004). *Right hand, left hand: The origins of asymmetry in brains, bodies, atoms and cultures.* Cambridge, MA: Harvard University Press.

McNaughton, D., & Bryen, D. (2007). AAC-technologies to enhance participation and access to meaningful societal roles for adolescents and adults with developmental disabilities who require AAC. *Augmentative and Alternative Communication, 23,* 217–229.

McNeil, M. R., & Prescott, T. H. (1978). *Revised token test.* Baltimore, MD: University Park Press.

McNeill, D. (1985). So you think gestures are nonverbal? *Psychological Review, 92*(3), 350–371.

Meador, H. E., & Zazove, P. (2005). Health care interactions with deaf culture. *The Journal of the American Board of Family Practice, 18*(3), 218–222.

MedicineNet.com. (2008). Retrieved from http://www.medterms.com/script/main/art.asp?articlekey=33271

MedicineNet.com. (2009). Retrieved April 8, 2009, from http://www.medterms.com/script/main/art.asp?articlekey=2940

MedicineNet, Inc. (2008). Retrieved May 25, 2008, from http://www.medterms.com

Medicine World. (2008). Medical dictionary. Retrieved from http://www.medicineword.com/tractus+corticobulbaris.shtml

Meduna, L. J. (1948). Alteration of neurotic pattern by use of CO2 inhalations. *Journal of Nervous and Mental Diseases, 108*, 373–374.

Mendel, L., Danhauer, J., & Singh, S. (1999). *Singular dictionary of audiology.* San Diego, CA: Singular.

Menyuk, P., Chesnick, M., Liebergott, J. W., Korngold, B., D'Agostino, R., & Belanger, A. (1991). Predicting reading problems in at-risk children. *Journal of Speech and Hearing Research, 34*(4), 893–903.

Menyuk, P. (1992). Early communicative and language behavior. In J. F. Rosenblith (Ed.) *In the beginning: Development from conception to age 2 (2nd ed.).* Newbury Park, CA: Sage, 430–455.

Merriam-Webster. (2008). Retrieved May 24, 2008, from http://www.merriam-webster.com/dictionary/minimalpairs

Merriam-Webster's collegiate dictionary (10th ed.). (1993). Springfield, MA: Merriam-Webster.

Merriam-Webster's medical dictionary. (2007). Springfield, MA: Merriam-Webster.

Merriam-Webster Online Dictionary. (2009). Retrieved November 12, 2009, from http://www.merriam-webster.com/dictionary/affect

Merril Advanced Studies Center, University of Kansas. (2004). Top 10 things you should know about children with specific language impairment. Retrieved from http://merrill.ku.edu/IntheKnow/sciencearticles/SLIfacts.html

Merson, R. M. (2003). *Auditory sidetone and the management of stuttering: From Wollensak to SpeechEasy.* Paper presented at International Stuttering Awareness Day Conference. Retrieved from http://www.mnsu.edu/comdis/isad6/papers/merson6.html

Miccio, A. W., Gallagher, E., Grossman, C. B., Yont, K. M., & Vernon-Feagans, L. (2001). Influence of chronic otitis media on phonological acquisition. *Clinical Linguistics & Phonetics, 15*(1–2), 47–51. doi:10.3109/02699200109167629.

Millar, D. C., Light, J. C. & Schlosser, R. (2006). The impact of augmentative and alternative communication intervention on the speech production of individuals with developmental disabilities: A research review. *Journal of Speech, Language, and Hearing Research, 49*, 248–264.

Miller, J., & Iglesias, A. (2006). *Systematic Analysis of Language Transcripts (SALT), English & Spanish, Version 9.* Madison: University of Wisconsin–Madison.

Miller, R. M., & Groher, M. E. (1993). Speech-language pathology and dysphagia: A brief historical perspective. *Dysphagia, 8*, 180–184.

Minifie, F., Hixon, T. J., & Williams, F. (1973). *Normal aspects of speech, hearing, and language.* Englewood Cliffs, NJ: Prentice-Hall.

Minigh, J. L. (2007). *Sports medicine.* West Port, CT: Greenwood Press.

Molt, L. F. (1998). A perspective on neuropharmacological agents and stuttering: Are there implications for a cause as well as a cure? In *Proceedings of the First International Stuttering Awareness Day Online Conference*, Mankato State University, Mankato, MN.

Molt, L. (2002). Fluency master/Speakeasy devices. In S. Hood, J. Kuster, D. Mallard, W. Manning, L. Molt, B. Quesal, et al. (Eds.), *Office Hours: The Professor is in. International Stuttering Awareness Day Conference*, October, 2002. Retrieved at: http://www.mnsu.edu/comdis/isad5/isadcon5.html

Montgomery, J. (1995). Sentence comprehension in children with specific language impairment: The role of phonological working memory. *Journal of Speech and Hearing Research, 138,* 187–199.

Montgomery, J. (2002). Understanding the language difficulties of children with specific language impairments: Does verbal working memory matter? *American Journal of Speech-Language Pathology, 11,* 77–91.

Moore, W. H. (1976). Bilateral tachistoscopic word perception of stutterers and normal subjects. *Brain and Language, 3,* 434–442.

Mundy, P., Sigman, M., Kasari, C., & Yirmiya, N. (1988). Nonverbal communication skills in Down syndrome children. *Child Development, 59,* 235–249.

Mundy, P., & Stella, J. (2000). Joint attention, social orienting and nonverbal communication in autism. In A. M. Wetherby & B. M. Prizant (Eds.), *Autism spectrum disorders: A transactional developmental perspective* (pp. 55–77). Baltimore: Brookes.

Murray, J. (1999). *Manual of dysphagia assessment in adults.* San Diego, CA: Singular.

Nathan, L., Stackhouse, J., Goulandris, N., & Snowling, M. J. (2004). The development of early literacy skills among children with speech difficulties: A test of the "critical age hypothesis". *Journal of Speech, Language, and Hearing Research: JSLHR, 47*(2), 377–391.

National Association of Future Doctors of Audiology. (2007). Retrieved from: http://www.nafda.org.

National Cancer Institute. (2008). Retrieved May 25, 2008, from http://www.cancer.gov

National Center for Injury Prevention and Control. (2009). What is traumatic brain injury? Retrieved September 18, 2009, from http://www.cdc.gov/ncipc/tbi/TBI.htm

National Highway Safety Administration. (2008). *Motorcycle helmet use laws* (DOT Publication No. HS 810 887W). Washington, DC: Author.

National Institute on Deafness and Other Communication Disorders. (2009). Information retrieved June 10, 2009, from http://www.nidcd.nih.gov/health/statistics/vsl.asp

National Institute of Neurological Disorders and Stroke. (2009a). Dementia: Hope through research. Retrieved September 18, 2009, from http://www.ninds.nih.gov/disorders/dementias/detail_dementia.htm?css=print#1366519213

National Institute of Neurological Disorders and Stroke. (2009b). NINDS aphasia information page. Retrieved April 8, 2009, from http://www.ninds.nih.gov/disorders/aphasia/aphasia.htm

National Science Foundation. (2007, August 3). Language and linguistics: Language acquisition. Retrieved October 14, 2007, from http://www.nsf.gov/news/special_reports/linguistics/learn.jsp

Nazzi, T., Jusczyk, P. W., & Johnson, E. K. (2000). Language discrimination by English-learning 5-month-olds: Effects of rhythm and familiarity. *Journal of Memory and Language, 43,* 1–19.

Neale, J. M., & Liebert, R. M. (1986). *Science and behavior: An introduction to methods and research.* Englewood Cliffs, NJ: Prentice-Hall.

Nicolosi, L., Harryman, E., & Krescheck, J. (1989). *Terminology of communication disorders: Speech-language-hearing* (3rd ed.). Baltimore: Williams & Wilkins.

Nicolosi, L., Harryman, E., & Krescheck, J. (2004). *Terminology of communication disorders: Speech-language-hearing* (5th ed.). Baltimore: Lippincott Williams & Wilkins.

Occam's razor (2004). *Cunningham and Cunningham, Inc.* At: http://c2.com/cgi/wiki?OccamsRazor.

Office on Aging of the American Psychological Association. (2009). What practitioners should know about working with older adults. Retrieved September 18, 2009, from http://www.apa.org/pi/aging/practitioners/homepage.html

Onslow, M., Packman, A., & Harrison, E. (2003). The Lidcombe program of early stuttering intervention. In *Overview of the Lidcombe program* (pp. 3–15). Austin, TX: Pro-Ed.

Owens, R. E., Metz, D. E., & Haas, A. (2000). *Introduction to communication disorders: A lifespan perspective.* Boston: Allyn & Bacon.

Owens, R. E., Metz, D. E., & Haas, A. (2007). *Introduction to communication disorders: A lifespan perspective* (3rd ed.). Boston: Allyn & Bacon.

Pannbacker, M. (1998). Voice treatment techniques: A review and recommendations for outcome studies. *American Journal of Speech-Language Pathology, 7*(3), 49–64.

Pang, V. O., & Cheng, L. L. (1998). *Struggling to be heard: The unmet needs of Asian Pacific American children.* New York: State University of New York.

Paradis, M. (2001). *Manifestations of aphasia symptoms in different languages.* Bingley, UK: Emerald.

Paradise, J. L., Dollaghan, C. A., Campbell, T. F., Feldman, H. M., Bernard, B. S., Colborn, D. K., ... Smith, C. G. (2000). Language, speech sound production, and cognition in three-year-old children in relation to otitis media in their first three years of life. *Pediatrics, 105*(5), 1119–1130.

Paradise, J. L., Feldman, H. M., Campbell, T. F., Dollaghan, C. A., Colborn, D. K., Bernard, B. S., ... Smith, C. G. (2001). Effect of early or delayed insertion of tympanostomy tubes for persistent otitis media on developmental outcomes at the age of three years. *The New England Journal of Medicine, 344*(16), 1179–1187.

Park, R. (2000). *Voodoo Science: The Road from Foolishness to Fraud:* New York: Oxford University Press.

Peckham, C. S. (1973). Speech defects in a national sample of children aged seven years. *The British Journal of Disorders of Communication, 8*(1), 2–8.

Perlis, S. M. (2001). Sexual orientation and multi perspective identity on a small, Catholic campus: An analysis of the cultural climate and multicultural organizational change. *Dissertation Abstracts International,* AAT3014468.

Perrie, S., & Core, C. (2006). *Challenges facing monolingual speech-language pathologists in south Florida.* Presentation at the ASHA Annual Convention, Miami, FL. Retrieved from http://convention.asha.org/2006/handouts/855_0502Core_Cynthia__W._090440_111506122233.doc

Petinou, K. C., Schwartz, R. G., Gravel, J. S., & Raphael, L. J. (2001). A preliminary account of phonological and morphophonological perception in young children with and without otitis media. *International Journal of Language & Communication Disorders/Royal College of Speech & Language Therapists, 36*(1), 21–42.

Popper, K. R. (1965). *Conjectures and refutations: The growth of scientific knowledge.* New York: Harper and Row.

Porch, B. (2001). Porch Index of Communicative Abilities-Revised. Albuquerque, NM: PICA PROGRAMS.

Powers, G. R. (2000). Communication sciences and disorders: The discipline. In R. B. Gillam, T. P. Marquardt, & F. N. Martin (Eds.), *Communication sciences and disorders: From science to clinical practice*. San Diego, CA: Singular.

Psychiatry24x7.com. (2009). Memory loss with aging: What is normal, what is not? Retrieved September 18, 2009, from http://www.psychiatry24x7.com/bgdisplay.jhtml?itemname=dementia_memoryloss)

Quesal, B. (1999). One size fits all (or: When the only tool you have is a hammer...). *International Stuttering Awareness Day Conference*. Available at: http://www.mnsu.edu/dept/comdis/isad2/papers/quesal2.html.

Ramig, L. O., & Verdolini, K. (1998). Treatment efficacy: Voice disorders. *Journal of Speech, Language, and Hearing Research, 41*, S101–S116.

Ramig, P. R. (1993). High reported spontaneous stuttering recovery rates: Fact or fiction? *Language, Speech, and Hearing Services in Schools, 24*, 156–160.

Ramig, P. R. (2003). Counseling adults in group therapy. In *Effective Counseling in Stuttering Therapy*. Memphis: Stuttering Foundation of America.

Ramig, P. R., & Dodge, D. M. (2004). Fluency shaping intervention: Helpful, but why it is important to know more. *International Stuttering Awareness Day Conference*. Retrieved from http://www.mnsu.edu/comdis/isad7/papers/ramig7.html

Ramig, P. R., & Dodge, D. M. (2005). *The child and adolescent stuttering treatment and activity resource guide*. Clifton Park, NY: Thomson/Delmar/Singular.

Ramig, P. R., Ellis, J. B., Pollard, R., & Finan, D. (2010). Application of the SpeechEasy to stuttering treatment: Introduction, background, and preliminary observations. In B. Guitar & R. McCauley (Eds.), *Treatment of stuttering: Conventional and emerging interventions*. Baltimore: Lippincott, Williams & Wilkins, 310–326.

Ramsden, G., & Botting, N. (2000). Social and behavioural difficulties in children with language impairment. *Child Language Teaching and Therapy, 16*, 105–120.

Raymond, M., Pontier, D., Dufour, A., & Moller, A. P. (1996). Frequency-dependent maintenance of left-handedness in humans. *Proceedings: Biological Sciences, 263*(1377), 1627–1633.

Reitan, R. M. (1991). Reitan-Indiana Aphasia Screening Test. Dallas, TX: The Neuropsychology Center.

Results of survey on electronic devices. (2004, Winter). *Stuttering Foundation of America* (newsletter).

Ringo, C. C., & Dietrich, S. (1995). Neurogenic stuttering: An analysis and critique. *Journal of Medical Speech-Language Pathology, 3*, 111–222.

Robbins, J., Fisher, H. B., Blom, E. C., & Singer, M. I. (1984). A comparative acoustic study of normal, esophageal and tracheoesophageal speech production. *Journal of Speech and Hearing Disorders, 49*, 202–210.

Robey, R. R., & Schultz, M. C. (1993). Optimizing theories and experiments. San Francisco, CA: Singular.

Roseberry-McKibbin, C. (2001). *The source for bilingual students with language disorders*. East Moline, IL: LinguiSystems.

Roseberry-McKibbin, C. (2006). *Language disorders in children. A multicultural and case perspective*. Boston: Allyn & Bacon.

Roseberry-McKibbin, C., Brice, A., & O'Hanlon, L. (2005). Serving English language learners in public school settings: A national survey. *Language, Speech, and Hearing Services in Schools, 36,* 48–61.

Roseberry-McKibbin, C., & Eicholtz G. (1994). Serving children with limited English proficiency in the schools. *Language, Speech, and Hearing Services in Schools, 25,* 156–164.

Rosenthal, H. (2003). *Human services dictionary.* New York: Brunner-Routledge.

Roth, F. P., & Worthington, C. K. (2001). *Treatment resource manual for speech-language pathology (2nd edition).* San Diego, CA: Singular Thomson Learning.

Roth, I., & Beal, D. (1999). Teasing and bullying of children who stutter. Retrieved from the Stuttering home page at http://www.mnsu.edu/comdis/kuster/journal/roth.html

Roth, P., Speece, D. L., & Cooper, D. H. (2002). A longitudinal analysis of the connection between oral language and early reading. *Journal of Educational Research, 95*(5), 259–272.

Roueche, J. (1980). *Dysphagia: An assessment and management program for the adult.* Minneapolis, MN: Sister Kenny Institute.

Rouse, C. E., & Krueger, A. B. (2004). Putting computerized instruction to the test: A randomized evaluation of a "scientifically based" reading program. *Economics of Education Review, 23,* 323–338. doi:10.1016/j.econedurev.2003.10.005.

Ruscello, D. M. (2008). Nonspeech oral motor treatment issues related to children with developmental speech sound disorders. *Language, Speech, and Hearing Services in Schools, 39,* 380–391.

Ryan, B. P. (2003). Treatment efficacy research and clinical treatment. *Perspectives on Fluency and Fluency Disorders, 13*(1), 31–33.

Sabbagh, M. (2008). *The Alzheimer's answer: Reduce your risk and keep your brain healthy.* Hoboken, NJ: Wiley.

Sagan, C. (1995). *The demon-haunted world.* New York: Random House.

Sakihara, Y., & Parving, A. (1999). Clinical otosclerosis, prevalence estimates and spontaneous progress. *Acta Otolaryngology, 119*(4), 468–472.

Saladin, K. S. (2005). *Anatomy and physiology: The unity of form and function* (3rd ed.). Boston: McGraw-Hill.

Sarno, M. T. (1969). Functional Communication Profile-Revised. Moline, IL: LinguiSystems.

Saul, R. (1989). Quality Indicators in Clinical Practice. Presentation to Veterans Administration Department Management Team, VA Medical Center, Miami.

Savage, R., Evans, L., & Savage, J. (1981). *Psychology and communication in deaf children.* Sydney, Australia: Grune & Stratton.

Schiavetti, N., & Metz, D. E. (2006). *Evaluating research in communicative disorders.* Boston: Allyn & Bacon.

Schlosser, R. W. (2003). *The efficacy of augmentative and alternative communication.* San Diego, CA: Academic Press.

Schmid, N. (2007). Filial love in Buddhism. In Y. K. Greenberg (Ed.), *Love in world religions* (pp. 215–216). Oxford, UK: ABC CLIO.

Schuell, H. (1973). Minnesota Test for the Differential Diagnosis of Aphasia. San Antonio, TX: Pearson Education, Inc.

Schuler, H. (1998). Glossary. Retrieved July 31, 2010, from http://www.personal-psychologie.com/glossary.html

Schwartz, H. D. (1999). *A primer for stuttering therapy.* Needham Heights, MA: Allyn & Bacon.

Scott, J., Clark, C., & Brady, M. P. (2000). *Students with autism: Characteristics and instructional programming for special educators.* San Diego: Singular Publishing Group.

Seikel, A. J., & Drumright, D. (2004). *Essentials of anatomy and physiology for communication disorders.* New York: Thomas Delmar Learning.

Seikel, J. A., King, D. W., & Drumright, D. G. (2005). *Anatomy and physiology for speech, language, and hearing.* Clifton Park, NY: Thomson Delmar Learning.

Shames, G. H., & Florence, C. L. (1980). *Stutter-free speech: A goal for therapy.* Columbus, OH: Merrill.

Shapiro, D. A. (1999). *Stuttering intervention: A collaborative journey to fluency freedom.* Austin, TX: Pro-Ed Inc.

Sheehan, V., Williams, D. F., & Dugan, P. (2001). Stuttering therapy: Treating the whole disorder. American Academy of Private Practice in Speech Pathology and Audiology Spring Conference Institute, Delray Beach, FL, May, 2001.

Shenker, R. C., Kully, D., & Meltzer, A. (1998). Letter to the editor concerning the leadership conference. *American Speech-Language-Hearing Association Special Interest Division 4, Fluency and Fluency Disorders Newsletter, 8*(3), 9–10.

Shindo, M. L., & Hanson, D. G. (1990). Geriatric voice and laryngeal dysfunction. *Otolaryngologic Clinics of North America, 23,* 1035–1044.

Shipley, K. G., & McAfee, J. G. (2004). *Assessment in speech-language pathology: A resource manual* (3rd ed.). Clifton Park, NY: Delmar Learning.

Shriberg, L. D., Aram, D. M., & Kwiatkowski, J. (1997). Developmental apraxia of speech: I. Descriptive and theoretical perspectives. *Journal of Speech, Language, and Hearing Research, 40,* 273–285.

Shriberg, L. D., Flipsen, P., Jr., Thielke, H., Kwiatkowski, J., Kertoy, M. K., Katcher, M. L., & Block, M. G. (2000). Risk for speech disorder associated with early recurrent otitis media with effusion: Two retrospective studies. *Journal of Speech, Language, and Hearing Research: JSLHR, 43*(1), 79–99.

Shriberg, L. D., Ballard, K. J., Tomblin, J. B., Duffy, J. R., Odell, K. H., & Williams, C. A. (2006). Speech, prosody, and voice characteristics of a mother and daughter with a 7;13 translocation affecting FOXP2. *Journal of Speech, Language, and Hearing Research: JSLHR, 49*(3), 500–525. doi:10.1044/1092-4388(2006/038).

Shriberg, L. D., Kwiatkowski, J., & Gruber, F. A. (1992, November). *Short-term and long-term normalization in developmental phonological disorders.* Paper presented at the annual Convention of the American Speech-Language-Hearing Association, San Antonio, TX.

Shriberg, L. D., Tomblin, J. B., McSweeny, J. L. (1999). Prevalance of speech delay in 6-year-old children and comorbidity with language impairment. *Journal of Speech and Lamman Research, 42*(6), 1461–1481.

Shuster, L. I. (2005, March 1). Aphasia theories and treatment. *The ASHA Leader,* pp. 8–9, 15–16.

Siegel, G. M., & Gold, C. (1999). Principles and practices of current stuttering therapy. In R. F. Curlee (Ed.), *Stuttering and related disorders of fluency.* New York: Thieme.

Silliman, E. R., & Diehl, S. F. (2002). Assessing children with language learning disabilities, In D. K. Bernstein & E. Tiegerman-Farber (Eds.), *Language and communication disorders in children* (5th ed., pp. 181–255). Boston: Allyn & Bacon, 289–297.

Silliman, E. R, Wilkinson, L. C., & Brea-Spahn, M. R. (2004). *Policy and practice imperatives for language and literacy learning: who will be left behind?* In C. A. Stone, E. R. Silliman, B. J. Shren, & K. Apels (Eds.). *Handbook of language and literacy.* NY: Guilford, 97–129.

Silverman, F. H., & Bongey, T. A. (1997). Nurses' attitudes toward physicians who stutter. *Journal of Fluency Disorders*, 22, 61–62.

Silverman, F. H., & Paynter, K. K. (1990). Impact of stuttering on perception of occupational competence. *Journal of Fluency Disorders*, 15, 87–91.

Simmons, C. (2007). Love in Islam. In Y. K. Greenberg (Ed.), *Love in world religions* (pp. 219–220). Oxford, UK: ABC-CLIO.

Singh, S., & Kent, R. D. (2000). *Singular's illustrated dictionary of speech-language pathology.* San Diego, CA: Singular.

Sklar, M. (1983). *Sklar aphasia scale-revised.* Los Angeles, CA: Western Psychological Services.

Sleeter, C. (1995). An analysis of the critiques of multicultural education. In J. A. Banks (Ed.), *Handbook of research on multicultural education* (pp. 65–80). New York: Macmillan.

Small, L. H. (2005). *Fundamentals of phonetics: A practical guide for students* (2nd ed.). Boston: Pearson Education.

Smiley, L. R., & Goldstein, P. A. (1998). *Language delays and disorders from research to practice.* San Diego, CA: Singular.

Smit, A. B., Hand, L., Freilinger, J. J., Bernthal, J. E., & Bird, A. (1990). The Iowa articulation norms project and its Nebraska replication. *Journal of Speech and Hearing Disorders*, 55, 779–798.

Smith, D. D. (2006). *Introduction to special education making a difference.* Boston: Pearson/Allen & Bacon.

Smith, M. (2005). *Literacy and augmentative and alternative communication* (Augmentative and alternative communication perspectives series). Burlington, MA: Elsevier Academic Press.

Smith, A., & Kelly, E. (1997). Stuttering: A dynamic, multifactorial model. In R. F. Curlee & G. M. Siegel (Eds.), *Nature and treatment of stuttering.* Boston: Allyn & Bacon, 97–127.

Smith, S. D., Pennington, B. F., Boada, R., & Shriberg, L. D. (2005). Linkage of speech sound disorder to reading disability loci. *Journal of Child Psychology and Psychiatry, and Allied Disciplines*, 46(10), 1057–1066.

Snowling, M. J. (1991). Developmental reading disorders. *Journal of Child Psychology and Psychiatry*, 32, 49–77.

Soto, G. (1994). A cultural perspective on augmentative and alternative communication. *American Speech-Language-Hearing Association Special Interest Division 12*, 3(2), 6.

Soto, G., Muller E., Hunt, P., & Goetz, L. (2001). Professional skills for serving students who use AAC in general education classrooms: A team perspective. *Language, Speech, and Hearing Services in Schools*, 3, 51–56.

Sports Legacy Institute. (2007, September 6). *Wrestler Chris Benoit brain's forensic exam consistent with numerous brain injuries.* Boston: Sports Legacy Institute.

Stach, B. A. (1998). *Clinical audiology: An introduction*. New York: Thomas Delmar Learning.

Stach, B. A. (2003). *Comprehensive dictionary of audiology: Illustrated* (2nd ed.). New York: Thomas Delmar Learning.

Stampe, D. (1973). A dissertation on natural phonology. Bloomington: IULC.

Stark, R. E. (1986). Prespeech segmental feature development. In *Studies in language acquisition*, P. Fletcher & M. Garman (Eds.), Cambridge, MA: Cambridge University Press, 149–173.

Starkweather, C. W. (1987). *Fluency and stuttering*. Englewood Cliffs, NJ: Prentice-Hall.

Starkweather, C. W., & Givens-Ackerman, C. R. (1997). *Stuttering*. Austin, TX: Pro-Ed.

Stedman, T. L. (2006). *Stedman's medical dictionary*. Philadelphia: Lippincott Williams & Wilkins.

Stemple, J. (2000). *Voice therapy clinical studies*. Clifton Park, NY: Delmar Cengage.

Stockman, I. (1986). Language acquisition in culturally diverse populations: The black child as a case study. In O. L. Taylor (Ed.), *Nature of communication disorders in culturally and linguistically diverse populations* (pp. 117–155). San Diego, CA: College Hill.

Stokoe, W. C. (1980). Sign language structure. *Annual Review of Anthropology, 9*, 365–470.

Strand, E. A., & Debertine, P. (2000). The efficacy of integral stimulation intervention with developmental apraxia of speech. *Journal of Medical Speech Language Pathology, 8*(4), 295–300.

Strand, E. A., Stoeckel, R., & Baas, B. (2006). Treatment of severe childhood apraxia of speech: A treatment efficacy study. *Journal of Medical Speech Language Pathology, 14*, 297–306.

Stroke Education Ltd. (2006). Retrieved June 9, 2011 from http://www.stroke-education.com/info/strokeinfo.do.

Susca, M. (1997). The normalization of speech patterns in people who stutter: A treatment process. Paper presented at the Second World Congress on Fluency Disorders, San Francisco.

Tallal, P., Miller, S. L., Bedi, G., Byma, G., Wang, X., Nagarajam, S., et al. (1996). Language comprehension in language-learning impaired children improved with acoustically modified speech. *Science, 271*, 81–84.

Tan, A. (2003). *The opposite of fate*. New York: Putnam.

Tanner, D. C. (2007). *The family guide to surviving stroke and communication disorders*. Needham Heights, MA: Allyn & Bacon.

Tanner, D., & Culbertson, W. (1999). Quick Assessment for Aphasia. Oceanside, CA: Academic Communication Associates, Inc.

Teasdale, G., & Jennett, B. (1974). Assessment of coma and impaired consciousness: A practical scale, *Lancet, 2* (7872), 81–84.

Thibodeau, G., A., & Patton, K., T. (2003). *Anatomy and physiology* (5th ed.). St. Louis: Mosby.

Tillery, K. (2009). Central auditory processing evaluation: A test battery approach. In J. Katz, L. Medwetsky, R. Burkard, & L. Hood (Eds.). *Handbook of clinical audiology*. Baltimore: Lippincott Williams & Wilkins, 631–633.

Todman, J., & Alm, N. (2003). Modeling conversational pragmatics in communication aids. *Journal of Pragmatics, 35*, 523–538.

Tomblin, B. J., & Buckwalter, P., R. (1994). Studies of genetics of specific language impairment. In R. V. Watkins & M. L. Rice (Eds.), *Specific language impairments in children*. Baltimore: Brookes, 17–34.

Tomblin, J. B., Records, N. L., Buckwalter, P., Zhang, X., Smith, E., & O'Brien, M. (1997). Prevalence of specific language impairment in kindergarten children. *Journal of Speech, Language, and Hearing Research: JSLHR, 40*(6), 1245–1260.

Torgesen, J. K. (1998, February). *Individual differences in response to reading intervention*. Paper presented at the Pacific Coast Research Conference, La Jolla, CA.

U. S. Bureau of the Census. (2000). Statistical abstract of the United States. Retrieved from http://www.census.gov/compendia/statab/

U. S. Bureau of the Census. (2005). Statistical abstract of the United States. Retrieved from http://www.census.gov/compendia/statab/

U.S. Bureau of the Census. (2007). American community survey. Retrieved June 10, 2011 from http://www.census.gov/acs/

Vanderheiden, G., & Lloyd, L. L. (1986). Communication systems and their components. In S. Blackstone (Ed.), *Augmentative communication: An introduction*. Rockville, MD: American Speech-Language-Hearing Association, 186–202.

Van Dyne, L. (2005–2006). Cultural intelligence (CQ). Retrieved from http://www.linnvandyne.com.cq.html

Van Riper, C. (1957). Symptomatic therapy for stuttering. New York: Appleton Century Croft.

Van Riper, C. (1973). *The treatment of stuttering*. Englewood Cliffs, NJ: Prentice-Hall.

Van Riper, C. (1978). *Speech correction: Principles and methods*. (6th ed.). Englewood Cliffs, NJ: Prentice-Hall.

Waldrop, W. F., & Gould, M. A. (1994). *Your new voice*. Chicago: ACS.

Wall, M., & Myers, F. L. (1995). *Clinical management of stuttering*. Austin, TX: Pro-Ed.

Webster, D. B. (1999). *Neuroscience of communication*. San Diego, CA: Singular.

Wells, P. G., & Malcolm, M. T. (1971). Controlled trial of the treatment of 36 stutterers. *British Journal of Psychiatry, 119*, 603–604.

Wener, D. L. (1998). Theories of language development. In L. R. Smiley & P. A. Goldstein (Eds.), *Language delays and disorders*. San Diego, CA: Singular.

Westby, C. (2005, September 27). Language, culture, and literacy. *The ASHA Leader*, pp. 16, 30.

Westby, C., & Watson, S. (2004). Perspectives on attention deficit hyperactivity disorder: Executive functions, working memory, and language disabilities. *Seminars in Speech and Language, 25*(3), 241–254.

White, P. A., & Collins, S. R. C. (1984). Stereotype formation by inference: A possible explanation for the "stutterer" stereotype. *Journal of Speech and Hearing Research, 27*, 567–570.

Whiteman, B. C., Simpson, G. B., & Compton, W. C. (1986). Relationship of otitis media and language impairment in adolescents with Down syndrome. *American Journal of Mental Retardation, 24*, 353–356.

Whurr, R. (1997). *Aphasia screening test, 2nd ed.* Florence, KY: Taylor & Francis Group.

Wildemuth, B. (1984). Alternatives to standardized tests. *Eric Digest, ED286938*, 1–3. Retrieved October 14, 2007, from http://eric.ed.gov/ERICDocs/data/ericdocs2sql/content_storage_01/0000019b/80/1b/f6/71.pdf

Williams, A. L. (2000). Multiple oppositions: Case studies of variables in phonological intervention. *American Journal of Speech-Language Pathology, 9*, 289–299.

Williams, D. (1992, May 4). Remembering Wendell Johnson. *Daily Iowan*, 433–435.

Williams, D. F. (1993). Voice disorders associated with schizophrenia. *The Rose Peddler, 7*(1), 2–4.

Williams, D. F. (1999). Matching stuttering therapy procedures with client traits: A preliminary investigation. *The Florida Journal of Communication Disorders, 19*, 16–24.

Williams, D. F. (2006). *Stuttering recovery: Personal and empirical perspectives.* Mahwah, NJ: Erlbaum.

Williams, D. F., & Dugan, P. (2002). Administering stuttering modification therapy in school settings. *Thieme Seminars in Speech and Language, 23*, 187–194.

Williams, D. F., & Williams, M. L. (2000, March). Helping the child who stutters: Guidelines for parents. *Parenting Plus, 16*, 52–53.

Winitz, H., & Darley, F. (1980). Speech production. In P. LaBenz & A. LaBenz (Eds.), *Early correlates of speech, language and hearing.* Littleton, MA:PSG, 232–265.

Wolfram, W. (1993). A proactive role for speech-language pathologists in sociolinguistic education. *Language, Speech, and Hearing Services in Schools, 24*, 181–185.

Woods, C. L., & Williams, D. E. (1976). Traits attributed to stuttering and normally fluent males. *Journal of Speech and Hearing Research, 19*, 267–278.

World Health Organization (WHO). 1980. *International classification of impairments, disabilities and handicaps.* Geneva, Switzerland: WHO.

Yairi, E., & Carrico, D. M. (1992). Early childhood stuttering: Pediatricians' attitudes and practices. *American Journal of Speech-Language Pathology, 1*, 54–62.

Yairi, E., & Williams, D. E. (1970). Speech clinicians' stereotypes of elementary-school boys who stutter. *Journal of Communication Disorders, 3*, 161–170.

Yaruss, J. S. (1998). Documenting treatment outcomes in stuttering: measuring impairment, disability, and handicap. *International Stuttering Awareness Day Conference.* Available at: http://www.mankato.msus.edu/dept/comdis/isad/papers/yaruss.html.

Yaruss, J. S., & Quesal, R. W. (2001). The many faces of stuttering: identifying appropriate treatment goals. *ASHA Leader, 6*, (21) 4–5; 14.

Yaruss, J. S., & Quesal, R. W. (2002). Research-based stuttering therapy revisited. *Perspectives on Fluency and Fluency Disorders* (Newsletter of American Speech-Language-Hearing Association Division 4), *12*(2), 22–24.

Yaruss, J. S., Quesal, R. W., Reeves, L., Molt, L. F., Kluetz, B., Caruso, A. J., et al. (2002). Speech treatment and support group experiences of people who participate in the National Stuttering Association. *Journal of Fluency Disorders, 27*, 115–135.

Yeakle, M. K., & Cooper, E. B. (1986). Teacher perceptions of stuttering. *Journal of Fluency Disorders, 11*, 345–359.

Zangari, C., Lloyd, L. L., & Vicker, B. (1994). Augmentative and alternative communication: An historic perspective. *AAC: Augmentative and Alternative Communication, 10*(1), 27–59.

Zhu, H. (2002). *Phonological development in specific contexts: Studies of Chinese-speaking children.* Clevedon, UK: Multilingual Matters.

AUTHOR INDEX

SUBJECT INDEX

A

AAA, *see* American Academy of Audiology
AAC, *see* Augmentative and alternative
        communication
AAE, *see* African American English
AAV, *see* African American Vernacular
Abdomen, 205
Abductor spasmodic dysphonia, 220
Acalculia, 120
Acetylcholine, 219
Acquired communication disorders, 282
Acquired disorders, 109
Acquired laryngeal webbing, 210
Acquired stuttering, 184
Acute laryngitis, 218
AD, *see* Alzheimer's disease
Adaptation, 180
Additions, 172
Adductor spasmodic dysphonia, 219
Adenoids, 68
Adult language disorders, 110
Affect, deficits in, 138
African American English (AAE), 323, 329
African American Vernacular (AAV), 323
Age equivalency, 65
Agnosia, 115
Agrammatism, 115
Agraphia, 115, 120
AH, *see* Audiologic habilitation
Aided communication, 278
Alexia, 116
Alzheimer's disease (AD), 148–149
American Academy of Audiology (AAA), 370
American Speech-Language-Hearing
        Association (ASHA), 369
Amnesia, 141
Amplitude perturbation, 223
Anomia, 113, 118
Anomic aphasia, 118
    general characteristics, 118
    location of neurological damage, 118
    prominent speech and language
        characteristics, 118
Anosognosia, 118
AOS, *see* Apraxia of speech

Aphasia, 110–134
    acute onset of, 111
    assessment tools, 133
    atypical syndromes, 123–126
        bilingual individual and aphasia,
            124–125
        crossed aphasia, 126
        left-handed individual and aphasia,
            125–126
        special populations, 124–126
        subcortical aphasias, 123–124
    bilingual, 336
    differential diagnosis, 136–137
    evaluation and treatment, 126–134
        assessment, 130–131
        considerations, 126–127
        intervention, 131–134
        medical considerations, 127–130
    fluent aphasias, 116–120
        anomic aphasia, 118
        conduction aphasia, 119–120
        transcortical sensory aphasia, 120
        Wernicke's aphasia, 117–118
    insidious onset, 111
    nonfluent aphasias, 121– 123
        Broca's aphasia, 121–122
        global or mixed aphasia, 122
        transcortical motor aphasia, 122–123
    screening and comprehensive
            diagnostic tests for, 132
    social perspective of, 111
    syndromes, 116–126
Aphemia, 121
Aphonia, 210
Appalachian English, 323
Apraxia of speech (AOS), 153–154
AR, *see* Audiologic rehabilitation
Arteriosclerosis, 111
Articulation delay, 162
Articulation disorder, 162
ASHA, *see* American
        Speech-Language-Hearing
        Association
Aspiration, 115, 212, 298
Aspiration pneumonia, 115, 299
Assessment, 55
Assimilation, 20